14

Develop Web applications using EGL

IBM Enterprise Generation Language (EGL) is a business application centric procedural programming language and environment used to develop batch, text user interface (TUI), and Web applications. When developing an EGL Web application, the developer creates the EGL source files using wizards and the source editor. Java/J2EE source is generated from the EGL source files so that the application can then be deployed to WebSphere Application Server.

In this chapter we introduce the concepts, benefits, and architecture of the IBM Enterprise Generation Language. We have included a working example that describes how to develop Web applications using EGL and JSF with the tooling provided in IBM Rational Application Developer V6.0.

The chapter is organized into the following sections:

- Introduction to EGL
- IBM EGL tooling in Rational Developer products
- Prepare for the sample application
- Develop the Web application using EGL
- Import and run the sample Web application
- Considerations for exporting an EGL project

14.1 Introduction to EGL

Throughout this chapter, we explore the features of EGL and tooling provided in IBM Rational Application Developer V6.0 used to develop EGL applications.

This section is organized as follows:
- Programming paradigms
- IBM Enterprise Generation Language
- IBM EGL and Rational brand software
- IBM EGL feature enhancements
- Where to find more information on EGL

14.1.1 Programming paradigms

The objective of this section is to describe the classes of programming paradigms to better understand why EGL is well suited for business application development.

System vs. business application programming

From a granular perspective, there are system programs and business application programs. Examples of systems programming include creating operating systems, spreadsheets, or word processors. Some examples of business application programming include creating an employee time and attendance system, customer order entry system, or a bill payment system.

Generally it can be said that business application programming involves slightly less software theory or invention, and more focus on applying the technology with the purpose of achieving a tangible business goal.

Computer programming languages that can provide for systems programming are general purpose in that they have fewer if any higher level constructs. For example, if you wanted to provide the end user with a data entry screen form and functions using the C language, you might have to write 2000 lines of program source code. When using a business application programming language, the same user interface might be developed in 200 lines of source code. Using the appropriate programming language can dramatically increase productivity.

Declarative programming languages

A declarative programming language describes what output is desired, not how to generate it. Examples of declarative languages include Structured Query Language (SQL), Extensible Markup Language (XML), and Hyper Text Markup Language (HTML).

Procedural programming languages

Procedure programming languages are modular in that they allow the programmer to group the code into modules, procedures, and/or functions. Examples of procedural languages include C, Fortran, Pascal, COBOL, and Basic.

Object-oriented programming languages

An object-oriented programming language supports the following constructs:

- Objects
- Abstraction
- Encapsulation
- Polymorphism
- Inheritance

Examples of object-oriented programming languages include Java, Smalltalk, C++, and C#. Object-oriented programming languages generally offer a language with many advanced capabilities over structured languages. These capabilities aid in software re-use, ease of maintenance, and numerous other desirable features. If there is a caveat to object-oriented programming languages, it is that they are considered to have a longer and more expensive learning curve than procedural programming languages.

Fourth generation programming languages (4GL)

Fourth generation programming languages, also known as 4GLs, are focused on business application programming. Using a 4GL minimizes programming skill requirements, development time, and total development cost.

14.1.2 IBM Enterprise Generation Language

IBM Enterprise Generation Language is a procedural language with a number of higher level 4GL language constructs. For example, EGL contains a two-word command verb that allows the developer to produce a dynamically retrieved array of tabular data for display, update, or other purposes.

IBM EGL provides the ability to develop a wide range of business application programs including applications with no user interface, a text user interface (TUI), or a multi-tier graphical Web interface. The IBM EGL compiler will generate Java source code for either Java 2 Platform Standard Edition or Java 2 Platform Enterprise Edition, as required.

Additionally, IBM EGL supports software re-use, ease of maintenance, and other features normally associated with object-oriented programming languages by following the Model-View-Controller (MVC) design pattern.

In summary, EGL offers the benefits of J2EE, while providing a simple procedural programming environment for non-Java developers, which facilitates rapid Web application development.

Target audience of IBM EGL

Since IBM EGL is geared toward business application development, the developers tend to have a greater focus on understanding the business needs and less so on technology. Java 2 Platform Enterprise Edition offers many benefits and is extremely powerful; however, this platform requires developers to have extensive programming knowledge, which can be an impediment for developers who are new to Java. EGL provides the ease of use of a procedural programming language with the power of Java 2 Platform Enterprise Edition, which is generated by the EGL tooling.

We have listed some common types of developers that use EGL:

- Business application programmers in need of higher productivity
- Programmers needing to deploy to diverse platforms
- Business-oriented developers
    - 4GL developers (Oracle Forms, Natural, CA Ideal, Mantis, Cool:Gen, reports)
    - Visual Basic developers
    - RPG developers
    - COBOL/PL1 developers
    - VisualAge® Generator developers
    - IBM/Informix 4GL developers

History of EGL

In 1981 IBM introduced the Cross System Product (CSP). This programming language began the concept of a platform neutral, singular programming language and environment that would allow enterprise-wide application development and support.

Generally speaking, the objectives of a cross-platform solution are as follows:

- Abstraction: Hide the platform-specific differences from the developer and end user.
- Code generation: Using code generation to bridge abstract and concrete applications
- Platform and language neutrality.
- Rich client and debugger support.

The benefits of a cross-platform strategy include:

- Less program code to write (not platform specific)
- Reduction of training requirements
- Provide easier transition to new technologies
- Provide tested performance and code quality

In 1994 the IBM VisualAge Generator product (VisualGen®) product was released. VisualAge Generator V4.0 allowed for the creation of Web programs without knowledge of Java. Later releases of VisualAge introduced the EGL-like ability to output COBOL.

In 2001, the WebSphere Studio tools were introduced. In 2003, IBM acquired Rational software, which was known as a leader in software engineering technologies, methodologies, and software. In 2004, IBM officially transferred the WebSphere Studio development tooling to the IBM Rational division to consolidate software under one brand supporting the entire software development life cycle. During this same time period, IBM joined forces with many strategic companies to contribute to the Eclipse project. Today Eclipse 3.0 is used as the base for which the IBM Rational Software Development Platform is built. Rational Application Developer, as well as much other Rational tooling, shares this common base. For more information on Eclipse and Rational products refer to 1.3.3, "Eclipse and IBM Rational Software Development Platform" on page 19.

The IBM Enterprise Generation Language emerged from many IBM 4GL predecessors (for example, VisualAge Generator and CSP). Today IBM EGL incorporates the ability to generate source output for Java 2 Platform Standard Edition, Java 2 Platform Enterprise Edition, COBOL, and PL1. It also includes migration tools for other 4GL languages.

IBM EGL value proposition

The IBM Enterprise Generation Language increases the developer's productivity and value to the business in three key areas. First, EGL is an easy-to-learn procedural programming language. Second, EGL is a business application centric programming language, which allows you focus and complete business applications more rapidly than other languages. Third, since the Rational Application Developer EGL tooling can generate Java and Java 2 Platform Enterprise Edition source code, you can take advantage of the benefits of the open, scalable, and potent Java and J2EE programming environments.

When evaluating infrastructure choices for Web applications, there are two major competing models, Java 2 Platform Enterprise Edition and Microsoft .NET. Java 2 Platform Enterprise Edition is the platform of choice of IBM and many businesses. Although Java 2 Platform Enterprise Edition does deliver on its great promises and is an excellent platform, it can take developers a great deal of time to master and be proficient. EGL addresses the learning curve issue of Java 2 Platform Enterprise Edition by offering a simple procedural and business application centric programming model, which with the use of the EGL tooling provided by Rational Developer products, can be generated into Java or Java 2 Platform Enterprise Edition resources.

As IBM EGL outputs Java/J2EE, IBM EGL acts as an abstract layer from changes in the Java/J2EE platform. Parts of Java/J2EE are mature. Parts of Java.J2EE are emerging and changing. IBM EGL offers to insulate programmers from this volatility.

In summary, IBM EGL provides the great productivity gains of a procedural and business centric programming language, with the many benefits of Java and Java 2 Platform Enterprise Edition.

Application architecture

IBM EGL can be used to deliver business application programs with no user interface (batch jobs), text user interface programs, and Web applications. In this section, we explore the architecture of Web applications.

Figure 14-1 displays the architecture of a standard Web application. While Web applications can be delivered via a number of computing infrastructure choices, we focus on J2EE.

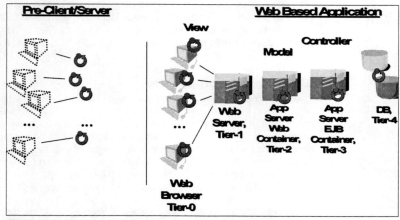

Figure 14-1   Architecture for a standard Web-based application

Using Java/J2EE, the following is held to be true:

- The end user operates from Tier-0. Tier-0 has no runtime or software requirements other than a Web browser and access to a network.
- Tier-1 supports a Web server and communicates with the end user using an HTTP communication protocol (for example, IBM HTTP Server).
- Generally, the Web server handles requests for static resources—GIF files, JPEG files, static HTML, and more. The Web server maintains a list of file types, if you will, and is configured to forward requests it does not understand to another agent. This agent, also referred to as a Web server plug-in, is a dynamic linked library (DLL) or shared object (a "*.so" file). Generally, the Web server plug-in forwards requests to Tier-2.
- Tier-2 supports a Java/J2EE-compliant Web container, a Java/J2EE-compliant application server such as WebSphere Application Server.
- Tier-2 receives inbound communication requests, parses the input, and formulates a response. Within Java/J2EE, the primary objects being programmed here are Java filters, Java servlets, and Java server pages. In short, Java servlets handle inbound communication, and Java server pages handle output.
- In the Model-View-Controller design pattern, Java servlets are the controller, and JSPs are used for the view.
- Tier-3 supports a Java/J2EE-compliant EJB container, a Java/J2EE application server such as IBM WebSphere Application Server.
- As seen in Figure 14-1 on page 756, Tier-3 is used to provide an advanced data persistence layer; access to a relational database server such as DB2 Universal Database.
- In the Model-View-Controller design pattern, Java beans or Enterprise Java Beans are models.
- Tier-4 supports the database server.

Java/J2EE is fabulous in that it is open, proven to scale, and offers numerous other advantages. If there is one criticism with Java/J2EE, it is the steep learning curve. First one must learn object-oriented programming, then Java, then Java/J2EE. There are numerous and distinct objects one must learn inside Java/J2SE and Java/J2EE—Java filters, Java servlets, Java server pages, Java beans, and/or Enterprise Java beans. IBM EGL is procedural and measurably less difficult to lean than Java/J2EE.

IBM EGL outputs Java/J2SE and Java/J2EE. For a Web application, IBM EGL uses one procedural language with no objects with 4GL level productivity. The interface is developed using Faces JSPs with small EGL page handlers to respond to page events, page loads, and action buttons.

14.1.3 IBM EGL and Rational brand software

The IBM Rational software brand includes products focused on design and construction, process and portfolio management, software configuration management, and software quality. The IBM EGL tooling and environment are included with the Rational Developer products on Windows and Linux platforms for the following editions (see Figure 14-2):

- IBM Rational Web Developer V6.0
- IBM Rational Application Developer V6.0
- IBM Rational Software Architect V6.0
- IBM WebSphere Studio Enterprise Developer
- IBM WebSphere Studio Integration Developer

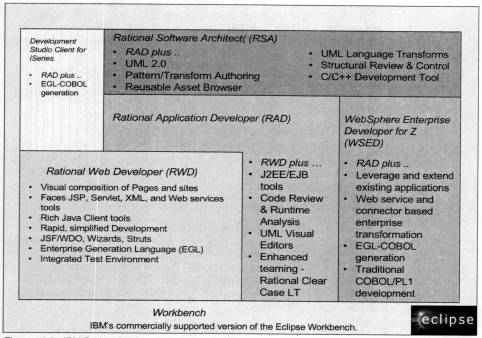

Figure 14-2   IBM Rational software containing IBM EGL

To keep the Rational Developer product base install image as small as possible, EGL is installable as an optional component. Figure 14-5 on page 769 displays a picture of the IBM Enterprise Generation Language (EGL) component in the IBM Rational Application Developer V6.0 Installer.

IBM WebSphere Studio Enterprise Edition has additional EGL capabilities including the ability to output COBOL program code that can execute on the IBM zSeries® (zOS) and IBM iSeries platforms (OS/400®), in addition to generate Java source output.

IBM EGL Web applications can be deployed to J2EE-compliant application servers, including the WebSphere Application Server V6.0, Express, Base, and Network Deployment Editions, as well as IBM WebSphere Application Server Enterprise Edition (V5.x).

14.1.4 IBM EGL feature enhancements

At the time of completing this book, we learned of EGL feature enhancements that would be delivered point releases of IBM Rational Web Developer V6.x and IBM Rational Application Developer V6.x. Although we were not able to test these new features, we want to make people aware of this new functionality.

Version 6.0.01 feature enhancements

The following section describes the key feature enhancements to EGL included in IBM Rational Developer products V6.0.01. This list is by no means exhaustive.

- TUI Editor for EGL: This is an Eclipse-based WYSIWYG editor for the construction of Text User Interfaces (TUIs) for EGL. This allows EGL customers to define EGL TUIs that will deploy as 5250 or 3270 applications running against iSeries or zSeries, respectively. The EGL TUIs can also be run on distributed Java platforms. This is useful for VisualAge Generator customers migrating their TUI applications from these platforms to EGL.

- EGL runtime support for HP/UX and SUN Solaris: Support for HP/UX V11.0, V11.11, V11.23, and SUN Solaris V7, V8, V9.

- Debugger support for Jasper Reports: EGL provides the ability to debug an EGL ReportHandler, including breakpoints, variable inspection, etc.

- i4GL Migration Utility: This utility provides enhanced tooling integrated with IBM Rational's Software Development Platform to increase productivity of Informix application developers. The Informix 4GL to EGL Conversion Utility is available as an iFix004 iFeature with the Rational Developer V6.0 products.

This release of IBM Informix 4GL to EGL Conversion Utility offers the following key features and benefits:

- Uniform Conversion from 4GL to EGL to retain the look-and-feel of your 4GL program with the equivalent EGL program after conversion.
- Graphical Conversion Wizard steps you through each step of the conversion process.
- Command Line Conversion - Scripted or automated usage.

Informix 4GL to EGL Conversion Utility iFix004 iFeature should be installed via the Update Manager functionality with any of the following products:

- IBM Rational Web Developer V6.0
- IBM Rational Application Developer V6.0
- IBM Rational Software Architect V6.0
- IBM WebSphere Application Server Express V6.0

Version 6.0.1 feature enhancements

This section describes the key feature enhancements to EGL included in IBM Rational Developer products V6.0.1. This list is by no means exhaustive.

▶ EGL Parts Reference View Enhancements:

- Part wizard: This wizard allows you to (optionally) create a part that does not exist. Currently a message saying the part does not exist will be displayed if the part is not defined.
- Flat layout: This layout lists all the parts that are referenced in a flat table. We show part name, part type (icon), project, package, and file name in the table. The customer can toggle between viewing in the flat layout versus the existing hierarchical layout.
- Search declarations and references: Allows you to search declarations and references to a part within a given scope. This is similar to the Java Development Tooling (JDT) in Eclipse.
- Find part: Ability to search the view (find capability) for a given part name.

▶ EGL Language Enhancements for IMS™ and DLI Support: This includes the addition of part types to allow access to data stored in DL/I databases, which includes parts to represent PCBs and SSPs, in addition to a DL/I record.

▶ EGL Support for MS SQL Server: EGL supports Microsoft SQL Server 2000.

▶ EGL Data Item Part Source Assistant: This assistant provides a dialog that groups the various properties available on EGL Data items and facilitates the entry of appropriate values via a graphical dialog instead of the EGL Source editor.

14.1.5 Where to find more information on EGL

For more information on IBM EGL, refer to the following:

- IBM developerWorks EGL home page:

    http://www.ibm.com/developerworks/rational/products/egl/

- *Generating Java using EGL and JSF with WebSphere Studio Site Developer V5.1.2*, white paper found at:

    http://www.ibm.com/developerworks/websphere/library/techarticles/0408_barosa/0408_barosa.html

- *Transitioning: Informix 4GL to Enterprise Generation Language (EGL)*, SG24-6673, redbook; expected publish date is June 2005

14.2 IBM EGL tooling in Rational Developer products

This section highlights the IBM EGL tooling and support included in Rational Developer products.

> **Important:** After installing the Rational Application Developer EGL component, you must enable the EGL development capability in order to access the EGL preferences and features.
>
> - For details on installation refer to 14.3.1, "Install the EGL component of Rational Application Developer" on page 768.
> - For details on enabling the EGL development capability refer to 14.3.2, "Enable the EGL development capability" on page 771.

14.2.1 EGL preferences

The EGL preferences allow you to define EGL development environment settings.

Once you have enabled the EGL development capability from the Workbench preferences, you can access the EGL preferences. Select **Window** → **Preferences**. Click the **EGL** tab. From the EGL preferences you will be able to customize the settings highlighted in Figure 14-3 on page 762.

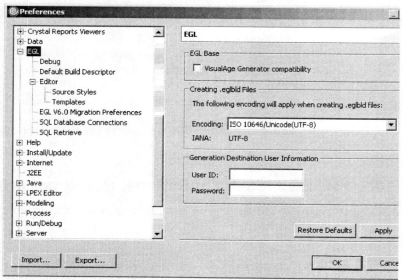

Figure 14-3 EGL preferences

14.2.2 EGL perspective and views

Within IBM Rational Application Developer V6, there is an EGL perspective and supporting views for EGL application development.

To open the EGL perspective, select **Window → Open Perspective → Other**. When the Select Perspective dialog appears, check **Show all**, select **EGL**, and then click **OK**.

EGL includes the following views, which can be accessed by selecting **Window → Show View**:

- EGL Debug Validation Errors
- EGL Generation Results
- EGL Parts Reference
- EGL SQL Errors
- EGL Validation Results

14.2.3 EGL projects

When working with EGL, it is important to understand the difference between an EGL Project and an EGL Web Project.

EGL Project
An EGL Project is used to develop EGL batch and text user interface (TUI) applications.

EGL Web Project
An EGL Web Project is a Dynamic Web Project with EGL support enabled and is used to develop applications with a Web interface. For the working example in this chapter, we demonstrate how to create an EGL Web Project in preparation for developing a Web application using EGL.

For details on creating an EGL Web Project, refer to 14.3.4, "Create an EGL Web Project" on page 773.

14.2.4 EGL wizards

IBM Rational Application Developer V6 includes several EGL wizards that can be used to generate the EGL source with the objective of speeding development tasks. For example, if you have created an EGL Web Project, right-click the project in the EGL perspective. Select **New** → **EGL** and then select one of the following EGL wizards:

- EGL Build File: The build descriptor controls the generation process. Within the context of Rational Application Developer, the EGL output type is Java/J2EE. The build descriptor is part of the EGL build file.
- EGL Source Folder (EGLSource): The EGLSource folder is the location where the EGL source files will be stored within the a project.
- EGL Package: EGL packages are used to group common types of code (for example, data, libraries, pagehandlers).
- EGL Source File: When using the EGL Source File wizard, the EGL file is created with the given name in the EGLSource folder.
- Faces JSP File: When creating a Faces JSP within an EGL Web Project, an EGL page handler source file is created in addition to the Faces JSP Java source being created.
- Program: An EGL program part is the main logical unit used to generate a Java program, Java wrapper, or Enterprise JavaBean session bean.
- Library: An EGL Library Part contains a set of functions, variables, and constructs that can be used by programs, page handlers, and other libraries.

- Data Table: An EGL Data Table Part associates a data structure with an array of initial values for the structure.
- Form Group: An EGL Form Group Part defines a collection of text and print forms.
- EGL Data Parts: The EGL Data Parts wizard is used to create SQL records, as well as data-item parts and library-based function parts, from one or more relational database tables or pre-existing views. The working example demonstrates how to use this wizard.
- EGL Data Parts and Pages: The EGL Data Parts and Pages wizard provides a method to create an EGL Web Project, data parts, and Faces JSPs for a given application in one simplified process.

14.2.5 EGL migration

IBM Rational Application Developer V6 includes EGL migration tooling for the following:

- EGL migration to V6.0

    The EGL migration to V6.0 tooling is used to migrate previous EGL versions to EGL V6.0 with Interim Fix 0004.

    This is enabled in through **Workbench** → **Capabilities** → **EGL Developer** → **EGL V6.0 Migration**. Once the capability is enabled, you can right-click on the project and select **Migrate** → **EGL V6.0 Migration** to migrate the EGL source code to the new level.

    Note: If you have developed an EGL application with IBM Rational Application Developer V6 .0 (original release), you will need to migrate the source code and manually copy the runtime libraries in your project after installing Rational Application Developer V6.0 - Interim Fix 0004. There are significant changes in the EGL language syntax that require that you migrate.

- VisualAge Generator to EGL migration

    The VisualAge Generator to EGL migration is used to migrate code developed in VisualAge Generator to EGL V6.0 with Interim Fix 004.

    Enabled this by selecting **Workbench** → **Capabilities** → **EGL Developer** → **VisualAge Generator to EGL Migration**. Once the capability is enabled, you can right-click the project and select **VisualAge Generator to EGL Migration** to migrate to EGL.

- Informix 4GL to EGL Conversion Utility

    The Informix 4GL migration is used to migrate Informix 4GL to EGL.

This feature requires that the *Informix 4GL to EGL Conversion Utility* be installed using the Rational Product Updater Optional Features tab.

Once this feature is installed, you will need to enable the *Informix 4GL to EGL Conversion* capability by selecting **Window** → **Preferences** → **Workbench** → **Capabilities** → **EGL Developer**, and checking the Informix 4GL to EGL Conversion check box.

For details on the Informix 4GL to EGL Conversion Utility refer to the following:

- *IBM Informix 4GL to EGL Conversion Utility User's Guide*, G251-2485, found in the following directory after installing the optional feature:

  `<rad_home>\egl\eclipse\plugins\com.ibm.etools.i4gl.conversion_6.0.0.2`

- *Transitioning: Informix 4GL to Enterprise Generation Language (EGL)*, SG24-6673, redbook (expected to be published June 2005)

14.2.6 EGL debug support

IBM Rational Application Developer V6 includes support for debugging applications developed in EGL. Like other development environments and languages within Rational Application Developer, EGL can be run and debugged on the WebSphere Application Server V6.0 or WebSphere Application Server V5.1 Test Environments.

From the Server view, right-click the server started in debug mode, and select **Enable/Disable EGL Debugging**.

14.2.7 EGL Web application components

In the previous sections we highlighted the EGL tools and features included in Rational Application Developer used to develop an EGL application. In this section, we describe the components generated by the wizards that make up an EGL Web application.

Figure 14-4 on page 767 displays the components of an EGL Web Project in the Project Explorer view. We have outlined the key resources to provide a better understanding of an EGL Web application.

- BankEGLEAR: The BankEGLEAR is created in the Enterprise Applications folder.
- Deployment Descriptor: BankEGLEAR: We will modify the enhanced EAR settings to define the deployment database in a later step.
- BankEGL: The BankEGL EGL Web Project is created in the Dynamic Web Projects folder.

- EGLSource: This folder will contain the EGL resources created for the application.
    - data: Folder includes EGL source files containing data records.
    - libraries: Folder includes EGL source files containing functions.
    - pagehandlers: Folder includes EGL page handler source files used to define the EGL functionality within a Faces JSP. For example, the page handler will contain the code to be executed when a button within the Faces JSP, such as Logout, is clicked.
- BankEGL.eglbld: The BankEGL.eglbld is the EGL Build Descriptor that was generated when we created the new EGL Web Project and selected to create new project build descriptor(s) automatically. This file contains the preferences that will be used for the EGL Web Project.
- JavaSource: This folder contains Java source files that have been generated from the EGL source files found in the EGLSource folder.
- WebContent: This folder contains Faces JSPs with EGL references (page handlers, libraries, data).

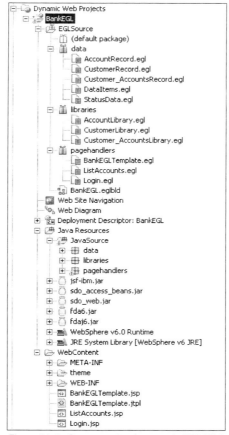

Figure 14-4   Components of a sample EGL Web application

14.3 Prepare for the sample application

Prior to developing the sample application using EGL, you will need to complete the following tasks described in this section:

- Install the EGL component of Rational Application Developer.
- Enable the EGL development capability.

- Install DB2 Universal Database.
- Create an EGL Web Project.
- Set up the sample database.
- Configure EGL preferences for SQL database connection.
- Configure the data source.

> **Note:** A completed version of the ITSO RedBank Web application built using EGL can be found in the c:\6449code\egl\BankEGL.zip Project Interchange file. If you do not wish to create the sample yourself, but want to see it run, follow the procedures described in 14.5, "Import and run the sample Web application" on page 816.

14.3.1 Install the EGL component of Rational Application Developer

This section describes the configuration requirements for using IBM EGL within IBM Rational Application Developer V6.0.

Install IBM Enterprise Generation Language

The IBM Enterprise Generation Language is optionally installed as a component of the Rational Application Developer installation, as seen in Figure 14-5 on page 769.

> **Note:** Within the context of this book, the installation of EGL requires that you have installed IBM Rational Application Developer V6.0 with the WebSphere Application Server V6.0 Integrated Test Environment.

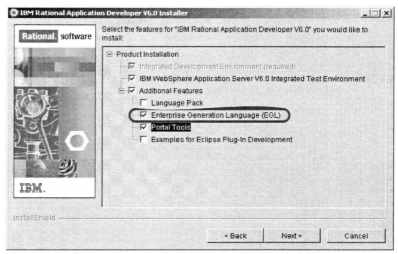

Figure 14-5   EGL component of Rational Application Developer installation

Interim fix

At the time of writing this chapter and sample application, we used IBM Rational Application Developer V6.0 - Interim Fix 0004. We suggest that you install the latest available interim fix level.

Refer to the following URL for details on the contents and instructions for installing the latest IBM Rational Application Developer V6.0 - Interim Fix:

http://www.ibm.com/support/search.wss?rs=2043&tc=SSRTLW%2BSSRTLW&q=interim+fix

> **Attention:** EGL applications developed with IBM Rational Application Developer V6.0 need to be migrated for the source code to adhere to the new EGL language syntax included in Interim Fix 0004 (or 0001).
>
> 1. Migrate the EGL source.
>
>   a. Enable EGL V6.0 Migration capability by selecting **Window** → **Preferences**. Expand **Workbench** and select **Capabilities**. Expand **EGL Developer** and check **EGL V6.0 Migration**. Click **OK**.
>
>   b. Right-click the **EGLSource** folder, and select **EGL V6.0 Migration** → **Migrate**.
>
> 2. Manually copy the new EGL runtime libraries listed in Table 14-2 on page 820 from a newly created EGL Web Project (contains correct level of runtime files) to the same folder of the project being migrated.

Verify EGL plug-ins exist

After installing the Enterprise Generation Language component, verify that the EGL plug-ins are configured.

1. From the menu bar of Rational Application Developer, select **Help** → **About IBM Rational Software Development Platform**.
2. Click **Plug-in Details**.
3. Scroll down the page until you see plug-ins with **IBM** in the Provider column.
4. Find the plug-ins that begin with EGL. You should see something like Figure 14-6 on page 771.

Figure 14-6 Enterprise Generation Language plug-ins

14.3.2 Enable the EGL development capability

The Rational Application Developer Workbench hides certain features by default. The EGL development capability is disabled by default.

To enable the EGL development capability, do the following:

1. From the menu bar, select **Window** → **Preferences**.
2. Expand **Workbench** → **Capabilities**.
3. Select and expand EGL Developer. Depending on your needs, check the appropriate sub features, as seen in Figure 14-7.
   - Check **EGL Developer** - Required for EGL development
   - Check **EGL V6.0 Migration** - Required for V6.0 to V6.0 + Interim Fix 0004

   > **Note:** We needed this feature to migrate an EGL Web Project created with the IBM Rational Application Developer V6.0, since Interim Fix 0001 and 0004 contain an EGL version that has new EGL language syntax.

   - VisualAge Generator to EGL Migration (as needed)
4. Click **OK**.

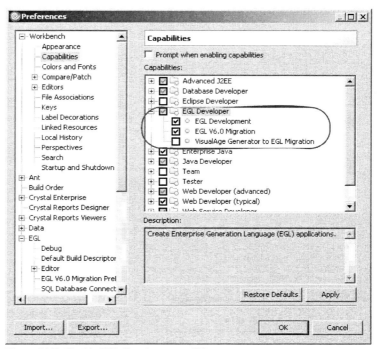

Figure 14-7 Enable EGL Developer capability

14.3.3 Install DB2 Universal Database

For the working example, we installed IBM DB2 Universal Database V8.2 Express Edition included with the IBM Rational Application Developer V6.0 packaging.

Refer to "IBM DB2 Universal Database V8.2 installation" on page 1387 for details on installing DB2 Universal Database.

14.3.4 Create an EGL Web Project

To create an EGL Web Project for the redbook sample application, do the following:

1. Open the EGL perspective.

a. From the menu bar, select **Window** → **Open Perspective** → **Other**.
   b. When the Select Perspectives dialog appears, check **Show All**.
   c. Select **EGL** and click **OK**.
2. From the menu bar, select **File** → **New** → **Project**.
3. When the New Project dialog appears, expand **EGL**, select **EGL Web Project**, and then click **Next**.
4. When the New EGL Web Project dialog appears, do the following (as seen in Figure 14-8 on page 775), and then click **Next**:
   – Name: `BankEGL`
   – Build Descriptor Options: Select **Create new project build descriptor(s) automatically**.
   – JNDI name for SQL connection: `jdbc/BankDS`

   This value should match the value entered in 14.3.6, "Configure EGL preferences for SQL database connection" on page 779.

   > **Note:** Should you need to change the JNDI name after creating the EGL Web Project, you will need to also modify the sqlJNDIName in the EGL build descriptor (for example, EGLSource\BankEGL.eglbld).

   – Click **Show Advanced**.

   If other EAR projects exist prior to creating the EGL Web Project, you may need to specify the EAR project by clicking **New**. In our example, no other EAR projects existed; thus, the wizard supplied BankEGLEAR as the EAR project name.

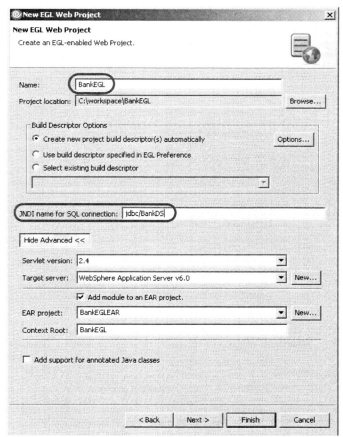

Figure 14-8   New EGL Web Project

5. When the New EGL Web Project - Features dialog appears, notice that Add EGL Support and JSP Standard Tag Library are checked, as seen in Figure 14-9 on page 776. Click **Finish**.

Note: An EGL Web Project is a Dynamic Web Project with Add EGL Support and JSP Standard Tag Library enabled.

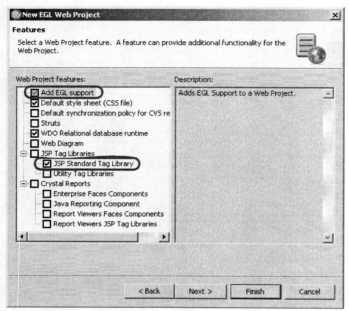

Figure 14-9 New EGL Web Project - Features

Add EGL support to an existing Dynamic Web Project

You can also add EGL support to an existing Dynamic Web Project by doing the following:

1. Open the Web perspective Project Explorer view.
2. Right-click the Dynamic Web Project that you wish to add EGL support to and select **Properties**.
3. In the Properties dialog select **Web Project Features**.
4. From the Available Web Project Features select **Add EGL Support** and **JSP Standard Tag Library**.
5. Click the **Apply** button.

14.3.5 Set up the sample database

This section provides instructions for deploying the BANK sample database and populating the database with sample data. For example, we chose to use IBM DB2 Universal Database V8.2 Express Edition.

To create the database, create the connection, and create and populate the tables for the BANK sample from within Rational Application Developer, do the following:

1. Create the BANK database in DB2 Universal Database.

   For details refer to "Create DB2 UDB database via a DB2 command window" on page 346.

2. Create the database connection from within Rational Application Developer to the BANK database.

   For details refer to "Create a database connection" on page 347.

   > **Note:** When using DB2 or Oracle you will have to provide the user information by providing the user ID and password. Also, you may need to update the class location. Once the user ID and password have been entered, you can click **Test Connection**.

3. Create the BANK database tables from within Rational Application Developer.

   For details refer to "Create DB2 UDB database tables via a DB2 command window" on page 351.

4. Populate the BANK database tables with sample data from within Rational Application Developer.

   For details refer to "Populate the tables via a DB2 UDB command window" on page 354.

After creating the BANK database, tables, and loading the sample data, view the database tables by opening the Database Explorer in the Data perspective, as seen in Figure 14-10 on page 778.

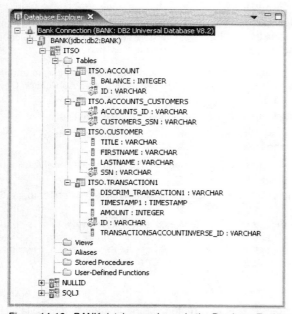

Figure 14-10   BANK database schema in the Database Explorer view

Right-click the **ITSO.CUSTOMER** table, and select **Sample contents**. You should see results like Figure 14-11 in the DB Output view.

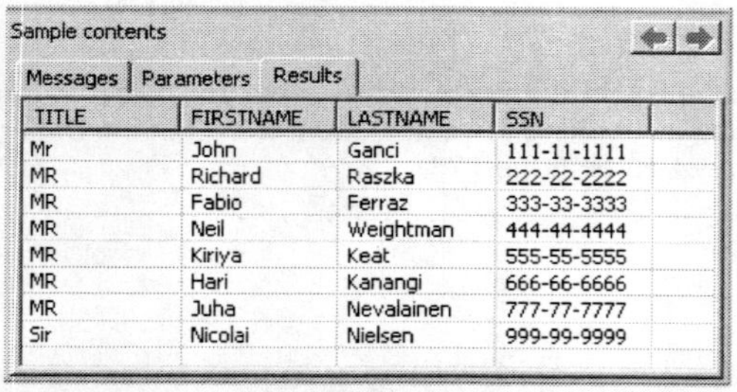

TITLE	FIRSTNAME	LASTNAME	SSN
Mr	John	Ganci	111-11-1111
MR	Richard	Raszka	222-22-2222
MR	Fabio	Ferraz	333-33-3333
MR	Neil	Weightman	444-44-4444
MR	Kiriya	Keat	555-55-5555
MR	Hari	Kanangi	666-66-6666
MR	Juha	Nevalainen	777-77-7777
Sir	Nicolai	Nielsen	999-99-9999

Figure 14-11   ITSO.CUSTOMER table sample data in DB Output view

14.3.6 Configure EGL preferences for SQL database connection

The EGL wizards rely upon the SQL database connection being configured. To configure the EGL preferences with the appropriate DB2 SQL database connection, do the following:

1. Select **Window** → **Preferences**.
2. When the Preferences dialog appears, expand **EGL and select SQL Database Connection**.
3. When the SQL Database Connection dialog appears, enter the following (as seen in Figure 14-12 on page 780), and then click **OK**:
   - Connection URL: `jdbc:db2:BANK`
   - Database: `BANK`
   - Database vendor type: Select **DB2 Universal Database Express V8.2**.
   - JDBC driver: Select **IBM DB2 App Driver**.
   - JDBC driver class: `COM.ibm.db2.jdbc.app.DB2Driver`
   - Class location: `C:\Program Files\IBM\SQLLIB\java\db2java.zip`
   - Connection JNDI name: `jdbc/BankDS`

   > **Note:** This value should match the value entered when creating the EGL Web Project in 14.3.4, "Create an EGL Web Project" on page 773.

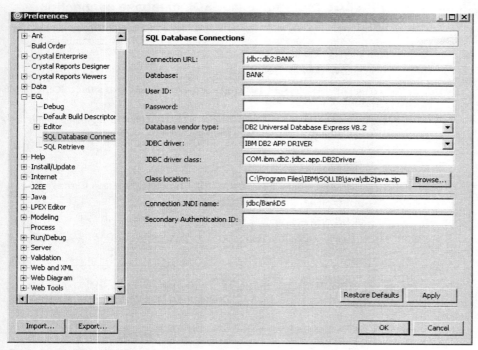

Figure 14-12   EGL preferences

14.3.7 Configure the data source

There are a couple methods that can be used to configure the datasource, including using the WebSphere Administrative Console or using the WebSphere Enhanced EAR, which stores the configuration in the deployment descriptor and is deployed with the application.

This section describes how to configure the datasource using the WebSphere Enhanced EAR capabilities. The enhanced EAR is configured in the Deployment tab of the EAR deployment descriptor.

The procedure found in this section considers two scenarios for using the enhanced EAR:

- If you choose to import the complete sample code, you will only need to verify that the value of the databaseName property in the deployment descriptor matches the location of your database.
- If you are going to complete the working example Web application found in this chapter, you will need to create the JDBC provider and datasource, and update the databaseName property.

Note: For more information on configuring data sources and general deployment issues, refer to Chapter 23, "Deploy enterprise applications" on page 1189.

Configure authentication

To configure the authentication settings in the enterprise application deployment descriptor where the enhanced EAR settings are defined, do the following:

1. Open the Web perspective Project Explorer view.
2. Expand **Enterprise Applications** → **BankEGLEAR**.
3. Double-click **Deployment Descriptor : BankEGLEAR** to open the file in the Deployment Descriptor Editor.
4. Click the **Deployment** tab.
5. Click **Authentication** (lower left of page).
6. Click **Add**.
7. When the Add JASS Authentication Entry dialog appears, enter the following and then click **OK**:
   - Alias: dbuser
   - User ID: db2admin
   - Password: <your_db2admin_password>

Configure a new JDBC provider

To create a new JDBC provider for DB2 Universal Database, do the following:

1. From the Deployment tab of the Application Deployment Descriptor, click **Add** under the JDBC provider list.
2. When the Create a JDBC Provider dialog appears, select **IBM DB2** as the Database type, select **DB2 Universal Database JDBC Driver Provider (XA)** as the JDBC provider type, and then click **Next**.
3. Enter DB2 Universal JDBC Driver Provider (XA) in the Name field (as seen in Figure 14-13 on page 782), and then click **Finish**.

Note: Our example only requires the db2jcc.jar and db2jcc_license_cu.jar.

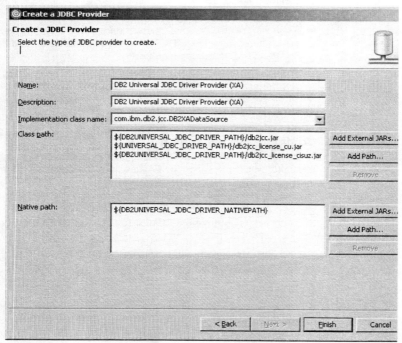

Figure 14-13 Add new JDBC provider

Configure the data source

To configure a new data source using the enhanced EAR capability in the deployment descriptor, do the following:

1. From the Deployment tab of the Application Deployment Descriptor, click the JDBC provider created in the previous step.
2. Click **Add** next to data source.
3. When the Create a Data Source dialog appears, select **DB2 Universal Database JDBC Driver Provider (XA)** under the JDBC provider, select **Version 5.0 data source**, and then click **Next**.

4. When the Create a Data Source dialog appears, enter the following and click **Finish**:
   – Name: BankDS
   – JNDI name: jdbc/BankDS
   – Component managed authentication alias: Select **dbuser**.

   > **Note:** The user is configured in "Configure authentication" on page 781.

Configure the databaseName property

To configure the databaseName in the new data source using the enhanced EAR capability in the deployment descriptor to define the location of the database for your environment, do the following:

1. Select the data source created in the previous section.
2. Select the **databaseName** property under the Resource properties.
3. Click **Edit** next to Resource properties to change the value for the databaseName.
4. When the Edit a resource property dialog appears, enter BANK in the Value field and then click **OK**.
5. Save the Application Deployment Descriptor.

14.3.8 Configure the DB2 JDBC class path environment variables

The JDBC provider for DB2 Universal Database, which we configured in "Configure a new JDBC provider" on page 781, depends upon environment variables being defined. We chose to update the environment variable values for the WebSphere Application Server environment in which the application will be deployed via the WebSphere Administrative Console.

Table 14-1   DB2 Universal Database JDBC driver classpath environment variables

Variable name	Path value
DB2UNIVERSAL_JDBC_DRIVER_PATH	C:\Program Files\IBM\SQLLIB\java
UNIVERSAL_JDBC_DRIVER_PATH	${WAS_INSTALL_ROOT}/universalDriver/lib

To configure the DB2 Universal Database JDBC driver classpath environment variables listed in Table 14-1, do the following:

1. Open the Web perspective.
2. From the Servers view, right-click the WebSphere Application Server v6.0 test server, and select **Start**.

3. After the server is started, right-click the WebSphere Application Server V6.0 test server, and select **Run administrative console**.
4. When prompted for a user ID, you can enter an ID or simply click **Log in** since WebSphere security is not enabled.
5. Expand **Environment**.
6. Click **WebSphere Variables**.
7. Ensure that the variables listed in Table 14-1 on page 783 are configured correctly for your environment at the node level. If they are not configured, enter the appropriate path values. Click **OK**.
8. Click **Save**, and then **Save to Master**.
9. Click **Logout**.
10. Restart the WebSphere Application Server V6.0 test server.

14.4 Develop the Web application using EGL

This section provides a working example describing how to develop a Web application using EGL. The application will use EGL for database access (records, libraries) and Faces JSPs with EGL page handlers for the user interface.

This section includes the following tasks:

- Create the EGL data parts.
- Create and customize a page template.
- Create the Faces JSPs using the Web Diagram tool.
- Add EGL components to the Faces JSPs.

When developing a Web application using EGL, there are several options that can be used to get started, including:

- EGL Data Parts and Pages wizard.

    When using the EGL Data Parts and Pages wizard, you will be guided through a sequence of dialogs that result in creating an EGL Web Project.

    Within minutes you will have a simple working application, customized for your database schema, ready for you to further customize.

    The down side to this approach is that you have less control of what is being created. Furthermore, the wizard can only be used to initially create a project, not update the contents of an existing project.

- Create EGL Web Project, Data Parts, and Faces JSPs individually.

When using this approach, we will still take advantage of the EGL wizards and tooling provided, with more control with what resources are created.

In our working example, we chose this approach. We will first create an EGL Web Project. Then we will create the EGL source for database access using the EGL Data Parts wizard. Finally we will create the Faces JSPs and EGL page handlers. We will then generate the Java resources and test the Web application on the WebSphere Application Server V6.0 test server.

14.4.1 Create the EGL data parts

There are a few methods of creating EGL data parts. In our example, we chose to use the EGL Data Parts wizard to create the EGL source files that define an SQL record type and reusable functions associated for the record type.

This section is organized as follows:

- Create records and libraries via the EGL Data Parts wizard.
- Summary of code created by the EGL Data Parts wizard.
- Generate the Java code for the EGL file.
- Create the Customer to Account relationship.
- Modify the SQL in the EGL source code.

Create records and libraries via the EGL Data Parts wizard

To create the records and libraries for customers and account, using the EGL Data Parts wizard, do the following:

1. Open the EGL perspective, Project Explorer view.
2. Expand **Dynamic Web Projects** → **BankEGL**.
3. Right-click the **EGLSource** folder, and select **New** → **EGL Data Parts**.
4. When the Generate EGL Components dialog appears, do the following:

    a. EGL project name: Select **BankEGL**.

    b. Database connection: Click **Add**.

> **Note:** At the time of writing, when using the EGL Data Parts wizard, only database connections for *DB2 aliases* worked. If a database connection was created with the *Database Manager and JDBC driver* option, you will not be able to use the database connection in the EGL Data Parts wizard (once selected, the wizard will not allow you to click Next).
>
> Additionally, we found that once a database connection is used by the EGL Data Parts wizard, it cannot be used again to create a new record with the EGL Data Parts wizard.
>
> You can manage database connections in the Database Explorer view of the Data perspective.

    c. When the Establish a connection to a database dialog appears, select **Choose a DB2 alias**, enter `EGL Bank Connection` in the Connection name field, and then click **Next**.

    d. When the Specify connection parameters dialog appears, do the following:

        i. For the JDBC driver, select **IBM DB2 Universal**.

        ii. For the Alias, select **BANK**.

        iii. Click **Test Connection** to verify the settings. You should see the message `Connection to BANK is successful`. Click **OK**.

        iv. Click **Finish**.

    e. When you return to the Generate EGL Components dialog, select **ACCOUNT** and **CUSTOMERS** under the Select your data column, and click the **>** to add to the column on the right of the dialog. When done the dialog should look like Figure 14-14 on page 787. Click **Next**.

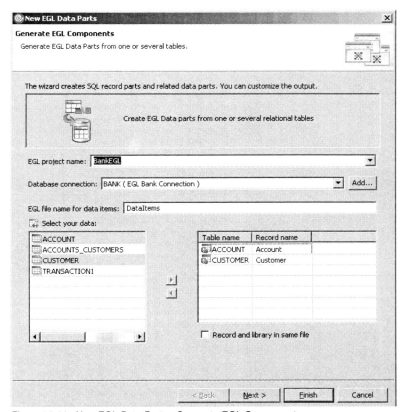

Figure 14-14 New EGL Data Parts - Generate EGL Components

> **Note:** The "Record and library in same file" check box seen in Figure 14-14 on page 787 allows us to keep the record and library content in the same file. In our example, we chose to keep them separate (default).

5. When the Define the Fields dialog appears, as seen in Figure 14-15 on page 788, we accepted the default settings and clicked **Next**.

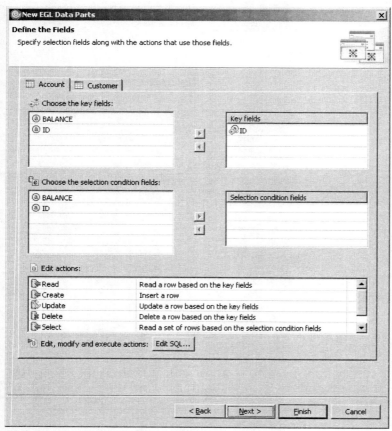

Figure 14-15   New EGL Data Parts - Define the Fields

6. When the Generate EGL Data Parts Summary dialog appears, as seen in Figure 14-16 on page 789, we accepted the default settings and clicked **Finish**.

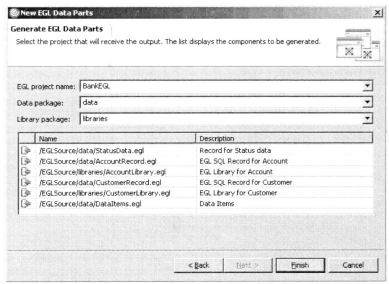

Figure 14-16 New EGL Data Parts - Summary

7. You should see a dialog with the message Successful Generation. Click **OK**.

Summary of code created by the EGL Data Parts wizard

The objective of this section is to provide a basic understanding of what was created by the EGL Data Parts wizard.

Figure 14-17 on page 790 displays the EGL and Java source files generated by the EGL Data Parts wizard for the sample. Notice there are data and libraries package folders under the EGLSource folder. Also, notice there is a JavaSource folder that has corresponding packages for data and libraries. When the EGL Generate feature is executed on the EGL source, the Java source will be generated in the appropriate JavaSource sub folder.

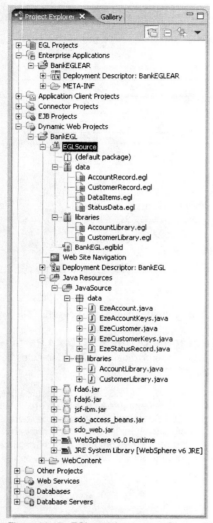

Figure 14-17 EGL and Java source files generated by the EGL Data Parts wizard

The data folder in the EGLSource contains EGL source files with record definitions for the database schema. For example, the CustomerRecord.egl file contains the record definition for the Customer table, as seen in Example 14-1.

Example 14-1   Sample CustomerRecord.egl

```
package data;

Record Customer type SQLRecord

    { tableNames = [["ITSO.CUSTOMER"]],
      keyitems = ["ssn"] }

    title TITLE {column = "TITLE", sqlVariableLen = yes, maxlen = 250, isNullable = yes};
    firstname FIRSTNAME {column = "FIRSTNAME", sqlVariableLen = yes, maxlen = 250, isNullable = yes};
    lastname LASTNAME {column = "LASTNAME", sqlVariableLen = yes, maxlen = 250, isNullable = yes};
    ssn SSN       {column = "SSN", sqlVariableLen = yes, maxlen = 250};

// used in arrays: index of the row
    indexInArray int {persistent = no};
end

// define the data to store in the session for a detail of Customer
 Record CustomerKeys type BasicRecord
   ssn SSN;
end

// define the data to store in the session for a list of Customer
 Record CustomerSessionListData type BasicRecord
// index of the first item of the current page
    indexOfCurrentPage int;
end
```

The record definition in Example 14-1 uses the type names SSN, TITLE, FIRSTNAME, and LASTNAME to define the types for the fields of the record. These are not built-in types, but defined in the file DataItems.egl, placed in the same folder as the record definition. Example 14-2 displays the contents of the DataItems.egl file. In addition to the type definitions for the Customer record, Example 14-2 also contains type definitions for the fields ID and BALANCE from the Account record.

Example 14-2   Sample DataItems.egl

```
package data;

DataItem BALANCE int {displayName = "BALANCE"} end
```

```
DataItem ID string {displayName = "ID"} end
DataItem SSN string {displayName = "SSN"} end
DataItem LASTNAME string {displayName = "LASTNAME"} end
DataItem FIRSTNAME string {displayName = "FIRSTNAME"} end
DataItem TITLE string {displayName = "TITLE"} end
```

To access the record, functions were created in the CustomerLibrary.egl file found in the libraries directory. Example 14-3 lists the contents of the CustomerLibrary.egl containing functions to manipulate the Customer record.

Example 14-3 Sample CustomerLibrary.egl

```
package libraries;
import data.StatusRecord;
import data.Customer;
import data.CustomerKeys;

Library CustomerLibrary

    /* Pass ssn in via Customer argument.
    Customer is returned if found. Status is returned with success or failure */
    Function readCustomer (customer Customer, sqlStatusData StatusRecord)

        try
            get customer;
            sqlStatusData.sqlStatus = 0;
        onException
            sqlStatusData.sqlStatus = sysvar.sqlCode;
            sqlStatusData.description = syslib.currentException.description;
        end
    end

    /* Pass ssn in via CustomerKeys argument.
    Customer is returned if found. Status is returned with success or failure */
    Function readCustomerFromKeyRecord (customer Customer, CustomerKeys customerKeys,
sqlStatusData StatusRecord)

        customer.ssn = customerKeys.ssn;
        readCustomer (customer, sqlStatusData);
    end

    /* Pass Customer to be created argument.
    Status is returned with success or failure */
    Function createCustomer (customer Customer, sqlStatusData StatusRecord)

        try
            add customer;
            sqlStatusData.sqlStatus = 0;
        onException
```

```
         sqlStatusData.sqlStatus = sysvar.sqlCode;
         sqlStatusData.description = syslib.currentException.description;
      end
end

/* Pass Customer to be deleted argument.
Status is returned with success or failure */
Function deleteCustomer (customer Customer, sqlStatusData StatusRecord)

   try
      execute #sql{
       DELETE FROM ITSO.CUSTOMER WHERE CUSTOMER.SSN = :customer.ssn
      };
      sqlStatusData.sqlStatus = 0;
   onException
      sqlStatusData.sqlStatus = sysvar.sqlCode;
      sqlStatusData.description = syslib.currentException.description;
   end
end

/* Pass Customer to be updated argument.
Status is returned with success or failure */
Function updateCustomer (customer Customer, sqlStatusData StatusRecord)
   try
      execute #sql{
        UPDATE ITSO.CUSTOMER SET TITLE = :customer.title, FIRSTNAME = :customer.firstname,
          LASTNAME = :customer.lastname WHERE CUSTOMER.SSN = :customer.ssn
      };
      sqlStatusData.sqlStatus = 0;
   onException
      sqlStatusData.sqlStatus = sysvar.sqlCode;
      sqlStatusData.description = syslib.currentException.description;
   end
end

/* Pass Customer[] dynamic array to be returned with data.
Status is returned with success or failure */
Function selectCustomer (customer Customer[], sqlStatusData StatusRecord)

   try
      get customer;
      sqlStatusData.sqlStatus = 0;
   onException
      sqlStatusData.sqlStatus = sysvar.sqlCode;
      sqlStatusData.description = syslib.currentException.description;
   end
end
```

end

Generate the Java code for the EGL file

In our example, the Java source code was generated from the EGL source files automatically by the EGL Data Parts wizard. After modifying the EGL source files, the files are typically generated automatically. On occasion, you will need to run the Generate feature manually to generate the corresponding Java source.

Generate Java from an individual EGL library source file

To generate Java from an individual EGL library source file, do the following:

1. Open the EGL perspective Project Explorer view.
2. Expand **Dynamic Web Projects** → **BankEGL** → **EGLSource**.
3. Right-click the EGL library source file, and select **Generate**.

    Alternatively, in the Source Editor view of an EGL source file, right-click and then select **Generate** (or press CTRL+G).

> **Attention:** Java source for EGL data (records) source files are only generated when a EGL library source file that references the record is being generated.
>
> Although it is possible to select an EGL record source file and run the Generate task, it will not generate Java source. You must run the Generate task on an EGL library source file that references the record.

Generate all EGL files in a EGL Web Project

To generate EGL files in a EGL Web Project, do the following:

1. From the EGL perspective, expand **Dynamic Web Projects**.
2. Right-click **BankEGL**, and select **Generate With Wizard**.
3. When the Generate wizard appears, click **Select All**, and click **Next**.
4. Select **Use one build descriptor for all parts**, select **BankEGLWebBuildOptions <BankEGL/EGLSource/BankEGL.eglbld>** from the drop-down list, and then click **Finish**.

Create the Customer to Account relationship

In our example, we needed to create an EGL record that joins the Accounts and Accounts_Customers tables, so that we can retrieve all account information for a customer. At the time of writing, the EGL tooling did not provide this capability; therefore, we needed to add the EGL source manually.

Create the Customer_AccountsRecord.egl

To create the Customer_AccountsRecord.egl, do the following:

1. Open the EGL perspective.
2. Expand Dynamic **Web Projects** → **BankEGL** → **EGLSource**.
3. Right-click **data**, and select **New** → **EGL Source File**.
4. When the New EGL Source file dialog appears, enter Customer_AccountsRecord in the EGL source file name field, and click **Finish**.
5. Open the Customer_AccountsRecord.egl file.
6. Enter the contents of Example 14-4 into the Customer_AccountsRecord.egl file.

> **Note:** The code in Example 14-4 can be found in c:\6449code\egl\Customer_AccountsRecordSnippet.txt.

Example 14-4   Add contents to Customer_AccountsRecord.egl

```
package data;

Record Customer_Accounts type SQLRecord {
   tableNames = [["ITSO.ACCOUNTS_CUSTOMERS", "AC"], ["ITSO.ACCOUNT", "A"]],
   defaultSelectCondition = #sqlCondition{
        AC.ACCOUNTS_ID=A.ID
        and AC.CUSTOMERS_SSN=:customers_ssn }}
end
```

7. Place the cursor inside the record, and press Ctrl+Shift+R to retrieve the record data.

   After running the SQL retrieve, the Customer_AccountsRecord.egl file should look similar to Example 14-5 (SQL formatted for readability).

> **Note:** The code in Example 14-5 can be found in c:\6449code\egl\Customer_AccountsRecord.egl.

Example 14-5   After SQL retrieve - Customer_AccountsRecord.egl

```
package data;

Record Customer_Accounts type SQLRecord {
   tableNames = [["ITSO.ACCOUNTS_CUSTOMERS", "AC"], ["ITSO.ACCOUNT", "A"]],
   defaultSelectCondition = #sqlCondition{
        AC.ACCOUNTS_ID=A.ID
        and AC.CUSTOMERS_SSN=:customers_ssn },
   keyItems=["ACCOUNTS_ID", "CUSTOMERS_SSN", "ID"]}
```

```
    ACCOUNTS_ID string {
         column="AC.ACCOUNTS_ID", isReadOnly=yes,
         sqlVariableLen=yes, maxLen=250};
    CUSTOMERS_SSN string {
         column="AC.CUSTOMERS_SSN", isReadOnly=yes,
         sqlVariableLen=yes, maxLen=250};
    BALANCE int {
         column="A.BALANCE", isReadOnly=yes};
    ID string {
         column="A.ID", isReadOnly=yes,
         sqlVariableLen=yes, maxLen=250};
end
```

8. Save the Customer_AccountsRecord.egl file.

Create the Customer_AccountsLibrary.egl

To create the Customer_AccountsLibrary.egl, do the following:

1. Open the EGL perspective.
2. Expand Dynamic **Web Projects** → **BankEGL** → **EGLSource**.
3. Right-click **library**, and select **New** → **EGL Source File**.
4. When the New EGL Source file dialog appears, enter Customer_AccountsLibrary in the EGL source file name field, and click **Finish**.
5. Open the Customer_AccountsLibrary.egl file.
6. Enter the contents of Example 14-6 into the Customers_AccountsLibrary.egl file.

> **Note:** The contents of Example 14-4 can be found in the c:\6449code\egl\Customer_AccountsLibrary.egl.

Example 14-6   Add contents to Customer_AccountsLibrary.egl

```
package libraries;
import data.StatusRecord;
import data.Customer;
import data.Customer_Accounts;
import data.Customer_AccountsKeys;

Library Customer_AccountsLibrary


    Function getCustomerAccountsByCustomer(
          customer Customer,
```

```
                customerAccounts Customer_Accounts[],
                sqlStatusData StatusRecord)
        returns (int)

        customers_ssn char(250);

        customers_ssn = Customer.ssn;

        try
            get customerAccounts usingkeys customers_ssn;
            sqlStatusData.sqlStatus = 0;
        onException
            sqlStatusData.sqlStatus = sysvar.sqlCode;
            sqlStatusData.description = syslib.currentException.description;
        end
    end
end
```

7. Save the Customers_AccountsLibrary.egl file.
8. Generate the Java source from the EGL library.

    For details refer to "Generate Java from an individual EGL library source file" on page 794.

Modify the SQL in the EGL source code

At the time of writing, we found that the EGL Data Parts wizard prefixed table names with the schema name in the FROM clause; however, the wizard prefixed the column names with the table name, without the schema name. This results in an invalid SQL statement, which requires that you modify the code manually.

> **Note:** While creating our sample, we only tested with the following software:
> - IBM Rational Application Developer V6.0 with Interim Fix 0004
> - IBM DB2 Universal Database V8.2 Express Edition (included with Rational Application Developer)
>
> We were not able to verify if this issue applies to other database platforms.

While testing our sample application, we found that our database update function for customer data did not work properly due to this issue. We have included a sample of the generated and modified source to resolve this issue:

- Generated EGL library source for deleting a customer (formatted for readability):

```
DELETE FROM ITSO.CUSTOMER
WHERE CUSTOMER.SSN = :customer.ssn
```

- Corrected EGL library source for deleting a customer:

  ```
  DELETE FROM ITSO.CUSTOMER
  WHERE ITSO.CUSTOMER.SSN = :customer.ssn
  ```

- Generated EGL library source for updating a customer (formatted for readability):

  ```
  UPDATE ITSO.CUSTOMER
  SET    TITLE = :customer.title,
         FIRSTNAME = :customer.firstname,
         LASTNAME = :customer.lastname
  WHERE CUSTOMER.SSN = :customer.ssn
  ```

- Corrected EGL library source for updating a customer:

  ```
  UPDATE ITSO.CUSTOMER
  SET    TITLE = :customer.title,
         FIRSTNAME = :customer.firstname,
         LASTNAME = :customer.lastname
  WHERE ITSO.CUSTOMER.SSN = :customer.ssn
  ```

To work around this issue for our sample application, we modified the EGL library source file generated by the EGL Data Parts wizard to include the schema name.

1. Open the Web perspective.
2. Expand the **Dynamic Web Projects** → **BankEGL** → **EGLSource** → **libraries**.
3. Double-click **CustomerLibrary.egl** to open in the source editor.
4. Modify the generated SQL code to match the corrected SQL that includes the schema name (ITSO) as follows:

   – Generated:

   ```
   UPDATE ITSO.CUSTOMER
   SET    TITLE = :customer.title,
          FIRSTNAME = :customer.firstname,
          LASTNAME = :customer.lastname
   WHERE CUSTOMER.SSN = :customer.ssn
   ```

   – Corrected:

   ```
   UPDATE ITSO.CUSTOMER
   SET    TITLE = :customer.title,
          FIRSTNAME = :customer.firstname,
          LASTNAME = :customer.lastname
   WHERE ITSO.CUSTOMER.SSN = :customer.ssn
   ```

5. Save the CustomerLibrary.egl file.
6. Generate the CustomerLibrary.egl by pressing Ctrl+G.

14.4.2 Create and customize a page template

This section describes how to create and customize a page template. We will use the page template in a later section to provide a common look and feel for the JSF pages.

> **Note:** For more detailed information on creating and customizing page templates used by JSF pages, refer to the following:
> - 13.3.1, "Create a page template" on page 684
> - 13.3.2, "Useful views for editing page template files" on page 687
> - 13.3.3, "Customize the page template" on page 695

Create a page template

To create a page template containing JSF components, do the following:

1. Open the Web perspective Project Explorer view.
2. Expand **Dynamic Web Projects**.
3. Right-click the **BankEGL** project, and select **New** → **Page Template File** from the context menu.
4. When the New Page Template wizard appears, enter the following and then click **Finish**:
   - Folder: /BankEGL/WebContent
   - File name: BankEGLTemplate
   - Model: Select **Template containing Faces Components**.
5. When prompted with the message A page template must contain at least one Content Area which is later filled in by the pages that use the template, click **OK**. We will add a content area as part of our page template customization.

Customize the page template

Now that you have created a page template, it is likely that you will want to customize the page. This section demonstrates how to make the following common customizations to a page template:

- Customize the logo image and title of the page template.
- Customize the style of the page template.
- Add the content area to the page template.

Customize the logo image and title of the page template

To customize the page template to include the ITSO logo image and ITSO RedBank title, do the following:

1. Open the Web perspective.

2. Import the itso_logo.gif image.
    a. Expand **Dynamic Web Projects** → **BankEGL** → **WebContent** → **theme**.
    b. Right-click the **theme** folder, and select **Import**.
    c. Select **File System** and click **Next**.
    d. Enter `c:\6449code\web` in the From directory, check **itso_logo.gif**, and then click **Finish**.
3. Expand **Dynamic Web Projects** → **BankEGL** → **WebContent**.
4. Double-click **BankEGLTemplate.jtpl** to open the file.
5. Click the **Design** tab.
6. Select the text **Place content here**, right-click, and select **Delete**.
7. From the Palettes view, expand **Faces Components**.
8. Select the **Panel - Group Box** and drag it onto the page.
9. When the Select Type dialog appears, select **List** and then click **OK**.
10. You should now see a box on your page with the text `box1: Drag and Drop Items from the palette to this area to populate this region`. From the Faces Components, select **Image** and drag it to the panel.
11. Update the image values in the Properties view.
    a. Select the image on the page to highlight the image.
    b. In the Properties view, enter `headerImage` in the Id field.
    c. Click the folder icon next to File and select **Import**. Enter the path to the image and click **Open**. In our example, we entered /WebContent/themes/itso_logo.gif to import the image.
    d. You will notice that the absolute reference has been entered. We need to make it a relative reference by removing the /BankEGL/ from the File field. After making the change, it will be theme/itso_logo.gif without any leading slash.
12. From the Faces Components palette, select **Output** and drag it under the image.
13. In the Properties view enter `ITSO RedBank` into the Value field.
14. Select the Output box (ITSO RedBank) and drag it to the right of the image.

Customize the style of the page template

To customize the style of the page template, do the following:

1. Select the Output text box on the page.
2. In the Properties view, click the button next to the Style: Props: field.

3. Change the Size field value to 18.
4. Select **Arial** for the Font and click **Add**.
5. Select **sans-serif** (rule of thumb) for the Font and click **Add**.
6. Click **OK**.

Add the content area to the page template

To add the required content area to the page template, do the following:

1. Right-click under the Output field and from the context menu select **Insert** → **Horizontal Rule**.
2. Expand **Page Template** in the Palette view.
3. From the Page Template, select the **Content Area** and drag it under the horizontal rule.
4. When the Insert Content Area for Page Template dialog appears, accept the default name (bodyarea) and click **OK**.
5. Right-click under the content area and from the context menu select **Insert** → **Horizontal Rule**.
6. Save the page template file.

The customized page template file should look similar to Figure 14-18.

Figure 14-18 Customized page template - BankEGLTemplate.jtpl

14.4.3 Create the Faces JSPs using the Web Diagram tool

This section demonstrates how to create the Faces JSPs using the Web Diagram tool, including the following tasks:

- Create a Web diagram.
- Create a Web page using the Web Diagram tool.
- Create a Faces JSP file.
- Create connections between Faces JSPs.

The sample application consists of the following pages:

- Login page (Login.jsp): Validate the entered CustomerSSN. If it is valid it will then display the Customer details for the entered customer.
- Customer account details page (ListAccounts.jsp): Display the customer's account details.

Create a Web diagram

By default, and EGL Web Project does not include a Web diagram like other Web Projects. To add a Web diagram to the EGL Web Project, do the following:

1. Open the Web perspective.
2. Expand Dynamic **Web Projects**.
3. Right-click **BankEGL**, and select **New** → **Other**.
4. Expand **Web**, select **Web Diagram**, and click **Next**.
5. When the Web Diagram dialog appears, enter `BankEGL Web Diagram` in the File name field, and then click **Finish**.

> **Note:** Although at a file system level the Web diagram is named Bank EGL Web Diagram.gph, within the Project Explorer it will be named Web diagram if there is only one diagram. After creating more than one Web diagram, they will be displayed with the actual file name in a folder called Web diagrams.

Create a Web page using the Web Diagram tool

To create a page using the Web Diagram tool, do the following:

1. Open the Web perspective Project Explorer view.
2. Expand Dynamic **Web Projects** → **BankEGL**.
3. Double-click **Web Diagram** to open.
4. When the Web diagram appears in the Web Diagram Editor, select **Web Page** from the Web Parts palette and drag it onto the page.

5. In the Properties view change Web Page Path value to /Login.jsp, and change the description to The login page.

   Note: Now that we have created a Web page in the Web Diagram tool, you may notice that the BankJSFLogin.jsp icon has a gray-blue tint. The reason for this is that it is not linked to an actual JSP file. We will use this diagram to create the actual JSP file that this icon will link to in a later step.

6. Repeat the process to create a Web page for /ListAccounts.jsp.

Create a Faces JSP file

To create the Faces JSP file from a page template using the Web diagram, do the following:

1. Double-click the **Login.jsp** in the Web diagram.
2. When the New Faces JSP File wizard appears, enter the following and then click **Next**:
   - Folder: /BankEGL/WebContent
   - File name: Login.jsp
   - Options: Check **Create from page template**.

   Note: If you have not already created the page template, refer to 14.4.2, "Create and customize a page template" on page 799, to create one.

3. When the Page Template File Selection page appears, select **User-defined page template**, select **BankEGLTemplate.jtpl**, and then click **Finish**.
4. The new Faces JSP file will be loaded into the Page Designer. At this point, the newly create JSF page should look like the page template.
5. Double-click **Web Diagram** to repeat the process to create the ListAccounts.jsf Faces JSPs using the BankEGLTemplate.jtpl page template.
6. Save the Web diagram.

   Now that the pages have been realized, the Web page icons should have color and the title icons displayed in bold.

Figure 14-19 on page 804 displays the EGL page handlers and corresponding Faces JSPs in the Project Explorer view. The EGL page handlers are created automatically when the Faces JSPs are created (realized in the Web diagram) within the EGL Web Project.

The EGL page handlers are used to define the EGL functionality within a Faces JSP. For example, the page handler will contain the code to be executed when a button within the Faces JSP, such as Logout, is clicked.

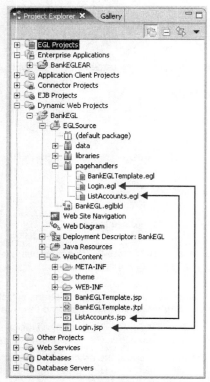

Figure 14-19 Creation of EGL pagehandlers when creating JSF page

Create connections between Faces JSPs

Now that the pages have been created, we can create connections between the pages.

To add connections between pages, do the following:

1. Create a connection from Login.jsp to ListAccounts.jsp.

    a. Click **Connection** from the Palette. Click **Login.jsp**, and then click **ListAccounts.jsp**.

> **Note:** The Connection palette item is not dragged to the Web diagram like the remaining palette items.

   b. When the Choose a Connection dialog appears, select **Faces Outcome** → **ListAccounts** (defaults to target name), as seen in Figure 14-20, and then click **OK**.

Figure 14-20 Choose a Connection dialog

2. Create a connection from ListAccounts.jsp to Login.jsp.

   a. Click **Connection** ![Connection] from the Palette, click **ListAccounts.jsp**, and then click **Login.jsp**.

   b. When the Choose a Connection dialog appears, select **Faces Outcome** → **<new>** and then click **OK**.

   c. Click **<new>** and change the name to `Logout`.

   d. Double-click **connection** and click **OK**.

When done, your Web diagram should look like Figure 14-21 on page 806.

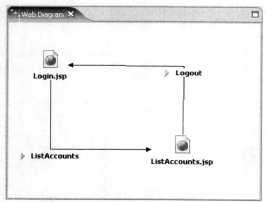

Figure 14-21   Web diagram

14.4.4 Add EGL components to the Faces JSPs

This section describes how to add the EGL components created in 14.4.1, "Create the EGL data parts" on page 785, to the Faces JSPs such that the application will have database access to read and update the database.

Add the content to the Login.jsp

To add the content to the JSP file, do the following:

1. Open the Web perspective, Project Explorer view.
2. Expand **Dynamic Web Projects** → **BankEGL** → **WebContent**
3. Double-click **Login.jsp** to open in the editor.
4. Click the **Design** tab.
5. Select the text **Default content of bodyarea**, and press Delete.
6. In the Palette, expand **EGL**.
7. Click **Record** and drag it to the page data view.
8. When the Select a Record Part dialog appears, do the following (as seen in Figure 14-22 on page 807), and then click **OK**:
   – Select **Customer (data/CustomerRecord.egl)**.
   – Enter the name of the field: `customer` (default)
   – Uncheck **Add controls to display the EGL element on the Web page**.

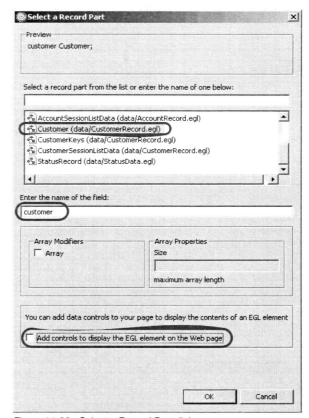

Figure 14-22 Select a Record Part dialog

The Page Data view will now display the customer, as shown in Figure 14-23 on page 808.

Figure 14-23   Page Data view

9. In the Page Data view, expand **Login** → **customer - Customer**.

10. Select the **ssn - SSN** field from the customer record and drag it onto the page.

11. When the Insert Control dialog appears, do the following:

    a. Select **Updating an existing record**.

    b. For the Label enter `Enter Customer SSN:`

    c. Select **Input field** for the Control Type.

    d. Click **Options**.

    e. When the Options dialog appears, uncheck **Delete button**, enter `Login` in the Label field (as seen in Figure 14-24), and then click **OK**.

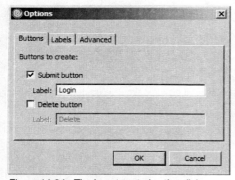

Figure 14-24   The insert control option dialog

12. The Insert Control page should look like Figure 14-25 on page 809. Click **Finish**.

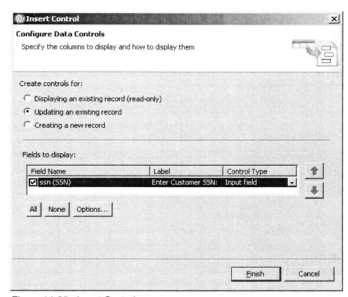

Figure 14-25   Insert Control

The resulting Login page should look similar to Figure 14-26 on page 810 in the Design view.

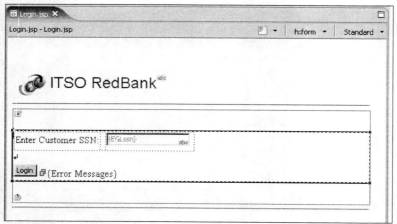

Figure 14-26   Login.jsp page

13. To add an EGL action to the login button:

    a. Select the **Login** button on the page.
    b. Open the Quick Edit view.
    c. Insert the code from Example 14-7 into the quick edit view.

    > **Note:** The Login source code found in Example 14-7 can be found in the c:\6449\egl\login_handler.txt.

Example 14-7   Login button code
```
// define SQL status area
sqlStatusData StatusRecord;

// lookup customer
libraries.CustomerLibrary.readCustomer(customer, sqlStatusData);

if (sqlStatusData.sqlStatus == 0)
   // SQL code 0 = No error. Record found.
   // Add the customer's SSN to the session variable customerSSN
   // and forward to the accounts page.
   J2EELib.setSessionAttr("customerSSN", customer.SSN);
   forward to "ListAccounts";
else
   if (sqlStatusData.sqlStatus == 100)
```

```
        // SQL code 100 = No row found. Set error code to display.
        setError("Customer does not exist");
    else
        // Unknown database error
        setError("Customer retrieval failed - database error");
    end
end
```

Before we can test the login screen we must first create a session scope variable, a navigation rule, and a new jsp file to be forwarded to.

14. Add a new Session Scope variable called `customerSSN`.

    a. In the Page Data view, right-click and select **New** → **ScriptingVariable** → **Session Scope Variable**.

    b. When the Add Session Scope Variable dialog appears, enter `customerSSN` in the Variable name field, enter `java.lang.String` in the Type field, and then click **OK**.

Add content to the ListAccounts.jsp

This section describes the steps required to complete the ListAccounts.jsp.

Add customer data

To add the content to the JSP file, do the following:

1. Open the Web perspective, Project Explorer view.
2. Expand **Dynamic Web Projects** → **BankEGL** → **WebContent**
3. Double-click **ListAccounts.jsp** to open in the editor.
4. Click the **Design** tab.
5. Select the text **Default content of bodyarea**, and press Delete.
6. In the Palette, expand **EGL**.
7. Click **Record** and drag it to the Page Data view.
8. When the Select a Record Part dialog appears, do the following (as seen in Figure 14-22 on page 807), and then click **OK**:
    - Select **Customer (data/CustomerRecord.egl)**.
    - Enter the name of the field: `customer`(default)
    - Check **Add controls to display the EGL element on the Web page**.
9. When the Configure Data Controls dialog appears, do the following:

    a. Select **Updating a existing record**.

    b. Uncheck **indexInArray**.

    c. Change the labels as seen in Figure 14-27 on page 812.

Chapter 14. Develop Web applications using EGL   **811**

d. In the Control Type drop-down for SSN, select **Output field**.
e. Click **Options**.
   i. Uncheck **Delete**.
   ii. Change the label to Update.
   iii. Click **OK**.
f. Click **Finish**.

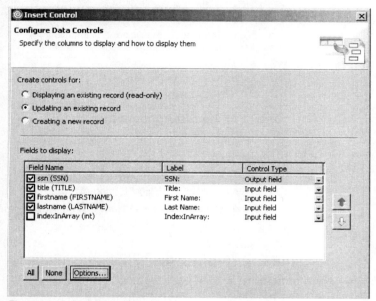

Figure 14-27   Insert customer record

10. Define action code for the Update button.
    a. Select the **Update** button.
    b. Enter the code found in Example 14-8 into the Quick Edit view.

Example 14-8   Add code for Update button to the page

```
// define SQL status area
sqlStatusData StatusRecord;

CustomerLibrary.updateCustomer(customer, sqlStatusData);
```

```
if (sqlStatusData.sqlStatus != 0)
   setError("Error updating customer");
end
```

Add the Logout button and action code

To add the Logout button and action code, do the following:

1. In the Design tab of the ListAccounts.jsp, expand **Faces Components**.
2. Click **Command - Button** and drag it to the area below the Account data list.
3. In the Properties, enter **Logout** in the Button label field.
4. Define action code for the Logout button.
   a. Switch to the Quick Edit view.
   b. Select the **Logout** button.
   c. Enter the code found in Example 14-9 into the Quick Edit view.

Example 14-9   Add code for Logout button to the page

```
j2eelib.clearSessionAttr("customerSSN");
forward to label "Logout";
```

Add account data

To add the account data to be displayed for a customer on the ListAccounts.egl, do the following:

1. Open the Web perspective, Project Explorer view.
2. Expand **Dynamic Web Projects** → **BankEGL** → **EGLSource** → **pagehandlers**.
3. Double-click **ListAccounts.egl** to open in the editor.
4. Click the **Design** tab.
5. Enter the contents of Example 14-10 into the ListAccounts.egl file.

   > **Note:** The contents of Example 14-10 can be found in the c:\6449code\egl\ListAccounts.egl.

Example 14-10   Add contents to ListAccounts.egl

```
package pagehandlers;

import data.*;
import libraries.*;
```

```
PageHandler ListAccounts {view="ListAccounts.jsp",
onPageLoadFunction=onPageLoad}

    customer Customer;
    customerAccounts Customer_Accounts[];

    Function onPageLoad()
       // define SQL status area
       sqlStatusData StatusRecord;

       J2EELib.getSessionAttr("customerSSN", customer.ssn);
       try
          get customer;
          sqlStatusData.sqlStatus = 0;
       onException
          sqlStatusData.sqlStatus = sysVar.sqlcode;
       end

       if (sqlStatusData.sqlStatus == 0)
          Customer_AccountsLibrary.getCustomerAccountsByCustomer(customer,
                customerAccounts, sqlStatusData);
          case (sqlStatusData.sqlStatus)
             when (0)
                ;
             when (100)
                ;
             otherwise
                setError("Error retrieving accouts for customer");
          end
       else
          setError("Error retrieving customer");
       end
    End
End
```

6. Save the ListAccounts.egl file.
7. Expand **Dynamic Web Projects** → **BankEGL** → **WebContent**.
8. Double-click **ListAccounts.jsp** to open in the editor.
9. Click the **Design** tab.
10. In the Page Data view, expand **ListAccounts** and drag **customerAccounts - Customer_Accounts[]** to the right of the Error Messages tag.

> **Note:** We found that in some cases, the tooling allowed dropping the CustomerAccounts - Customer_Accounts on the page but did not add the code after clicking Finish. Ensure that you drop the record in the proper location of the content area.

11. When the Configure Data Controls dialog appears, do the following:

    a. Uncheck **CUSTOMERS_SSN** and **ID**.

    b. Change the labels as seen in Figure 14-28.

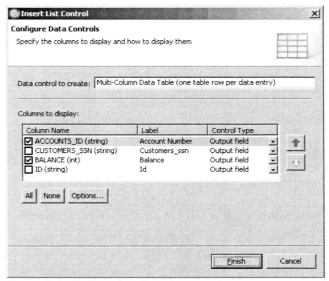

Figure 14-28   Configure Data Controls

    c. Click **Finish**.

12. Test the sample Web application.

    Refer to 14.5.4, "Run the sample EGL Web application" on page 818.

14.5 Import and run the sample Web application

This section describes how to import the completed Web application built using EGL, and run it within the WebSphere Application Server V6.0 Test Environment.

14.5.1 Import the EGL Web application sample

The imported sample project interchange file will use the project name BankEGL.

To import the completed sample EGL Web application, do the following:

1. Open the EGL perspective Project Explorer view.
2. Select **File → Import**.
3. When the Import Wizard wizard appears, select **Project Interchange** and click **Next**.
4. In the Import Projects screen, browse to the c:\6449code\egl folder and select **BankEGL.zip**. Click **Open**.
5. Check the **BankEGL** and **BankEGLEAR** projects, and click **Finish**.

Rational Application Developer will import the BankEGL and BankEGLEAR projects. Since the projects were packaged without the EGL runtime libraries to reduce the file of the sample code zip file, you will have a number of errors in your workspace after the import. These will be fixed when you generate in 14.5.3, "Generate Java from EGL source" on page 817, since the runtime libraries are automatically added back to the appropriate folder during the Generate task.

14.5.2 Prerequisites

If you have worked your way through this chapter, it is likely that you have completed the following prerequisite steps.

Ensure the you have completed the following prerequisite steps:

1. Ensure that the IBM Rational Application Developer V6.0 EGL component is installed, and that you have installed Interim Fix 0004.

   For details refer to "Install the EGL component of Rational Application Developer" on page 768.

2. Ensure that the EGL development capability is enabled under the Workbench preferences.

   For details refer to "Enable the EGL development capability" on page 771.

3. Ensure that IBM DB2 Universal Database V8.2 is installed, as this is a required for the EGL Web application sample.

For details refer to "Install DB2 Universal Database" on page 773.

4. Ensure that the BANK sample database and tables have been created, the sample data has been loaded, and a connection has been created in Rational Application Developer.

   For details refer to "Set up the sample database" on page 777.

5. Ensure that the EGL preferences for the SQL database connection defining the database and datasource have been configured.

   For details refer to "Configure EGL preferences for SQL database connection" on page 779.

   Note: This step is not necessary if you simply want to run the sample application in the test environment. If you wish to further customize the sample you will need this option configured.

6. Ensure that the JDBC provider and datasource have been configured in the application deployment descriptor (enhanced EAR feature). This information will be used during deployment to create the datasource on the target test server.

   For details refer to "Configure the data source" on page 780.

7. Ensure that the DB2 Universal Database JDBC class path environment variable variables have been defined for the WebSphere Application Server V6.0 test server via the WebSphere Administrative Console.

   For details refer to "Configure the DB2 JDBC class path environment variables" on page 783.

14.5.3 Generate Java from EGL source

The BankEGL.zip Project Interchange file shipped with the redbook sample code was modified manually to remove some EGL runtime libraries. This was done to reduce the size of the BankEGL.zip for distribution purposes. For more information regarding this issue refer to 14.6, "Considerations for exporting an EGL project" on page 820.

We will run the Generate task on the EGL source to generate the Java used for deployment. This also has the effect of copying the EGL runtime libraries back to the \WebContent\WEB-INF\lib folder.

1. From the EGL perspective, expand **Dynamic Web Projects**.
2. Right-click **BankEGL**, and select **Generate With Wizard**.
3. When the Generate wizard appears, click **Select All**, and click **Next**.

4. Select **Use one build descriptor for all parts**, select
   BankEGLWebBuildOptions <BankEGL/EGLSource/BankEGL.eglbld>
   from the drop-down list, and then click **Finish**.

   The Generate task should resolve all the errors for the BankEGL Web Project. Some warnings may still exist.

14.5.4 Run the sample EGL Web application

To run the Web application sample built using EGL, do the following:

1. Open the Web perspective Package Explorer view.
2. Expand **Dynamic Web Projects** → **BankEGL** → **WebContent**.
3. Right-click **Login.jsp**, and select **Run** → **Run on Server** from the context menu.
4. When the Server Selection dialog appears, select **Choose and existing server**, select **WebSphere Application Server v6.0**, and click **Finish**.

   This operation will start the server and publish the application to the server.

5. When the Login page appears, enter 111-11-1111 in the Customer SSN field (as seen in Figure 14-29 on page 819), and then click the **Login** button.

   > **Note:** At the time of writing, we found that we had to enter the Customer SSN input again after clicking Login, due to a problem with JSF input validation. This is only necessary after the first time the application is run.

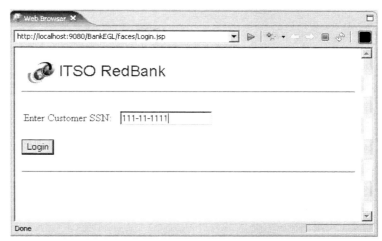

Figure 14-29 EGL Web application sample: Login page

6. The Accounts page should be displayed (as seen in Figure 14-30 on page 820) with the customer account information retrieved from the BANK database.

   From the page you can do the following:

   – You can modify the values in the Title, Firstname, and Lastname fields and then click **Update**.
   – You can log out by clicking **Logout**.

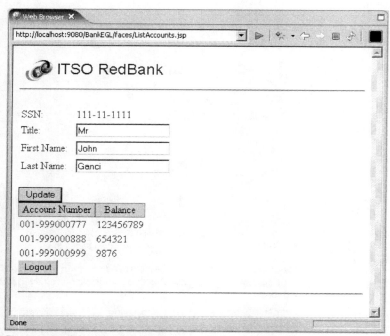

Figure 14-30 EGL Web application sample - Customer accounts

14.6 Considerations for exporting an EGL project

Table 14-2 lists the EGL runtime libraries added to the \WebContent\WEB-INF\lib folder of an EGL Web Project.

Table 14-2 EGL and supporting runtime libraries

EGL and supporting runtime libraries	Time of addition to EGL Web Project
jsf-ibm.jar	When project is created
sdo_access_beans.jar	When project is created
sdo_web.jar	When project is created
fda6.jar	When project is created and when Generate is executed

EGL and supporting runtime libraries	Time of addition to EGL Web Project
fdaj6.jar	When project is created and when Generate is executed
eglintdebug.jar	When 1st Faces JSP added and when Generate is executed
eglintdebugsupport.jar	When 1st Faces JSP added and when Generate is executed

At the time of writing, we discovered several issues when exporting an EGL Web Project to a Project Interchange file, WAR and EAR:

- Project Interchange and WAR file size: We found that a simple EGL Web Project when exported was fairly large. For example, the eglintdebugsupport.jar is 14 MB, when using IBM Rational Application Developer V6.0 and Interim Fix 0004, and is packaged in the Project Interchange file.

    Refer to 14.6.1, "Reduce the file size of the Project Interchange file" on page 821, for a work-around procedure to address this issue for Project Interchange files.

- Migration of runtime libraries: We found that the EGL V6.0 Migration tooling used to migrate EGL V6.0 to V6.0 with Interim Fix 0001 or 0004, did not migrate the EGL runtime libraries; thus, the migrated EGL source is out of synch with the EGL runtime libraries.

    Refer to 14.6.2, "Manually adding the runtime libraries after migration" on page 822, for a work-around procedure to address the issue of migrating the runtime libraries.

- Export WAR/EAR with source: We found that when checking Export source during the export of a WAR or EAR file containing an EGL Web Project, the EGL source was not exported. Only the generated Java source was exported. We were informed this is working as designed.

    Refer to "Export WAR/EAR with source" on page 823 for a work-around procedure to address the issue of including the EGL source in a WAR/EAR.

14.6.1 Reduce the file size of the Project Interchange file

Project Interchange files are a very useful means of packaging the contents of projects. Since the size of the EGL runtime files is likely to be much larger than the size of the EGL and generated Java source, it is desirable to remove some of the runtime files before exporting the EGL Web Project to a Project Interchange file.

We found that eglintdebug.jar, eglintdebugsupport.jar, fda6.jar, and fdaj6.jar were added back into the \WebContent\WEB-INF\lib folder when the EGL Generate task was run. Due to this behavior, we found that we could remove the noted files before exporting to a Project Interchange file, and thus greatly reduce the size of the file. For example, when using this technique our sample BankEGL.zip Project Interchange file was reduced from 15 MB to 800 KB (and that is a good thing).

14.6.2 Manually adding the runtime libraries after migration

When originally developing the EGL Web application sample, we used IBM Rational Application Developer V6.0, which includes EGL V6.0. We later upgraded to Interim Fix 0004. Interim Fix 0004 includes a significant number of changes to the EGL language syntax and requires that projects created in EGL V6.0 be migrated to EGL V6.0 with Interim Fix 0004.

We successfully migrated our sample source code by right-clicking the EGL Web Project and selecting **EGL V6.0 Migration → Migrate**.

After the migration, we discovered that the EGL runtime libraries listed in Table 14-2 on page 820 had not been migrated.

To manually update the EGL runtime libraries, do the following:

1. Expand **Dynamic Web Projects → BankEGL → WebContent → WEB-INF → lib**.

   Where *BankEGL* is the EGL Web Project that has been migrated and has the old level of the EGL runtime libraries.

2. Back up the files found in the lib directory. This step is only included for precautionary purposes.

3. Delete all files listed in Table 14-2 on page 820 from the lib directory.

4. Create a new EGL Web Project called EGLv601.

   The newly created EGL Web Project will contain the proper level of the EGL runtime files. We will use this project as a source of the desired EGL runtime files.

5. Expand **Dynamic Web Projects → EGLv601 → WebContent → WEB-INF → lib**.

6. Copy all files found in the lib folder EGLv601 project lib directory to the migrated project lib directory.

7. Generate the BankEGL project, which will automatically add the remaining EGL runtime libraries.

14.6.3 Export WAR/EAR with source

Although WAR/EAR files can be used to package source code, they are primarily intended as deployment packages. We recommend that developers use Project Interchange files as a method of exchanging project resources, such as source code. If you do decide to use WAR/EARs and would like to include EGL source in the EAR/WAR files, you will need to understand and complete the following work-around.

> **Note:** When using this procedure, the EGL source files will always be included in the WAR file, regardless of the setting of the Export source files check box in the WAR/EAR export wizard. Once configured as described in "Adding EGL source to WAR" on page 823, you can temporarily disable this work-around by following the procedure outlined in "Disable export of EGL source" on page 824.

Adding EGL source to WAR

To enable the inclusion of EGL source code to exported WAR files, do the following:

1. Right-click the **BankEGL** project, and select **Properties**.

   Where *BankEGL* is the EGL Web Project you wish to configure.

2. Select **Java Build Path**.
3. Select the **Source** tab.
4. Check **Allow output folders for source folders**.
5. Click **Add Folder**.
6. Check **EGLSource** and click **OK**.
7. Expand the **BankEGL/EGLSource**, select **Output folder**, and click **Edit**.
8. When the Source Folder Output Location dialog appears, select **Specific output folder**, enter `WebContent/WEB-INF/EGLSource` (as seen in Figure 14-31 on page 824), and then click **OK**.

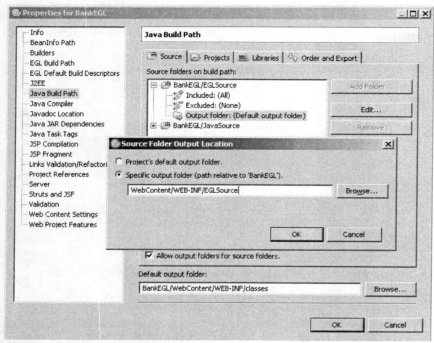

Figure 14-31   Source Folder Output Location

9. Click **OK**.

Now when you perform the Export of an EAR or WAR, the EGL source files will be found in the folder WEB-INF/EGLSource of the WAR file.

Disable export of EGL source
To exclude EGL source code from exported WAR files, do the following:

> **Note:** When the work-around is disabled using the procedure mentioned here, the exported WAR files will still contain a folder named WEB-INF/EGLSource. However, this folder will be empty.

1. Right-click the *BankEGL* project, and select **Properties**.

   Where *BankEGL* is the EGL Web Project you wish to configure.

2. Select **Java Build Path**.
3. Select the **Source** tab.
4. Expand the **BankEGL/EGLSource**, select **Excluded**, and click **Edit**.
5. When the Inclusion and Exclusion Patterns window appears, click **Add** in the Exclusion patterns section.
6. When the Add Exclusion Pattern window appears, enter **/* and click **OK**.
7. Click **OK** to close the Inclusion and Exclusion Patterns window.
8. The Properties window should now look similar to Figure 14-32. Click **OK**.

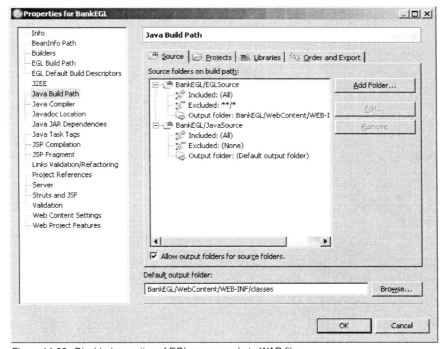

Figure 14-32   Disabled exporting of EGL source code to WAR files

15

Develop Web applications using EJBs

This chapter introduces Enterprise JavaBeans (EJB) and demonstrates by example how to create, maintain, and test such components.

We will describe how to develop entity beans, relationships between the entity beans, a session bean, and integrate the EJBs with a front-end Web application for the ITSO Bank sample. We will include examples for creating the EJBs using the Visual UML tooling as well as the Deployment Descriptor Editor.

The chapter is organized into the following topics:

- Introduction to Enterprise JavaBeans
- RedBank sample application overview
- Prepare for the sample
- Develop an EJB application
- Testing EJB with the Universal Test Client
- Adapting the Web application

15.1 Introduction to Enterprise JavaBeans

Enterprise JavaBeans (EJBs) is an architecture for server-centric, component-based, distributed object-oriented business applications written in the Java programming language.

> **Note:** This chapter provides a condensed description of the EJB architecture and several coding examples. For more complete coverage on EJBs refer to the *EJB 2.0 Development with WebSphere Studio Application Developer*, SG24-6819. Although IBM Rational Application Developer V6 includes support for EJB 2.1, much of the information is still relevant.

15.1.1 What is new

The following features, supported by IBM Rational Application Developer V6.0, are new to the EJB 2.1 specification and require a J2EE 1.4 compatible application server, such as WebSphere Application Server V6.0:

- Stateless session beans can now implement a Web service endpoint.
- Enterprise beans of any type may utilize external Web services.
- The container-managed Timer service.
- Message-driven beans support more messaging types in addition to JMS.
- The EJB Query Language has been enhanced to include support for aggregate functions, ordering of results, and additional scalar functions. Also, the rules for allowing null values to be returned by finder and select methods have been clarified.

15.1.2 Enterprise JavaBeans overview

Since its introduction in December 1999, the technology has gained momentum among platform providers and enterprise development teams. This is because the EJB component model simplifies the development of business components that are:

- Secure: Certain types of applications have security restrictions that have previously made them difficult and time consuming to implement in Java. For example, an insurance application may have to restrict access to patient data in order to meet regulatory guidelines. Until the advent of enterprise beans, there was no inherent way to restrict access to an object or method by a particular user. Previously, restricting access at the database level and then catching errors thrown at the JDBC level, or restricting access at the application level by custom security code, would have been the only implementation options.

Enterprise JavaBeans allow the declaration of method-level security rules for any bean. Users and user groups can be granted or denied execution rights to any bean or method. In WebSphere, these same user groups can be granted or denied access to Web resources (servlets, JSPs, and HTML pages), and the user IDs can be in a seamless way passed from the Web resources to the EJBs by the underlying security framework. Not only that, but the authenticated credentials may also be forwarded to other systems, possibly legacy systems (compatible LTPA clients).

- Distributed: Enterprise JavaBeans automatically provide distribution capabilities to your application, allowing for the building of enterprise-scale systems. In short, this means that your system's modules can be deployed to many different physical machines and many separate OS processes to achieve your performance, scalability, and availability requirements. Better yet, you may start small with just a single process and grow to as many different machines as you want without ever having to touch your code.

- Persistent: Making an object persistent means preserving its persistent state (the values of its non-transient variables) even after the termination of the system that created that object.

    In most cases, the state of a persistent object is stored in a relational database. Unfortunately, the OO and relational paradigms differ a lot from each other. Relational models are less expressive than OO models because they provide no way to represent behavior, encapsulation, or complex relationships like inheritance. Additionally, SQL data types do not exactly match Java data types, leading to conversion problems. All these problems may be automatically solved when using EJBs.

- Transactional: Transactions give us four fundamental guarantees including atomicity, consistency, isolation, and durability (ACID):

    – *Atomicity* means that delimited sets of operations have to be executed as a single unit of work. If any single operation fails, the whole set must fail as well.

    – *Consistency* guarantees that no matter what the transaction outcome is, the system is going to be left in a consistent state.

    – *Isolation* means that even though you may have many transactions being performed at the same time, your system will be under the impression that these transactions occur one after the other.

    – *Durability* means that the effects of transactions are to be persistent. Once committed, they cannot be rolled-back.

    Enterprise beans support multiple concurrent transactions with commit and rollback capabilities across multiple data sources in a full two-phase commit-capable environment for distributed transactions.

- Scalable: Over the past several years customers have found that fat-client systems simply do not scale up, as Web-based systems do, to the thousands or millions of users that they may have. At the same time, software distribution problems have led to a desire to "trim down" fat clients. The 24-hour, 7-day-a-week nature of the Web has also made uptime a crucial issue for businesses. However, not everyone needs a system designed for 24x7 operation or that is able to handle millions of concurrent users. We should be able to design a system so that scalability can be achieved without sacrificing ease of development, or standardization.

  So, what customers need is a way to write business logic that can scale up to meet these kinds of requirements. WebSphere's EJB support can provide this kind of highly scalable, highly available system. It does so by utilizing the following features:

  – Object caching and pooling: WebSphere Application Server automatically pools enterprise beans at the server level, reducing the amount of time spent in object creation and garbage collection. This results in more processing cycles being available to do real work.

  – Workload optimization: WebSphere Application Server Network Deployment provides advanced EJB workload optimization features. Servers can be grouped in clusters and then managed together using a single administration facility. Weights can be assigned to each server to account for their individual capabilities. When you install an application on a cluster, the application is automatically installed on all cluster members, providing for weighted load balancing. In addition, you can configure and run multiple application servers on one machine, taking advantage of multiprocessor architectures.

  – Automatic fail-over support: With several servers available in a cluster to handle requests, it is less likely that occasional hardware and software failures will produce throughput and reliability issues. In a clustered environment, tasks are assigned to servers that have the capacity to perform the task operations. If one server is unavailable to perform the task, it is assigned to another cluster member. No changes to the code are necessary to take advantage of these features.

- Portable: A strategic issue for businesses nowadays is achieving platform and vendor independence. The EJB architecture, which is an industry standard, can help achieve this goal. EJBs developed for the J2EE platform can be deployed to any compliant application servers. This promise has been demonstrated at the June 1999 JavaOne conference, where the same car dealer application was deployed on multiple application servers, from multiple vendors. While in the short-term it is often easier and faster to take advantage of features that may precede standardization, standardization provides the best long-term advantage.

The EJB architecture depicted in Figure 15-1 reduces the complexity of developing business components by providing automatic (non-programmatic) support for such system level services, thus allowing developers to concentrate on the development of business logic. Such focus can bring a competitive advantage to a business.

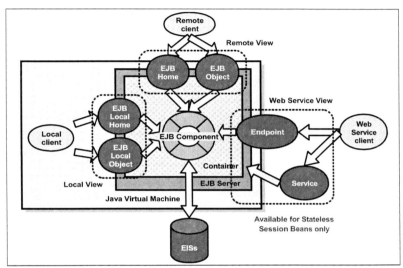

Figure 15-1   EJB architecture overview

In the following sections we briefly explain each of the EJB architecture elements depicted in:

- EJB server
- EJB container
- EJB components

15.1.3 EJB server

An EJB server is the part of an application server that hosts EJB containers. It is sometimes referred to as an Enterprise Java Server (EJS).

The EJB server provides the implementation for the common services available to all EJBs. The EJB server's responsibility is to hide the complexities of these services from the component requiring them. The EJB specification outlines eight services that must be provided by an EJB server:

- Naming
- Transaction
- Security
- Persistence
- Concurrency
- Life cycle
- Messaging
- Timer

Bear in mind that the EJB container and the EJB server are not very clearly separated constructs from the component point of view. EJBs do not interact directly with the EJB server (there is no standard API for that), but rather do so through the EJB container. So, from the EJBs' perspective, it appears as if the EJB container is providing those services, when in fact it might not. The specification defines a bean-container contract, but not a container-server contract, so determining who actually does what is somewhat ambiguous and platform dependent.

15.1.4 EJB container

The EJB container functions as a runtime environment for enterprise beans by managing and applying the primary services that are needed for bean management at runtime. In addition to being an intermediary to the services provided by the EJB server, the EJB container will also provide for EJB instance life cycle management and EJB instance identification. EJB containers create bean instances, manage pools of instances, and destroy them.

Containers are transparent to the client in that there is no client API to manipulate the container, and there is no way for a client to tell in which container an enterprise bean is deployed.

One of the container's primary responsibilities is to provide the means for remote clients to access components that live within them. Remote accessibility enables remote invocation of a native component by converting it into a network component. EJB containers use the Java RMI interfaces to specify remote accessibility to clients of the EJBs.

The responsibilities that an EJB container must satisfy can be defined in terms of the primary services. Specific EJB container responsibilities are as follows:

- Naming

- Transaction
- Security
- Persistence
- Concurrency
- Life cycle
- Messaging
- Timer

Note the similarity to the list in 15.1.3, "EJB server" on page 831. This is due to the unspecified division of responsibilities between the EJB server and container.

Naming
The container is responsible for registering the unique lookup name in the JNDI namespace when the server starts up, and binding the appropriate object type into the JNDI namespace.

Transaction
The EJB container may handle the demarcation of transactions automatically, depending on the EJB type and the transaction type attribute, both described in the EJB module's deployment descriptor. When the container demarcates the transactions, applications can be written without explicit transaction demarcation code (for example, begin, commit, rollback).

Security
The container provides security realms for enterprise beans. It is responsible for enforcing the security policies defined at the deployment time whenever there is a method call, through access control lists (ACL). An ACL is a list of users, the groups they belong to, and their rights, and it ensures that users access only those resources and perform those tasks for which they have been given permission.

Persistence
The container is also responsible for managing the persistence of a certain type of bean (discussed later in this chapter) by synchronizing the state of the bean's instance in memory with the respective record in the data source.

Concurrency
The container is responsible for managing the concurrent access to components, according to the rules of each bean type.

Life cycle

The container controls the life cycle of the deployed components. As EJB clients start sending requests to the container, the container dynamically instantiates, destroys, and reuses the beans as appropriate. The specific life cycle management that the container performs is dependent upon the type of bean. The container may ultimately provide for some resource utilization optimizations, and employ techniques for bean instance pooling.

Messaging

The container must provide for the reliable routing of asynchronous messages from messaging clients (JMS or otherwise) to message-driven beans (MDBs). These messages can follow either the peer-to-peer (queue-based) or publish/subscribe (topic-based) communication patterns.

Timer

Enterprise applications may model business processes that are dependent on temporal events. To implement this characteristic, the container must provide a reliable and transactional EJB Timer Service that allows callbacks to be scheduled for time-based events. Timer notifications may be scheduled to occur at a specific time, after a specific elapsed duration, or at specific recurring intervals. Note that this service is not intended for the modeling of real-time events.

15.1.5 EJB components

EJB components run inside an EJB container, their runtime environment. The container offers life-cycle services to these components, and provides them with an interface to the EJB server. It also manages the connections to the enterprise information systems (EISs), including databases and legacy systems.

Client views

For client objects to send messages to an EJB component, the component must provide a view. A view is a client interface to the bean, and may be local or remote:

- A local view can be used only by local clients (clients that reside in the same JVM as the server component) to access the EJB.
- A remote view allows any client (possibly distributed) to access the component.

The motivation for local interfaces is that remote calls are more expensive than local calls. Which one to use is influenced by how the bean itself is to be used by its clients, because local and remote depict the clients' view of the bean. An EJB client may be a remote client, such as a servlet running on another process, or may be a local client, such as another EJB in the same container.

> **Note:** Even though a component may expose both a local and a remote view at the same time, this is typically not the case. EJBs that play the role of facades usually offer only a remote interface. The rest of the components generally expose only a local interface.
>
> In remote invocation, method arguments and return values are passed by value. This means that the complete objects, including their non-transient reference graphs, have to be serialized and sent over the network to the remote party, which reconstructs them as new objects. Both the object serialization and network overhead can be a costly proposition, ultimately reducing the response time of the request.
>
> On the other hand, remote interfaces have the advantage of being location independent. The same method can be called by a client that is inside or outside of the container.

Additionally, Web Service clients may access stateless session beans through the Web Service client view. The view is described by the WSDL document for the Web Service the bean implements, and corresponds to the bean's Web Service endpoint interface.

Which interfaces to use, classes to extend, and other rules of bean construction are governed by the type of bean you choose to develop. A quick introduction to the types of enterprise beans and their uses is presented here.

EJB types

There are three main types of EJBs: Entity beans, session beans, and message-driven beans (see Figure 15-2).

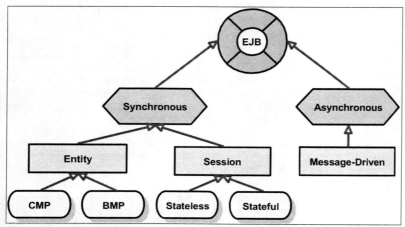

Figure 15-2   EJB types

- Entity beans: Entity beans are modeled to represent business or domain specific concepts, and are typically the nouns of your system, such as *customer* and *account*. Entity beans are persistent; that is, they maintain their internal state (attribute values) between invocations and across server restarts. Due to their persistent nature, entity beans usually represent data (entities) stored in a database.

   While the container determines *when* an entity bean is stored in persistent storage, *how* the bean is stored can either be controlled by the container, through *container-managed persistence* (CMP), or by the bean itself, through *bean-managed persistence* (BMP). Container-managed persistence is typically obtained by defining the mapping between the fields of the entity bean and columns in a relational database to the EJB server.

- Session beans: A session bean is modeled to represent a task or workflow of a system, and to provide coordination of those activities. It is commonly used to implement the facade of EJB modules. Although some session beans may maintain state data, this data is not persistent, it is just conversational.

   Session beans can either be *stateless* or *stateful*. Stateless session beans are beans that maintain no conversational state, and are pooled by the container to be reused. Stateful session beans are beans that keep track of the conversational state with a specific client. Thus, they cannot be shared among clients.

- Message-driven beans (MDB): Like session beans, message-driven beans may also be modeled to represent tasks. However, they are invoked by the receipt of asynchronous messages, instead of synchronous ones. The bean either listens for or subscribes to messages that it is to receive.

> **Note:** Although the bean flavors (CMP versus BMP, stateful versus stateless) are often referred to as EJB types, this is not the case. EJBs with different persistent management or stateness are not different types in the sense that there are no new classes or interfaces to represent these types. They are still just entity or session beans. Rather, how the container manages these beans is what makes them different. All information regarding the way the container has to handle these different bean flavors is managed in the deployment descriptor.

Entity and session beans are accessed synchronously through a remote or local EJB interface method invocation. This is referred to as synchronous invocation, because when a client makes an invocation request, it will be blocked, waiting for the return. Clients of EJBs invoke methods on session and entity beans. An EJB client may be remote, such as a servlet, or local, such as another EJB within the same JVM.

Message-driven beans are not accessible through remote or a local interfaces. The only way for an EJB client to communicate with a message-driven bean is by sending a JMS message. This is an example of asynchronous communication. The client does not invoke the method on the bean directly, but rather, uses JMS constructs to send a message. The container delegates the message to a suitable message-driven bean instance to handle the invocation. EJBs of any type can also be accessed asynchronously by means of a timer event, fired by the EJB Timer Service.

Interfaces and classes

An EJB component consists of the following primary elements, depending on the type of bean:

- EJB bean class: Contains the bean's business logic implementation. Bean classes must implement one of the enterprise bean interfaces, depending on the bean type: javax.ejb.SessionBean, javax.ejb.EntityBean, javax.ejb.MessageDrivenBean. Beans willing to be notified of timer events must implement the javax.ejb.TimedObject, so that the container may call the bean back when a timer expires. Message-driven beans must also implement the javax.jms.MessageListener interface, to allow the container to register the bean as a JMS message listener and to call it back when a new message arrives.

- EJB component interface: Declares which of the bean's business methods should be exposed to the bean's public interface. Clients will use this interface to access such methods. Clients may not access methods that are not declared in this interface. A bean may implement a local component interface, a remote component interface, or both, depending on the kinds of clients it expects to serve. The local component interface is also known as an EJB local object, because of the javax.ejb.EJBLocalObject interface that it extends. The remote component interface, in turn, is also known as EJB object, due to the javax.ejb.EJBObject interface that it extends.

- EJB home interface: Declares which bean's life-cycle methods (to create, find, and remove beans instances) are available to clients, functioning very much like a factory. Local beans have local home interfaces that extend javax.ejb.EJBLocalHome. Remote beans have remote home interfaces that extend javax.ejb.EJBHome.

- Primary key class: Entity beans must also have a primary key class. Instances of this class uniquely identify an instance of the entity type in the database. Even though not formally enforced, primary key classes must also correctly implement the equals and hashCode methods. As you will see, Rational Application Developer takes care of that for you. The primary key class may be an existing class, such as java.lang.Integer or java.lang.String, or a new class created specifically for this purpose.

Relationships

Relations are a key component of object-oriented software development. Non-trivial object models can form complex networks with these relationships.

The container automatically manages the state of CMP entity beans. This management includes synchronizing the state of the bean with the underlying database when necessary and also managing any container-managed relationships (CMRs) with other entity beans. The bean developer is relieved of the burden that is writing database-specific code and, instead, can focus on business logic.

Multiplicity is an important characteristic of relations. Relations can have the following multiplicities:

- One-to-one: In a one-to-one (1:1) relationship, a CMP entity bean is associated with a single instance of another CMP entity bean. If you come up with a one-to-one composition or aggregation relationship, remember to check if you are not, in fact, modeling the same concept as two different entities.

- One-to-many: In a one-to-many (1:m) relationship, a CMP entity bean is associated with multiple instances of another CMP entity bean. For example, an `Account` **bean could be associated with multiple instances of a** `Transaction` **bea**n, kept as a log of transactions.
- Many-to-many: In a many-to-many (m:m) relationship, multiple instances of a CMP entity bean **are associated with multiple instances of another CMP entity bean. For example, a** `Customer` **bean may be associated with multiple instances of an** `Account` **bean, and a single** `Account` **bean may, in turn, be associated with many** `Customer` **beans.**

There are also three different types of relationships:

- Association: An association is a loose relationship between two independent objects.
- Aggregation: Aggregation identifies that an object is made up of separate parts. That is, the aggregating object is dependent on the aggregated objects. The lifetime of the aggregated objects is not controlled by the aggregator. If the aggregating object is destroyed, the aggregated objects are not necessarily destroyed.
- Composition: Composition defines a stronger dependency between the objects. Composition is similar to aggregation, but with composition, the lifetime of the objects that make up the whole are controlled by the compositor.

It is the developer's task to implement the differences among the three kinds of relationships. These differences may require considerations of characteristics such as the navigation of the relationship and the encapsulation of the related objects.

Component-level inheritance is still not in the EJB 2.1 specification, even though it is planned for future releases. In want of standardized component-level inheritance, IBM WebSphere Application Server V6.0 and IBM Rational Application Developer V6.0 implements proprietary component-level inheritance.

EJB query language (EJB QL)

The EJB query language is a query specification language, similar to SQL, for entity beans with container-managed persistence. With it, the Bean Provider is able to specify the semantics of custom finder or EJB select methods in a portable way and in terms of the object model's entities, instead of the relational model's entities. This is possible because EJB QL is based on the abstract schema types of the entity beans.

> **Note:** Both finder and EJB select methods are used to query the backend where the actual data is stored. The difference is that finder methods are accessible to the entity beans' clients, whereas select methods are internal to the implementation and not visible to clients.

An EJB QL query is a string consisting of the following clauses:

- A SELECT clause, which determines the type of the objects or values to be selected.
- A FROM clause, which provides declarations that designate the domain to which the specified expressions apply.
- An optional WHERE clause, which may be used to restrict the results that are returned by the query.
- An optional ORDER BY clause, which may be used to order the results that are returned by the query.
- The result type can be an EJBLocalObject, an EJBObject, a CMP-field value, a collection of any of these types, or the result of an aggregate function.

EJB QL queries are defined by the Bean Provider in the deployment descriptor. The SQL statements for the actual database access is generated automatically by the deployment tooling. As an example, this query retrieves customers that have accounts with a large balance:

```
select object(c) from Customer c, in(c.accounts) a where a.balance > ?1
```

As you can see, this EJB QL statement is independent of the database implementation. It follows a CMR relationship from customer to account and queries the account balance. Finder and EJB select methods specified using EJB QL are portable to any EJB 2.1 environment.

> **Note:** These finder and EJB select methods may also be portable to EJB 2.0 environments if they do not use the new order and aggregate features defined by the EJB 2.1 specification.

15.2 RedBank sample application overview

In this chapter, we reuse the design of the RedBank application, described in Chapter 11, "Develop Web applications using JSPs and servlets" on page 499. The focus of this chapter is on implementing EJBs for the business model, instead of regular JavaBeans. The rest of the application's layers (control and view) still apply exactly as designed.

Note: While the sample application in this chapter extends the sample application developed in the Web application chapter (Chapter 11, "Develop Web applications using JSPs and servlets" on page 499), the content of this chapter does not strictly depend on it.

If your focus is on developing EJBs and testing them using the Universal Test Client, you can complete the sample in this chapter without knowledge of the sample developed in the Web application chapter.

Also, since the completed sample application from the Web application chapter is included with the additional material for this book, you can choose to import the finished sample application from the Web application chapter in order to get a running application at the end of this chapter.

Figure 15-3 depicts the RedBank application model layer design.

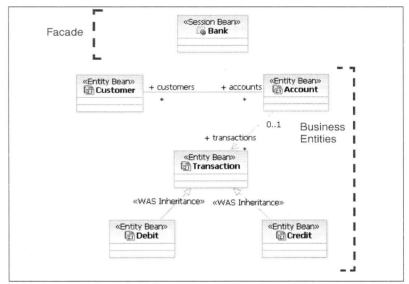

Figure 15-3 EJB module's class diagram for RedBank application

If you compare the model depicted in Figure 15-3 on page 841 to the Web application model shown in Figure 11-8 on page 514, the Bank session bean will act as a facade for the EJB model. A new coordinator, EJBBank will replace the MemoryBank coordinator shown in Figure 11-8.

Our business entities (Customer, Account, Transaction, Credit, and Debit) are implemented as CMP entity beans with local interfaces, as opposed to regular JavaBeans. By doing so, we automatically gain persistence, security, distribution, and transaction management services. On the other hand, this also implies that the control and view layers will not be able to reference these entities directly, because they may be placed in a different JVM. Only the session bean (Bank) will be able to access the business entities through their local home interfaces.

You may be asking yourself then why we do not expose a remote interface for the entity beans as well? The problem with doing that is two-fold. First, in such a design, clients would probably make many remote calls to the model in order to resolve each client request. This is not a recommended practice because remote calls are much more expensive than local ones. Finally, allowing clients to see into the model breaks the layer's encapsulation, promoting unwanted dependencies and coupling.

As the control layer will not be able to reference the model's objects directly, we will reuse the Customer, Account, Transaction, Credit, and Debit from the Web application from Chapter 11, "Develop Web applications using JSPs and servlets" on page 499, as data transfer object, carrying data to the servlets and JSPs, but allowing no direct access to the underlying model.

> **Note:** The data transfer object, also known as value object or transfer object, is documented in many J2EE architecture books. The objective is to limit inter-layer data sharing to serializable JavaBeans, thus avoiding remote references. The DTOs can be created by the session facade or by a builder object (according to the *Builder* design pattern) on its behalf, in case the building process is too complicated or needs validation steps.

Figure 15-4 shows the application component model and the flow of events.

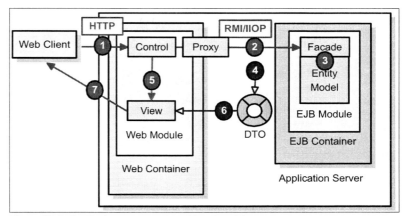

Figure 15-4   Application component model and workflow

The flow of events, as shown in Figure 15-4 on page 843, is:

1. The first event that occurs is the HTTP request issued by the Web client to the server. This request is answered by a servlet in the control layer, also known as the front controller, which extracts the parameters from the request. The servlet sends the request to the appropriate control JavaBean. This bean verifies whether the request is valid in the current user and application states.

2. If so, the control layer sends the request through the JavaBean proxy to the session EJB facade. This involves using JNDI to locate the session bean's home interface and creating a new instance of the bean.

3. The session EJB executes the appropriate business logic related to the request. This includes having to access entity beans in the model layer.

4. The facade creates a new DTO and populates it with the response data. The DTO is returned to the calling controller servlet.

5. The front controller servlet sets the response DTO as a request attribute and forwards the request to the appropriate JSP in the view layer, responsible for rendering the response back to the client.

6. The view JSP accesses the response DTO to build the user response.

7. The result view, possibly in HTML, is returned to the client.

Please note that the intent of this chapter is to introduce you to the Rational Application Developer tools that make the development of EJBs and enterprise applications possible. Together we will work only on a single session bean and three entity beans.

15.3 Prepare for the sample

This section describes the steps to prepare for developing the sample EJB application.

15.3.1 Required software

To complete the EJB development sample in this chapter, you will need the following software installed:

- IBM Rational Application Developer V6.0
- Database software:
  - Cloudscape V5.1 (installed by default with Rational Application Developer)

  Or:
  - IBM DB2 Universal Database V8.2

> **Note:** For more information on installing the software, refer to Appendix A, "IBM product installation and configuration tips" on page 1371.

15.3.2 Create and configure the EJB projects

In Rational Application Developer, you create and maintain Enterprise JavaBeans and associated Java resources in EJB projects. The environment has facilities that help you create all three types of EJBs, define relationships (association and inheritance), and create resources such as access beans, converters, and composers. Within an EJB project, these resources can be treated as a portable, cohesive unit.

> **Note:** Converters and composers are used for non-standard relational mapping. A converter allows you to transform a user-defined Java type to an SQL type back and forth. Composers are used when entity attributes have multi-column relational representations.

An EJB module typically contains components that work together to perform some business logic. This logic may be self-contained, or access external data and functions as needed. It should be comprised of a facade and the business entities. The facade is usually implemented using one or more remote session beans and message-driven beans. The model is commonly implemented with related local entity beans.

In this chapter we develop the entity beans shown in Figure 15-3 on page 841.

15.3.3 Create an EJB project

In order to develop EJBs, you must create an EJB project. When creating an EJB project, you need to create an EJB client project to hold the deployed code. It is also typical to create an Enterprise Application project that will be the container for deploying the EJB project.

To create a J2EE EJB project, do the following:

1. From the Workbench, select **File** → **New** → **Project**.
2. When the New Project dialog appears, select **EJB** → **EJB Project** and click **Next**.

   Tip: From the Project Explorer, it is possible to access the New EJB Project wizard by right-clicking **EJB Projects** and selecting **File** → **New** → **EJB Project**.

3. When the New EJB Project dialog appears, enter BankEJB in the Name field (as shown in Figure 15-5 on page 846), and click **Next**.

   If you click the **Show Advanced** button, additional options are displayed. The following lists the selections that should be done for advanced options:

   – EJB version: Select **2.1** (default).
   – Target server: Select **WebSphere Application Server V6.0**.

     Note: The New button allows you to define a new installed server runtime environment.

   – Check **Add module to EAR project** (default).

     You can choose to add the EJB module being created to an EAR project. The default behavior for that end is to create a new EAR project, but you can also select an existing one from the drop-down combo box. If you would like to create a new project and also configure its location, click the **New** button. For our example, we will use the given default value.

   – Check **Create an EJB Client JAR Project to hold client interfaces and classes** (default).

     You can also choose to create an EJB client JAR project, which is optional under the EJB 2.1 specification but considered a best practice. The EJB client jar holds the home and component interfaces of the project's enterprise beans, and other classes that these interfaces depend on, such as their superclasses and implemented interfaces, the classes and interfaces used as method parameters, results, and exceptions.

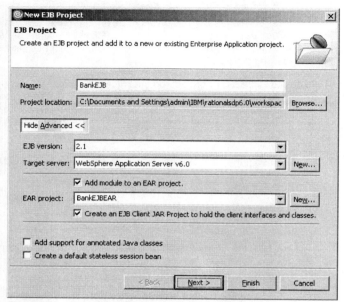

Figure 15-5   Create an EJB project wizard (page 1)

Finally, on the last section of the Figure 15-5 dialog, you can select whether you want to add support for annotated Java classes or create a default stateless session bean (always named DefaultSession).

> **Note:** Annotation-based programming provides an extensible mechanism for generating application artifacts, packaging the application, and readying it for execution. Annotation-based programming offers a set of tags and a processing mechanism that allow you to embed additional metadata in your source code. This additional metadata is used to derive the artifacts required to execute the application in a J2EE environment.
>
> The goal of annotation-based programming is to minimize the number of artifacts that you have to create and maintain, thereby simplifying the development process.
>
> For example, consider a CMP entity EJB. With annotation-based programming, you simply create a simple Java source file containing the bean implementation logic, and a few tags indicating that you want to deploy this class as an EJB. Using this single artifact, Rational Application Developer can create:
>
> - The home and remote interfaces and the key class
> - The EJB deployment descriptor
> - WebSphere-specific binding data
>
> You can also use annotations to edit the bean's characteristics later, such as which methods should be exposed to the home and remote interfaces, which attributes the bean has, and which of those belong to the primary key.
>
> Unfortunately, this extremely interesting capability is not yet fully integrated to the rest of the environment. If you choose to use it, you will not be able to edit some of the enterprise beans' characteristics through other means provided by the tool, such as the deployment descriptor or the graphical interface. Because of this, we chose not to use it at this time in the book.
>
> Annotations are an integral part of J2SE 1.5 and will probably be integrated to a future J2EE 1.5 specification.

4. When the EJB client JAR Creation window appears, enter the following (as shown in Figure 15-6 on page 848), and then click **Finish**:
   - Client JAR URI: BankEJBClient.jar
   - Name: BankEJBClient

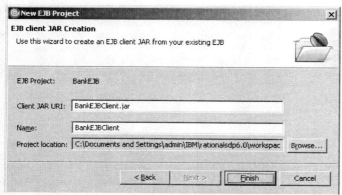

Figure 15-6 Create an EJB project wizard (page 2)

If the current perspective was not the J2EE Perspective when you created the project, Rational Application Developer will prompt if you want to switch to the J2EE Perspective. Click **Yes**.

5. Verify that when complete, the resulting workspace structure and created project components should look like Figure 15-7.

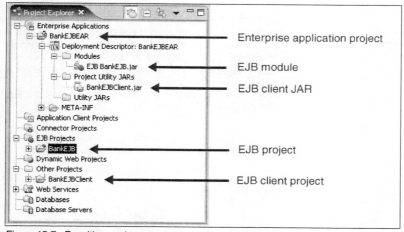

Figure 15-7 Resulting workspace structure after project creation

15.3.4 Configure the EJB projects

Before we can develop the EJB code, we need to prepare the project settings. The following needs to be done:

1. Add a new source folder, ejbDeploy, in the BankEJB project.
2. Set up the ned folder to be used for deployment source code.
3. Configure the BankEJB project to not produce warnings for unused imports.
4. Configure the BankEJBClient project to not produce warnings for unused imports.

Do the following to perform these changes to the workspace:

1. Configure the Java Build Path properties.

    We will now make some changes to the EJB project's structure in order to facilitate development and maintenance:

    a. From the Project Explorer view, right-click **EJB Project** → **BankEJB** and select **Properties**.
    b. When the Properties for BankEJB dialog appears, select **Java Build Path**.
    c. When the Java Build Path panel appears, click the **Source** tab and click **Add Folder**, as seen Figure 15-8.

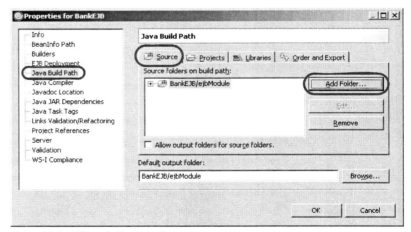

Figure 15-8   EJB project's properties

    d. When the Source Folder Selection dialog appears, click **Create New Folder**.

Chapter 15. Develop Web applications using EJBs   **849**

e. When the New Folder dialog appears, enter ejbDeploy as the folder name and then click **OK** (see Figure 15-9).

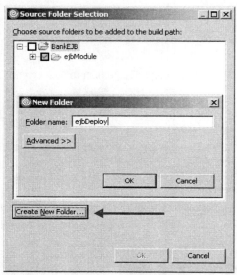

Figure 15-9   Source folder selection dialog

    f. Click **OK** in the Source Folder Selection window to add the folder.

    g. Click **OK** in the Properties for BankEJB window to apply the changes.

2. Configure the EJB Deployment properties.

   This step describes how to configure the Rational Application Developer folder where the deployment code will be generated and keep it independent of the code we will develop. This will make it easier to later develop and maintain the beans by keeping the ejbModule directory structure clean.

   a. From the Project Explorer view, select **EJB Project → BankEJB**, right-click, and select **Properties**.

   b. When the Properties for BankEJB dialog appears, select **EJB Deployment**.

   c. Check the **ejbDeploy** folder (only one folder can be checked) (as seen in Figure 15-10 on page 851), and click **OK**.

   This selects the source folder to store the EJBs deployment code to be the ejbDeploy folder that was created in the previous step.

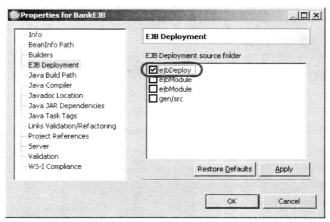

Figure 15-10 EJB Deployment properties

3. Configure the Java Compiler properties.

   a. From the Project Explorer view, select **EJB Project** → **BankEJB**, right-click, and select **Properties**.

   b. When the Properties for BankEJB window appears, select **Java Compiler**.

   c. Select **Use project settings**, as seen in Figure 15-11 on page 852.

   d. Select the **Unused Code** tab and select **Ignore** in the Unused imports drop-down.

   > **Note:** Since Eclipse 3.0, the Java compiler's default behavior is to warn about unused imports. This is a very nice feature, but in EJB and EJB client projects this can be an annoyance. The code that Java's RMI compiler (RMIC) generates is full of unused imports, so if we do not disable the verification we will get a lot of warnings in the Problems view.

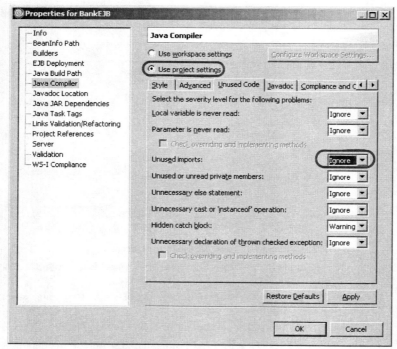

Figure 15-11   Java compiler settings

- e. Click **OK** to close the properties dialog.
- f. When the Compiler Settings Changed dialog appears, click **Yes**.

    The dialog is displayed to let you know that the compiler settings have changed and that a project rebuild is required for the changes to take effect. Clicking **Yes** will perform the rebuild.

4. Repeat the previous step for the BankEJBClient project:

    a. From the Project Explorer view, select **Other Projects → BankEJBClient**, right-click, and select **Properties**.

    b. When the Properties for BankEJB window appears, select **Java Compiler**.

    c. Select **Use project settings**.

d. Select the **Unused Code** tab and select **Ignore** in the Unused imports drop-down.
e. Click **OK** to close the properties dialog.
f. When the Compiler Settings Changed dialog appears, click **Yes** to rebuild the project.

15.3.5 Import BankBasicWeb Project

In order to finish the EJB application, we need resources from the Web Project, which was developed in Chapter 11, "Develop Web applications using JSPs and servlets" on page 499.

Do the following to import the BankBasicWeb project from the additional material (refer to Appendix B, "Additional material" on page 1395, for more information about the additional material for this Redbook):

1. From the Workbench, select **File** → **Import**.
2. When the Import dialog appears, select **Project Interchange** and click **Next**.
3. When the Import Projects dialog appears, enter `c:\6449code\web\BankBasicWeb.zip` in the From zip file field and select **BankBasicWeb** in the project list.

> **Tip:** It can take a while for the project list to populate. To force it to populate, click anywhere on the list box, or click **Back**, followed by **Next** to switch to the previous page, and **Back** again.

4. Click **Finish**.

Now we need to add the new BankBasicWeb project to the BankEJBEAR Enterprise Application. Do the following to add the Web Project to the EAR:

1. In the Project Explorer, expand **Enterprise Applications** → **BankEJBEAR**.
2. Double-click **Deployment Descriptor: BankEJBEAR** to open the Deployment Descriptor editor.
3. Click the **Module** tab.
4. In the Modules section you will see `EJB BankEJB.jar` listed; click **Add**.
5. When the Add Module dialog appears, select **BankBasicWeb** and click **Finish**.
6. Press Ctrl+S to save the deployment descriptor, and close the editor.

We need to reference the exceptions and data objects defined in the Web project from both the EJB project and EJB Client, as well as from the Web project itself. We have to move these classes to the EJB Client project.

1. In the Project Explorer, expand **Dynamic Web Projects** → **BankBasicWeb** → **Java Resources** → **JavaSource**.
2. Select **itso.bank.exception** and **itso.bank.model**, right-click, and select **Refactor** → **Move**.
3. When the Move dialog appears, expand and select **BankEJBClient** → **ejbModule** and click **OK**.
4. When the Confirm overwriting dialog appears, click **Yes To All**.

Several errors will appear in the Problems view. This is due to the fact that the BankBasicWeb project cannot see the classes that we just moved. To fix this, do the following:

1. In the Project Explorer, expand and right-click **Dynamic Web Projects** → **BankBasicWeb** and select **Properties**.
2. When the Properties for BankBasicWeb dialog appears, select **Java JAR Dependencies**.
3. Select **Use EJB client JARs**, check **BankEJBClient.jar**, and click **OK**.

You will notice that the build errors related to the exception and model classes have disappeared.

15.3.6 Set up the sample database

Before we can define the EJB to RDB mapping, we need to create and populate the database, as well as define a database connection within Rational Application Developer that the mapping tools will use to extract schema information from the database.

This section provides instructions for deploying the BANK sample database and populating the database with sample data. For simplicity we will use the built-in Cloudscape database.

To create the database, create the connection, and create and populate the tables for the BANK sample from within Rational Application Developer, do the following:

1. Create the database and connection to the Cloudscape BANK database from within Rational Application Developer.

    For details refer to "Create a database connection" on page 347.

2. Create the BANK database tables from within Rational Application Developer.

For details refer to "Create database tables via Rational Application Developer" on page 350.

3. Populate the BANK database tables with sample data from within Rational Application Developer.

   For details refer to "Populate the tables within Rational Application Developer" on page 352.

4. Import database metadata.

   Now that the database tables have been created, we need to import the metadata (database schema) into the EJB project. This has to be done in order for the mapping tools to be able to map the EJBs to the database.

   a. From from Database Explorer view, right-click the **Bank Connection**, and select **Copy to Project**.

   b. When the Copy to Project dialog appears, click **Browse**, expand and select **BankEJB** → **ejbModule** → **META-INF**, and click **OK**.

   c. Check **Use default schema folder for EJB projects**. The folder path is then automatically entered for the appropriate database type.

   d. Click **Finish** (see Figure 15-12 on page 855).

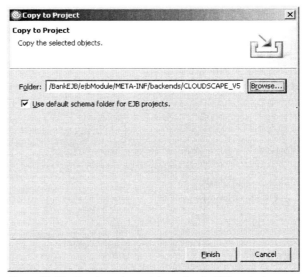

Figure 15-12   Copying schema information to EJB project

e. When the Confirm Folder Create dialog appears, click **Yes**.

15.3.7 Configure the data source

There are a couple of methods that can be used to configure the data source, including using the WebSphere Administrative Console or using the WebSphere Enhanced EAR, which stores the configuration in the deployment descriptor and is deployed with the application.

This section describes how to configure the data source using the WebSphere Enhanced EAR capabilities. The enhanced EAR is configured in the Deployment tab of the EAR deployment descriptor.

The procedure found in this section considers two scenarios for using the enhanced EAR:

- If you choose to import the complete sample code, you will only need to verify that the value of the databaseName property in the deployment descriptor matches the location of your database.
- If you are going to complete the working example Web application found in this chapter, you will need to create the JDBC provider and data source, and update the databaseName property.

> **Note:** For more information on configuring data sources and general deployment issues, refer to Chapter 23, "Deploy enterprise applications" on page 1189.

Access the deployment descriptor

To access the deployment descriptor where the enhanced EAR settings are defined, do the following:

1. Open the J2EE Perspective Project Explorer view.
2. Expand **Enterprise Applications** → **BankEJBEAR**.
3. Double-click **Deployment Descriptor: BankEJBEAR** to open the file in the Deployment Descriptor Editor.
4. Click the **Deployment** tab.

> **Note:** For JAAS authentication, when using Cloudscape, the configuration of the user ID and password for the JAAS authentication is not needed.
>
> When using DB2 Universal Database or other database types that require a user ID and password you will need to configure the JAAS authentication.

Configure a new JDBC provider

To configure a new JDBC provider using the enhanced EAR capability in the deployment descriptor, do the following:

1. From the Deployment tab of the Application Deployment Descriptor, click **Add** under the JDBC provider list.

2. When the Create a JDBC Provider dialog appears, select **Cloudscape** as the Database type, select **Cloudscape JDBC Provider** as the JDBC provider type, and then click **Next**.

   > **Note:** The JDBC provider type list for Cloudscape will contain two entries:
   > - Cloudscape JDBC Provider
   > - Cloudscape JDBC Provider (XA)
   >
   > Since we will not need support for two-phase commits, we choose to use the non-XA JDBC provider for Cloudscape.

3. Enter `Cloudscape JDBC Provider - BankEJB` in the Name field and then click **Finish**.

Configure the data source

To configure a new data source using the enhanced EAR capability in the deployment descriptor, do the following:

1. From the Deployment tab of the Application Deployment Descriptor, select the JDBC provider created in the previous step.

2. Click **Add** next to data source.

3. When the Create a Data Source dialog appears, select **Cloudscape JDBC Provider** under the JDBC provider, select **Version 5.0 data source**, and then click **Next**.

4. When the Create a Data Source dialog appears, enter the following and then click **Finish**:
   - Name: `BankDS`
   - JNDI name: `jdbc/BankDS`
   - Description: `Bank Data Source`

Configure the databaseName property

To configure the databaseName in the new data source using the enhanced EAR capability in the deployment descriptor to define the location of the database for your environment, do the following:

1. Select the data source created in the previous section.

2. Select the **databaseName** property under the Resource properties.
3. Click **Edit** next to Resource properties to change the value for the databaseName.
4. When the Edit a resource property dialog appears, enter `c:\databases\BANK` in the Value field and then click **OK**.

> **Important:** The Edit a resource property dialog allows you to edit the entire resource property, including the name. Ensure that you only change the value of the databaseName property, not the name.

In our example, c:\databases\BANK is the database created for our sample application in 15.3.6, "Set up the sample database" on page 854.

5. Save the Application Deployment Descriptor.
6. Restart the test server for the changes to the deployment descriptor to take effect.

Set up the default CMP data source

Several data sources can be defined for an enterprise application. In order for the EJB container to be able to determine which data source should be used, we must configure the BankEJBEAR project to point to the newly created data source as follows:

1. Open the J2EE Perspective Project Explorer view.
2. Expand **EJB Projects** → **BankEJB**.
3. Double-click **Deployment Descriptor: BankEJB** to open the file in the Deployment Descriptor Editor.
4. On the Overview tab, scroll down to the JNDI - CMP Connection Factory Binding section.
5. Enter `jdbc/BankDS` in the JNDI name field.
6. Press Ctrl+S followed by Ctrl+F4 to save and close the deployment descriptor.

15.4 Develop an EJB application

Our first step towards implementing the RedBank's model with EJBs is creating the following entity beans (as seen in Figure 15-13 on page 859):

- Customer
- Account
- Transaction

- Debit
- Credit

In this section, we focus on defining and implementing the business logic for the entity beans. In 15.4.5, "Object-relational mapping" on page 892, we define the mapping to the relational database.

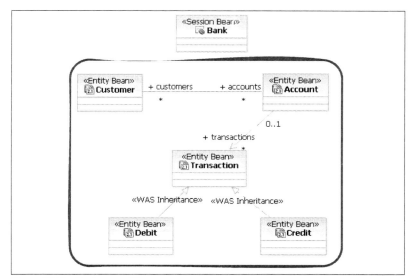

Figure 15-13   Business entities

15.4.1 Create the entity beans

This section describes how to implement the RedBank entity beans in the following sequence:

- Define the Customer bean.
- Define the Account and Transaction beans.
- Define the Credit and Debit derived beans.

Define the Customer bean

To define the Customer bean, do the following:

1. Select and expand **EJB Projects** → **BankEJB** from the Project Explorer view.

2. Select **File → New → Enterprise Bean**.

> **Tip:** This can also be done by right-clicking the Deployment Descriptor for the EJB project and selecting **New → Enterprise Bean**.

3. When the Create an Enterprise Bean dialog appears, do the following (as seen in Figure 15-14):
   - Select **Entity bean with container-managed persistence (CMP) fields**.
   - Bean name: Customer
   - Default package: itso.bank.model.ejb
   - Leave the remaining options with the default values and click **Next**.

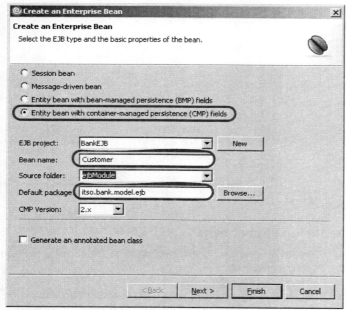

Figure 15-14 Create an enterprise bean (page 1)

4. When the Enterprise Bean Details dialog appears, we entered the information below (as seen in Figure 15-15 on page 862).

This page lets you select the bean supertype, allowing you to define the inheritance structures. We will do this in "Define the Credit and Debit derived beans" on page 870. For now, we leave the supertype blank.

Additionally, you can define type names, which views you would like to create, and finally the key class and CMP attributes.

– *Do not* check Remote client view.

> **Note:** Most of the time the suggested values for the type names (derived from the bean name) are fine, so you do not have to worry about them. According to the design, entity beans should have only local interfaces, so make sure not to select the Remote client view check box. Rational Application Developer knows about this best practice, so it will only select Local client view by default.

– Check **Local client view** (default).
– CMP attributes: Select **id:java.lang.Integer** and then click **Remove**.

> **Note:** The Customer class will have a key field, but it will be named ssn and be of type java.lang.String.

– Add the CMP attributes by clicking **Add**.

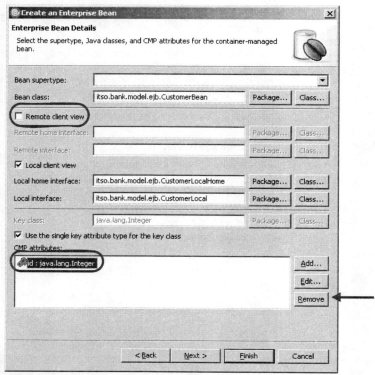

Figure 15-15   Create an entity bean (page 2)

5. When the Create CMP Attribute dialog appears, we entered the following, as seen in Figure 15-16 on page 863. This dialog lets you specify the characteristics of the new CMP attribute you would like to add to the entity bean.

   – Name: ssn
   – Type: Select **java.lang.String**.
   – Check **Key field**.
   – Click **Apply**.

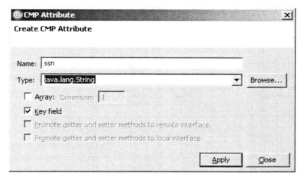

Figure 15-16   Create CMP attributes

> **Note:** Create CMP Attributes.
>
> If you do not define at least one key CMP attribute, you may not create the CMP entity bean.
>
> ► Array: If the attribute is an array, select the **Array** check box and specify the number of the dimensions for it.
>
> ► Key field: By selecting the **Key field** check box, you indicate that the new field should be part of the entity's unique identifier. You may declare as many attributes as you want to perform this role. Rational Application Developer is very smart here. If you specify just one key attribute of an object type, it will declare that type as the *key class*. If you select an attribute of a non-object type (like int or double), or if you select more than one key attribute, the environment will automatically create a new key class for you, implement all its methods (including equals and hashCode), and declare it as the key class.
>
> ► The two last check boxes let you indicate whether you want to promote the new attribute (through its getter and setter) to either the remote or the local interfaces, or to both. The availability of these options depends on which client views you selected, and if the attribute is a key field.

6. For the Customer bean, repeat the process of adding a CMP attribute for the fields listed in Table 15-1. Click **Apply** after adding each attribute. Click **Close** when done.

Chapter 15. Develop Web applications using EJBs   **863**

> **Tip:** You can enter String, instead of java.lang.String, in the Type field. Rational Application Developer will automatically change the type to be java.lang.String.

Table 15-1   Customer bean's CMP attributes

Name	Type	Attribute type check box
ssn	java.lang.String	Key field
title	java.lang.String	Promote getter and setter methods to local interface
firstName	java.lang.String	Promote getter and setter methods to local interface
lastName	java.lang.String	Promote getter and setter methods to local interface

7. After closing the CMP Attribute dialog, the Enterprise Bean Details page should look similar to Figure 15-17 on page 865. Check **Use the single key attribute type for the key class**.

    – If you have one key attribute and it is of an object type, such as String, Integer, Float, BigDecimal, and so forth, then a separate key class is not required.

    – Key wrapper classes are required for the simple data types (int, float, char) or if there is more than one key attribute.

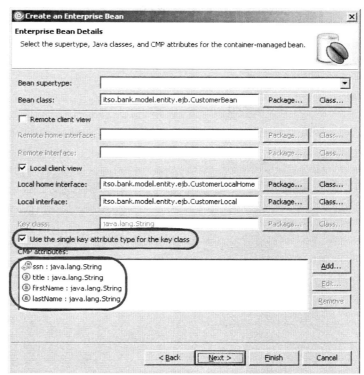

Figure 15-17 Creating an entity bean (page 2) after adding CMP attributes

8. When the EJB Java Class Details page appears, we accepted the defaults and clicked **Next**.

> **Important:** The Bean superclass on the EJB Java Class Detail, shown in Figure 15-18 on page 866, is not related to the Bean supertype field on the previous page, shown in Figure 15-17. The former is used to define Java class inheritance for the implementation classes that make up the EJB. The latter is used to define the EJB inheritance hierarchy. Refer to "Define a bean supertype" on page 871 for use of the Bean supertype and EJB inheritance feature.

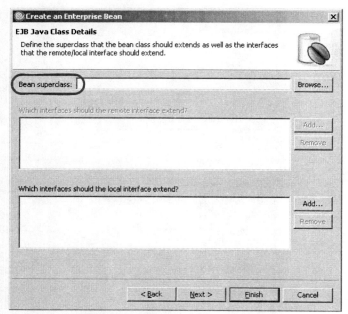

Figure 15-18   EJB Class Details page

9. When the Select Class Diagram for Visualization dialog appears, click **New**.

10. When the New Class Diagram dialog appears, enter `BankEJB/diagrams` in the Enter or select the parent folder field and `ejbs` in the File name field, as seen in Figure 15-19 on page 867, and click **Finish**.

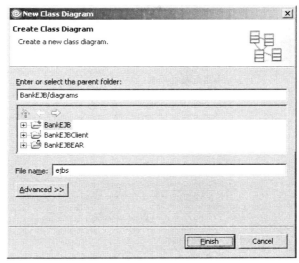

Figure 15-19   Creating a class diagram for EJBs

11. When the dialog closes, expand and select **BankEJB** → **diagrams** → **ejbs.dnx**, as shown in Figure 15-20 on page 868, and click **Finish**.

> **Note:** Although this page allows you to specify a class diagram, we found that it defaulted to use the diagram named default.dnx, located in the root of the BankEJB project. We chose to place all diagrams in a separate folder named diagrams.

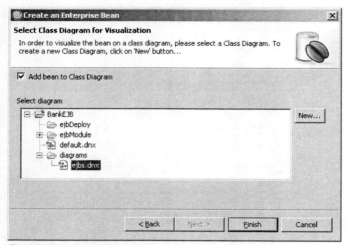

Figure 15-20   Creating an entity bean (page 4)

The new UML class diagram should be displayed with the Customer entity bean, as seen in Figure 15-21 on page 868.

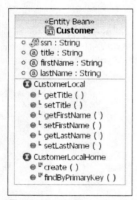

Figure 15-21   Class diagram with Customer entity bean

12. Select **File → Save**, or press Ctrl+S, to save the diagram, and then close the window.

Define the Account and Transaction beans

Repeat the same process for the next two CMP entity beans, Account and Transaction, according to the data on Table 15-2 and Table 15-3.

> **Important:** Make sure to select **Use the single key attribute type for the key class**, as shown on Figure 15-17 on page 865.

Table 15-2   Account bean CMP attributes

Name	Type	Attribute type check box
id	java.lang.String	Key field
balance	int	Promote getter and setter methods to local interface.

Table 15-3   Transaction bean CMP attributes

Name	Type	Attribute type check box
id	java.lang.String	Key field
amount	int	Promote getter and setter methods to local interface
timestamp	java.util.Date	Promote getter and setter methods to local interface

> **Tip:** Approaches to resolve no natural unique identifier follow.
>
> It is common to find entities that do not have a natural unique identifier, as is the case with our Account and Transaction objects. The EJB 2.0 specification approached this problem when it introduced the unknown primary key class for CMP entity beans. Even though WebSphere Application Server has implemented this part of the specification since Version 5, IBM Rational Application Developer V6.0 does not include support for this.
>
> There are basically two approaches to the problem. The first is to have the back-end database generate the unique identifiers. This is feasible because even though you may have as many application servers as you may like, the data pertinent to a single entity will hopefully be stored in just one database. The downside to this approach is that every time an entity is created, a database table must be locked in order to generate the ID, and thus becomes a bottleneck in the process. The upside is that sequential identifiers may be generated this way. This was our selected approach for the Account bean.
>
> The second approach would be to generate the universally unique identifiers (UUIDs, unique even among distributed systems) in the application server tier. This is a little tricky, but can be accomplished. One way to do it is to come up with a utility class that generates the UUIDs based on a unique JVM identifier, the machine's IP address, the system time, and an internal counter. This technique is usually more efficient than having the back-end database generate UIDs because it does not involve table locking. This was our selected approach for the Transaction bean. We used the class com.ibm.ejs.util.Uuid to generate UUIDs. This class ships with Rational Application Developer and WebSphere Application Server.

Define the Credit and Debit derived beans

Complete the creation of our business entities by defining the last two beans: Credit and Debit. Both are subtypes of Transaction, so the process of creating them is slightly different.

1. Select and expand **EJB Projects** → **BankEJB** from the Project Explorer view.
2. Select **File** → **New** → **Enterprise Bean**.
3. When the Create an Enterprise Bean dialog appears, do the following to define the Credit bean (subtype of Transaction):
   - Select **Entity bean with container-managed persistence (CMP) fields**.
   - Bean name: `Credit`
   - Default package: `itso.bank.model.ejb`
   - Leave the remaining options with the default values and click **Next**.

4. When the Enterprise Bean Details dialog appears, select **Transaction** in the Bean supertype drop-down, as seen in Figure 15-22, and click **Next**.

   This page lets you select the supertype (allowing you to define the inheritance structures), type names, which views you would like to create, and finally the key class and CMP attributes.

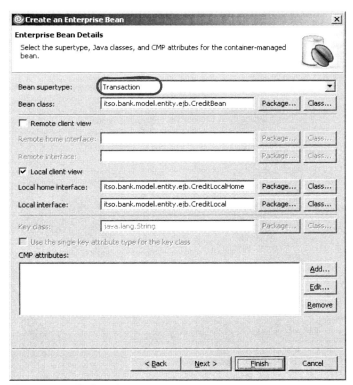

Figure 15-22 Define a bean supertype

5. When the EJB Java Class Details page appears, click **Next**.

   Note: As mentioned earlier, this page has nothing to do with EJB inheritance. As such, we leave the page blank.

6. When the Select Class Diagram for Visualization page appears, expand and select **BankEJB** → **diagrams** → **ejbs.dnx** and click **Finish**.
7. Repeat the process for the Debit bean. None of the beans have additional attributes, apart from the attributes inherited from the Transaction EJB. They only differ in behavior.
8. At this point, we have all the five entities created (Customer, Account, Transaction, Credit, and Debit). Your class diagram should look like Figure 15-23. As you can see, for each entity bean, we have a primary key attribute, regular attributes, and home and component interfaces.
9. Save the diagram, and the close the editor.

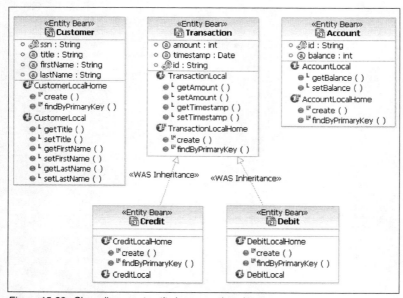

Figure 15-23   Class diagram at entity bean creation phase

15.4.2 Create the entity relationships

Now that the five business entities have been created, it is time to specify their relationships: A one-to-many unidirectional association, implementing an analysis composition, and a many-to-many bidirectional association (see Figure 15-24 on page 873).

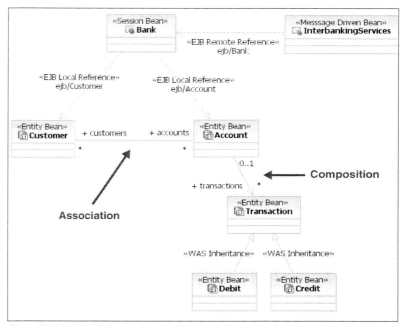

Figure 15-24 Association relationships in the model

Rational Application Developer offers a couple of facilities to streamline the process of both creating and maintaining container-managed relationships (CMRs). You can, for instance, visually create relationships with the UML Diagram Editor, and the environment will automatically generate all the necessary code and deployment descriptor changes. You may, alternatively, edit the deployment descriptor directly, and Rational Application Developer will also generate the appropriate code changes. Finally, you can use the environment's menus to accomplish the same task.

In the following sections, we will use the first two strategies described above to create the association and the composition relationships, respectively.

Customer Account association relationship

The first relationship that we will add is the association between the Customer bean and the Account bean. In this example, we demonstrate how to define relationships using the UML Diagram Editor.

1. From the Project Explorer view, expand **EJB Projects** → **BankEJB** → **diagrams**.
2. Double-click **ejbs.dnx** to open it with the UML Editor.
3. When the editor opens, click the down-arrow to the right of `0..1:0..1 CMP Relationship` in the Palette and select **0..*:0..* CMP Relationship**, as shown in Figure 15-25 on page 874.

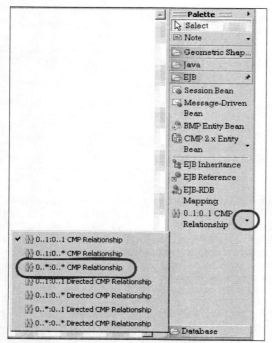

Figure 15-25 Selecting the relationship type and multiplicity

4. Left-click and hold the mouse arrow over the **Customer** bean, and then drag the mouse towards the **Account** bean. Release the button over the **Account** bean to create the association relationship, as shown in Figure 15-26.

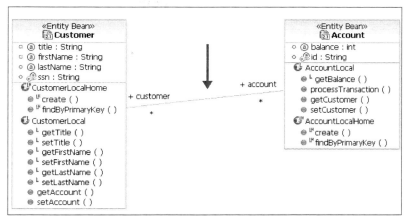

Figure 15-26   Association relationship between Customer and Account (part 1)

> **Note:** The names at the ends of the association (in this case customer and account) are used to generate accessor methods in the two beans' interface.
>
> The plus sign (+) means that the relationship is visible to the associated entity at the respective end.

5. Double-click **+ customer** and change to **+ customers**.
6. Double-click **+ account** and change to **+ accounts**.

The resulting relationship and the added methods to support it should look similar to Figure 15-27.

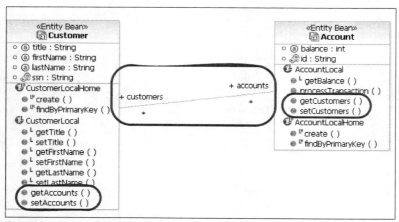

Figure 15-27   Finished customer account relationship

7. Save the changes and close the editor.

> **Important:** If you ever need to delete the relationship, you need to select it, open its context menu, and select **Delete from Deployment Descriptor**.
>
> If you select Delete from Diagram, or simply press Delete, the relationship is only removed from the diagram, but stays in the model.
>
> If a relationship is deleted from the diagram but stays in the model, it can be redrawn by right-clicking one of the related entities and selecting **Filters → Show / Hide Relationships**. The resulting Show/Hide Relationships dialog can then be used to show or hide specific relationship types.

Account Transaction composition relationship

The second relationship that needs to be created is the composition between the Account and the Transaction beans. It represents the account's transaction log that has to be maintained over time. In this example, we create the relationship using the Deployment Descriptor Editor to demonstrate an alternative to the UML Diagram Editor.

1. In the Project Explorer view, expand **EJB Projects → BankEJB → Deployment Descriptor: BankEJB → Entity Beans**.

2. Double-click the **Account** bean to open the EJB Deployment Descriptor Editor. The Deployment Descriptor Editor will open on the Bean tab with the Account bean selected.
3. Scroll down to the Relationships section, as shown in Figure 15-28.

> **Tip:** There are alternative ways to open the EJB deployment descriptor. On the Project Explorer view, you can double-click **Deployment Descriptor: BankEJB**, or navigate **BankEJB** → **ejbModule** → **META-INF** and double-click **ejb-jar.xml**.

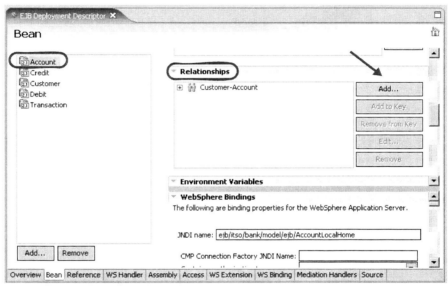

Figure 15-28 Defining relationships with the EJB Deployment Descriptor Editor

4. Click **Add** to create a new relationship for the Account bean.
5. The Add Relationship wizard opens, showing an UML view of the relationship, with the Account bean already displaying on the left-hand side.

   Select the **Transaction** bean on the right-hand side list box. The wizard should automatically fill in the remaining Role name field, as shown in Figure 15-29.

Chapter 15. Develop Web applications using EJBs   **877**

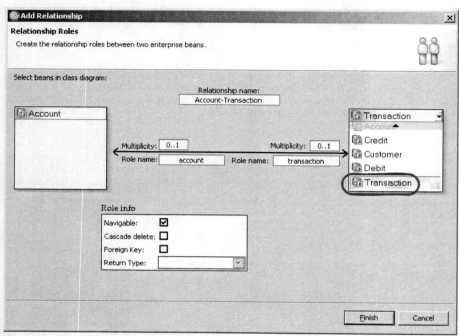

Figure 15-29   Add relationship wizard (part 1)

6. Modify the relationships.

   a. Modify the Transaction bean multiplicity. The Account bean's role name and multiplicity are already correct, but the Transaction's are not and need to be edited as follows:

      i. Modify the Transaction multiplicity by double-clicking **0..1** and changing it to `0..*`

      ii. Modify the Transaction role name to be plural, due to the relationship's multiplicity (one account may be associated with many transactions) by double-clicking the **transaction** role name and changing it to `transactions`.

   b. We also want to guarantee that the same transaction is not added to the account twice. Hover the mouse cursor over the Transaction's end of the relationship and select the return type of **java.util.Set**.

c. Hover the mouse cursor over the Account's end of the relationship to display the its role information. As this relationship is a composition relationship, the composed objects should have no knowledge about the composer. Uncheck the **Navigable** check box, as seen in Figure 15-30.

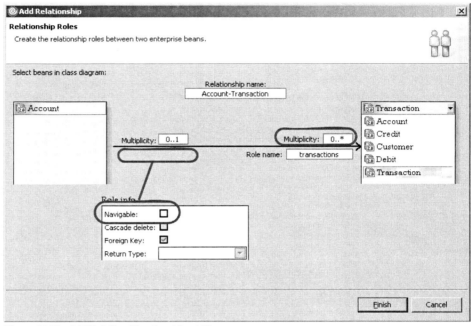

Figure 15-30 Add Relationship wizard (part 2)

7. Click **Finish** to complete the wizard.
8. Save the deployment descriptor to apply the changes just made and close it.
9. You may now inspect the changes the wizard made to your EJBs. Among them are the ones made to the Account bean.

    a. In the Project Explorer view, double-click the **AccountLocal** interface under the Account bean to open it with the Java editor.
    b. The following methods will have been added:
    ```
    public java.util.Collection getCustomers();
    public void setCustomers(java.util.Collection aCustomers);
    public java.util.Set getTransactions();
    ```

Chapter 15. Develop Web applications using EJBs **879**

```
            public void setTransactions(java.util.Set aTransactions);
```
c. Close the editor.

15.4.3 Customize the entity beans and add business logic

Now that our five entity beans have been created, it is time for us to do a little programming. For each of the beans created, three types were generated: The bean class, the home interface, and the local component interface.

1. View the Account bean, for instance, to see the generated code, as these types are shown in Figure 15-31.

    From the Project explorer view, select and expand **EJB Projects** → **BankEJB** → **Deployment Descriptor: BankEJB** → **Entity Beans** → **Account**.

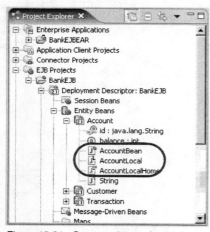

Figure 15-31   Generated types for the Account bean

> **Note:** There is a fourth type associated with the Account bean: String. It is the primary key class. If we had chosen a non-object key field or multiple key fields, a key class would also have been generated.

2. Double-click the **AccountBean** class.
3. Select the **Outline** view. It should look similar to Figure 15-32 on page 881.

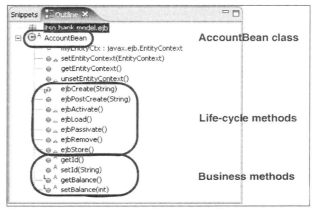

Figure 15-32 Outline view of the AccountBean class

There are two kinds of methods generated (see Figure 15-32):

- Life-cycle methods, which are the callback methods used by the EJB container at predefined events
- Business methods, which manipulate the CMP attributes

Manage the home and component interfaces

As you can see, Rational Application Developer has already generated the life-cycle methods and some business methods for us. The latest, of course, are the getters and setters. Some of these methods belong to the bean's home interface. Others belong to the local interface. Some of them are simply private to the component and should not be exposed.

Whether a method is exposed to the interface or not is a design choice. We will make some modifications to the generated interfaces in order to accommodate our design decisions.

Limit access to the Transaction bean

We do not want clients to instantiate the Transaction EJB or modify fields in an already created instance. The reason for the former is that in our model, this represents an abstract entity. While there is no such thing as an abstract EJB, in the same sense as an abstract Java class, we can obtain a similar behavior by removing any ejbCreate methods from the remote and home interfaces. The reason why we do not want clients to change a transaction object is that these should appear immutable, as they represent a log of historical transactions.

In order to block access for clients to the setter methods, as well as the constructor and setters for the Transaction EJB, do the following:

1. In the Outline view for the AccountBean class, right-click **setBalance** and select **Enterprise Bean → Demote from Local Interface**.

   Notice that the L-shaped icon next to `setBalance` disappears. The seBalance method is now inaccessible to clients.

2. In the Project Explorer, expand **EJB Projects → BankEJB → Deployment Descriptor: BankEJB → Entity Beans → Transaction**.

3. Double-click **TransactionBean** to open TransactionBean.java in the Java editor.

4. In the Outline view, right-click **ejbCreate(String)** and select **Enterprise Bean → Demote from Local Home Interface**.

   Notice that the LH-shaped icon next to ejbCreate(String) disappears.

5. In the Outline view, right-click **setAmount(int)** and select **Enterprise Bean → Demote from Local Interface**.

6. In the Outline view, right-click **setTimestamp(int)** and select **Enterprise Bean → Demote from Local Interface**.

Modify constructors for Transaction, Credit, and Debit

When creating a transaction object, we want to be able to specify the transaction amount and let the bean generate the identifier and timestamp automatically. Do the following to accomplish this.

> **Tip:** The Java code for this section can be copied from the file c:\6449code\ejb\source\Transactions.jpage, included with the additional material for this book.

1. In the Project Explorer, expand **EJB Projects → BankEJB → Deployment Descriptor: BankEJB → Entity Beans → Transaction**.

2. Double-click **TransactionBean** to open TransactionBean.java in the Java editor.

3. Modify the ejbCreate and ejbPostCreate methods so they look like Example 15-1 on page 883. Save when done.

   > **Note:** As noted earlier, the class com.ibm.ejs.util.Uuid, referenced in Example 15-1, is used to generate unique identifiers. We use it here to automatically generate identifiers for any transaction object. Clients will thus not have to worry about this.

Example 15-1   TransactionBean ejbCreate and ejbPostCreate

```
public java.lang.String ejbCreate(int amount)
   throws javax.ejb.CreateException {

   setId((new com.ibm.ejs.util.Uuid()).toString());
   setAmount(amount);
   setTimestamp(new java.util.Date());
   return null;
}

public void ejbPostCreate(int amount)
   throws javax.ejb.CreateException {
}
```

> **Note:** At this stage you will likely see the following two warning messages in the Problems view:
>
> CHKJ2504W: The ejbCreate matching method must exist on itso.bank.model.ejb.CreditBean (EJB 2.0: 10.6.12)
>
> CHKJ2504W: The ejbCreate matching method must exist on itso.bank.model.ejb.DebitBean (EJB 2.0: 10.6.12)
>
> This is simply a message that we need to align the subtypes Credit and Debit with the new Transaction constructor. We will do this in the next two steps.

4. In the Project Explorer, expand **EJB Projects** → **BankEJB** → **Deployment Descriptor: BankEJB** → **Entity Beans** → **Transaction** → **Credit**.

5. Double-click **CreditLocalHome** to open CreditLocalHome.java in the Java editor.

6. Modify the create method signature to match Example 15-2. Save when done.

Example 15-2   Modify create method in CreditLocalHome.java

```
public itso.bank.model.ejb.CreditLocal create(int amount)
      throws javax.ejb.CreateException;
```

7. In the Project Explorer, expand **EJB Projects** → **BankEJB** → **Deployment Descriptor: BankEJB** → **Entity Beans** → **Transaction** → **Debit**.

8. Double-click **DebitLocalHome** to open DebitLocalHome.java in the Java editor.

9. Modify the create method signature to match Example 15-3. Save when done.

Example 15-3   Modify create method in DebitLocalHome.java

```
public itso.bank.model.ejb.DebitLocal create(int amount)
      throws javax.ejb.CreateException;
```

Add the business logic

Getters and setters are generated automatically, but the business methods must be implemented manually.

We will need to add business logic to the Transaction, Credit, Debit, and Account EJBs. We will add a new method, getSignedAmount, to the transaction EJBs. This method will return the transaction amount with a sign that denotes the transaction "direction" in such a way that the return value added to the pre-transaction account balance will yield the post-transaction account balance.

We will then add the method processTransaction to the Account EJB. This method will, given a Transaction instance, update the account balance, utilizing the new getSignedAmount method.

> **Tip:** The Java code for this section can be copied from the file c:\6449code\ejb\source\Transactions.jpage, included with the additional material for this book.

Add business logic to the transaction EJBs

To add the getSignedAmount method to the transaction EJBs, do the following:

1. Open TransactionBean.java for editing.

2. Add the method getSignedAmount, shown in Example 15-4, to the TransactionBean class.

Example 15-4   TransactionBean getSignedAmount method

```
public int getSignedAmount()
      throws itso.bank.exception.ApplicationException
{
   throw new itso.bank.exception.ApplicationException(
         "Transaction.getSignedAmount invoked!");
}
```

The implementation of the getSignedAmount method is not relevant in the base Transaction bean, since the method is conceptually abstract. In a Java class hierarchy, this method would be made abstract, but this is not possible in an EJB hierarchy. If we were to define the getSignedAmount as abstract, the deployed code would have errors, and the EJB would not be deployable.

We thus choose to throw an exception from the method in case a programming error results in the execution of the method.

3. Promote the newly created getSignedAmount method to the bean's local interface.

   a. In the Outline view, right-click **getSignedAmount** and select **Enterprise Bean** → **Promote to Local Interface**.

   b. Save the changes and close the Java editor.

4. Modify the CreditBean class.

   a. Double-click the **CreditBean** class on the Project Explorer view to open the class in the Java editor.

   b. Insert the declarations in Example 15-5 to the CreditBean.java file.

Example 15-5 CreditBean extensions to TransactionBean

```
/**
 * Insert before the first method
 */
public static final String TYPE_KEY = "Credit";

/**
 * Insert after the last method
 */
public int getSignedAmount()
      throws itso.bank.exception.ApplicationException
{
    return getAmount();
}
```

> **Tip:** As getSignedAmount is an inherited method, the code can be alternatively created by Rational Application Developer's sourcing facility, relieving you from having to type it.
>
> 1. Select the **CreditBean** class from the Outline view, right-click, and select **Source** → **Override/Implement Methods**.
>
> 2. On the resulting dialog, click **Deselect All** to make sure that no other methods have their signatures generated. Next, check the **getSignedAmount** method and click **OK**.
>
> 3. Manually add the following after the CreditBean class:
>
>   `public static final String TYPE_KEY = "Credit";`

   c. Save your changes and close the editor.

4. Modify the DebitBean class.

a. Double-click the **DebitBean** class on the Project Explorer view to open the class up on the Java editor.

b. Insert the declarations in Example 15-6 to the CreditBean.java file.

Example 15-6   DebitBean extensions to TransactionBean

```
/**
 * Insert before the first method
 */
public static final String TYPE_KEY = "Debit";

/**
 * Insert after the last method
 */
public int getSignedAmount()
      throws itso.bank.exception.ApplicationException
{
    return -getAmount();
}
```

c. Save the changes and close the editor.

> **Note:** The TYPE_KEY constant defined in the Debit and Credit classes is used by the EJB container to determine what type a given record in the database refers to, since both Credit and Debit instances will be persisted to the same database table. The value of this constant is compared to the value of the DISCRIM_<*tablename*> column, where <*tablename*> is the name of the table that the EJB is being persisted to.

Add business logic to the Account bean

When we specified the account bean's CMP fields, for instance, we configured the wizard to expose both the setter and the getter for the balance attribute to the bean's local interface. This is why there is a small L-shaped icon next to the getBalance and setBalance methods. While it is fine for a client to retrieve an account's balance, we do not want the clients to change the balance by calling the setBalance method. Later we will implement and expose another business method, processTransaction, that manipulates the balance, adhering to business rules.

From a business perspective, it makes no sense to allow the creation of accounts that are not associated to any customers. Thus, the first modification that we want to make is to guarantee that accounts are not created unless a primary customer is specified.

> **Tip:** The Java code for this section can be copied from the file c:\6449code\ejb\source\AccountBean.jpage, included with the additional material for this book.

1. Open the **AccountBean** class by double-clicking it from the Project Explorer view.
2. Refactor the ejbCreate(String) method signature.

   > **Tip:** For refactoring, if you need to edit the signature of any method that already belongs to either the remote or home interface, the easiest way is as follows:
   >
   > - First demote the method from the interface.
   > - Edit the signature.
   > - Promote the method back to the interface.
   >
   > If you do not demote the method from the interfaces first, you will have to manually edit the method signatures in these interfaces. Using the approach mentioned here, you let Rational Application Developer update the method signatures in the interfaces when the method is promoted back to the interfaces.
   >
   > Since the *throws* clause for a method is part of the method signature, this procedure should also be followed when changing this clause.

   a. From the Outline view, select the existing **ejbCreate(String)** method.
   b. Right-click and select **Enterprise Bean → Demote from Local Home Interface** to remove the create method declaration from the bean's home interface.
   c. Modify the ejbCreate(String) and ejbPostCreate(String) methods so that they look like the definitions in Example 15-7.

Example 15-7   Account bean's ejbCreate and ejbPostCreate methods

```
public java.lang.String ejbCreate(CustomerLocal primaryCustomer)
      throws javax.ejb.CreateException
{
   setId((new com.ibm.ejs.util.Uuid()).toString());
   return null;
}

public void ejbPostCreate(CustomerLocal primaryCustomer)
      throws javax.ejb.CreateException
{
```

```
getCustomers().add(primaryCustomer);
}
```

> **Important:** The getCustomers method was generated when we created the association relationship between the Account and the Customer beans. This method cannot be called from the Account's ejbCreate method. According to the specification, during ejbCreate the instance cannot acquire references to the associated entity objects.
>
> In the ejbPostCreate method, on the other hand, the instance may reference the associated entity objects. Thus, a call to getCustomers can be made.

    d. Now add the create method back to the Account bean's home interface by selecting the **ejbCreate(CustomerLocal)** method on the Outline view, right-clicking it, and selecting **Enterprise Bean** → **Promote to Local Home Interface**.

3. When we created the relationship between the Account and the Customer beans, the method *setCustomers(Collection)* was created. It does not have to be available to the bean's clients. Right-click **setCustomers(Collection)** in the Outline view and demote it from the local interface by selecting **Enterprise Bean** → **Demote from Local Interface**.

4. Demote the accessors for the transactions relation.

   As you may recall, the relationship between the Account bean and the Transaction bean is a composition. This means that references to transaction objects cannot be exported to objects outside of the Account bean.

   When we created the relationship, getTransactions and setTransactions(Set) methods were generated and added to the local interface for the Account bean. We want clients to be able to check the transaction log. If we were to allow access to these methods, clients would be able not only to do so, but also to add transactions to the log without correctly processing them using the processTransaction method, which we will define later in this section. The result would be that the affected account object would be put into an invalid state. This would be breaching the object's encapsulation, and thus should not be allowed.

   Demote both getTransactions and setTransactions(Set) methods, then add the getLog method as follows:

       a. Right-click **getTransactions** from the Outline view, and select **Enterprise Bean** → **Demote from Local Interface**.

       b. Right-click **setTransactions(Set)** from the Outline view, and select **Enterprise Bean** → **Demote from Local Interface**.

c. Add the getLog method, as seen in Example 15-8, to the AccountBean.java.

Example 15-8   Account bean's getLog method

```
public java.util.Set getLog()
{
   return java.util.Collections.unmodifiableSet(getTransactions());
}
```

d. Right-click **getLog** from the Outline view, and select **Enterprise Bean** → **Promote from Local Interface**.

5. Add the processTransaction method to the AccountBean class.

   a. Double-click **AccountBean** in the Project Explorer view to open the class in the Java editor.

   b. Insert the declarations in Example 15-9 in to the AccountBean.java file to add the processTransaction method.

Example 15-9   AccountBean processTransaction method

```
public void processTransaction(TransactionLocal transaction)
      throws itso.bank.exception.ApplicationException
{
   setBalance(getBalance() + transaction.getSignedAmount());
   getTransactions().add(transaction);
}
```

The processTransaction method receives a transaction object local reference and changes the account's balance by adding the transaction's signed amount to it. Later in this chapter, we will alter this method to also add the transaction reference into a transaction log.

c. Save the changes and close the editor.

6. Promote the processTransaction method to the bean's local interface.

   a. Add the method to the bean's local interface by right-clicking **processTransaction** from the Outline view.

   b. Select **Enterprise Bean** → **Promote to Local Interface**.

15.4.4 Creating custom finders

When you create an entity bean, you always get the findByPrimaryKey finder method on the home interface. Sometimes, though, you need to find an entity based on criteria other than just the primary key. For these occasions, the EJB 2.1 specification provides a query language called EJB QL. Custom finder methods are declared in the home interface and defined in the EJB deployment descriptor using the EJB QL.

Our example requires two similar simple custom finders: One for the Account bean and the other for the Customer bean. To add them, do the following:

1. From the Project Explorer, expand and double-click **EJB Projects** → **BankEJB** → **diagrams** → **ejbs.dnx** to open the class diagram in the UML Diagram Editor.
2. Modify the Account bean to create a findAll query.

    a. Right-click the **Account** bean to open its context menu and then select **Add EJB** → **Query**.

    b. When the Add Finder Descriptor wizard appears, do the following:

    - Method: Select **New**.

      The only finder we have in our AccountLocalHome interface is the default findByPrimaryKey. Rational Application Developer will take care of updating the home interface for you by adding the declaration of the new finder method.

    - Method Type: Select **find method**.

      The Method Type field lets you select whether you want to create a descriptor for a finder method or for an ejbSelect method. The difference between the two is that finder methods get promoted to the bean's home interface, whereas ejbSelect methods do not. The ejbSelect methods are useful as internal helper methods, as they cannot be called by clients.

    - Type: Check **Local**.

      The Type field lets you select to which home interface, either local or remote, you would like the finder method promoted.

      > **Note:** We found that in some cases, the Remote check box was enabled, since the Account bean only exposes a local view. If you check Remote, the query is only added to the deployment descriptor, but no changes are made to the home interface. Make sure that only **Local** is checked.

- Name: findAll
- Return type: Select **java.util.Collection**.

The dialog should look like Figure 15-33 on page 891 after making the selections. Click **Next** to continue.

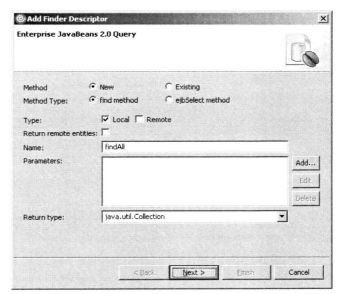

Figure 15-33   Adding a new finder descriptor (page 1)

　　c. When the Add Finder Descriptor dialog appears, select **Find All Query** and click **Finish** (see Figure 15-34 on page 892).

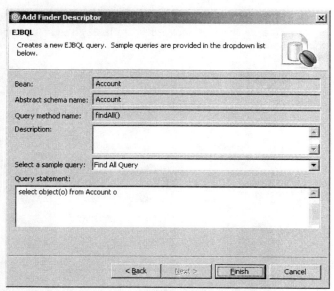

Figure 15-34 Adding a new finder descriptor (page 2)

3. Repeat the same steps for the Customer bean to create a findAll query.
4. Your changes should already be saved, so you may close the editor.

15.4.5 Object-relational mapping

Container-managed persistence (CMP) entity beans delegate their persistence to the container. As mentioned in "EJB types" on page 836, this means that it is the responsibility of the EJB container to handle the details of how to store the internal state of the EJBs.

In order for the container to be able to do this, we need to provide information about how the EJB fields should be mapped to the relational database. This information is stored in the deployment descriptor, and during deployment, the JDBC code to perform the operations is generated by the container.

When the beans are actually deployed, associations to real data sources can be made to dynamically bind the bean to the data. In this way, the CMPs are abstract classes that associate to data, but do not provide any implementation for accessing data themselves.

To facilitate development, deployment, and testing, Rational Application Developer contains the tools for the developer to both define the mappings and create deployment bindings.

The advantages to separating the development and persistence concerns are numerous. Apart from achieving database implementation independence, the developer is free to work with object views of the domain data instead of data views and writing SQL, and is allowed to focus on the business logic, instead of the technical details of accessing the database.

As mentioned, the CMP can be developed largely independently of the data source, and allows a clear separation of business and data access logic. This is one of the fundamental axioms of aspect-oriented programming, where the aspect of persistence can be removed from the development process and applied later, in this case at deployment time.

Rational Application Developer offers three different mapping strategies:

- *Top down* is when you start from an object-oriented model and let the environment generate the data model automatically for you, including the object-relational mapping and the DDL that you would use to create the tables in the database.

    Note: This strategy is preferred when the data backend does not exist and will be created from scratch.

- *Bottom up* is when you start from a data model and let Rational Application Developer generate the object model automatically for you, including the creation of the entity beans based on tables and columns that you select.

    Note: This strategy is not recommended for object-oriented applications, because the data model is less expressive than the object model. It should be used only for prototyping purposes.

- *Meet in the middle* is the compromise strategy, in which you keep both your existing object-oriented and data models, creating a mapping between the two. The mapping process is usually started by Rational Application Developer, based on cues like attribute names and types, and completed manually by the Developer.

For the ITSO Bank application, we will use the meet in the middle strategy because we do have an existing database for application data.

The BANK database schema

This chapter uses the same relational model created in Chapter 8, "Develop Java database applications" on page 333. Figure 15-35 shows the existing data model.

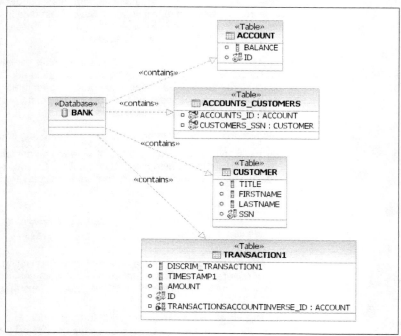

Figure 15-35 Existing relational model

Our objective is to map the object model created in 15.4, "Develop an EJB application" on page 858, to the existing relational model. As mentioned, this is a more realistic approach than creating a new top-down mapping from scratch, although a top-down mapping would be simpler and more convenient if a relational database model did not already exist.

Generate EJB-to-RDB mapping

We now create a mapping between the object-oriented EJB model and the relational database model, as defined by the BANK database schema. To generate the EJB-to-RDB mapping, do the following:

1. In the Project Explorer view of the J2EE perspective, right-click **EJB Projects** → **BankEJB** and select **EJB to RDB Mapping** → **Generate Map** from the context menu.

2. When the EJB to RDB Mapping wizard appears, select **Use an existing backend folder**. Select **CLOUDSCAPE_V51_1** and click **Next** (see Figure 15-36 on page 895).

   Note: This is the folder that was created when we copied the database metadata to the EJB project folder in 15.3.6, "Set up the sample database" on page 854.

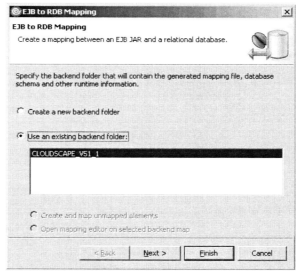

Figure 15-36 Using an existing backend folder

3. When the Create new EJB / RDB Mapping dialog appears, select **Meet In the Middle** and click **Next** (Figure 15-37 on page 896).

The Create new EJB / RDB Mapping page lets you select which kind of mapping you would like to create. The options displayed are the ones discussed earlier:

- Bottom-Up, which creates a new set of EJBs based on an existing database schema.
- Top-Down, which automatically generates a new database schema supporting the existing enterprise beans and the mapping between the existing object model and the new relational model. This option is greyed out since we chose to use an existing backend folder on the previous page.
- Meet-In-The-Middle, which generates a map between the existing object and relational models.

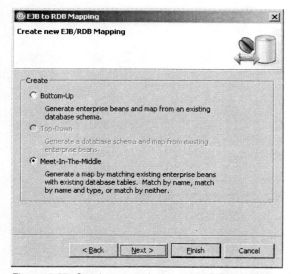

Figure 15-37 Creating a meet-in-the-middle EJB-to-RDB mapping

4. When the Select Meet-in-Middle Mapping options page appears, select **Match by Name** (as seen in Figure 15-39 on page 898) and click **Finish**.

When selecting Match by Name, Rational Application Developer will attempt to match the entity beans to table names and entity bean field names to column names. When the EJBs and their fields are appropriately named, the amount of manual work will be minimized.

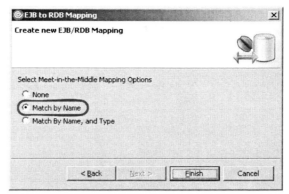

Figure 15-38 Select meet-in-the-middle option

Completing the EJB-to-RDB mapping

After completing the EJB to RDB wizard from the previous section, the Map.mapxmi editor will open. The display should look similar to Figure 15-39 on page 898.

As you can see, the wizard has already mapped the Customer and Account beans to the correct tables, and some of the fields are mapped to the correct columns. The mapped items carry a little triangle as an indicator, and they are listed in the bottom pane.

There are two possible methods of completing the mapping: Drag-and-drop, and using the context menus and choosing **Create Mapping**.

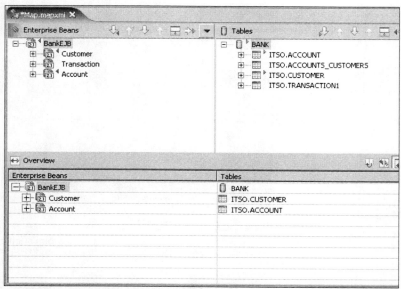

Figure 15-39   Generated object-relational mapping

To complete the EJB-to-RDB mapping using the drag-and-drop approach, do the following:

1. Map the EJBs to tables.

   A bean must be mapped to a table before you can map the attributes of the bean to the columns.

   a. Drag the **Transaction** EJB and drop it on the ITSO.TRANSACTION1 table.
   b. Expand the **Transaction** EJB.
   c. Drag the **Credit** EJB and drop it on the ITSO.TRANSACTION1 table.
   d. Drag the **Debit** EJB and drop it on the ITSO.TRANSACTION1 table.

> **Tip:** The DISCRIM_TRANSACTION1 column of the ITSO.TRANSACTION1 table is the discriminator field. It is used to tell whether a transaction is a debit or a credit. The contents of this column correspond to the value of the TYPE_KEY constant field, which was added to the Credit and Debit beans in "Modify constructors for Transaction, Credit, and Debit" on page 882.
>
> The DISCRIM_ prefix is reserved for use by the persistence manager.

2. Map the EJB attributes to the table columns.

    Some fields have not been matched automatically. We can perform the manual mapping by dragging and dropping attributes in the left pane to relational columns on the right, or vice-versa.

    a. Expand the **Transaction EJB** and the **TRANSACTION1** table.
    b. Drag the **id** attribute of the Transaction EJB to the ID column of the ITSO.TRANSACTION1 table.
    c. Drag the **amount** attribute of the Transaction EJB to the AMOUNT column of the ITSO.TRANSACTION1 table.
    d. Drag the **timestamp** attribute of the Transaction EJB to the TIMESTAMP1 column of the ITSO.TRANSACTION1 table.

3. Map the EJB container-managed relationships to the foreign key relationships between the database tables.

    a. Right-click the **ITSO.TRANSACTION1** table and select **Open Table Editor**.
    b. When the Table Editor opens, switch to the **Foreign Keys** tab.
    c. Click **Add Another**.

        Several edit fields, along with a Source Columns area that allows you to select columns for the foreign key, will appear in the right side of the page, as shown in Figure 15-40 on page 900.

        The value in the Foreign key name field is generated automatically and will have a different value for you.

    d. Enter `FK_TRANSACTION_ACCOUNT` in the Foreign key name field
    e. Select **ITSO.ACCOUNT** in the Target Table drop-down list.
    f. Select **TRANSACTIONSACCOUNTINVERSE_ID** on the source column and click > to add it to the list on the right.
    g. Save and close the Table Editor.

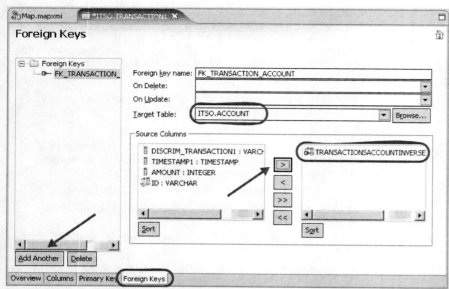

Figure 15-40 Creating a foreign key with the table editor

    h. In the Map.mapxmi editor, drag **[0..1] account : Account** from the Transaction bean and drop it on FK_TRANSACTION_ACCOUNT.

    i. Right-click the **ITSO.ACCOUNTS_CUSTOMERS** table and select **Open Table Editor**.

    j. Create two foreign keys:

        i. Right-click the **ITSO.ACCOUNTS_CUSTOMERS** table and select **Open Table Editor**.

        ii. Switch to the **Foreign Keys** tab.

        iii. Click **Add Another**.

        iv. Enter `FK_CUSTOMER_ACCOUNT` in the Foreign key name field.

        v. Select **ITSO.ACCOUNT** in the Target Table drop-down list.

        vi. Select **ACCOUNTS_ID** on the source column and click **>** to add it to the list on the right.

        vii. Click **Add Another**.

        viii. Enter `FK_ACCOUNT_CUSTOMER` in the Foreign key name field.

ix. Select **ITSO.CUSTOMER** in the Target Table drop-down list.

x. Select **CUSTOMERS_SSN** on the source column and click **>** to add it to the list on the right.

xi. Save and close the Table Editor.

k. Expand the **Customer** EJB, and the **ITSO.ACCOUNT_CUSTOMERS** table. Drag **[0..*] accounts: Account** to FK_CUSTOMER_ACCOUNT.

l. Expand the **Account** EJB. Drag the **[0..*] customers: Customer** to FK_ACCOUNT_CUSTOMER.

The Outline view of the mapping editor summarizes our mapping activities (Figure 15-41).

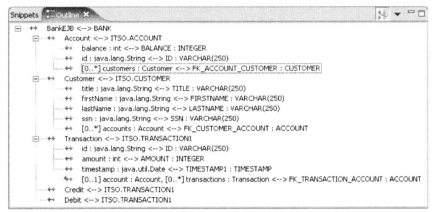

Figure 15-41   Outline view of the mapping editor

4. Save the mapping by pressing Ctrl+S and close the Map Editor.

15.4.6 Implement the session facade

The next EJB that we have to build is the session facade: The Bank stateless session bean (Figure 15-42).

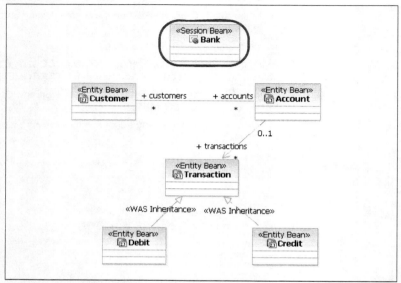

Figure 15-42   Business model session facade

Create the Bank session bean

To create the session bean, do the following:

1. In the Project Explorer view, expand **EJB Projects** → **BankEJB** → **diagrams**.
2. Double-click the **ejbs.dnx** diagram file to open it in the diagram editor.
3. In the Palette view, select **EJB** → **Session Bean** and click the canvas.
4. When the Create a new Session bean dialog appears, enter the following (as seen in Figure 15-43 on page 903), and then click **Next**:
   – EJB project: Select **BankEJB**.
   – Bean name: Bank
   – Source folder: ejbModule
   – Default package: itso.bank.facade.ejb

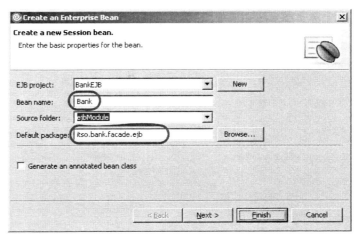

Figure 15-43 Creating a new session bean (page 1)

5. When the Enterprise Bean Details dialog appears, ensure that **Stateless** is selected in the Session type listbox and **Container** is selected in the Transaction type listbox, as shown in Figure 15-44 on page 904, and click **Finish**.

    Note that the default selection for the session bean is to create a remote client view instead of a local client view, as for the entity beans (see Figure 15-15 on page 862). This is because the environment knows that session beans are normally used to implement the model's facade and, as such, need remote interfaces as opposed to local ones.

6. Save the diagram to apply your changes, and close the UML Editor.

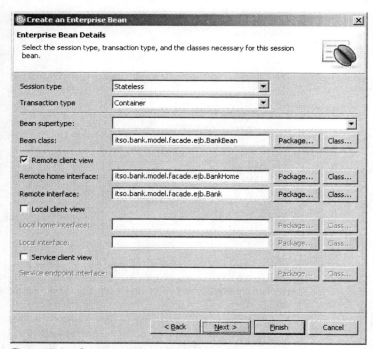

Figure 15-44   Creating a new session bean (page 2)

Edit the session bean

We will now add the facade methods that will be used by clients to perform banking operations.

> **Tip:** The Java code for this section can be copied from the file c:\6449code\ejb\source\BankBean.jpage, included with the additional material for this book.

1. In the Project Explorer view of the J2EE Perspective, expand **EJB Projects** → **BankEJB** → **Deployment Descriptor: BankEJB** → **Session Beans** → **Bank**.
2. Double-click **BankBean** to open BankBean.java in the Java source editor.
3. Add the import statements from Example 15-10 to the file.

Example 15-10   Import statements for BankBean.java

```
import itso.bank.exception.*;
import itso.bank.model.*;
import itso.bank.model.ejb.*;

import java.util.Collection;
import java.util.Iterator;
import java.util.Set;
```

4. Complete the getCustomer method.

   a. Enter the method stub for the getCustomer method shown in Example 15-11 after the last method of the BankBean class.

Example 15-11   The getCustomer method stub

```
public Customer getCustomer(String ssn)
       throws UnknownCustomerException
{
}
```

   b. Place the cursor in the getCustomer method body.
   c. Switch to the Snippets view and double-click **EJB** → **Call an EJB "find" method**.

   > **Tip:** The Snippets view is usually located in the same panel as the Outline view. If it is not visible, change to the Outline view and select **Window** → **Show View** → **Other**, and then select **Basic** → **Snippets** and click **OK**.

   d. When the Insert EJB Find wizard appears, click **New EJB Reference**.
   e. When the Add EJB Reference dialog appears, select **Enterprise Beans in the workspace**, expand and select **BankEJBEAR** → **BankEJB** → **Customer**, ensure that **Local** is selected in the Ref type drop-down, and click **Finish**.

   > **Note:** The name defaults to ejb/*<BeanName>*, where *<BeanName>* is the name of the bean that you are adding a reference to. You can change this, but we choose to use the default.

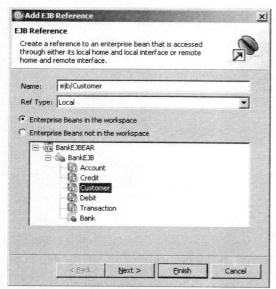

Figure 15-45 Adding the ejb/Customer EJB reference

    f. When you return the Insert EJB Find wizard, click **Next**.

    g. When the Select Method page appears, select **findByPrimaryKey(String primaryKey)** and click **Next**.

    h. When the Enter Parameter Values page appears, enter ssn in the Value column of the first row and click **Finish**.

Several things will have happened when you are returned to the Java editor:

- A new EJB reference has been added to the Bank session bean, as shown in Figure 15-46 on page 908.
- A new line of code, shown in Example 15-12, has been added at the current cursor location.

Example 15-12 New code to find a Customer bean by its primary key

```
CustomerLocal aCustomerLocal = find_CustomerLocalHome_findByPrimaryKey(ssn);
```

- Example 15-12 invokes a new local method, find_CustomerLocalHome_findByPrimaryKey, which has been added after the last method of the class. The code for this method is shown in Example 15-13.

Example 15-13   Generated find_CustomerLocalHome_findByPrimaryKey method

```
protected CustomerLocal find_CustomerLocalHome_findByPrimaryKey(
     String primaryKey) {
  CustomerLocalHome aCustomerLocalHome = (CustomerLocalHome) ServiceLocatorManager
      .getLocalHome(STATIC_CustomerLocalHome_REF_NAME,
          STATIC_CustomerLocalHome_CLASS);
  try {
     if (aCustomerLocalHome != null)
        return aCustomerLocalHome.findByPrimaryKey(primaryKey);
  } catch (javax.ejb.FinderException fe) {
     // TODO Auto-generated catch block
     fe.printStackTrace();
  }
  return null;
}
```

– Example 15-13 uses some constants, which have been added before the first method in the class. The definition for these is shown in Example 15-14.

Example 15-14   Constants to support the find_CustomerLocalHome_findByPrimaryKey method

```
private final static String STATIC_CustomerLocalHome_REF_NAME = "ejb/Customer";
private final static Class STATIC_CustomerLocalHome_CLASS = CustomerLocalHome.class;
```

– Additionally, the import statements, shown in Example 15-15, have been added at the top of the file.

Example 15-15   Imports added to the BankBean.java file

```
import itso.bank.model.ejb.CustomerLocal;
import com.ibm.etools.service.locator.ServiceLocatorManager;
import itso.bank.model.ejb.CustomerLocalHome;
```

– Finally, the JAR file serviceLocatorMgr.jar is added to the BankEJBEAR Enterprise Application, as shown in Figure 15-46 on page 908. This JAR, which contains the implementation of the ServiceLocatorManager class used in Example 15-13, is also added to the Java build path and the Java JAR Dependencies for the BankEJB project.

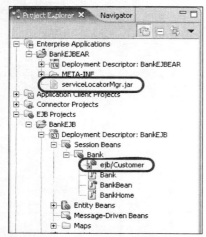

Figure 15-46 New JAR and EJB Reference to the Customer bean for the Bank bean

    i. Modify the find_CustomerLocalHome_findByPrimaryKey method to match the code in Example 15-16. The difference, which consists of throwing an application-specific exception when the customer cannot be found, is highlighted in bold.

Example 15-16 Modified find_CustomerLocalHome_findByPrimaryKey method

```
protected CustomerLocal find_CustomerLocalHome_findByPrimaryKey(String primaryKey)
      throws UnknownCustomerException
{
   CustomerLocalHome aCustomerLocalHome = (CustomerLocalHome) ServiceLocatorManager
         .getLocalHome(STATIC_CustomerLocalHome_REF_NAME,
               STATIC_CustomerLocalHome_CLASS);
   try {
      if (aCustomerLocalHome != null)
         return aCustomerLocalHome.findByPrimaryKey(primaryKey);
   } catch (javax.ejb.FinderException fe) {
      // Customer not found
      throw new UnknownCustomerException(primaryKey);
   }
   return null;
}
```

    j. Complete the getCustomer method, as shown in Example 15-17. The method uses the find_CustomerLocalHome_findByPrimaryKey method to look up the customer in the database and then builds a data transfer object and returns that to the caller.

Example 15-17   Completed getCustomer method

```
public Customer getCustomer(String ssn)
      throws UnknownCustomerException
{
   CustomerLocal aCustomerLocal = find_CustomerLocalHome_findByPrimaryKey(ssn);
   Customer customer = new Customer();
   customer.setSsn(ssn);
   customer.setTitle(aCustomerLocal.getTitle());
   customer.setFirstName(aCustomerLocal.getFirstName());
   customer.setLastName(aCustomerLocal.getLastName());
   return customer;
}
```

5. Complete the getAccount method using a similar approach to the getCustomer method. The finished getAccount method is shown in Example 15-18.

Example 15-18   Completed getAccount method

```
public Account getAccount(String accountNumber)
      throws UnknownAccountException
{
   AccountLocal anAccountLocal = find_AccountLocalHome_findByPrimaryKey(accountNumber);

   Account account = new Account();
   account.setAccountNumber(accountNumber);
   account.setBalance(anAccountLocal.getBalance());

   return account;
}
```

Example 15-19 shows the find_AccountLocalHome_findByPrimaryKey method, modified to throw the application-specific exception UnknownAccountException.

Example 15-19   Completed find_AccountLocalHome_findByPrimaryKey method

```
protected AccountLocal find_AccountLocalHome_findByPrimaryKey(String primaryKey)
      throws UnknownAccountException
{
   AccountLocalHome anAccountLocalHome = (AccountLocalHome) ServiceLocatorManager
         .getLocalHome(STATIC_AccountLocalHome_REF_NAME,
             STATIC_AccountLocalHome_CLASS);
   try {
      if (anAccountLocalHome != null)
         return anAccountLocalHome.findByPrimaryKey(primaryKey);
```

```
      } catch (javax.ejb.FinderException fe) {
         // Account does not exist
         throw new UnknownAccountException(primaryKey);
      }
      return null;
}
```

6. Now that we have utility functions to look up accounts and customers, we can implement the methods for updating a customer (updateCustomer), retrieving the accounts for a customer (getAccounts), and the transactions for an account (getTransactions). These are shown in Example 15-20.

Example 15-20   Completed updateCustomer, getAccounts, and getTransactions methods

```
public void updateCustomer(String ssn, String title, String firstName, String lastName)
      throws UnknownCustomerException
{
   CustomerLocal aCustomerLocal = find_CustomerLocalHome_findByPrimaryKey(ssn);

   aCustomerLocal.setTitle(title);
   aCustomerLocal.setFirstName(firstName);
   aCustomerLocal.setLastName(lastName);
}

public Account[] getAccounts(String ssn)
      throws UnknownCustomerException
{
   CustomerLocal aCustomerLocal = find_CustomerLocalHome_findByPrimaryKey(ssn);

   Collection colAccounts = aCustomerLocal.getAccounts();
   Iterator itAccounts = colAccounts.iterator();
   Account[] arrAccount = new Account[colAccounts.size()];
   int i = 0;
   while (itAccounts.hasNext()) {
      AccountLocal accountLocal = (AccountLocal) itAccounts.next();
      Account account = new Account();
      account.setAccountNumber(accountLocal.getPrimaryKey().toString());
      account.setBalance(accountLocal.getBalance());
      arrAccount[i++] = account;
   }

   return arrAccount;
}

public Transaction[] getTransactions(String accountNumber)
      throws UnknownAccountException
{
   AccountLocal anAccountLocal = find_AccountLocalHome_findByPrimaryKey(accountNumber);
   Set setTransactions = anAccountLocal.getLog();
```

```
    Iterator itTransactions = setTransactions.iterator();
    Transaction[] arrTransaction = new Transaction[setTransactions.size()];
    int i = 0;
    while (itTransactions.hasNext()) {
       TransactionLocal transactionLocal = (TransactionLocal) itTransactions
             .next();
       Transaction transaction = null;
       if (transactionLocal instanceof CreditLocal) {
          transaction = new Credit();
       } else {
          transaction = new Debit();
       }
       transaction.setAccountNumber(accountNumber);
       transaction.setAmount(transactionLocal.getAmount());
       transaction.setTimestamp(transactionLocal.getTimestamp());
       arrTransaction[i++] = transaction;
    }

    return arrTransaction;
 }
```

7. In order to implement the transaction methods, we need code to create a new transaction. The method is similar to creating code for an EJB lookup method:

    a. Create a method stub for the deposit method, as shown in Example 15-21, placing the cursor inside the method body.

    Example 15-21   Method stub for the deposit method

    ```
    public void deposit(String accountNumber, int amount)
          throws UnknownAccountException, ApplicationException
    {
    }
    ```

    b. In the Snippets view, double-click **EJB** → **Call an EJB "create" method**.

    c. When the Insert EJB Create wizard appears, click **New EJB Reference**.

    d. When the Add EJB Reference dialog appears, select **Enterprise Beans in the workspace**, expand and select **BankEJBEAR** → **BankEJB** → **Credit**, ensure that **Local** is selected in the Ref type drop-down, and click **Finish**.

    e. When you return the Insert EJB Create wizard, click **Finish**.

    Similar resources to the Insert EJB Find wizard are created for you:

    - An EJB reference named ejb/Credit is created for the Bank session bean.
    - A createCreditLocal method is created in the BankBean class.

- Constants STATIC_CreditLocalHome_REF_NAME and STATIC_CreditLocalHome_CLASS are added to the BankBean class.
- Import statements for itso.bank.model.ejb.CreditLocalHome and itso.bank.model.ejb.CreditLocal are added to BankBean.java.

f. Modify the generated createCreditLocal method to match the code shown in Example 15-22.

Example 15-22 Completed createCreditLocal method, customizations shown in bold

```
protected CreditLocal createCreditLocal(int amount)
      throws ApplicationException
{
   CreditLocalHome aCreditLocalHome = (CreditLocalHome) ServiceLocatorManager
         .getLocalHome(STATIC_CreditLocalHome_REF_NAME,
               STATIC_CreditLocalHome_CLASS);
   try {
      if (aCreditLocalHome != null)
         return aCreditLocalHome.create(amount);
   } catch (javax.ejb.CreateException ce) {
      throw new ApplicationException(
            "Unable to create credit transaction (amount="+amount+")", ce);
   }
   return null;
}
```

g. Complete the deposit method, as shown in Example 15-23.

Example 15-23 Completed deposit method

```
public void deposit(String accountNumber, int amount)
      throws UnknownAccountException, ApplicationException
{
   AccountLocal anAccountLocal = find_AccountLocalHome_findByPrimaryKey(accountNumber);

   CreditLocal aCreditLocal = createCreditLocal(amount);

   anAccountLocal.processTransaction(aCreditLocal);
}
```

8. Implement the withdraw method, using the same process as the deposit method, except that you use the Insert EJB Create wizard to generate code to create a Debit bean. The completed code for the withdraw, transfer, and createDebitLocal methods is shown in Example 15-24. Again, the modified parts of the createDebitLocal method are highlighted in bold.

Example 15-24 Completed withdraw, transfer, and createDebitLocal method

```
public void withdraw(String accountNumber, int amount)
```

```
      throws UnknownAccountException, InsufficientFundsException, ApplicationException
{
   AccountLocal anAccountLocal = find_AccountLocalHome_findByPrimaryKey(accountNumber);

   DebitLocal aDebitLocal = createDebitLocal(amount);

   anAccountLocal.processTransaction(aDebitLocal);
}

public void transfer(String debitAccountNumber, String creditAccountNumber, int amount)
      throws UnknownAccountException, InsufficientFundsException, ApplicationException
{
   withdraw(debitAccountNumber, amount);
   deposit(creditAccountNumber, amount);
}

protected DebitLocal createDebitLocal(int amount)
      throws ApplicationException
{
   DebitLocalHome aDebitLocalHome = (DebitLocalHome) ServiceLocatorManager
         .getLocalHome(STATIC_DebitLocalHome_REF_NAME,
               STATIC_DebitLocalHome_CLASS);
   try {
      if (aDebitLocalHome != null)
         return aDebitLocalHome.create(amount);
   } catch (javax.ejb.CreateException ce) {
      throw new ApplicationException(
            "Unable to create debit transaction (amount="+amount+")", ce);
   }
   return null;
}
```

9. Promote the facade methods to the remote interface, as follows:

   a. In the Outline view, highlight the following methods, as shown in Figure 15-47 on page 914:
      - getCustomer(String)
      - getAccount(String)
      - updateCustomer(String, String, String, String)
      - getAccounts(String)
      - getTransactions(String)
      - deposit(String, int)
      - withdraw(String, int)
      - transfer(String, String, int)

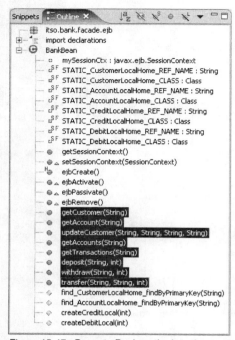

Figure 15-47 Promote Bank methods to the remote interface

  b. Right-click one of the selected methods and select **Enterprise Bean → Promote to Remote Interface**.

  > **Note:** We found that sometimes the R-shaped icons (which mean that the method exists in the remote interface) would not appear after promoting the methods. Closing and reopening the Java editor would fix this.

The Bank session bean is now complete. In the following sections we first test the EJBs using the Universal Test Client and then proceed to integrate the EJBs with the ITSO Web Bank application.

15.5 Testing EJB with the Universal Test Client

Before we integrate the EJB application with the Web application, imported in 15.3.5, "Import BankBasicWeb Project" on page 853, we will test the Bank session bean to see that it works as expected. We will use the enterprise application Universal Test Client (UTC), which is contained within Rational Application Developer.

In this section we describe some of the operations you can perform with the Universal Test Client. We will use the test client to find the Customer EJB home, find and create instances of the Customer bean, and send messages to those instances.

To test the EJBs, do the following:

1. From the Project Explorer of the J2EE Perspective, right-click **EJB Projects** → **BankEJB** and select **Run** → **Run on Server**.
2. When the Server Selection dialog appears, select **WebSphere Application Server v6.0** and click **Finish**.

    The server will be started and the EJB project will be deployed, if necessary. This may take a while.

3. When the Universal Test Client Welcome page appears, as shown in Figure 15-48, click **JNDI Explorer**.

    Tip: The default URL of the test client is http://localhost:9080/UTC/, so you can also access it through an external browser. If you want to access it from another machine, just substitute `localhost` with the hostname or IP address of the developer machine.

Figure 15-48   Universal Test Client home page

4. When the JNDI Explorer page appears, expand **[Local EJB Beans]** → **ejb** → **itso** → **bank** → **model** → **ejb**, **ejb** → **itso** → **bank** → **facade** → **ejb** and **jdbc**.

   The page should look similar to Figure 15-49. Notice that our five entity beans appear in the section for local EJBs, because they have no remote interface, while the Bank session bean appears in the remotely accessible scope. Also, the data source that we defined in 15.3.7, "Configure the data source" on page 856, appears in the JNDI explorer view. All EJBs appear as Web links.

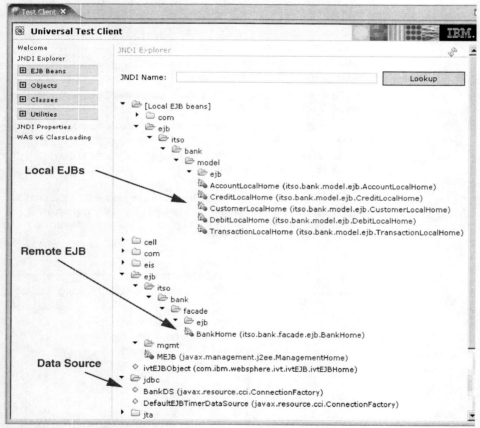

Figure 15-49 The UTC JNDI Explorer

> **Note:** If the EJBs do not show up as links, we suggest that you unpublish the application from the server, restart the server, and start again by running the BankEJB project on the server.

5. Click **BankHome (itso.bank.facade.ejb.BankHome)**. The result is that the Bank bean is added to the EJB Beans list.
6. Expand **EJB Beans** → **BankHome** → **Bank** and click **Bank create()**.
7. The method signature for the create method is displayed. Click **Invoke**. The page should look similar to Figure 15-50.

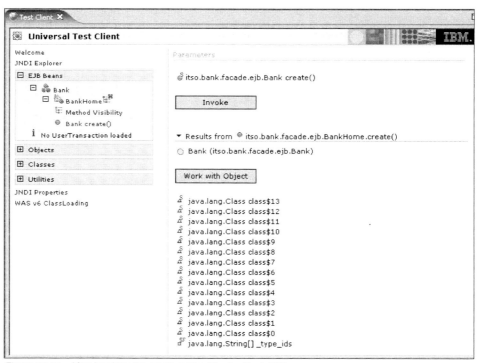

Figure 15-50 After invoking the create method for the Bank EJB

8. Click **Work with Object**. UTC will display the following message below the menu:

   ```
   Recently added:
   Bank 1
   ```

   Additionally, the object Bank 1 will appear below the existing BankHome object in the EJB Beans compartment of the menu.

9. Expand **EJB Beans** → **Bank 1** and click **Account[] getAccounts(String)**. The method signature for the getAccounts method will appear with a table, allowing you to specify the method parameters (in this case, only one String parameter).

10. Enter 111-11-1111 in the Value field and click **Invoke**. The resulting page should look similar to Figure 15-51. As you can see, three objects of the type itso.bank.model.Account were returned.

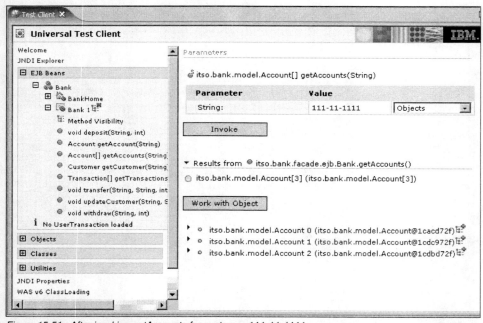

Figure 15-51   After invoking getAccounts for customer 111-11-1111

11. Click **Work with Object**. Notice how the object is added to the Objects compartment and not the EJB Beans.

The test client cannot inspect objects in arrays, so we will have to convert it to a java.util.List:

a. Expand **Utilities** and click **Object[] -> List**.

b. When the Object[] -> List page appears, select **Account[3]** and click **Convert**.

c. Click **Work with Contained Objects**.

Three Account objects will be added to the Objects compartment. Invoke their getAccountNumber and getBalance methods to inspect their contents.

You can play with the UTC to make sure all of your EJBs work. When you are done, close the browser window and stop the server in the Servers view.

15.6 Adapting the Web application

The Web application, developed in Chapter 11, "Develop Web applications using JSPs and servlets" on page 499, was imported and added to the BankEJBEAR project in 15.3.5, "Import BankBasicWeb Project" on page 853. We will now add client code to the Web application, in order to utilize the EJBs developed and tested in this chapter.

> **Tip:** The Java code for the EJBBank class can be copied from the file c:\6449code\ejb\source\EJBBank.java, included with the additional material for this book.

1. In the Project Explorer, expand **Dynamic Web Projects → BankBasicWeb → diagrams**.

2. Double-click **model.dnx** to open the class diagram in the UML Editor.

3. The UML Editor will open.

   Notice that the model and exception classes and their relationship lines appear with crossed-out circles. This is the UML Editor's way of telling us that it cannot find the source for these resources.

4. Select the model and exception classes and press Delete to remove them from the diagram.

5. Select **itso.bank.facade** and press Delete to remove the package from the diagram.

6. In the Palette, select **Java → Class** and click the canvas.

7. When the New Java Class wizard appears, do the following and click **Finish**:
   - Name: EJBBank
   - Package: itso.bank.facade
   - Superclass: Bank
   - Select **Inherited abstract methods**.
8. When the new class has been added to the diagram, double-click it to open EJBBank.java in the Java source editor.
9. Add the code from Example 15-25 to the class.

Example 15-25   Method stub for getBankEJB

```
// add before the first method of the class
private itso.bank.facade.ejb.Bank bankEJB = null;

// add after the last method of the class
private itso.bank.facade.ejb.Bank getBankEJB()
      throws ApplicationException
{
   if (bankEJB == null) {
      // place the cursor on the next line

   }
   return bankEJB;
}
```

10. Place the cursor over the if statement and double-click **EJB → Call an EJB "create" method** in the Snippets view.
11. When the Insert EJB Create wizard appears, click **New EJB Reference**.
12. When the Add EJB Reference dialog appears, select **Enterprise Beans in the workspace**, expand and select **BankEJBEAR → BankEJB → Bank**, ensure that **Remote** is selected in the Ref type drop-down, and click **Finish**.
13. When you return the Insert EJB Create wizard, click **Finish**.
14. When the wizard is done adding configuration data and code, replace the getBankEJB and generated createBank methods with the code shown in Example 15-26.

Example 15-26   Completed getBankEJB method

```
private itso.bank.facade.ejb.Bank getBankEJB() throws ApplicationException {
   if (bankEJB == null) {
      BankHome aBankHome = (BankHome) ServiceLocatorManager.getRemoteHome(
            STATIC_BankHome_REF_NAME, STATIC_BankHome_CLASS);
      try {
         if (aBankHome != null)
            bankEJB = aBankHome.create();
```

```
      } catch (javax.ejb.CreateException ce) {
         throw new ApplicationException("Unable to create EJB: "+
                  STATIC_BankHome_REF_NAME, ce);
      } catch (RemoteException re) {
         throw new ApplicationException("Unable to create EJB: "+
                  STATIC_BankHome_REF_NAME, re);
      }
   }
   return bankEJB;
}
```

15. Remove the following import statement:

    ```
    import itso.bank.facade.ejb.Bank;
    ```

    This import statement was created by the Insert EJB Create wizard.

16. Replace the method stubs that were generated by the New Java Class wizard with the methods shown in Example 15-27. These methods will forward all calls to the Bank EJB.

Example 15-27   Completed EJBBank facade methods invoke the Bank EJB

```
public Account getAccount(String accountNumber)
      throws UnknownAccountException, ApplicationException {
   try {
      return getBankEJB().getAccount(accountNumber);
   } catch (RemoteException e) {
      throw new ApplicationException("Unable to retrieve account: "+
               accountNumber, e);
   }
}

public Account[] getAccounts(String customerNumber)
      throws UnknownCustomerException, ApplicationException {
   try {
      return getBankEJB().getAccounts(customerNumber);
   } catch (RemoteException e) {
      throw new ApplicationException("Unable to retrieve accounts for: "+
               customerNumber, e);
   }
}

public Customer getCustomer(String customerNumber)
      throws UnknownCustomerException, ApplicationException {
   try {
      return getBankEJB().getCustomer(customerNumber);
   } catch (RemoteException e) {
      throw new ApplicationException("Unable to retrieve accounts for: "+
               customerNumber, e);
```

```java
        }
    }

    public Transaction[] getTransactions(String accountId)
            throws UnknownAccountException, ApplicationException {
        try {
            return getBankEJB().getTransactions(accountId);
        } catch (RemoteException e) {
            throw new ApplicationException("Unable to retrieve transactions for: "+
                    accountId, e);
        }
    }

    public void deposit(String accountId, int amount)
            throws UnknownAccountException, ApplicationException {
        try {
            getBankEJB().deposit(accountId, amount);
        } catch (RemoteException e) {
            throw new ApplicationException("Unable to deposit "+amount+
                    " to "+accountId, e);
        }
    }

    public void withdraw(String accountId, int amount)
            throws UnknownAccountException, InsufficientFundsException,
            ApplicationException {
        try {
            getBankEJB().withdraw(accountId, amount);
        } catch (RemoteException e) {
            throw new ApplicationException("Unable to withdraw "+amount+" from
"+accountId, e);
        }
    }

    public void transfer(String debitAccountNumber, String creditAccountNumber,
            int amount)
            throws UnknownAccountException, InsufficientFundsException,
ApplicationException {
        try {
            getBankEJB().transfer(debitAccountNumber, creditAccountNumber, amount);
        } catch (RemoteException e) {
            throw new ApplicationException("Unable to transfer "+amount+
                    " from "+debitAccountNumber+" to "+creditAccountNumber, e);
        }
    }

    public void updateCustomer(String ssn, String title,
            String firstName, String lastName)
            throws UnknownCustomerException, ApplicationException {
```

```
   try {
      getBankEJB().updateCustomer(ssn, title, firstName, lastName);
   } catch (RemoteException e) {
      throw new ApplicationException("Unable to update customer "+ssn, e);
   }
}
```

17. Now that we have completed the EJBBank facade, we need to update the abstract class itso.bank.facade.Bank to return an instance to the EJBBank class when its getBank method is called. Modify the getBank method of the Bank class as shown in Example 15-28.

Example 15-28 New getBank method for the Bank facade

```
public static Bank getBank() throws ApplicationException {
    if (singleton == null) {
        // no singleton has been created yet - create one
        singleton = new EJBBank();
    }

    return singleton;
}
```

> **Tip:** The Java code for the getBank method can be copied from the file c:\6449code\ejb\source\Bank.jpage, included with the additional material for this book.

18. Restart the server.
19. Follow the instructions in 11.7, "Test the application" on page 610, to test the Web application.

> **Persistence:** In the first implementation, every time you started the Web application you got the same data because it was created from memory. Now we are running with EJBs accessing the underlying BANK database. All the updates are persistent. The updated balance is stored in the database and the transaction records accumulate for each account.
>
> When testing, try to restart the server to see the persistence.

16

Develop J2EE application clients

This chapter provides an introduction to J2EE application clients and the facilities supplied by the J2EE application client container. In addition, we highlight the features provided by Rational Application Developer for developing and testing J2EE application clients.

The chapter is organized into the following sections:

- Introduction to J2EE application clients
- Overview of the sample application
- Preparing for the sample application
- Develop the J2EE application client
- Test the J2EE application client
- Package the application client project

16.1 Introduction to J2EE application clients

A J2EE application server is capable of making several different types of resources available for remote access, such as:

- Enterprise JavaBeans (EJBs)
- JDBC Data Sources
- Java Message Service (JMS) resources (Queues and Topics)
- Java Naming and Directory Interface (JNDI) services

These resources are most often accessed from a component that is running within the J2EE application server itself, such as an EJB, servlet, or JSP. However, these resources can also be used from a stand-alone Java application running in its own Java Virtual Machine (JVM), possibly on a different computer from the server. This is known as a J2EE application client. Figure 16-1 depicts the resource access scenarios described.

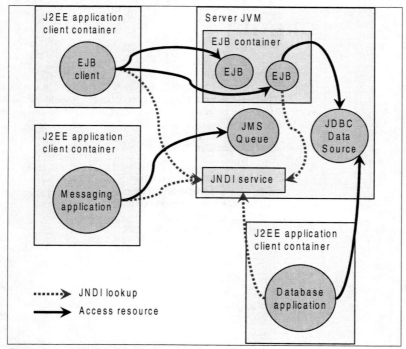

Figure 16-1   Java applications using J2EE server resources

> **Note:** The clients shown in Figure 16-1 on page 926 may conceptually be running on the same physical node, or even in the same JVM as the application server. The focus in this chapter, however, is clients running in distributed environments. During the course of this chapter, we will develop an EJB client, invoking the EJBs from Chapter 15, "Develop Web applications using EJBs" on page 827, to provide a simple ITSO Bank client application.

Since a regular JVM does not support accessing such application server resources, additional setup for the runtime environment is required for a J2EE application. There are two methods to achieve this:

- Add the required packages to the Java Runtime Environment manually.
- Package the application according to the J2EE application client specification and execute the application in a J2EE application client container.

In this chapter, we focus on the second of these options. In addition to providing the correct runtime resources for Java applications wishing to access J2EE server resources, the J2EE application client container provides additional features, such as mapping references to JNDI names and integration with server security features.

> **Note:** For more detailed information on J2EE application clients, refer to the J2EE specification (Chapter 9, "Application Clients") found at:
>
> http://java.sun.com/j2ee/

The specification defines the runtime requirements for J2EE application clients, particularly in the areas of security, transactions, and naming (JNDI). It also specifies which programming APIs are required in addition to those provided by Java 2 Standard Edition (J2SE):

- Enterprise JavaBeans (EJB) 2.1 (client-side APIs)
- Java Message Service (JMS) 1.1
- JavaMail 1.3
- JavaBeans Activation Framework (JAF) 1.0
- Java APIs for XML Processing (JAXP) 1.2
- Web Services 1.1
- Java API for XML-based Remote Procedure Call (JAX-RPC) 1.1
- SOAP with Attachments API for Java (SAAJ) 1.2
- Java API for XML Registries (JAXR) 1.0
- J2EE Management 1.0
- Java Management Extensions (JMX) 1.2

In addition, the J2EE specification describes the packaging format to be used for J2EE application clients (based on the JAR file format) and the contents of the the deployment descriptor for the J2EE application client.

IBM WebSphere Application Server V6.0 includes a J2EE application client container and a facility for launching J2EE application clients. The J2EE application client container, known as *Application Client for WebSphere Application Server*, can be installed separately from the WebSphere Application Server installation CDs, or downloaded from developerWorks, and runs a completely separate JVM on the client machine. When the JVM starts it loads the necessary runtime support classes to make it possible to communicate with WebSphere Application Server and to support J2EE application clients that will use server-side resources. Refer to the WebSphere Application Server Information Center for more information about installing and using the Application Client for WebSphere Application Server.

> **Note:** Although the J2EE specification describes the JAR format as the packaging format for J2EE application clients, the Application Client for WebSphere Application Server expects the application to be packaged as a JAR inside an enterprise application archive (EAR). The Application Client for WebSphere Application Server does not support execution of a standalone J2EE client JAR.

IBM Rational Application Developer V6.0 includes tooling to assist with developing and configuring J2EE application clients and a test facility that allows J2EE application clients to be executed in an appropriate container. The focus of this chapter is on the Rational Application Developer tooling for J2EE application clients, so we will be looking only at this facility.

16.2 Overview of the sample application

The application that will be developed in the course of this chapter is a very simple client application. It will use the EJB application that was developed in Chapter 15, "Develop Web applications using EJBs" on page 827, to look up the customer information and account overview from a specified customer SSN.

The application will use a graphical user interface, implemented with Swing components, as shown in Figure 16-2, which displays the details for the customer with SSN 111-11-1111.

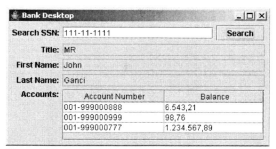

Figure 16-2   Interface for the sample application client

Referring to Figure 16-1 on page 926, the sample J2EE application client is an EJB client that uses the services of the Bank EJB, created in Chapter 15, "Develop Web applications using EJBs" on page 827, to access account information for customers in the ITSO Bank.

Figure 16-3 on page 930 shows a class diagram of the finished sample application. The classes on the right-hand side of the class diagram are classes from the EJB enterprise application, while the three left-hand classes are part of the application client. As the class diagram outlines, the application client controller class, BankDesktopController, uses the Bank EJB to retrieve Customer and Account object instances, representing the customer and associated account(s) that is being retrieved from the server database.

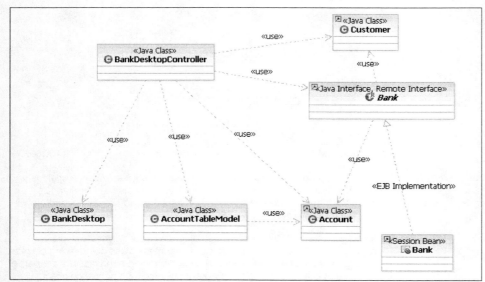

Figure 16-3 Class diagram for the ITSO Bank J2EE application client

To illustrate the deployment units for the finished application, Figure 16-4 on page 931 shows the Project Explorer view with all projects and the deployment descriptors for the two enterprise applications expanded. When deployed to a working environment, the BankAppClientEAR is deployed on the client node, while the BankEJBEAR is deployed on an application server.

As Figure 16-4 on page 931 shows, the two enterprise applications share the two utility JARs BankEJBClient.jar and serviceLocatorMgr.jar. The former is the client code necessary to use the EJBs from the BankEJB project, deployed within the BankEJBEAR enterprise application, while the latter contains utility classes for looking up and instantiating EJBs from a client application.

The projects BankAppClientEAR and BankAppClient are created during the course of this chapter, while the remaining projects were implemented in Chapter 15, "Develop Web applications using EJBs" on page 827.

Figure 16-4   Project Explorer for the finished application client

16.3 Preparing for the sample application

Prior to working on the sample for this chapter, we need to set up the database for the sample application, import the EJB bank projects, and ensure that everything is working.

The preparation tasks are as follows:

- Import the base enterprise application sample.
- Set up the sample database.
- Configure the data source.
- Test the imported code.

16.3.1 Import the base enterprise application sample

To import the base enterprise application sample that we will use as a starting point for this chapter, do the following:

1. From the Project Explorer view in the J2EE perspective, select **File** → **Import...**.
2. When the Import dialog appears, select **Project Interchange** and click **Next**.
3. When the Import Project Interchange Contents dialog appears, enter `c:\6449code\ejb\BankEJB.zip` in the From zip file field, click **Select All**, and then **Finish**.

After the Import wizard has completed the import, the projects shown in Figure 16-5 should appear in the workspace.

Figure 16-5 Projects imported from the BankEJB sample application

> **Note:** You may notice that a number of warnings exist for the BankEJB and BankEJBClient projects. These are all related to unused import statements in code generated by Rational Application Developer, and can be safely ignored. To remove these warnings from the Problems view, you may follow the instructions in 15.3.4, "Configure the EJB projects" on page 849, for ignoring such warning messages.

The projects shown in Figure 16-5 are described as follows:

- BankEJBEAR: This is the deployable enterprise application, which functions as a container for the remaining projects. This enterprise application must be executed on an application server.

- BankEJB: This is the project, containing the EJBs, that makes up the business logic of the ITSO Bank. The Bank session bean acts as a facade for the EJB application.

    This project is packaged inside BankEJBEAR when exported and deployed on an application server.

- BankBasicWeb: This is a Web application that uses the EJBs to implement a Web interface for the ITSO Bank. During the course of this chapter, we develop a stand-alone J2EE client application with the same functionality as the ListAccounts servlet of this Web application.

    This project is packaged inside BankEJBEAR when exported and deployed on an application server.

- BankEJBClient: This is the client interface for the EJB application. This project is packaged with any application that will need to access the EJBs in the BankEJB project, including the BankBasicWeb project and the client application that will be developed during the course of this chapter.

16.3.2 Set up the sample database

If the Cloudscape database has already been configured for another sample in this book, you can skip the next step and go straight to 16.3.3, "Configure the data source" on page 934.

This section provides instructions for deploying the BANK sample database and populating the database with sample data. For simplicity we will use the built-in Cloudscape database.

To create the database, create the connection, and create and populate the tables for the BANK sample from within Rational Application Developer, do the following:

1. Create the database and connection to the Cloudscape BANK database from within Rational Application Developer.

    For details refer to "Create a database connection" on page 347.

2. Create the BANK database tables from within Rational Application Developer.

    For details refer to "Create database tables via Rational Application Developer" on page 350.

3. Populate the BANK database tables with sample data from within Rational Application Developer.

    For details refer to "Populate the tables within Rational Application Developer" on page 352.

16.3.3 Configure the data source

There are a couple of methods that can be used to configure the data source, including using the WebSphere Administrative Console or using the WebSphere Enhanced EAR, which stores the configuration in the deployment descriptor and is deployed with the application.

This section describes how to configure the data source using the WebSphere Enhanced EAR capabilities. The enhanced EAR is configured in the Deployment tab of the EAR deployment descriptor.

Access the deployment descriptor

To access the deployment descriptor where the enhanced EAR settings are defined, do the following:

1. Open the J2EE Perspective Project Explorer view.
2. Expand **Enterprise Applications** → **BankEJBEAR**.
3. Double-click **Deployment Descriptor: BankEJBEAR** to open the file in the Deployment Descriptor Editor.
4. Click the **Deployment** tab.

> **Note:** For JAAS Authentication, when using Cloudscape, the configuration of the user ID and password for the JAAS Authentication is not needed.
>
> When using DB2 Universal Database or other database types that require a user ID and password, you will need to configure the JAAS Authentication.

Configure a new JDBC provider

To configure a new JDBC provider using the enhanced EAR capability in the deployment descriptor, do the following:

1. From the Deployment tab of the Application Deployment Descriptor, click **Add** under the JDBC provider list.
2. When the Create a JDBC Provider dialog appears, select **Cloudscape** as the Database type, select **Cloudscape JDBC Provider** as the JDBC provider type, and then click **Next**.

> **Note:** The JDBC provider type list for Cloudscape will contain two entries:
> ▶ Cloudscape JDBC Provider
> ▶ Cloudscape JDBC Provider (XA)
>
> Since we will not need support for two-phase commits, we choose to use the non-XA JDBC provider for Cloudscape.

3. Enter `Cloudscape JDBC Provider - BankEJB` in the Name field and then click **Finish**.

Configure the data source

To configure a new data source using the enhanced EAR capability in the deployment descriptor, do the following:

1. From the Deployment tab of the Application Deployment Descriptor, select the JDBC provider created in the previous step.
2. Click **Add** next to data source.
3. When the Create a Data Source dialog appears, select **Cloudscape JDBC Provider** under the JDBC provider, select **Version 5.0 data source**, and then click **Next**.
4. When the Create a Data Source dialog appears, enter the following and then click **Finish**:
   - Name: `BankDS`
   - JNDI name: `jdbc/BankDS`
   - Description: `Bank Data Source`

Configure the databaseName property

To configure the databaseName in the new data source using the enhanced EAR capability in the deployment descriptor to define the location of the database for your environment, do the following:

1. Select the data source created in the previous section.
2. Select the **databaseName** property under the Resource properties.
3. Click **Edit** next to Resource properties to change the value for the databaseName.
4. When the Edit a resource property dialog appears, enter `c:\databases\BANK` in the Value field and then click **OK**.

> **Important:** The Edit a resource property dialog allows you to edit the entire resource property, including the name. Ensure that you only change the value of the databaseName property, not the name.

In our example, c:\databases\BANK is the database created for our sample application in 15.3.6, "Set up the sample database" on page 854.

5. Save the Application Deployment Descriptor.
6. Restart the test server for the changes to the deployment descriptor to take effect.

Set up the default CMP data source

Several data sources can be defined for an enterprise application. In order for the EJB container to be able to determine which data source should be used, we must configure the BankEJBEAR project to point to the newly created data source as follows:

1. Open the J2EE Perspective Project Explorer view.
2. Expand **EJB Projects** → **BankEJB**.
3. Double-click **Deployment Descriptor: BankEJB** to open the file in the Deployment Descriptor Editor.
4. From the Overview tab, scroll down to the JNDI - CMP Connection Factory Binding section.
5. Enter `jdbc/BankDS` in the JNDI name field.
6. Press Ctrl+S followed by Ctrl+F4 to save and close the deployment descriptor.

16.3.4 Test the imported code

Before continuing with the sample application, we suggest that you test the imported code. Follow the instructions in 15.5, "Testing EJB with the Universal Test Client" on page 915, to test the EJBs.

16.4 Develop the J2EE application client

We will now use Rational Application Developer to create a project containing a J2EE application client. This application client will be associated with its own enterprise application.

> **Note:** While it is possible to use the new client application with the existing BankEJBEAR enterprise application, this is not the recommended approach.
>
> The reason for this is that the enterprise application that contains the EJBs and other server resources will typically contain information that should not be distributed to the clients, such as passwords or proprietary business logic.

To finish the J2EE application client sample you need to complete the following tasks:

- Create the J2EE application client projects.
- Configure the J2EE application client projects.
- Import the graphical user interface and control classes.
- Create the BankDesktopController class.
- Complete the BankDesktopController class.
- Register the BankDesktopController class as the Main class.

16.4.1 Create the J2EE application client projects

To create the J2EE application projects, do the following:

1. In the Project Explorer view of the J2EE perspective, right-click **Application Client Projects** and select **New** → **Application Client Project** from the menu.

2. When the New Application Client Project wizard appears, enter `BankAppClient` in the Name field and click **Show Advanced**.

3. From the Show Advanced options, do the following (as seen in Figure 16-6), and then click **Finish**:

    - Ensure that the J2EE version is set to 1.4.
    - Check **Add module to an EAR project**.
    - Select **BankAppClientEAR**.
    - Uncheck **Create a default Main class**.

> **Note:** After the wizard has created the new projects, you will see the following error in the Problems view:
>
> ```
> IWAE0035E The Main-Class attribute must be defined in the
>     application client module.
> ```
>
> This is because we unchecked "Create a default Main Class" in the New Application Client Project wizard. We will create a main class, and thus resolve this problem in a subsequent step.

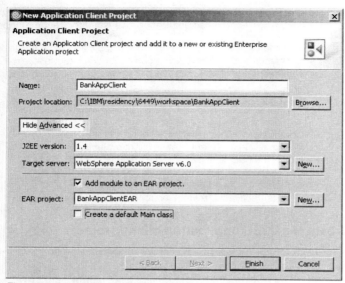

Figure 16-6 New Application Client Project wizard

When the wizard is complete, the following projects should have been created in your workspace:

- BankAppClientEAR: This is an enterprise application project that acts as a container for the code to be deployed on the application client node.
- BankAppClient: This project will contain the actual code for the ITSO Bank application client.

16.4.2 Configure the J2EE application client projects

As mentioned in 16.2, "Overview of the sample application" on page 928, the application client projects reference the BankEJBClient project that was imported in 16.3.1, "Import the base enterprise application sample" on page 932. In this section, we configure this dependency by completing the following tasks:

- Add BankEJBClient as a Utility JAR.
- Add BankEJBClient to the Java JAR Dependencies.

Add BankEJBClient as a Utility JAR

To add BankEJBClient as a Utility JAR for the BankAppClientEAR project, do the following:

1. In the Project Explorer view of the J2EE perspective, expand **Enterprise Applications** → **BankAppClientEAR**.
2. Double-click **Deployment Descriptor: BankAppClientEAR** to open in the Application Deployment Descriptor editor.
3. Select the **Module** tab.
4. Click **Add** in the Project Utility Jars section.
5. When the Add Utility JAR dialog appears, select **BankEJBClient** and click **Finish**.
6. Save and close the deployment descriptor.

Add BankEJBClient to the Java JAR Dependencies

To add BankEJBClient as a Java JAR Dependency for the BankAppClient project, do the following:

1. In the Project Explorer view of the J2EE perspective, expand **Application Client Projects**, right-click **BankAppClient**, and select **Properties** from the menu.
2. When the Properties for BankAppClient dialog appears, select **Java JAR Dependencies**.
3. Check **BankEJBClient.jar** and click **OK**.

16.4.3 Import the graphical user interface and control classes

In this section, we complete the graphical user interface (GUI) for the J2EE application client.

Since this chapter focuses on the aspects relating to development of J2EE application clients, we will import the finished user interface and focus on implementing the code for accessing the EJBs in the EJB project that was imported in 16.3.1, "Import the base enterprise application sample" on page 932.

To import the framework classes for the J2EE application client, do the following:

1. Expand **Application Client Projects** → **BankAppClient**, right-click **appClientModule**, and select **Import**.
2. When the Import dialog appears, select **Zip file** and click **Next**.
3. When the Zip file page appears, enter `c:\6449code\j2eeclt\BankAppClient_GUI.jar` in the From zip file field.

4. Expand **/** in the left panel and ensure that only **itso** is checked (as seen in Figure 16-7, and then click **Finish**.

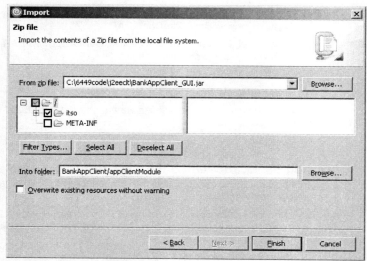

Figure 16-7 Import existing GUI class

When the wizard has completed the import, the following classes should have been added to the BankAppClient project:

- itso.bank.client.ui.BankDesktop

   This is a visual class, containing the view for the Bank J2EE application client.

- itso.bank.client.model.AccountTableModel

   This is an implementation of the interface javax.swing.table.TableModel. The class will provide the relevant TableModel interface, given an array of Account instances.

16.4.4 Create the BankDesktopController class

In this section, we create the controller class for the J2EE application client. This class will also be the main class for the application and will contain the EJB lookup code.

To create the BankDesktopController class, do the following:

1. Expand **Application Client Projects** → **BankAppClient**.

2. Right-click **appClientModule** and select **New** → **Class**.
3. When the New Java Class dialog appears, enter `itso.bank.client.control` in the Package field, `BankDesktopController` in the Name field, check **public static void main(String[] args)** and **Constructors from superclass**, and click **Add**.
4. When the Implemented Interfaces Selection dialog appears, enter `ActionListener` in the Choose interfaces field, select **java.awt.event** in the Qualifier list, and click **OK**.
5. When you return to the New Java Class wizard, it should look like Figure 16-8 on page 941. Click **Finish**.

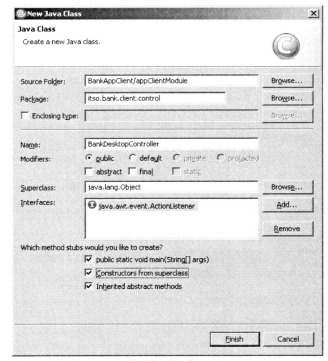

Figure 16-8 Create class BankDesktopController

The BankDesktopController class is now created. In the following section, you will add the logic to the class.

16.4.5 Complete the BankDesktopController class

The BankDesktopController class, which was created in the previous section, is an empty class with no logic. In this section we add control logic, as well as the code to look up customer and account information from the BankEJB enterprise application.

> **Note:** The code found in this section can be copied from the complete BankDesktopController class that is supplied with the additional material for this book. The class can be found in the file c:\6449code\j2eeclt\BankDesktopController.java.
>
> We suggest that you copy the sections as noted in our procedure from the completed BankDesktopController.java (step by step). If you simply import the BankDesktopController.java, the serviceLocatorMgr.jar will not be added as a Java JAR dependency to the BankAppClient project, and thus you will have *can not resolve* errors in the source code. The serviceLocatorMgr.jar is added by using the Insert EJB wizard.

To complete the BankDesktopController class, do the following:

1. In the Project Explorer view of the J2EE perspective, expand **Application Client Projects** → **BankAppClient** → **appClientModule** → **itso.bank.client.control**.
2. Double-click **BankDesktopController.java** to open the class in the Java editor.
3. Add the import statements shown in Example 16-1 to the Java file.

Example 16-1   Import statements to add to BankDesktopController.java

```
import itso.bank.client.ui.AccountTableModel;
import itso.bank.client.ui.BankDesktop;
import itso.bank.model.Account;
import itso.bank.model.Customer;
import itso.bank.exception.UnknownCustomerException;
```

4. Add the fields shown in Example 16-2 to the beginning of the class definition.

Example 16-2   Fields to add to the BankDesktopController class

```
private BankDesktop desktop = null;
private AccountTableModel accountTableModel = null;
```

5. Locate the constructor and modify it to look similar to Example 16-3. The new code is highlighted in bold.

Example 16-3   Constructor for the BankDesktopController class

```
public BankDesktopController() {

    desktop = new BankDesktop();

    desktop.getBtnSearch().addActionListener(this);

    desktop.setVisible(true);
}
```

6. Locate the main method stub and modify it to look similar to Example 16-4. The new code is highlighted in bold.

Example 16-4   Modify the main method

```
public static void main(String[] args) {

    BankDesktopController controller = new BankDesktopController();
}
```

7. Add the setAccounts method shown in Example 16-5 right before the main method.

Example 16-5   Add the setAccounts method

```
private void setAccounts(Account[] accounts) {
    if (accountTableModel == null) {
        // instantiate the model and associate it with the JTable, if it
        // hasn't been created yet.
        accountTableModel = new AccountTableModel();
        desktop.getTblAccounts().setModel(accountTableModel);
    }

    // update the JTable
    accountTableModel.setAccounts(accounts);
}
```

8. Locate the actionPerformed method stub and modify it to look similar to Example 16-6. The new code is highlighted in bold.

Example 16-6   Modify the actionPerformed method

```
public void actionPerformed(ActionEvent e) {
    // we know that we are only listening to action events from
    // the search button, so...

    String ssn = desktop.getTfSSN().getText();
```

}

9. Place the cursor on the last line of the actionPerformed method (the line between the ssn variable declaration and the ending curly brace).
10. In the Snippets view, expand **EJB** and double-click **Call an EJB "create" method**.
11. When the Insert EJB create dialog appears, click **New EJB Reference**.
12. When the Add EJB Reference dialog appears, select **Enterprise Beans in the workspace**, expand **BankEJBEAR** → **BankEJB**, select **Bank**, and click **Finish**.
13. When you return to the Insert EJB create dialog, click **Next**.
14. When the Enter Lookup Properties dialog appears, check **Use default context properties for doing a lookup on this reference** and click **Finish**.

> **Note:** By specifying to use the default context properties, we do not need to hard-code the server name in the code, or in other ways make the code location-aware.
>
> To allow the application client to run on a node, separate from the application server, just specify the server name when starting the J2EE client container.
>
> In the Application Client for WebSphere Application Server, this can be done by using the -CCBootstrapHost parameter to the launchClient script. Refer to the WebSphere Application Server InfoCenter for more information about using the Application Client for WebSphere Application Server.

The Insert EJB create wizard will do the following:

– Adds the following line at the cursor location in the actionPerformed method:

```
Bank aBank = createBank();
```

– Adds private fields STATIC_BankHome_REF_NAME and STATIC_BankHome_CLASS to the class.
– Adds a private method, createBank, to the class.
– Adds the JAR serviceLocatorMgr.jar as a Utility JAR to the BankAppClientEAR enterprise application project.
– Creates an EJB reference, ejb/Bank, to the deployment descriptor for the BankAppClient project.

– Adds the following import statements to the Java class file:

```
import com.ibm.etools.service.locator.ServiceLocatorManager;
import java.rmi.RemoteException;
import itso.bank.facade.ejb.BankHome;
import itso.bank.facade.ejb.Bank;
```

15. Complete the actionPerformed to look similar to Example 16-7. The new code is highlighted in bold.

Example 16-7   Complete the actionPerformed method

```
public void actionPerformed(ActionEvent e) {
   // we know that we are only listening to action events from
   // the search button, so...

   String ssn = desktop.getTfSSN().getText();

   Bank aBank = createBank();

   try {
      // look up the customer
      Customer customer = aBank.getCustomer(ssn);
      // look up the accounts
      Account[] accounts = aBank.getAccounts(ssn);

      // update the user interface
      desktop.getTfTitle().setText(customer.getTitle());
      desktop.getTfFirstName().setText(customer.getFirstName());
      desktop.getTfLastName().setText(customer.getLastName());
      setAccounts(accounts);
   }
   catch (UnknownCustomerException x) {
      // unknown customer. Report this using the output fields...
      desktop.getTfTitle().setText("(not found)");
      desktop.getTfFirstName().setText("(not found)");
      desktop.getTfLastName().setText("(not found)");
      setAccounts(new Account[0]);
   }
   catch (RemoteException x) {
      // unexpected RMI exception. Print it to the console and report it...
      x.printStackTrace();
      desktop.getTfTitle().setText("(internal error)");
      desktop.getTfFirstName().setText("(internal error)");
      desktop.getTfLastName().setText("(internal error)");
      setAccounts(new Account[0]);
   }
}
```

16. Save and close BankDesktopController.java.

The code for the ITSO Bank J2EE application client is now complete. Now we just need to register the BankDesktopController class as the main class for the application client.

16.4.6 Register the BankDesktopController class as the Main class

The BankDesktopController class, which was created in the previous section, contains the logic for the J2EE application client. We need to register that this is the main class for the application client, such that J2EE application client containers know how to launch the application.

To register the BankDesktopController class as the main class, do the following:

1. In the Project Explorer, expand **Application Client Projects** → **BankAppClient** → **appClientModule** → **META-INF**.
2. Right-click **MANIFEST.MF** and select **Open With** → **JAR Dependency Editor**.
3. When the JAR Dependency editor appears, click **Browse** next to the Main-Class entry field.
4. When the Type Selection dialog appears, enter `BankDesktopController` in the Select a class using field, ensure that **itso.bank.client.control.BankDesktopController** is selected in the Qualifier list, and click **OK**.
5. Save the file and close the JAR Dependency Editor.

   The error regarding the missing main class should disappear from the Problems view when the file is saved.

16.5 Test the J2EE application client

Now that the code has been updated, we can test the J2EE application client as follows:

1. Ensure that the server is started.

   a. In the J2EE perspective, switch to the **Servers** view.

   b. Check that the status shown for WebSphere Application Server v6.0 is `Started`. If not, right-click the server and select **Start**.

2. Ensure that the BankEJBEAR enterprise application is deployed on the server.

   a. In the J2EE perspective, switch to the Servers view.

b. Right-click **WebSphere Application Server v6.0** and select **Add and remove projects**.

c. When the Add and Remove Projects dialog appears, the BankEJBEAR project should appear in the Configured projects list, as shown in Figure 16-9 on page 947. If it does not, select **BankEJBEAR** and click **Add**.

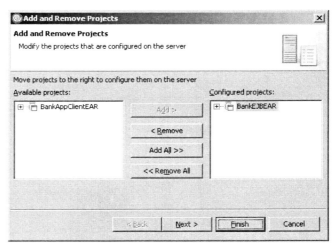

Figure 16-9 Add and Remove Projects dialog showing BankEJBEAR as deployed

d. Click **Finish**.

If you had to add the BankEJBEAR project to the list, Rational Application Developer will now deploy that project to the server. This may take a while.

> **Note:** We found that sometimes, the server would restart in Debug mode after adding or removing projects for the server. If this happens, for you, right-click the server in the Servers view and select **Restart → Start**.

3. In the Project Explorer, expand **Application Client Projects**, right-click **BankAppClient** and select **Run → Run...** from the menu.

4. When the Run dialog appears, select the **WebSphere v6.0 Application Client** in the Configurations list and click **New**.

The right-hand side of the dialog will change to allow you to set up the new Run configuration.

5. Enter BankAppClient in the Name field, as shown in Figure 16-10 on page 948, click **Apply** and then **Run**.

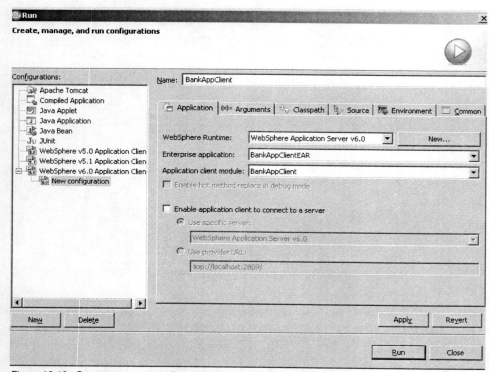

Figure 16-10   Create a new run configuration for the ITSO Bank application client

6. When the Bank Desktop window appears, enter 111-11-1111 in the Search SSN field and click **Search**. The results will be displayed as shown in Figure 16-11 on page 949. Try other SSN values, such as 222-22-2222 or 999-99-9999.

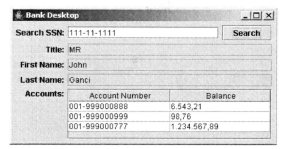

Figure 16-11   Showing the details for customer 111-11-1111

7. Enter an invalid value for the Search SSN and observe the output in the GUI.
8. When you have finished testing the J2EE application client, close the window.

We have successfully built and tested a J2EE application client.

16.6 Package the application client project

In order to run the application client outside Rational Application Developer, we need to package the application.

> **Note:** Although the J2EE specification names the JAR format as the principle means for distributing J2EE application clients, the WebSphere Application Server application client container, Application Client for WebSphere Application Server, expects an enterprise application archive (EAR) file.

To package the application client for deployment, do the following:

1. In the Project Explorer view of the J2EE perspective, expand **Enterprise Applications**, right-click **BankAppClientEAR**, and select **Export** → **EAR file** from the menu.

2. When the EAR Export dialog appears, enter the name of the EAR file (for example, `c:\deployment\BankAppClient.ear`) in the Destination field, and click **Finish**.

   > **Tip:** If you check the **Export source files** and **Include project build paths and meta-data files** check boxes, you will be able to later import the EAR file to Rational Application Developer.

The exported EAR file can now be deployed to a client node and executed using the Application Client for WebSphere Application Server.

17

Develop Web Services applications

This chapter introduces the concepts of a service-oriented architecture (SOA) and explains how such an architecture can be realized using the Java 2 Platform Enterprise Edition (J2EE) Web Services implementation.

We will explore the features provided by Rational Application Developer for Web Services development and look at two common examples: Create Web Services based on a JavaBean, and on an Enterprise JavaBean. We will also demonstrate how Rational Application Developer can help with testing Web Services and developing Web Services client applications.

The chapter is organized into the following sections:

- Introduction to Web Services
- Web Services tools in Application Developer
- Preparing for the samples
- Create a Web Service from a JavaBean
- Create a Web Service from an EJB
- Web Services security
- Publish a Web Service using UDDI

> **Note:** For more detailed information refer to *WebSphere Application Server V6: Web Services Development and Deployment*, SG24-6461.

17.1 Introduction to Web Services

This section introduces architecture and concepts of the service-oriented architecture (SOA) and Web Services.

17.1.1 Service-oriented architecture (SOA)

In a service-oriented architecture, applications are made up from loosely coupled software services, which interact to provide all the functionality needed by the application. Each service is generally designed to be very self-contained and stateless to simplify the communication that takes place between them.

There are three main roles involved in a service-oriented architecture:
- Service provider
- Service broker
- Service requester

The interactions between these roles are shown in Figure 17-1.

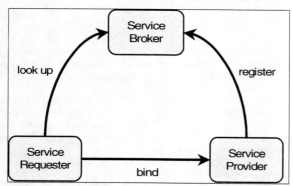

Figure 17-1   Service-oriented architecture

Service provider

The *service provider* creates a service and may publish its interface and access information to a *service broker*.

A service provider must decide which services to expose and how to expose them. There is often a trade-off between security and interoperability; the service provider must make technology decisions based on this trade-off. If the service provider is using a service broker, decisions must be made on how to categorize the service, and the service must be registered with the service broker using agreed-upon protocols.

Service broker

The *service broker,* also known as the *service registry,* is responsible for making the service interface and implementation access information available to any potential service requester.

The service broker will provide mechanisms for registering and finding services. A particular broker might be public (for example, available on the Internet) or private—only available to a limited audience (for example, on an intranet). The type and format of the information stored by a broker and the access mechanisms used will be implementation-dependent.

Service requester

The *service requester*, also know as a *service client*, discovers services and then uses them as part of its operation.

A service requester uses services provided by service providers. Using an agreed-upon protocol, the requester can find the required information about services using a broker (or this information can be obtained in some other way). Once the service requester has the necessary details of the service, it can bind or connect to the service and invoke operations on it. The binding is usually static, but the possibility of dynamically discovering the service details from a service broker and configuring the client accordingly makes dynamic binding possible.

17.1.2 Web Services as an SOA implementation

Web Services provides a technology foundation for implementing a service-oriented architecture. A major focus during the development of this technology is to make the functional building blocks accessible over standard Internet protocols which are independent of platforms and programming languages to ensure that very high levels of interoperability are possible.

Web Services are self-contained software services that can be accessed using simple protocols over a network. They can also be described using standard mechanisms, and these descriptions can be published and located using standard registries. Web Services can perform a wide variety of tasks, ranging from simple request-reply to full business process interactions.

Using tools like Rational Application Developer, existing resources can be exposed as Web Services very easily.

The core technologies used for Web Services are as follows:
- XML
- SOAP
- WSDL
- UDDI

XML

Extensible Markup Language (XML) is the markup language that underlies Web Services. XML is a generic language that can be used to describe any kind of content in a structured way, separated from its presentation to a specific device. All elements of Web Services use XML extensively, including XML namespaces and XML schemas.

The specification for XML is available at:

http://www.w3.org/XML/

SOAP

Simple Object Access Protocol (SOAP) is a network, transport, and programming language neutral protocol that allows a client to call a remote service. The message format is XML. SOAP is used for all communication between the service requester and the service provider. The format of the individual SOAP messages depends on the specific details of the service being used.

The specification for SOAP is available at:

http://www.w3.org/TR/soap/

WSDL

Web Services Description Language (WSDL) is an XML-based interface and implementation description language. The service provider uses a WSDL document in order to specify:

- The operations a Web Service provides
- The parameters and data types of these operations
- The service access information

WSDL is one way to make service interface and implementation information available in a UDDI registry. A server can use a WSDL document to deploy a Web Service. A service requester can use a WSDL document to work out how to access a Web Service (or a tool can be used for this purpose).

The specification for WSDL is available at:

http://www.w3.org/TR/wsdl/

UDDI

Universal Description, Discovery and Integration (UDDI) is both a client-side API and a SOAP-based server implementation that can be used to store and retrieve information on service providers and Web Services.

The specification for UDDI is available at:

http://www.uddi.org/

Figure 17-2 shows a how the Web Services technologies are used to implement an SOA.

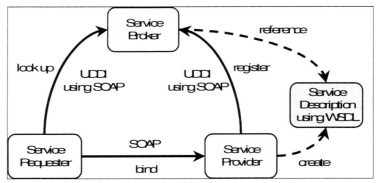

Figure 17-2   Web Services implementation of an SOA

17.1.3 Related Web Services standards

The basic technologies of XML, SOAP, WSDL, and UDDI are fundamental to Web Services, but many other standards have been developed to help with developing and using them.

An excellent resource for information on standards related to Web Services can be found at:

http://www.ibm.com/developerworks/views/webservices/standards.jsp

Web Services in J2EE V1.4

One of the main changes in moving from J2EE V1.3 to V1.4 is the incorporation of Web Services into the Platform standard. J2EE V1.4 provides support for Web

Services clients and also allows Web Services to be published. The main technologies in J2EE V1.4 that provide this support are as follows:

- Java API for XML-based Remote Procedure Calls (JAX-RPC): JAX-RPC provides an API for Web Services clients to invoke services using SOAP over HTTP. It also defines standard mappings between Java classes and XML types.
- SOAP with Attachments API for Java (SAAJ): Allows SOAP messages to be manipulated from within Java code. The API includes classes to represent such concepts as SOAP envelopes (the basic packaging mechanism within SOAP), SOAP faults (the SOAP equivalent of Java exceptions), SOAP connections, and attachments to SOAP messages.
- Web Services for J2EE: This specification deals with the deployment of Web Service clients and Web Services themselves. Under this specification, Web Services can be implemented using JavaBeans or stateless session EJBs.
- Java API for XML Registries (JAXR): This API deals with accessing XML registry servers, such as servers providing UDDI functionality.

The specifications for Web Services support in J2EE V1.4 are available at:

http://java.sun.com/j2ee/

Web Services interoperability

In an effort to improve the interoperability of Web Services, the Web Services Interoperability Organization (known as WS-I) was formed. WS-I produces a specification known as the *WS-I Basic Profile*, which describes the technology choices that maximize interoperability between Web Services and clients running on different platforms, using different runtime systems and written in different languages.

The WS-I Basic Profile is available at:

http://ws-i.org/deliverables/workinggroup.aspx?wg=basicprofile

Web Services security

Although not all runtimes support security for Web Services, a body of standards is evolving that describes how Web Services can be secured. The technical basis for these standards is known as *WS-Security*, which provides the basic encryption and digital signature technologies. In addition, several other specifications now use WS-Security for defining trust models, creating secure channels between Web Services and their clients, and ensuring that clients are authorized to use Web Services.

The specification for WS-Security is managed by OASIS:

http://www.oasis-open.org/

Web Services workflow

Business Process Execution Language for Web Services (BPEL4WS) provides a language for the specification of business processes and business interactions protocols, extending the basic Web Services model to include business transaction support.

The specification for BPEL4WS is available at:

http://www.ibm.com/developerworks/webservices/library/ws-bpel/

Web Services Inspection Language

Web Services Inspection Language (WS-IL) can be used as an alternative to registering Web Services using UDDI. With WS-IL, a site can be inspected for Web Services, and all the necessary information about the available Web Services can be obtained from this inspection.

The WS-IL specification is available at:

http://www.ibm.com/developerworks/webservices/library/ws-wsilspec.html

17.2 Web Services tools in Application Developer

Rational Application Developer provides tools to create Web Services from existing Java and other resources or from WSDL files, as well as tools for Web Services client development and for testing Web Services.

17.2.1 Creating a Web Service from existing resources

Application Developer provides wizards for exposing a variety of resources as Web Services. The following resources can be used to build a Web Service:

- JavaBean: The Web Service wizard assists you in creating a new Web Service from a simple Java class, configures it for deployment, and deploys the Web Service to a server. The server can be the WebSphere Application Server V6.0 Test Environment included with Rational Application Developer or another application server.

- EJB: The Web Service wizard assists you in creating a new Web Service from a stateless session EJB, configures it for deployment, and deploys the Web Service to a server.

- DADX: Document access definition extension (DADX) is an XML document format that specifies how to create a Web Service using a set of operations that are defined by DAD documents and SQL statements. A DADX Web Service enables you to expose DB2 XML Extender or regular SQL statements as a Web Service. The DADX file defines the operations available

- URL: The Web Service wizard assists you in creating a new Web Service that directly accesses a *servlet* running on a server.
- ISD: An ISD file is a legacy Web Service deployment descriptor. It provides information to the SOAP runtime about the service that should be made available to clients (for example, URI, methods, implementation classes, serializers, and deserializers). When using a Web Services runtime based on Apache SOAP, ISD files are concatenated into the SOAP deployment descriptor (dds.xml). This mechanism has been replaced in more recent Web Services runtimes, such as Apache Axis and J2EE Web Services runtimes.

17.2.2 Creating a skeleton Web Service

Rational Application Developer provides the functionality to create Web Services from a description in a WSDL (or WSIL) file:

- JavaBean from WSDL: The Web Service wizard assists you in creating a skeleton JavaBean from an existing WSDL document. The skeleton bean contains a set of methods that correspond to the operations described in the WSDL document. When the bean is created, each method has a trivial implementation that you replace by editing the bean.
- Enterprise JavaBean from WSDL: The Web Services tools support the generation of a skeleton EJB from an existing WSDL file. Apart from the type of component produced, the process is similar to that for JavaBeans.

17.2.3 Client development

To assist in development of Web Service clients, Rational Application Developer provides these features:

- Java client proxy from WSDL: The Web Service client wizard assists you in generating a proxy JavaBean. This proxy can be used within a client application to greatly simplify the client programming required to access a Web Service.
- Sample Web application from WSDL: Rational Application Developer can generate a sample Web application, which includes the proxy classes described above, and sample JSPs that use the proxy classes.

17.2.4 Testing tools for Web Services

To allow developers to test Web Services, Rational Application Developer provides a range of features:

- WebSphere Application Server V6.0 Test Environment: The V6.0 server is included with Rational Application Developer as a test server and can be used to host Web Services. It provides a range of Web Services runtimes, including an implementation of the J2EE specification standards.
- Sample Web application: The Web application mentioned above can be used to test Web Services and the generated proxy it uses.
- Web Services Explorer: This is a simple test environment that can be used to test any Web Service, based only on the WSDL file for the service. The service can be running on a local test server or anywhere else on the network.
- Universal Test Client: The Universal Test Client (UTC) is a very powerful and flexible test application that is normally used for testing EJBs. Its flexibility makes it possible to test ordinary Java classes, so it can be used to test the generated proxy classes created to simplify client development.
- TCP/IP Monitor: The TCP/IP Monitor works like a proxy server, passing TCP/IP requests on to another server and directing the returned responses back to the originating client. In the process of doing this, it records the TCP/IP messages that are exchanged, and can display these in a special view within Rational Application Developer.

17.3 Preparing for the samples

This section describes the steps required for preparing the environment for the Web Services application samples.

This section includes the following tasks:

- Import the sample code.
- Enable the Web Services Development capability.
- Set up the sample back-end database.
- Add Cloudscape JDBC driver (JAR) to the project.
- Define a server to test the application.
- Test the application.

17.3.1 Import the sample code

To prepare for this sample, we will import some sample code. This is a simple Web application that includes Java classes and an Enterprise JavaBean.

1. Switch to the J2EE perspective Project Explorer view.
2. Right-click **Enterprise Applications**, and select **Import...** → **EAR file**.
3. When the Enterprise Application Import dialog appears, click the **Browse** button next to the EAR file, navigate to and select the **BankWebServiceEAR.ear** from the c:\6449code\webservices folder, and click **Open**.

> **Note:** For information on downloading and unpacking the redbook sample code, refer to Appendix B, "Additional material" on page 1395.

4. Ensure that the Import EAR project is checked and click **Next >**.
5. Click **Select All** in the part of the next page dealing with Utility JARs and Web libraries, and then click **Finish**.

17.3.2 Enable the Web Services Development capability

By default, the Web Services Development capability is not enabled in IBM Rational Application Developer V6.0.

To enable the Web Services Development capability, do the following:

1. From the Workbench, select **Window** → **Preferences**.
2. Select **Workbench** → **Capabilities**.
3. Expand **Web Service Developer**.
4. Check **Web Services Development** and **Component Test for Web Services** (Core Database Development is already checked by default), as seen in Figure 17-3 on page 961, and then click **OK**.

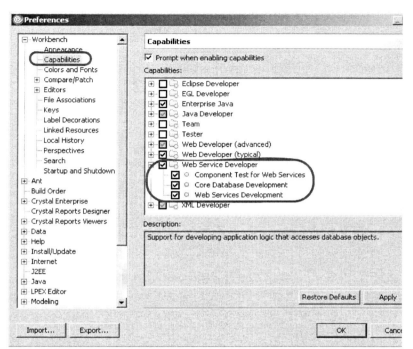

Figure 17-3 Enable Web Services Development capability

17.3.3 Set up the sample back-end database

This section provides instructions for deploying the BANK sample database and populating the database with sample data. For simplicity we will use the built-in Cloudscape database.

To create the database, create the connection, and create and populate the tables for the BANK sample from within Rational Application Developer, do the following:

1. Create the database and the connection to the Cloudscape BANK database from within Rational Application Developer.

    For details refer to "Create a database connection" on page 347.

2. Create the BANK database tables from within Rational Application Developer.

For details refer to "Create database tables via Rational Application Developer" on page 350.

3. Populate the BANK database tables with sample data from within Rational Application Developer.

For details refer to "Populate the tables within Rational Application Developer" on page 352.

17.3.4 Add Cloudscape JDBC driver (JAR) to the project

To add the Cloudscape JDBC driver (JAR) to the BankWebServiceUtility project, do the following:

1. From the J2EE perspective, expand **Other Projects**.
2. Select **BankWebServiceUtility**, right-click, and select **Properties**.
3. Select **Java Build Path**.
4. Select the **Libraries** tab at the top of the dialog and click **Add Variable...**.
5. A further dialog appears, allowing you to select from a list of predefined variables. By default, there is no variable defined for the JAR file we need, so we will have to create one.
6. Click **Configure Variables...** and in the resulting dialog click **New...**.
7. Enter `CLOUDSCAPE_DRIVER_JAR` in the Name field and click **File...**.
8. Find the appropriate JAR file, which is in <rad_home>\runtimes\base_v6\cloudscape\lib and is called db2j.jar.
9. Click **Open**, **OK**, and **OK** and you will be back at the New Variable Classpath Entry dialog.
10. Select the **CLOUDSCAPE_DRIVER_JAR** variable you just created and click **OK**.
11. Modify the sample code URL to point to the correct back-end database.

    a. From the J2EE perspective expand **Other Projects** → **BankWebServiceUtility** → **src** → **itso.bank.model.entity.java**.

    b. Open the **DatabaseManager.java** file.

    c. Modify the URL string for the database in the getConnection method to reflect the actual location of our database. For example:

    ```
    "jdbc:db2j:C:\\databases\\BANK"
    ```

    d. Save and close the file.

17.3.5 Define a server to test the application

Next, we need to define the server that the project will be added to to run and test the application. You can add the project to an existing server or create a new server.

Add project to an existing server
If you already have a server defined for testing purposes, do the following.

> **Note:** We chose this option for our example, since we already had a test server configured.

1. Right-click the server (for example, WebSphere Application Server v6.0), and select **Add and remove projects**.
2. When the Add and Remove Projects dialog appears, select **BankWebServiceEAR** under Available projects, and click **Add >**.
3. The BankWebServiceEAR should now appear under the Configured projects column. Click **Finish**.
4. Verify that the server can start and stop successfully.

Create a new server and add the project
To create a new server to run the application, do the following:

1. From the J2EE perspective, select the **Servers** view.
2. Right-click in the Servers view and select **New** → **Server**.
3. When the Define a New Server dialog appears, accept the default Host name as *localhost* and ensure that **WebSphere v6.0 Server** is selected under Select the server type. Click **Next >**.
4. When the WebSphere Server Settings dialog appears, accept the defaults and click **Next >**.
5. When the Add and Remove Projects dialog appears, select **BankWebServiceEAR** under Available projects, and click **Add >**.
6. The BankWebServiceEAR should now appear under the Configured projects column. Click **Finish**.

17.3.6 Test the application

To start and test the application, do the following:

1. Ensure that CView or another application is not connected to the sample BANK database.

2. Expand **Dynamic Web Projects** → **BankWebServiceWeb** → **WebContent**.
3. Right-click **search.html** and select **Run** → **Run on Server...**.
4. Select the **Choose an existing server** radio button and the desired server to run the application and then click **Finish**.
5. When search.html opens in a Web browser, enter an appropriate value in the Social Security field, such as 111-11-1111, and click **Search**.

   If everything is working correctly, you should see the details of the customer and one of the customer's accounts, which have been read from the database.
6. The stateless session EJB, CustomerFacade, can be tested using the Universal Test Client (UTC). See 15.5, "Testing EJB with the Universal Test Client" on page 915, for more information on using the UTC.

We now have some resources in preparation for the Web Services sample, including a Java class in the BankWebServicesWeb project and an EJB in the BankWebServicesEJB project. We will use these as a base for developing and testing the Web Services samples.

17.4 Create a Web Service from a JavaBean

As explained above, Web Services can be created in several different ways. In this first example, we will create a Web Service from an existing Java class.

The imported application contains a Java class called SimpleBankBean, which has various methods for querying the database.

This section is organized into the following tasks:

- Create a Web Service using the Web Service wizard.
- Resources generated by the Web Services wizard.
- Test the Web Service using the Web Services Explorer.
- Generate and test the client proxy.
- Monitor the Web Service using the TCP/IP Monitor.

17.4.1 Create a Web Service using the Web Service wizard

To create a Web Service using the Web Service wizard, do the following:

1. Ensure that the Web Services Development capability has been enabled.

   For details refer to "Enable the Web Services Development capability" on page 960.

2. Ensure the test server (WebSphere Application Server v6.0) is started. This is needed by the wizard to create a service endpoint interface.
3. From the J2EE perspective, select the **Dynamic Web Projects** folder.
4. Select **File** → **New** → **Other...**.
5. When the Select a Wizard dialog appears, select **Web Service** and then click **Next**.

> **Note:** If you have not previously enabled the Web Services Development capability within Rational Application Developer, you will see the dialog with the message `This action requires the "Web Services Development"`. `Enable the required capability?` Click **OK**.

6. When the Web Service dialog appears, we selected the following options (as seen in Figure 17-4 on page 966), and then clicked **Next**:
   - Web service type: Select **Java bean Web Service**.
   - Check **Start Web Service in Web project** (default).
   - Check **Create folders when necessary** (default).

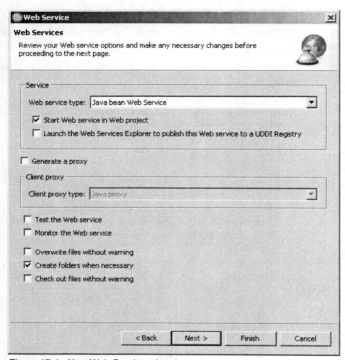

Figure 17-4   New Web Service wizard

7. When the Object Selection Page appears, click **Browse Classes...**, type `SimpleBankBean`, and click **OK**.
8. The Bean name should be itso.bank.model.simple.SimpleBankBean. Click **Next >**.
9. When the Service Deployment Configuration dialog appears, we accepted the values displayed in Figure 17-5 on page 967 (based on our previous settings), and then clicked **Next**.

    If these are not the value shown, you will need to click **Edit...** and set them as appropriate or choose them from the drop-down lists.

> **Tip:** We found that if the server was not started, we received a null pointer exception from the wizard when attempting to create the service endpoint interface in the next step. This is the reason we started the server prior to running the wizard.

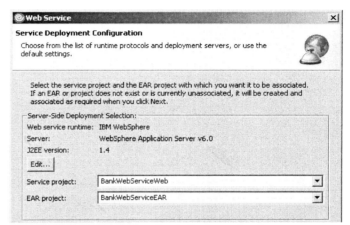

Figure 17-5   New Web Service wizard - Deployment settings

10. When the Service Endpoint Interface Selection dialog appears, accept the default ("Use an existing service endpoint interface" check box unchecked). This will cause the wizard to create a new service end point. Click **Next**.

11. When the Web Service Java Bean Identity dialog appears, we entered the following, as seen in Figure 17-6 on page 968:
    – WSDL File: SimpleBankBean.wsdl (default)
    – Methods:
      • Check **getNumAccounts(String)**.
      • Check **getAccountId(String,int)**.
      • Check **getCustomerFullName(String)**.
      • Check **getAccountBalance(String)**.
    – Style and use: select **Document/ Literal**.
    – Accept the default values for the remaining settings.

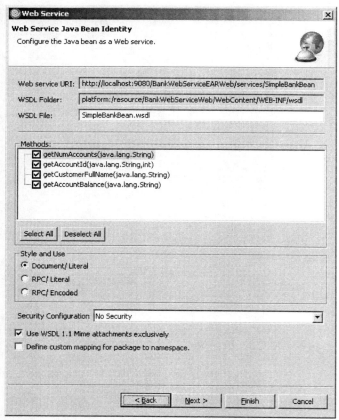

Figure 17-6 New Web Service wizard - Configure the Web Service

12. Click **Next >**.
13. Click **Finish**.

17.4.2 Resources generated by the Web Services wizard

The wizard generates a lot of files based on the choices made. Since the original Java classes are located in the BankWebServiceWeb project, all of the generated code is also located in the BankWebServiceWeb project. The generated files are visible in two different views, as seen in Figure 17-7 and Figure 17-8 on page 970.

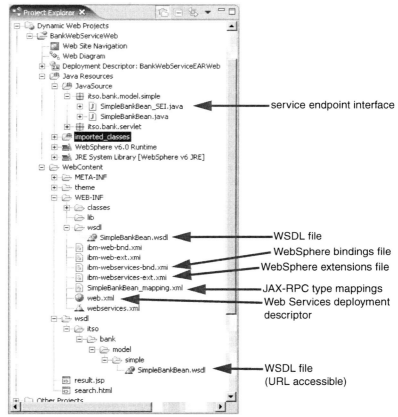

Figure 17-7   Web Services generated resources - Web project view

- The service endpoint interface is the Java interface that is implemented by the Web Service. This will include a subset of the public methods on the class that has been exposed as a Web Service.
- The WSDL file appears in two places:
  - WEB-INF folder: This copy is used by the server for deployment purposes, but is not accessible to external clients through HTTP (the Servlet

specification states that resources contained within the WEB-INF folder are not visible externally).

– wsdl folder: This copy is accessible to external clients and can therefore be used by a client to obtain all the necessary information about the Web Service.

- The WebSphere bindings file is used to map local names to global names (for example, to map EJB references to real names used to register EJBs in JNDI).
- The WebSphere extensions file stores information relating to WebSphere extensions to the J2EE specification. This acts as an extension to the information contained within the deployment descriptor.
- The JAX-RPC type mapping file contains information on the relationships between types used in Java code and their equivalents in XML.
- The Web Services deployment descriptor contains information used by the server to deploy the Web Services in the project. The format of this file is defined by the Web Services for J2EE specification.

Figure 17-8   Web Services generated files - Web Services view

This view only shows information about Web Services defined in projects within the workspace.

- The Service Classes section shows how the Web Service is registered in a Web project as a Servlet (this can also be seen in the Web project's deployment descriptor).
- The WSDL section shows the location of the internally visible copy of the WSDL file for the Web Service.

- The Handlers section (empty in this case) lists the handlers that are configured for this Web Service. These are similar in concept to Servlet filters.

17.4.3 Test the Web Service using the Web Services Explorer

Rational Application Developer includes a versatile tool for working with Web Services, called the Web Services Explorer. It works with WSDL files and automatically generates the appropriate interface for the Web Services being tested.

1. Ensure that you have closed other application connections to the sample BANK database (exit CView or disconnection from within Application Developer).
2. Open the J2EE perspective Project Explorer view.
3. Expand **Web Services** → **Services** → **SimpleBankBeanService**.

> **Note:** Alternatively, expand **Dynamic Web Projects** → **BankWebServiceWeb** → **WebContent** → **WEB-INF** → **wsdl**.

4. Right-click **SimpleBankBean.wsdl** from the SimpleBankBeanService folder, and select **Test with Web Services Explorer**, as seen in Figure 17-9 on page 972.

> **Note:** Alternatively, right-click **SimpleBankBean.wsdl**, and select **Web Services** → **Test with Web Services Explorer**.

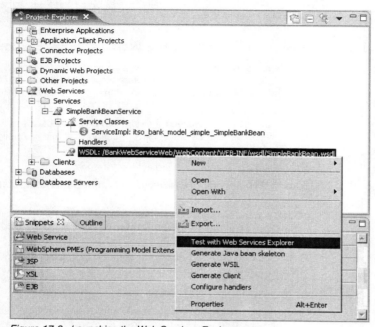

Figure 17-9 Launching the Web Services Explorer

5. When the Web Services Explorer edit dialog appears, expand **SimpleBankBeanSoapBinding** to see the methods available on the Web Service.
6. Select one of the methods (for example, getCustomerFullName).

   The Actions pane on the right displays a simple interface allowing you to enter values for the method parameters
7. Enter a value for the customerId, such as 111-11-1111, and click **Go**.

   The results of your Web Service invocation should appear in the Status pane at the bottom right of the Web Services Explorer.
8. Test the other methods in a similar way.

17.4.4 Generate and test the client proxy

We can also test out Web Service using a proxy class, which is generated by Rational Application Developer.

> **Note:** The proxy is generated using only the WSDL file, so in fact a proxy can be generated for any Web Service for which a WSDL file is available. The Web Service can be running anywhere on the Internet or on an intranet.
>
> The intention of this feature of Rational Application Developer is to simplify client development by encapsulating the lookup and invocation code in a simple Java class.
>
> For more information on using this feature refer to the *WebSphere Application Server V6: Web Services Development and Deployment*, SG24-6461, redbook.

To generate a client and test the client proxy, do the following:

1. Open the J2EE perspective Project Explorer view.
2. Expand **Web Services** → **Services** → **SimpleBankBeanService**.

   > **Note:** Alternatively, expand **Dynamic Web Projects** → **BankWebServiceWeb** → **WebContent** → **WEB-INF** → **wsdl**.

3. Right-click **SimpleBankBean.wsdl**, and select **Generate Client**.

   > **Note:** Alternatively, right-click **SimpleBankBean.wsdl**, and select **Web Services** → **Generate Client**.

4. When the Web Services Client dialog appears, we entered the following (as seen in Figure 17-10 on page 974), and then clicked **Next**:
   - Check **Test the Web Service**.
   - Check **Monitor the Web Service**.
   - Uncheck **Monitor the Web Service** (we will come to this shortly).

   In addition to creating the proxy, this will allow us to generate a sample application based on JSPs, which we can use to test the proxy.

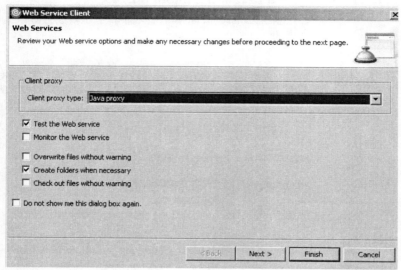

Figure 17-10   Generate Web Service client proxy

5. When the Web Service Selection Page dialog appears, we accepted the default (correct WSDL file selected) and clicked **Next >**.

6. When the Client Environment Configuration dialog appears, we entered the following and then clicked **Next**:
   - Web Service runtime: IBM WebSphere
   - Server: WebSphere Application Server v6.0
   - J2EE version: 1.4
   - Client type: Select **Web** (default). The other possible options include EJB, Application Client (J2EE), and Java (standalone application).
   - Client project: BankWSClient (This will be created for us.)
   - EAR project: Select **BankWebServiceEAR**.

7. When the Web Service Proxy Page dialog appears, we accepted the default (No Security) and clicked **Next**.

8. You may be prompted with Cannot create the file "web.xml" relative to the path "/BankWSClient/WebContent/WEB-INF" because automatic file overwriting has not been enabled. Do you want to enable it for this file? Click **Yes**.

9. When the Web Service Client Test dialog appears, we entered the following and then clicked Finish:

   – Check **Test the generated proxy**.
   – Test facility: Select **Web Service sample JSPs** (default). The test facility options include Web Service sample JSPs, Web Services Explorer, and Universal Test Client.
   – Folder: sampleSimpleBankBeanProxy (default)

     You can specify a different folder for the generated application if you wish.
   – Methods: Leave all methods checked.
   – Check **Run test on server**.

   The sample application should start and be displayed in a Web browser.

10. Select the **getCustomerFullName** method, enter a valid value in the customerId field such as 111-11-1111, and then click **Invoke**.

    The results should be displayed in the result pane, as seen in Figure 17-11.

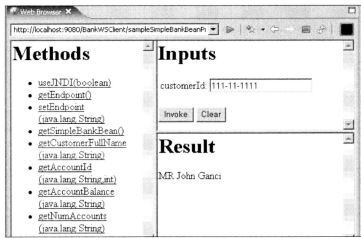

Figure 17-11   Sample JSP results

The code that uses the generated proxy is in Result.jsp and can be viewed in the Source view of the Page Designer editor, although it is not easy to read.

17.4.5 Monitor the Web Service using the TCP/IP Monitor

When developing Web Services, it is often useful to be able to observe the SOAP messages that are passed in both directions between the client and the Web Service. Rational Application Developer provides a tool to allow you to do this, known as the *TCP/IP Monitor*.

To monitor a Web Service using the Rational Application Developer TCP/IP Monitor, do the following:

1. Ensure that you have closed other application connections to the sample BANK database (exit CView or disconnection from within Application Developer).
2. Ensure the test server is started.
3. Create a server to act as the TCP/IP Monitor.
   a. From the Workbench, select **Window → Preferences**.
   b. Select **Internet → TCP/IP Monitor**.
   c. Ensure that **Show the TCP/IP Monitor view when there is activity** is checked.
   d. Under the TCP/IP Monitors lists, click Add.
   e. When the new Monitor dialog appears, we entered the following, as seen in Figure 17-12 on page 977:
      - Local Monitoring port: 9081

        Specify a unique port number on your local machine.
      - Host name: localhost

        Specify the hostname or IP address of the machine where the server is running.
      - Port: 9080

        Specify the port number of the remote server.
      - Type: Select **HTTP** (or TCP/IP).
   f. Select the newly added hostname to monitor and then click **Start**.
   g. Click **OK** to save preference settings.

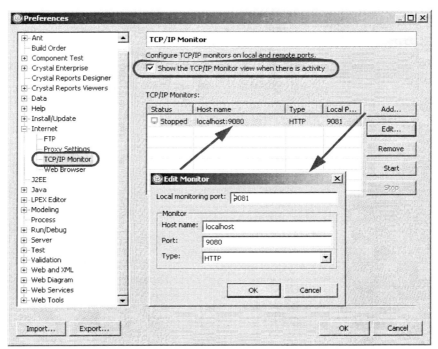

Figure 17-12   TCP/IP Monitor preferences

4. Open the J2EE perspective Project Explorer view.
5. Expand **Web Services** → **Services** → **SimpleBankBeanService**.

> **Note:** Alternatively, expand **Dynamic Web Projects** → **BankWebServiceWeb** → **WebContent** → **WEB-INF** → **wsdl**.

6. Right-click **SimpleBankBean.wsdl**, and select **Test with Web Services Explorer**.

> **Note:** Alternatively, right-click **SimpleBankBean.wsdl**, and select **Web Services** → **Test with Web Services Explorer**.

7. From the Web Services Explorer, select **SimpleBankBeanSoapBinding** in the Navigator pane.
8. Scroll down to the Endpoints section in the Actions pane and click **Add**.
9. A new editable endpoint address will appear, pre-filled with the original address. Change the port number from 9080 to 9081, so the new address will be as follows:

   `http://localhost:9081/BankWebServiceEARWeb/services/SimpleBankBean`
10. Check the new endpoint, and click **Go**.

    You should see a message `Endpoints were successfully updated`.
11. Select the method you wish to test. For example, select **getCustomerFullName**, and from the Endpoints list select the endpoint with 9081 as the port number.
12. Enter a suitable value for the customerId such as 555-55-5555 and click **Go**.

    The TCP/IP Monitor view will automatically open, as seen in Figure 17-13 on page 979.

    As long as port 9081 is used for the endpoint instead of 9080, all requests and responses will be routed through the TCP/IP monitor and will appear in the TCP/IP Monitor view.

    The TCP/IP Monitor view shows all the intercepted requests in the top pane, and when a request is selected, the messages passed in each direction are shown in the bottom panes (request in the left pane, response in the right). This can be a very useful tool in debugging Web Services and clients.

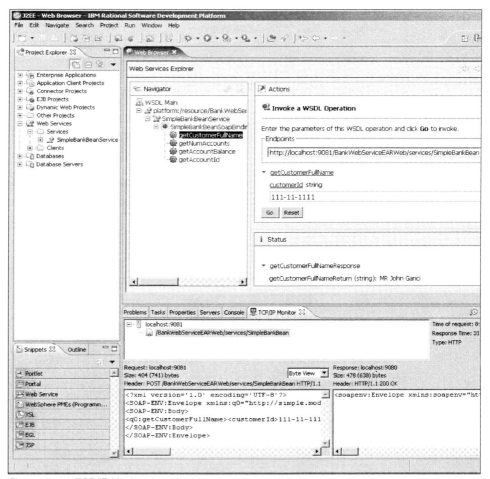

Figure 17-13 TCP/IP Monitor view

17.5 Create a Web Service from an EJB

The process of creating a Web Service from an EJB session bean is very similar to the process for a JavaBean.

1. Expand **EJB Projects** → **BankWebServiceEJB** → **Deployment Descriptor** → **Session Beans**.
2. Right-click **SimpleBankFacade**, and select **Web Services** → **Create Web Service**.
3. The **Web Service type** should be **EJB Web Service**. Leave all the other check boxes at their default values.
4. Click **Next >** and select the appropriate session EJB if it is not already selected.
5. Click **Next >** and **Next >** (these pages are the same as before).
6. On the page entitled Web Service EJB Configuration, you need to specify which Web project will contain the routing Servlet to forward requests to the EJB. We will use the same project we used for the other Web Service, so select **BankWebServiceWeb** from the list.
7. It is possible to invoke message-driven EJBs using SOAP over JMS as opposed to SOAP over HTTP (this is a WebSphere extension). We are using a stateless session EJB, so we need to leave the radio button set to SOAP over HTTP.
8. Click **Next >**.
9. On this page we can select which methods we want to make available to clients. Leave all the methods checked as before and click **Next >**.
10. Click **Finish** on the Web Service Publication page.

The mechanisms for testing Web Services based on stateless session EJBs are exactly the same as for services based on JavaBeans (or any other Web Service). Try testing your Web Service using the Web Services Explorer or the sample JSP application as described above. You will find the WSDL file in the EJB project under ejbModule META-INF wsdl.

17.6 Web Services security

Rational Application Developer allows you to create Web Services that communicate securely with clients. This can be selected in the wizard on the Web Service Java Bean Identity page, as shown in Figure 17-14 on page 982.

The options available are as follows:
- No security
- XML Digital Signature
- XML Encryption
- XML Digital Signature and XML Encryption

Although standards are evolving for Web Services security, they are not yet universally implemented, so the use of these security mechanisms is forbidden by the WS-I Basic Profile. Consequently, enabling any of these security options will produce the warning dialog shown in Figure 17-14 on page 982, stating `You have made a choice that may result in a Web Service that does not comply with WS-I Simple SOAP Basic Profile`. You can choose to ignore this message and continue to use secure Web Services, but this decision will impact the interoperability of your service with Web Services clients running on different technologies.

Secure Web Services can still be tested using the client proxy that is generated by Rational Application Developer, since the proxy includes the necessary code to communicate securely with the Web Service. The Web Services Explorer and the TCP/IP Monitor cannot be used effectively in this case, however.

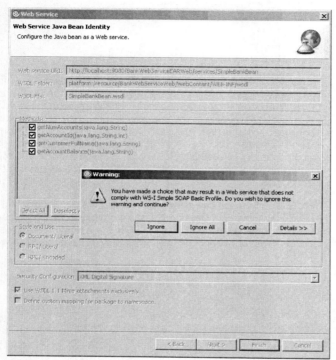

Figure 17-14   Web Services security

17.7 Publish a Web Service using UDDI

Rational Application Developer includes a test UDDI registry, which runs in the integrated WebSphere server and uses Cloudscape or DB2 as the back-end database. To create the test registry:

1. Select **File** → **New** → **Other...** → **Web Services** → **Unit Test UDDI** and click **Next >**.

2. Leave the first page of the wizard with the default values (Private UDDI Registry for WAS v6.0 with Cloudscape) and click **Next >**.

3. The second page of the wizard allows you to specify which server to use for the registry. Leave the default values and click **Finish**.

The wizard imports an EAR file, which includes Web and EJB components and sets up the necessary database tables and data sources in the server; this takes some time. The Web Services Explorer is opened on completion with the UDDI page open. This can be used to register and search for businesses and services using the test registry. The Web Services Explorer can also be used with other registries, such as the Public Business Registries available at locations such as `http://uddi.ibm.com/`.

18

Develop portal applications

This chapter describes the portal development tools and test environment for IBM WebSphere Portal that are now included with IBM Rational Application Developer V6.0. We will also highlight how the portal tools in Rational Application Developer can be used to develop a portal and associated portlet applications for WebSphere Portal. Lastly, we have included a development scenario to demonstrate how to use the new integrated portal tooling and test environment to develop a portal, customize the portal, and develop two portlets.

The chapter is organized into the following topics:

- Introduction to portals
- Developing applications for WebSphere Portal
- Portal development scenario

> **Note:** For more detailed information on IBM WebSphere Portal V5.0 and V5.1 application development, refer to the following:
>
> - *IBM WebSphere Portal V5 A Guide for Portlet Application Development*, SG24-6076
> - *IBM WebSphere Portal V5.1 Portlet Application Development*, SG24-6681

18.1 Introduction to portals

As J2EE technology has evolved, much emphasis has been placed on the challenges of building enterprise applications and bringing those applications to the Web. At the core of the challenges currently being faced by Web developers is the integration of disparate user content into a seamless Web application and well-designed user interface. Portal technology provides a framework to build such applications for the Web.

Because of the increasing popularity of portal technologies, the tooling and frameworks used to support the building of new portals has evolved. The main job of a portal is to aggregate content and functionality. Portal servers provide:

- A server to aggregate content
- A scalable infrastructure
- A framework to build portal components and extensions

Additionally, many portals offer personalization and customization features. Personalization enables the portal to deliver user-specific information targeting a user based on their unique information. Customization allows the user to organize the look and feel of the portal to suit their individual needs and preferences.

Portals are the next-generation desktop, delivering e-business applications over the Web to many types of client devices from PCs to PDAs. Portals provide site users with a single point of access to multiple types of information and applications. Regardless of where the information resides or what format it is in, a portal aggregates all of the information in a way that is relevant to the user.

The goal of implementing an Enterprise portal is to enable a working environment that integrates people, their work, personal activities, and supporting processes and technology.

18.1.1 Portal concepts and definitions

Before beginning development for portals, you should become familiar with some common definitions and descriptions of portal-related terminology.

Portal page
A portal page is a single Web page that can be used to display content aggregated from multiple sources. The content that appears on a portal page is displayed by an arrangement of one or more portlets. For example, a World Stock Market portal page might contain two portlets that display stock tickers for popular stock exchanges and a third portlet that displays the current exchange rates for world currencies.

Portlet

A portlet is an individual application that displays content on a portal page. To a user, a portlet is a single window or panel on the portal page that provides information or Web application functionality. To a developer, portlets are Java-based plugable modules that can access content from a source such as another Web site, an XML feed, or a database, and display this content to the user as part of the portal page.

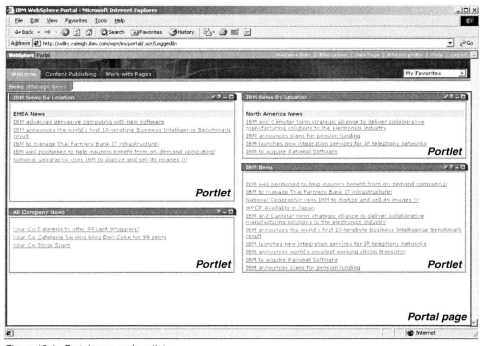

Figure 18-1 Portal page and portlets

Portlet application

Portlet applications are collections of related portlets and resources that are packaged together. Portlets within the same portlet application can exchange and share data and act as a unit. All portlets packaged together share the same context, which contains all resources such as images, properties files, and classes.

Chapter 18. Develop portal applications   **987**

Portlet states

Portlet states determine how individual portlets look when a user accesses them on the portal page. These states are very similar to minimize, restore, and maximize window states of applications run on any popular operating system just in a Web-based environment.

The state of the portlet is stored in the PortletWindow.State object and can be queried for changing the way a portlet looks or behaves based on its current state. The IBM portlet API defines three possible states for a portlet:

- Normal: The portlet is displayed in its initial state, as defined when it was installed.
- Minimized: Only the portlet title bar is visible on the portal page.
- Maximized: The portlet fills the entire body of the portal page, hiding all other portlets.

Portlet modes

Portlet modes allow the portlet to display a different *face* depending on how it is being used. This allows different content to be displayed within the same portlet, depending on its mode. Modes are most commonly used to allow users and administrators to configure portlets or to offer help to the users. There are four modes in the IBM Portlet API:

- View: Initial face of the portlet when created. The portlet normally functions in this mode.
- Edit: This mode allows the user to configure the portlet for their personal use (for example, specifying a city for a localized weather forecast).
- Help: If the portlet supports the help mode, this mode displays a help page to the user.
- Configure: If provided, this mode displays a face that allows the portal administrator to configure the portlet for a group of users or a single user.

Portlet events

Some portlets only display static content in independent windows. To allow users to interact with portlets and to allow portlets to interact with each other, portlet events are used. Portlet events contain information to which a portlet might need to respond. For example, when a user clicks a link or button, this generates an *action* event. To receive notification of a given event, the portlet must also have the appropriate *event listener* implemented within the portlet class. There are three commonly used types of portlet events:

- Action events: Generated when an HTTP request is received by the portlet that is associated with an action, such as when a user clicks a link.

- Message events: Generated when one portlet within a portlet application sends a message to another portlet.
- Window events: Generated when the user changes the state of the portlet window.

18.1.2 IBM WebSphere Portal

IBM WebSphere Portal provides an extensible framework that allows the end user to interact with enterprise applications, people, content, and processes. They can personalize and organize their own view of the portal, manage their own profiles, and publish and share documents. WebSphere Portal provides additional services such as Single Sign-On (SSO), security, credential vault, directory services, document management, Web content management, personalization, search, collaboration, search and taxonomy, support for mobile devices, accessibility support, internationalization, e-learning, integration to applications, and site analytics. Clients can further extend the portal solution to provide host integration and e-commerce.

WebSphere Portal allows you to plug in new features or extensions using portlets. In the same way that a servlet is an application within a Web server, a portlet is an application within WebSphere Portal. Developing portlets is the most important task when providing a portal that functions as the user's interface to information and tasks.

Portlets are an encapsulation of content and functionality. They are reusable components that combine Web-based content, application functionality, and access to resources. Portlets are assembled into portal pages that, in turn, make up a portal implementation.

Portal solutions such as IBM WebSphere Portal are proven to shorten the development time. Pre-built adapters and connectors are available so that customers can leverage on the company's existing investment by integrating with the existing legacy systems without re-inventing the wheel.

18.1.3 IBM Rational Application Developer

IBM Rational Application Developer provides development tools for applications destined to WebSphere Portal. Bundled with IBM Rational Application Developer V6.0 are a number of portal tools that allow you to create, test, debug, and deploy portal and portlet applications. These tools are described in more detail in 18.2, "Developing applications for WebSphere Portal" on page 992.

Portal tools

Unlike WebSphere Studio Application Developer where the tools where installed as a separate toolkit, Portal Tools can now be installed as a feature when installing IBM Rational Application Developer V6.0. For this reason, there is no longer a separate portal toolkit or separate installation procedure.

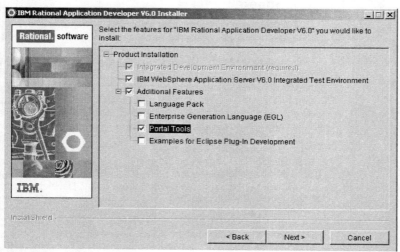

Figure 18-2   Portal tools installation

Portal test environments

As part of this tool set, Rational Application Developer provides an integrated test environment to run and test your portal and portlet projects from within the Rational Application Developer Workbench.

At the time IBM Rational Application Developer V6.0 was released, the WebSphere Portal V5.0.2.2 Test Environment was included as an installed component of the Rational Application Developer installer known as the Launchpad (see Figure 18-3 on page 991).

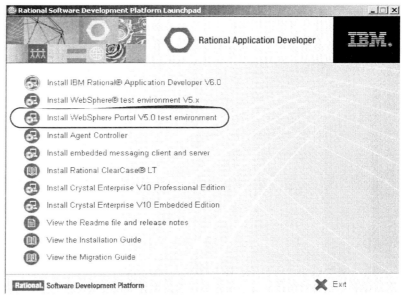

Figure 18-3   Product installation launchpad

CDs to install the WebSphere Portal V5.1 Test Environment are also included with the IBM Rational Application Developer V6.0 distribution. To install the WebSphere Portal V5.1 Test Environment, you must run the WebSphere Portal V5.1 setup program and select **Test Environment** as the setup type, as seen in Figure 18-4 on page 992. Follow the instructions in the InfoCenter to configure this test environment so that it works from within Rational Application Developer. The WebSphere Portal V5.0.2.2 and V5.1 Test Environments can co-exist within the same product installation.

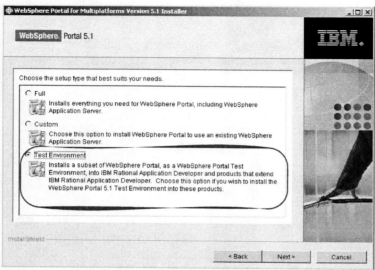

Figure 18-4 Installing the WebSphere Portal V5.1 Test Environment

18.2 Developing applications for WebSphere Portal

Rational Application Developer includes many tools to help you quickly develop portals and individual portlet applications. In this section, we cover some basic portlet development strategies and provide an overview of the tools included with IBM Rational Application Developer V6.0 to aid with development of WebSphere Portal.

18.2.1 Portal samples and tutorials

Rational Application Developer also comes with several samples and tutorials to aid you with the development of WebSphere Portal. The Samples Gallery provides sample portlet applications to illustrate portlet development.

To access portlet samples, click **Help → Samples Gallery**. Then expand **Technology samples** and **Portlet**. Here you can select a Basic Portlet, Faces Portlet, or Struts Portlet Framework to view sample portlet application projects that you can then modify and build upon for your own purposes.

The Tutorials Gallery provides detailed tutorials to illustrate portlet development. These are accessible by selecting **Help** → **Tutorials Gallery**. Then expand **Do and Learn**. You can select **Create a portal application** or **Examine the differences between portlet APIs** to view the content of these tutorials.

18.2.2 Development strategy

A portlet application consists of Java classes, JSP files, and other resources such as deployment descriptors and image files. Before beginning development, several decisions must be made regarding the development strategy and technologies that will be used to develop a portlet application.

Choosing an API - IBM or JSR 168

WebSphere Portal supports portlet development using the IBM portlet API and the JSR 168 portlet API standard. The portal tools included with IBM Rational Application Developer V6.0 support both APIs.

The IBM portlet API was initially supported in WebSphere Portal V4.x and will continue to be supported by WebSphere Portal. It is important to note that the IBM portlet API extends the servlet API. More information about the IBM portlet API can be found at:

http://www.ibm.com/developerworks/websphere/zones/portal/portlet/5.0api/WPS

JSR 168 is a Java specification from the Java Community Process Program that addresses the requirements of content aggregation, personalization, presentation, and security for portlets running in a portal environment. It was finalized in October of 2003. Portlets conforming to JSR 168 are more portable and reusable because they can be deployed to any JSR 168 compliant portal. Rational Application Developer supports Faces portlet development based on the JSR 168 specification.

Unlike the IBM portlet API, the JSR 168 API does not extend the servlet API. It does, however, share many of the same characteristics such as servlet specification, session management, and request dispatching. The JSR 168 API as implemented in WebSphere Portal V5.0.2.2 does not support Click-to-Action cooperative portlets or portlet messaging. However, in WebSphere Portal V5.1, the JSR 168 container has been enhanced with Property Broker support, which can act as a messaging broker for either portlet messaging or wired (automatic cooperating) portlets. At the time of writing, the support for Click-to-Action (user-initiated cooperating portlets) was still under development.

For new portlets, consider using JSR 168 when the functionality it provides is sufficient for the portlet's needs or when the portlet is expected to be published as a Web Service for Remote Portlets (WSRP) service.

IBM will further support JSR 168 in follow-on versions to make the JSR 168 portlet API as robust as the current IBM counterpart, and offer tooling to support JSR 168 development. IBM is committed to the wider adoption of open standards in WebSphere Portal.

More information can be found on JSR 168 at:

http://www.jcp.org/en/jsr/detail?id=168

Choosing markup languages

WebSphere Portal supports mobile devices by generating pages in any markup language. Three markup languages are officially supported in Rational Application Developer:

- HyperText Markup Language (HTML) is used for Web browsers on desktop computers. All portlet applications support HTML at a minimum.
- Wireless Markup Language (WML) is used for WAP devices that are typically Web-enabled mobile telephones.
- compact Hyper Text Markup Language (cHTML) is used for mobile devices in the NTT DoCoMo i-mode network. For more information on the i-mode network, visit the following Web site:

    http://www.nttdocomo.co.jp/english/

Adding emulator support for other markup languages

To run a portlet application that supports WML or cHTML, you must use an emulator provided by the device vendor. To add device emulator support to Rational Application Developer, do the following:

1. Select **Window → Preferences**.
2. Expand **Internet** and select **Web Browser**.
3. Click the **Add** button to locate the device emulator appropriate for the device that you wish to test and debug.

Enabling transcoding for development in other markup languages

Transcoding is the process by which WebSphere Portal makes portal content displayable on mobile devices. By default, it is *not enabled* in the WebSphere Portal Test Environment. Therefore, you need to make some configuration changes before you can test and debug applications on mobile device emulators. You will need to remove the comments from lines beginning with #Disable Transcoding from three files.

The PortletFilterService.properties and PortalFilterService.properties files are all located by default in the following directory:

<rad_home>\runtimes\portal_v50\shared\app\config\services

The services.properties file is located by default in the following directory:

`<rad_home>\runtimes\portal_v50\shared\app\config`

Choosing other technologies

Struts technology and JavaServer Faces technology can also be incorporated into a portlet development strategy.

Struts

Struts-based application development can be applied to portlets, similar to the way that Struts development is implemented in Web applications. The Struts Portal Framework (SPF) was developed to merge these two technologies. SPF support in Rational Application Developer simplifies the process of writing Struts portlet applications and eliminates the need to manage many of the underlying requirements of portlet applications. In addition, multiple wizards are present to help you create Struts portlet-related artifacts. These are the same wizards used in Struts development. These wizards include: Action Class, Action Mapping, ActionForm, Form-Bean Mapping, Struts Configuration, Struts Module, Struts Exception, and Web diagram. Refer to the Rational Application Developer Struts documentation for usage details.

In WebSphere Portal V5.0.2.2, Struts is only supported using the IBM portlet API. Struts is fully supported in both the IBM and JSR 168 APIs in WebSphere Portal V5.1; however, there is no tooling support in Rational Application Developer for this configuration.

More information on Struts can be found at:

`http://struts.apache.org/`

JavaServer Faces (JSF)

JavaServer Faces is a GUI framework for developing J2EE Web applications (JSR 127). It includes reusable user interface components, input validation, state management, server-side event handling, page lifecycle management, accessibility, and internationalization. Faces-based application development can be applied to portlets, similar to the way that Faces development is implemented in Web applications. Similar to Struts, there are many wizards to help you with Faces development. Both WebSphere Portal V5.0.2.2 and V5.1 support JavaServer Faces.

There are certain limitations to Faces portlet development in the current release. Service Data Objects (SDO), formerly referred to as WebSphere Data Objects (WDO), are limited to prototyping purposes only. Applications that rely on SDOs should be limited in a production environment. File upload and binary download are not supported for Faces components. Finally, document root-relative URLs are not supported for images.

Refer to the Rational Application Developer Faces documentation in the InfoCenter for usage details. Alternatively you can refer to the following Web site:

http://www.jcp.org/en/jsr/detail?id=127

Beginning development

After making these decisions, you can now begin development using the portal tools included with Rational Application Developer.

18.2.3 Portal tools for developing portals

A portal is essentially a J2EE Web application. It provides a framework where developers can associate many portlets and portlet applications via one or more portal pages.

Rational Application Developer includes several new portal site creation tools that enable you to visually customize portal page layout, themes, skins, and navigation.

Portal Import wizard

One way to create a new portal project is to import an existing portal site from a WebSphere Portal V5.0 server into Rational Application Developer. Importing is also useful for updating the configuration of a project that already exists in IBM Rational Application Developer.

The portal site configuration on WebSphere Portal server contains the following resources: The global settings, the resource definitions, the portal content tree, and the page layout. Importing these resources from WebSphere Portal server to Rational Application Developer overwrites duplicate resources within the existing portal project. Non-duplicate resources from the server configuration are copied into the existing portal project. Likewise, resources that are unique to the portal project are not affected by the import.

Rational Application Developer uses the XML configuration interface to import a server configuration, and optionally retrieves files under the websphere_installation_directory/installedApps/node/wps.ear directory. These files include the JSP, CSS, and image files for themes and skins. When creating a new portal project, retrieving files is mandatory. To retrieve files, Rational Application Developer must have access to this directory, as specified when you define a new server for this project.

You can access the Portal Import Wizard by selecting **File → Import**, then selecting **Portal**. You will need to specify the server and options for importing the project into Rational Application Developer.

Follow the instructions in the Help Topics on Developing Portal Applications to ensure that the configuration in the development environment accurately reflects that of the staging or runtime environment. If you do not do this, you may experience compilation errors after the product is imported or unexpected portal behaviors.

Portal Project wizard

The New Portal Project wizard will guide you through the process of creating a portal project within Rational Application Developer.

During this process, you are able to:

- Specify a project name.
- Specify the default server.
- Choose a default theme (optional).
- Choose a default skin for the theme (optional).

Important: You should not name your project *wps* or anything that resembles this string, in order to avoid internal naming conflicts.

The project that you create with this wizard will not have any portlet definitions, labels, or pages. The themes and skins that are available in this wizard are the same as if you had imported a portal site from a WebSphere Portal server.

You can access this wizard by clicking **File** → **New** → **Project** and then selecting **Portal Project** from the list. Figure 18-5 on page 998 displays the options to specify when creating a Portal Project after clicking the **Show Advanced** button.

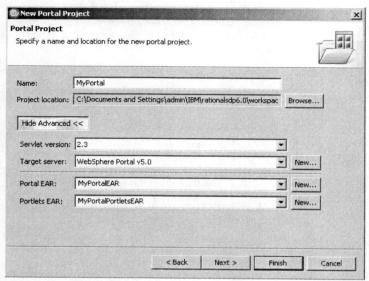

Figure 18-5   Portal Project wizard

Portal Designer

Rational Application Developer allows for editing both the graphic design and portlet layout within your portal. Portal Designer is the Workbench interface that you see upon opening a portal project.

When using Portal Designer, the portal page layout can be altered. The layout refers to the number of content areas within a page and the number of portlets within those content areas. Page content includes rows, columns, URLs, and portlets.

Once the project is published to the Portal server, Portal administrators can use the administration portlets to give site users permission to edit the page layout.

In terms of portal layout and appearance, you can think of Portal Designer as a What-You-See-Is-What-You-Get (WYSIWYG) editor. It will render graphic interface items such as themes, skins, and page layouts.

Portal Designer will also render the initial pages of JSF and Struts portlets within your portal pages, but not anything else with regard to portlet content.

Portal Designer provides the capability to alter the layout of the content within a portal page with respect to navigation (the hierarchy of your labels, pages, and URLs) and content (the arrangement of portlets via rows and columns on the portal pages).

Portal Configuration is the name of the layout source file that resides in the root of the portal project folder (see Figure 18-6). To open Portal Designer, double-click the file in the Project Explorer.

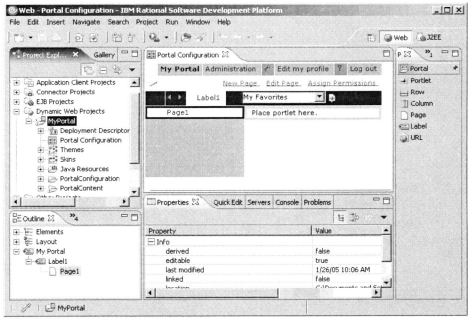

Figure 18-6   Portal Designer

Skin and theme design and editing

A skin is the border around each portlet within a portal page. Unlike themes, which apply to the overall look and feel of the portal, skins are limited to the look and feel of each portlet that you insert into your portal application.

The IBM Rational Application Developer installation includes pre-built themes and skins to use with portal projects. There are also wizards to create new themes and skins. Changing themes and skins was previously done through portal administration. In addition to these wizards for creating new skins and themes, there are tools that can be used to change or edit these.

Once created, skins and themes will be displayed in the Project Explorer view. Double-click a skin or theme to manually edit it.

New Skin wizard

In addition to using the pre-made skins that came with the installation, you can use the New Skin wizard to create customized skins for your project. Right-click the portal project in the Project Explorer view and select **New → Skin**.

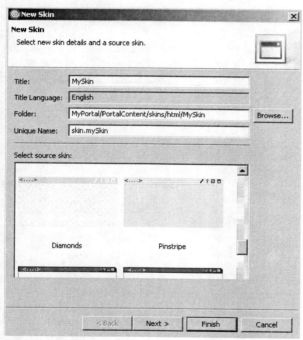

Figure 18-7 New Skin wizard

New Theme wizard

Themes provide the overall look and feel of your portal application. In addition to using the pre-existing themes, you can use the New Theme wizard to create customized themes for your project. Right-click the portal project in the Project Explorer view and select **New → Theme** (see Figure 18-8 on page 1001).

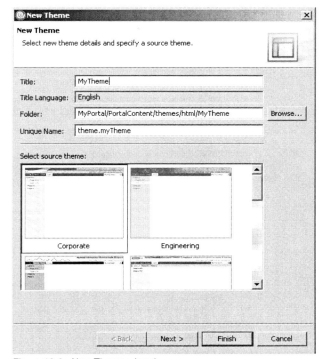

Figure 18-8 New Theme wizard

Deploying portal projects

From Rational Application Developer, you can choose to publish a portal project to a WebSphere Portal server either manually (export) or automatically (deploy).

There are two models of publishing your portal project to WebSphere Portal:

- *Export*: This method is recommended for publishing to a staging or production server. You need to manually copy the packaged portal project to the portal server. Since exporting does not require FTP or copy access to the portal server, there is very little chance of interruption during publishing.

    To export, select **File** → **Export**, then select **Portal Project Deploy Set**. You will need to specify the Portal EAR file and specify a target Portal server. The wizard examines the Portal server so that it can generate specific deploy information. It then generates a set of files for manually deploying the portal project to the Portal server. These files include:

- WPS.ear
- XmlAccess for deployment portal configuration (contained in the EAR)
- Readme file with instructions for deploying to a server
- WAR files for each portlet project used in the portal project
- XMLAccess script for deploying portlets

The wizard also created a file named DeployInstructions.txt, which is a set of instructions that will guide you through the process of manually deploying your exported project to the server.

> **Note:** Do not attempt to manually deploy the exported files to a portal server other than the one you specify. The export operation contains information from this portal server, and it will not work with other servers.

► *Deploy*: This method automatically publishes a configuration from a portal project to a Portal Server. The deploy method is recommended for publishing to a test, integration, or staging server.

If you are also transferring the theme and skin files during the deployment, you must also have FTP or copy access to the portal server.

To deploy a portal, right-click the portal project and select **Deploy Portal**. From here, a wizard will guide you through the deployment process. This will include specifying the portal server to where you are deploying.

Once you start the deploy process, do not interrupt it. Errors in a project or an unfinished deploy may cause a portal server to become inoperable. As such, you should not deploy directly to a production server. Before running deploy, it is recommended that you back up or image your server.

> **Note:** If a transfer interruption (for example, network failure) occurs during deployment, there is a slight chance that the portal server will become inoperable.

Since the portal project does not have any access control information, use administration portlets in the published Portal site to set appropriate access control.

18.2.4 Portal tools for developing portlets

Whether beginning or continuing development of individual portlets and portlet projects, Rational Application Developer has tools that can make this process easier.

Project Interchange files

If you are not using a software configuration management (SCM) system, such as ClearCase or CVS, and you want to share portlet projects with team members or develop a portlet application among multiple computers, you can use the Project Interchange feature.

There are other ways that you can share projects and files including manually copying the project's workspace and importing via WAR files. The recommended method of accomplishing project portability is using the Project Interchange feature. When you export using Project Interchange, the entire project structure is maintained, including metadata files. You can also export several unrelated projects or include required projects for an entire application. Projects exported using this feature can be easily imported into another workspace with a single action.

The Project Interchange mechanism exports projects as they exist in the Workbench, including the project property that specifies the target server runtime for the project. If a user imports the exported project and does not have the same target server runtime installed, the project will not compile. This can be corrected by modifying the target server for the project.

> **Important:** It is important that the IBM Rational Application Developer V6 install path is common for all team members sharing code to avoid absolute library path problems found in projects when importing.

Exporting a Project Interchange file

To export to a Project Interchange file, follow these steps:

1. Right-click the project that you want to export, and select **Export**.
2. Select **Project Interchange**, and click **Next**.
3. Select the projects that you want to export. You have the following options for selection:
   - Click **Select All** to select all projects in the window.
   - Click **Deselect All** to clear all the check boxes.
   - Click **Select Referenced** to automatically select projects that are referenced by any of the currently selected projects.
4. In the To zip file field, enter the full path, including the ZIP file name, where you want to export the selected projects.
5. Click **Finish**.

Import a Project Interchange file

To import a Project Interchange file, do the following:

1. Click **File** → **Import**.
2. Select **Project Interchange** and click **Next**.
3. In the From ZIP file field, click **Browse** to navigate to the ZIP file that contains the shared projects. The Import wizard lists the projects that are in the ZIP file.
4. Select the projects that you want to import. You have the following options for selection:
   - Click **Select All** to select all projects in the window.
   - Click **Deselect All** to clear all the check boxes.
   - Click **Select Referenced** to automatically select projects that are referenced by any of the currently selected projects.
5. Click **Finish**.

Import WAR files

An alternate method of transferring a portlet project to another computer is via a WAR file. WAR files package all pieces of a portlet project into a single file. They are most commonly used to manually deploy portlet projects to Portal Servers.

For development purposes, WAR files can be used to move portlet projects from one computer to another. WAR files are not optimized for this purpose, and moving projects in this way may result in lost meta data or lost time due to any reconfigurations that may be required upon import.

For portlet projects completed with a version of the Portal Toolkit prior to V5.0.2.2, importing by WAR file is the only supported migration path.

To import a project by WAR file, follow these steps:

1. Select **File** → **Import** and select **WAR File**. Then click **Next**.
2. Locate the WAR file to import by using the **Browse** button.
3. The wizard assumes you want to create a new Web project with the same name as the WAR file. Accepting these defaults will create a new project with the same servlet version as specified by the WAR file and in the same location. To override these settings, click **New** and specify the new settings in the Dynamic Web Project wizard.
4. To import a WAR file into an existing Web project, select the project from the Web project drop-down list. If this method is used, the option to overwrite existing resources without warning can be selected.

5. Click **Finish** to populate the Web project.

Note: When a portlet project is exported to a WAR file, the source files must be included. This procedure is detailed in "Export WAR Files" on page 1020.

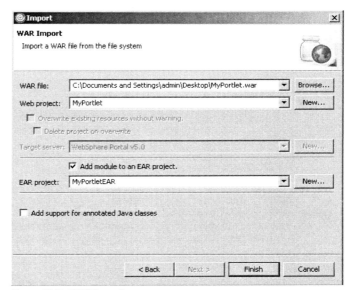

Figure 18-9 WAR Import screen

Portlet Project wizard

Portlet projects are used for developing portlet applications in Rational Application Developer. To create a portlet application, first create a portlet project using the Portlet Project wizard.

The Portlet Project wizard is a very powerful tool that automatically assembles a framework for a portlet project containing all the resources that are necessary for testing, debugging, or deploying a portlet.

To use the Portlet Project wizard, do the following:

1. Select **File** → **New** → **Project**.
2. Select **Portlet Project** and click **Next**.

3. On the first screen in the wizard, enter a project name. You can also specify an alternate project location by clicking the **Browse** button.
4. If you do not want to create the initial portlet definitions in the project, clear the **Create a portlet** check box. Typically, a portlet does not need to be created when importing a WAR file.
5. Click the **Show Advanced** button to see more options (see Figure 18-10 on page 1007).

    The advanced options allow changes to be made to the project's J2EE settings and runtime server environment. The Servlet version specifies the version of Servlet and JSP specifications to be included in your portlet.

    > **Tip:** Use the 2.2 Servlet version if importing a WebSphere Portal V4.x project WAR file. Note that features such as Servlet filters and life cycle event listeners are not supported if this level is chosen.

    Choosing a Servlet version also determines the choice of target servers that appear in the drop-down list. When choosing a server, do not accidentally select any WebSphere Application Server options.

    a. Deselect the **Add module to an EAR project** option only if you do not intend to deploy the portlet. Name an EAR project according to the name of the enterprise application project (EAR) that the portlet project should be associated with during deployment. All portlet applications associated with a single EAR project will run on a single session on a WebSphere Portal Server. You should use the same EAR project for portlet projects that are related.

    The context root is used as the top-level directory in the portlet project when the portlet is deployed. It must not be the same as ones used by other projects.

    b. Ensure that the **Add support for annotated Java classes** check box is selected if using model annotations to generate code in portlet projects.

    c. Click **Next** to continue with the Portlet Project wizard or **Finish** to generate a portlet project based on the defaults associated with a Basic IBM API portlet project.

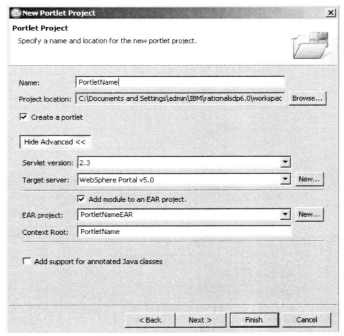

Figure 18-10   Portlet Project wizard

d. On the following screen, select a portlet type that is appropriate for the portlet project. There are four types of portlets (see Figure 18-11 on page 1008):

- Empty portlet: Creates a portlet application that extends the PortletAdapter class with minimum code included. This option is selected if importing a project from a WAR file or when customizing empty portlet projects from scratch.

- Basic portlet: Creates a basic portlet application that extends the PortletAdapter class comprised of a complete concrete portlet and concrete portlet application. It contains a portlet class, sample JSP files that are used when rendering the portlet, and a sample Java bean.

- Faces portlet: Creates a Faces portlet application based on Java Faces technology.

- Struts portlet: Creates a Struts portlet application based on Java Struts technology.

  e. When finished selecting options on this screen, click **Next**.

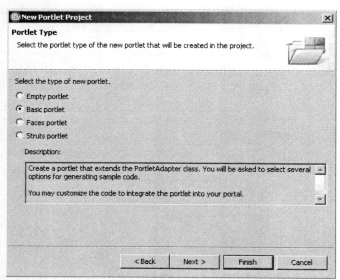

Figure 18-11 Portlet type screen

When creating a Faces portlet, you will be presented with the following screen.

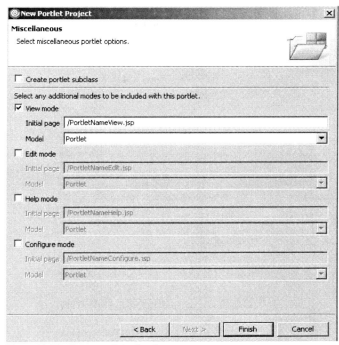

Figure 18-12 Faces portlet miscellaneous screen

When creating a Struts portlet, you will be presented with the following screen.

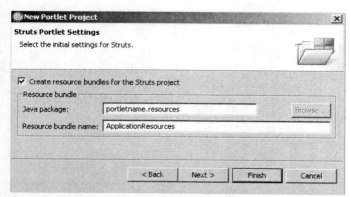

Figure 18-13 Struts Portlet Settings screen

When creating a Basic portlet, you will be presented with the following screen. It allows you to select features that provide additional functionality in the portlet application. Select features as necessary. Deselect the Web Diagram check box if you are creating a Basic or Empty portlet. Select **JSP Tag Libraries** to include the functionality of this technology in the portlet project.

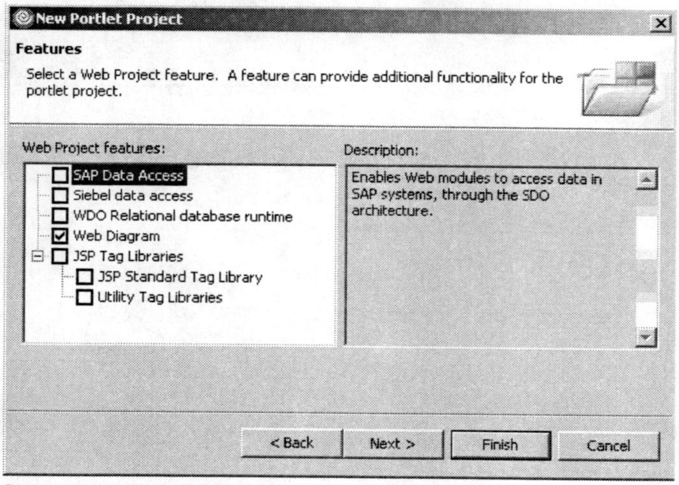

Figure 18-14 Portlet Features screen

On the Portlet Settings screen, update or add any general portlet settings. The application name is the name of the portlet application as used to manage it by the portal administrator. To update this name after generating your portlet project, use the deployment descriptor editor to modify portlet.xml. Modify the Display name of each concrete portlet application.

The portlet name is the name of the portlet. It is also used by the portal administrator. It also can be updated by using the deployment descriptor editor and modifying the Display name of each concrete portlet.

The default locale specifies a default locale to use if the client locale cannot be determined. You can add supported locale using the deployment descriptor editor and adding a locale to each concrete portlet.

The portlet title appears in the portlet title bar. To update this in the future, you can use the deployment descriptor editor to modify the title of each concrete portlet.

Change code generation options can be used to change the package and class prefixes.

Click **Next** to continue. If creating an empty portlet, the Miscellaneous screen (as seen in Figure 18-18 on page 1015) will be shown. If creating a Basic portlet, the Event Handling screen will be shown.

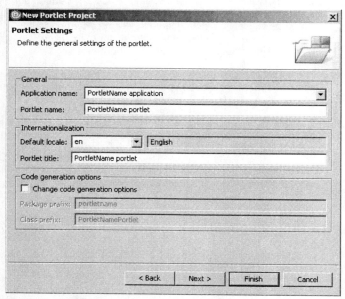

Figure 18-15   Portlet settings screen

On this screen, you have the ability to optionally add event handling capabilities to the portlet application. An action event is sent when an HTTP request is received that is associated with a portlet action. The Add action listener option implements the ActionListener interface to handle action events. The Add form sample option generates code to demonstrate action event handling with a simple form example.

Cooperative portlets provide a model for declaring, publishing, and sharing information with each other using the WebSphere Portal property broker. Cooperative portlets are only available when the Servlet level is 2.3. Cooperative portlets can run on WebSphere Portal V5.x servers. Create a portlet application that extends the PortletAdapter class. "Enable cooperative target" adds a sample WSDL file so that the Click-to-Action target can receive input properties. If you select this option with the Add form sample option in the Action Event handling section of this screen, the generated portlet project will be enabled as a Click-to-Action receiver. It is also possible to create an action handler and form and customize the WSDL file as required. The "Add Click-to-Action sender portlet sample" option adds a simple Click-to-Action sender portlet that is useful to test receiver function and provides sample code. The "Enable cooperative source" option adds the Click-to-Action tag library directive for JSP files of the Click-to-Action source portlet.

Message events can be sent from one portlet to others if the recipient portlets are placed on the same portal page as the sending portlet. To get a Java class that implements the MessageListener interface, select the **Add message listener** option. The "Add message sender portlet sample" option generates a sample message sender portlet.

To add a function showing events received by listeners in view mode select **Add event log viewer**. To select this option, you need to add at least one of the event listeners. The option to add edit panel allows you to change the default maximum event count while in edit mode.

Click **Next** to continue with the Portlet Project wizard.

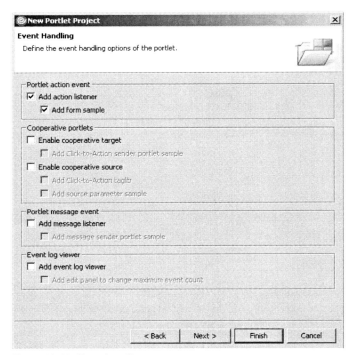

Figure 18-16   Event handling screen

Use the Single Sign-On screen to add sample code to support credential vault handling, which is used to safely store credentials that are used in portlet authentication. Portlets written to extract users' credentials from the credential vault can hide the login challenge from the user. A portlet private credential vault clot stores user credentials that are not shared among portlets. A shared credential vault slot shares user credentials among all of a user's portlets. The administrative credential vault slot allows each user to store their confidential information for accessing administrator-defined resources such as Lotus Notes® databases. A system credential vault slot stores system credentials where the actual confidential information is shared among all users and portlets.

The slot name defines the name of the credential vault slot to store and retrieve the credentials. The Show password option allows a password to be displayed on the screen while in View mode.

Click **Next** to continue with the Portlet Project wizard.

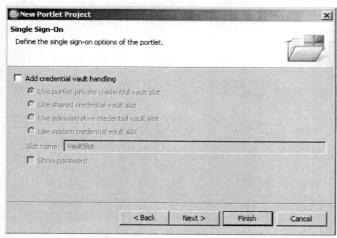

Figure 18-17   Single Sign-On screen

The Miscellaneous screen allows other supported markup languages and portlet modes to be selected. For more information on markup languages, see "Choosing markup languages" on page 994. For more information on modes, see "Portlet modes" on page 988.

Click **Finish** to generate the new portlet project. You may be presented with an option to switch to the Web perspective to work on this project. Click **Yes** if the Confirm Perspective Switch is shown.

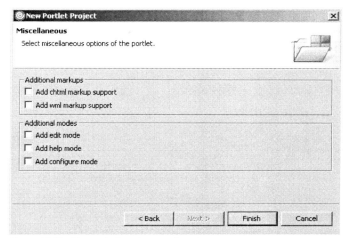

Figure 18-18   Supported markups and modes screen

Web perspective
The Web perspective combines views and editors that assist you with Web application development. This perspective is used to edit the project resources, such as HTML and JSP files, and deployment descriptors that make up the portlet project.

More information on the Web perspective can be found in 4.2.14, "Web perspective" on page 162.

Page Designer
Page Designer is an editor for HTML, XHTML, JSP, and Faces JSP files. It provides three representations of each file: Design, Source, and Preview. Each of these provides a different way to work with a file while it is being edited. You can switch between these by clicking the tabs at the bottom of the editor (see Figure 18-19 on page 1016):

- Design: The Design page provides a visual environment to create and work with a file while viewing its elements on the page.
- Source: The Source page enables you to view and directly work with a file's source code.

▶ Preview: The preview page shows you how the current page is likely to look when viewed in an external Web browser. Previewing dynamic content requires running the portlet or portal page on a local or remote test server.

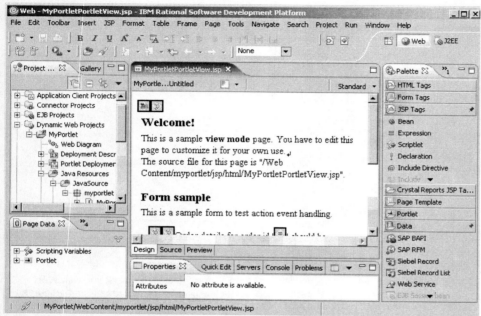

Figure 18-19   Page Designer showing the Design page

18.2.5 Portal tools for testing and debugging portlets

Once development is underway, you will need to test and debug your applications. Rational Application Developer provides many ways for you to do this. When defining a remote (server attach) server for testing, debugging, or profiling a portlet project, you must create and configure the server.

Portal server configuration

Portlet tools provide an additional type of server configuration, called the portal server configuration, which contains the server configuration information needed to publish your portlet application on a WebSphere Portal machine. After it is published, your target portlet will appear on the test page and the debug page of your WebSphere Portal. Source-level debugging is also supported.

Remote server test

When developing portlet projects, you have the option of testing and debugging on a remote server or in a local test environment (as described in the next section). To test portlets on a remote WebSphere Portal Server, you will use this feature.

Before testing portlets with a server attach server, you may need to configure the remote server. See the section titled *Preparing WebSphere Portal for remote testing and debugging* in the product help for more information. The configuration steps detailed in this section are required when performing any of the following tasks.

- Testing or debugging with multiple users to the same remote server
- Testing or debugging a JSR 168 portlet on WebSphere Portal 5.0.2
- Debugging to a remote Server Attach server
- Testing or debugging to a remote server behind a firewall
- Testing or debugging to a remote server running Linux

Important: If multiple users are testing portlets to the same portlet server, ensure that the UIDs of the portlets are unique. Otherwise, when the portlet is installed on the portlet server, it may replace the original portlet using that UID.

- For the IBM portlet API, modify the UID using the portlet deployment descriptor editor.
- For the JSR 168 portlet API, the UID is constructed using the ID attribute of the portlet-app element.
- If the ID attribute is not specified, the UID is generated automatically using the login user ID and project name.

To use the remote server testing feature, do the following:

1. Right-click your portlet project and select **Run** → **Run on Server**.
2. To use an existing server, select **Choose an existing server** and choose a **WebSphere Portal Server Attach** server from the list.
3. To define a new external test server, you will need to use the New Server wizard to configure it. See the section titled *Configuring remote servers for testing portlets* in the product help.
4. Click **Finish**.

   After the server starts and the portal is deployed, the Web browser opens to the URL of the portal application on the external server.

> **Note:** An XML Exception occurs and the server attach fails to start if the project name, the filename, the file directory structure, or the user ID for the WebSphere Portal login name are excessively long.
>
> To correct this, shorten the length of the filename, the file directory structure, or the user ID for WebSphere Portal login at the WebSphere Portal Server Attach server configuration.

WebSphere Portal Test Environment

Rational Application Developer includes the WebSphere Portal Test Environment to locally test and debug portlet applications.

The WebSphere Portal Universal Test Environment allows you to locally test and debug portlets developed with the portal tools from within the Rational Application Developer Workbench. This is similar to running a Java servlet webapp in the WebSphere (Application Server) Test Environment.

The test environment is a WebSphere Portal runtime built on top of the WebSphere Test Environment. By default, the test environment uses Cloudscape as the portal configuration database. This can be configured to use DB2 UDB or Oracle.

When using the WebSphere Portal Test Environment, the server is running against the resources that are in the workspace. It supports adding, changing, or removing a resource from the portlet project without needing to be restarted or republished for these changes to be reflected.

To run your project in the WebSphere Portal Test Environment, right-click the portlet project and select **Run → Run on Server**. The Server Selection dialog is displayed. You may either choose to run the application on an existing server or manually define a new server.

To define a new local test server, perform the following steps:

1. Choose the option to **Manually define a server**.
2. Select **WebSphere Portal v5.0 Test Environment** from the list of server types.

   > **Note:** You must have installed the WebSphere Portal V5.0 Test Environment when installing IBM Rational Application Developer for this option to be available.

3. Click **Next**.

4. On the WebSphere Server Configuration Settings page, select one of the following values:
   - Select **Use default port numbers** and set the HTTP port number to use the default HTTP port (9081).
   - Select **Use consecutive port numbers** and set the first port number to use port numbers other than the default numbers used by WebSphere Application Server.

     This setting causes the test environment to use sequential port numbers, starting with the number you specify. You must specify a port number that begins a range of port numbers that are not being used by another application. This option allows you to have an external portal server or WebSphere Application Server running on your system, and allows the test environment to use different port numbers. You can also configure the test environment server's HTTP port numbers by editing the server configuration, as explained below.

5. Click **Finish**.

   Additional options for local servers can be viewed and changed by double-clicking the server in the Servers view. This opens the server configuration editor. You can change any of the settings that were defined previously. In addition, the Portal tab has several additional settings that can be changed to suit your individual configuration.

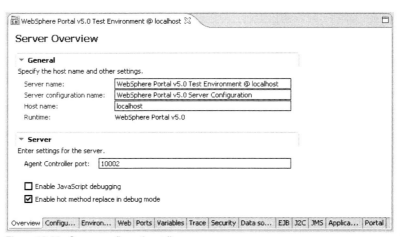

Figure 18-20 Server configuration editor

When you test a portlet on the local test environment server, the default theme and skin are used.

The test environment does not support features that rely on WebSphere Enterprise Edition (personalization and asynchronous rendering of portlets) or LDAP. Transcoding is also not enabled by default. It must be enabled to use a WML device emulator when developing portlets for mobile phones and other devices. See "Choosing markup languages" on page 994 for instructions on how to do this.

When testing or debugging, you may experience the following limitations:

- Help mode does not function correctly in the test environment while using the internal browser. Using an external browser corrects this issue.
- Single sign-on using LDAP is not supported when using the local test environment. LDAP is supported when testing portlets by remotely attaching to another WebSphere Portal server.
- You cannot create new portal users while in debug mode. Use the normal mode to create users.
- Portlet modifications are not previewed correctly when the portlet has been cached by the browser. Logging out and back in to the portal server corrects this.
- If using Linux, you may not be able to start the test environment server without the appropriate user permissions. Users need full permissions on <STUDIO_HOME>/runtimes/portal_v50/cloudscape/wps50.

18.2.6 Portal tools for deploying and managing portlets

When development is complete, these tools will help you to load your completed portlet project onto a WebSphere Portal Server.

Export WAR Files

Exporting a portlet project to a WAR file allows you to install it on a WebSphere Portal server. To export a WAR file for a portlet project, do the following:

1. Right-click the portlet project and select **Export** → **WAR** file. The Export wizard opens.
2. On the WAR Export page, select a destination directory for the WAR file. Enter a name for the WAR file or accept the default.
3. Select the **Export Source files** check box to include source files in the WAR file. When deploying to a WebSphere Portal Server, you do not need to include the source files. If you were exporting a WAR file to continue development on another machine, you would want to select this option.

4. Select the **Overwrite existing file** option to replace an existing WAR file with the same name.
5. Click **Finish**.

Install the WAR file on the WebSphere Portal server by using the WebSphere Portal administrative tools.

Remote Server Deploy

Remote Server Deploy is a function that allows portlets developed for a WebSphere Portal V5.0 Server to be deployed in an automated fashion.

This functionality is not available for WebSphere Portal V5.1 servers. To deploy portlets to a WebSphere Portal V5.1 server, you must export portlet projects to WAR files, and then install them to WebSphere Portal V5.1 using the WebSphere Portal administration interface. The process of exporting WAR files is described in "Export WAR Files" on page 1020.

To deploy a portlet project to a WebSphere Portal server, follow the steps below.

1. Right-click the portlet project and select **Deploy Portlet**. The Deploy Portlet wizard opens.
2. Select an existing server from the list or create a new one. Then click **Next**.
3. On the Portlets page, define these options for Portlet Overwriting:
   a. Select **Automatically overwrite portlets to replace existing portlets without warning**.
   b. Select the **Update** or the **Remove & Deploy** option.
      - Use the **Update** option to install the portlet, but preserve any customization data that was added in the configure or edit modes.
      - Use the **Remove & Deploy** option to remove and reinstall the portlet. During the removal process, all customization data is also removed, and portlets are removed from any pages where they were already placed. The install process only installs portlets, but does not restore customization data nor place portlets on pages. Use this option if you want to clean up portlet settings, or your portlet is not compatible with the old version.
4. Click **Finish**. Do not interrupt the deployment process.

> **Note:** An XML Exception occurs and the server attach fails to start if the project name, the filename, the file directory structure, or the user ID for the WebSphere Portal login name are excessively long. To correct this, shorten the length of the filename, the file directory structure, or the user ID for WebSphere Portal login at the WebSphere Portal Server Attach server configuration.

Portal administration

Administrative portlets can be enabled in the server configuration by using the Portal Server Configuration editor described in "Portal server configuration" on page 1016.

You can use the administrative portlets to configure advanced options when running portal and portlet projects.

There are several limitations to using the administrative portlets. You cannot install portlets using the administration portlets. In addition, any changes that are made are reset to the default values the next time the test environment is started.

It is recommended to only use this option when necessary. It affects the performance of the test environment.

To debug portlets in a particular layout, use the test and debug options of a portal project, not the administration portlets in the test environment.

18.2.7 Enterprise Application Integration Portal Tools

Rational Application Developer also includes some tools to help you with Enterprise Application Integration with SAP and Siebel.

Service Data Objects and Tools

Service Data Objects (SDO), the JSR 235 standard, is a new model for representing data, accessing persistent data, and passing data between tiers. It provides a single, consistent interface to any data source.

The JSF tools for SDO in IBM Rational Application Developer provide minimal or zero coding for building dynamic data-bound JSPs.

IBM has included SDO mediators for applications, including SAP and Siebel, that are supported on WebSphere Portal V5.1 servers.

SDO mediators are added to portlets through drag-and-drop from the Palette view and the Page Data view.

Business Process Portlet Development Tools

The portal tools in IBM Rational Application Developer V6.0 also include support for Business Process Execution Language (BPEL)-based business process portlet development. These portlets are supported on WebSphere Portal V5.1 servers.

To use these tools, process designers develop business processes by using the BPEL editor on WebSphere Studio Application Developer - Integration Edition V5.1.1 and test them in the WebSphere Test Environment.

You can then import the resultant business processes as JAR files to develop and compile task processing portlets using the remote server attach function for testing and debugging portlets.

18.2.8 Coexistence and migration of tools and applications

When installing multiple versions of IBM development software and working with portal and portlet projects developed with different versions of development software, there are some important issues to consider.

WebSphere Studio and Rational Application Developer

WebSphere Studio Application Developer and IBM Rational Application Developer can coexist with regards to the Portal Toolkit 5.0.x on WebSphere Studio 5.x.

Portlet Projects (Portal Toolkit 5.0.2.2 and later)

Portlet projects completed using the Portal Toolkit V5.0.2.2 will be migrated automatically to Rational Application Developer V6.0 Portal Tools by either migrating the Portal Toolkit workspace or importing the project using the Project Interchange feature.

During migration of Portal Toolkit V5.0.2.2 projects, some additional changes take place:

- The target server is set to WebSphere Portal V5.0, if no target server is set to the project.
- The portlet build path is corrected.
- A portlet project nature is added.

Portlet projects (Portal Toolkit earlier than V5.0.2.2)

If migrating portlet projects from earlier versions of Portal Toolkit (prior to V5.0.2.2), the best practice is to export your portlet projects to WAR files and then import the WAR files into new portlet projects within IBM Rational Application Developer V6.0.

Manually migrate your portlet projects by following these directions:

1. Export the existing project to a WAR file, and include its source files.
    a. Right-click the project and select **Export**.
    b. Select **WAR file** and **Export source files** and click **Finish**.
2. Import the portlet WAR file into a new portlet project:
    a. In the Portal Tools for Rational Application Developer V6.0, create a new empty portlet project.
        i. Select **File → New → Project → Portal → Portlet Project** or **Portlet Project (JSR 168)**.
        ii. Deselect **Create a portlet**.
        iii. Click **Show Advanced**.
        iv. If you are importing a WebSphere Portal V4.2 portlet, select **2.2** as the servlet version.
        v. Select **WebSphere Portal v5.0** as the target server, and click **Finish**.
    b. Import the WAR file to this new empty portlet project.
        i. Select **File → Import**.
        ii. Select **WAR file** and specify the WAR file from the portlet project that you exported.
        iii. Select the newly created empty portlet project.
        iv. Select **Overwrite existing resources without warning**.
        v. Do not select Delete project on overwrite.
        vi. Delete the TLD file.

            It is recommended that you delete the portlet TLD file from the project if it exists. Otherwise, you will get a warning message when you rebuild the project. Leaving it may cause a problem when the portlet project is deployed to WebSphere Portal and the TLD file of the portlet is different from the file in the server.

Note: If you are migrating a WebSphere Portal V4.2 portlet, you will need to migrate this migrated portlet project to WebSphere Portal V5.x. Backward compatibility of portlet projects is not supported.

18.3 Portal development scenario

To gain an understanding of the portal development process, this scenario demonstrates how the portal tools can be used to create a portal site.

The portal development scenario is organized into the following tasks:

- Prepare for the sample.
- Add and modify a portal page.
- Create and modify two portlets.
- Add portlets to a portal page.
- Run the project in the test environment.

> **Note:** The sample code described in this chapter can be completed by following along in the procedures documented. Alternatively, you can import the sample Portal code provided in the c:\6449code\portal\Portal.zip Project Interchange file. For details refer to Appendix B, "Additional material" on page 1395.
>
> When importing the Project Interchange file, we found some errors when using the IBM WebSphere Portal V5.0.2 Test Environment due to issues related files outside of the scope of the Project Interchange packaging (specifically, themes and related JSPs).

18.3.1 Prepare for the sample

Prior to working on the portal development scenario, ensure that you have prepared the environment by installing the Portal Tools and WebSphere Portal Test Environment (V5.0.2 or V5.1).

Install the Portal Tools

For details on installing the Portal Tools as a component of the Rational Application Developer installation, refer to "Rational Application Developer installation" on page 1372.

Install WebSphere Portal Test Environment

For the scenario in this chapter, you can install either the V5.0.2 or V5.1 WebSphere Portal Test Environments (sample applies to both).

For more information on installing the WebSphere Portal Test Environments refer to the following:

- IBM WebSphere Portal V5.0.2 Test Environment

    Refer to "WebSphere Portal V5.0 Test Environment installation" on page 1376

- IBM WebSphere Portal V5.1 Test Environment

    Refer to "WebSphere Portal V5.1 Test Environment installation" on page 1377.

Install the Rational Application Developer V6 Interim Fix

We recommend that you install the latest Rational Application Developer interim fixes. For details refer to "Rational Application Developer Product Updater - Interim Fix 0004" on page 1380.

Start Rational Application Developer

To begin, start the IBM Rational Application Developer Workbench. By default, click **Start** → **Programs** → **IBM Rational** → **IBM Rational Application Developer V6.0** → **Rational Application Developer**.

Once Developer is open, you will begin using the Portal Tools to develop a portal site, as instructed below.

18.3.2 Create a portal project

To create a portal project, do the following:

1. Select **File** → **New** → **Project**.
2. When the New Project dialog appears, select **Portal Project** and then click **Next**.
3. If prompted with the dialog displayed in Figure 18-21, click **OK** to enable portal development capabilities.

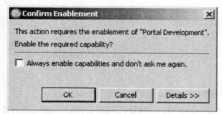

Figure 18-21   Enable portal development

4. When the Portal Project dialog appears, enter `MyPortal` in the Name field, click **Show Advanced** to see more options (we accepted the defaults), and then click **Next**.
5. When the Select Theme dialog appears, select the desired theme. For example, we select the **Corporate** theme and then clicked **Next**.

6. When the Select Skin dialog appears, select the desired skin. For example, we selected the **Outline** skin and then clicked **Finish**.

   This will generate the framework for the portal site.

7. If prompted to change to the Web perspective as seen in Figure 18-22, click **Yes**.

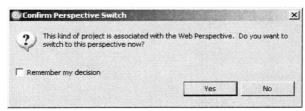

Figure 18-22   Confirm perspective switch

18.3.3 Add and modify a portal page

This section describes how to add and modify a portal page for a portal site.

To add a new portal page, do the following:

1. Drag-and-drop the **Page** button from the Palette and place it in the same column as the existing Page1 was created (see Figure 18-23 on page 1028).
2. Click **New Page**.
3. Select the **Title** tab from the Properties view at the bottom of the window.
4. Change the page names.

   Change the names of the pages *Page1* and *New Page* to `Top Page` and `Bottom page`, respectively.

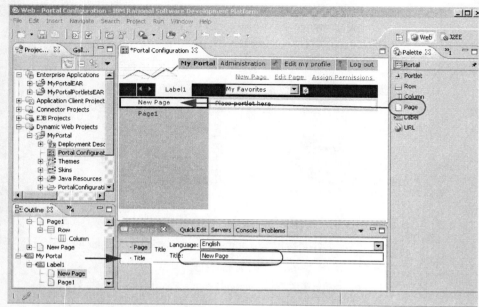

Figure 18-23   Insert a new page and modify title

5. Add a label to the page (see Figure 18-24 on page 1029).

   a. Drag and drop the **Label** button from the Palette view, and place it to the right of the existing Label1.

   b. Drag and drop the **Page** button from the Palette view onto the New Label to add a new page on which to place portlets.

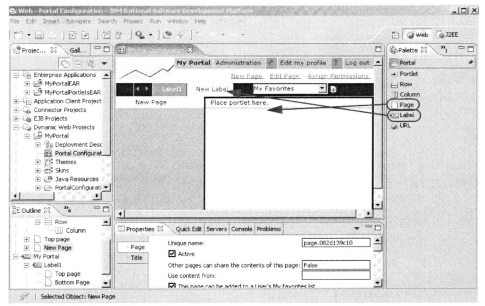

Figure 18-24   Add a new label and page

6. Change the label names (see Figure 18-25).

   In the same way that the titles of pages are modified, change the names of the two labels on the portal site. Name the right label `Right Label` and the left label `Left Label`.

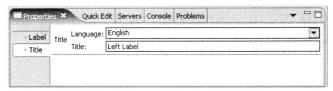

Figure 18-25   Changing label titles

7. Click **File** → **Save All** to save all the changes you have made.
8. By adding labels and pages, you are able to alter the navigational structure of the portal. You can also view an outline view of this structure by looking at the

Outline view, which appears in the lower left corner of the Workbench (see Figure 18-26).

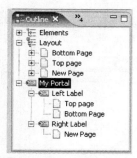

Figure 18-26   Outline view

18.3.4 Create and modify two portlets

Now that the portal site and its navigational structure have been defined, we can add content. Content is added to portals by placing portlets on each of the pages. We will create two portlet projects for our example in this section.

Create the first portlet

To create the first portlet, do the following:

1. Click **File** → **New** → **Project**.
2. When the New Project dialog appears, select **Portlet Project** and click **Next**.
3. Enter `Basic Portlet` in the Name field and click **Next**.
4. When the Portlet Type dialog appears, select the **Basic portlet** type and click **Next**.
5. When the Features dialog appears, uncheck **Web Diagram** and click **Next**.
6. When the Portlet Settings dialog appears, we accepted the default portlet settings and click **Next**.
7. When the Event Handling dialog appears, do the following and then click **Next**:
   – Uncheck **Add form sample**.
   – Uncheck **Add action listener**.
8. When the Single Sign-on dialog appears, accept the default values for credential vault handling and click **Next**.

9. When the Miscellaneous dialog appears, check **Add edit mode** on the miscellaneous settings page, and click **Finish** to generate your portlet code.

   The portlet's view mode JSP is now displayed in the Workbench to be edited.

10. Expand **Dynamic Web Projects** → **MyPortal** in the Project Explorer view (see Figure 18-27).

    Under this directory are all the resources associated with the portlet including the supporting JSP files, Java classes, and the portlet's deployment descriptor. You can double-click any resource to edit it in its default editor.

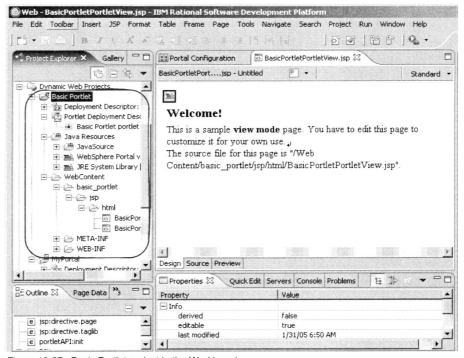

Figure 18-27 Basic Portlet project in the Workbench

Create the second portlet

Now, create a second portlet for the portal site. This portlet will process a form and display the results.

1. Select **File** → **New** → **Project**.

Chapter 18. Develop portal applications   **1031**

2. When the New Project dialog appears, select **Portlet Project**, and click **Next**.
3. Enter `Form Portlet` in the Name field and click **Next**.
4. When the Portlet Type dialog appears, select **Basic portlet** and click **Next**.
5. When the Features dialog appears, uncheck **Web Diagram**, check the **JSP Tag Libraries**, and then click **Next**.
6. When the Portlet Settings dialog appears, we accepted the default portlet settings, and clicked **Next**.
7. When the Event Handling dialog appears, accept the defaults on the event handling screen. The **Add action listener** and **Add form sample** options should be selected. Click **Next**.
8. When the Single Sign-on dialog appears, accept the default values for credential vault handling and click **Next**.
9. When the Miscellaneous dialog appears, accept the default and click **Finish** to generate your portlet code.
10. In the FormPortletPortletView.jsp file that is displayed on your screen, delete Welcome!
11. Figure 18-28 on page 1033 displays a sample view mode page. You have to edit this page to customize it for your own use.

    The source file for this page is as follows, leaving only the form sample to be displayed on this page:

    `/WebContent/form_portlet/jsp/html/FormPortletPortletView.jsp`

Figure 18-28 Modified second portlet

12. Click **File** → **Save All** to save all the changes made to the portlet projects.

18.3.5 Add portlets to a portal page

Now return to the Portal Configuration editor used in 18.3.3, "Add and modify a portal page" on page 1027, to add portlets to a portal page.

1. Expand **Dynamic Web Projects** → **MyPortal**.
2. Double-click **Portal Configuration** to open in the editor.
3. Add portlets to the Left Label of the Top Page.
   a. Select the **Left Label** of the Top Page.
   b. Drag and drop the **Column** button from the Palette view into the area of the Top Page that says **Place portlet here**.

   By doing this, the layout of the page is changed to accommodate two portlets side-by-side, as seen in Figure 18-29 on page 1034.

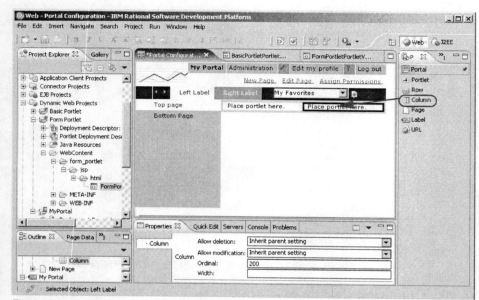

Figure 18-29   Adding a column

    c. Right-click the left column and click **Insert Portlet** → **As Child**.

    d. Select the **Basic Portlet portlet**, as seen in Figure 18-30 on page 1035, and click **OK**.

Figure 18-30   Select portlet to insert

4. Add portlets to the Left Label of the Bottom Page.

   a. Select the **Left Label** of the Bottom Page.

   b. Drag and drop the **Column** button from the Palette view into the area of the Bottom Page that says **Place portlet here**.

   c. Right-click the right column and click **Insert Portlet** → **As Child**.

   d. Select the **Form Portlet portlet** and click **OK**.

5. Perform the same action to insert the *Basic Portlet portlet* to the Left Label of the Bottom Page (see Figure 18-31 on page 1036).

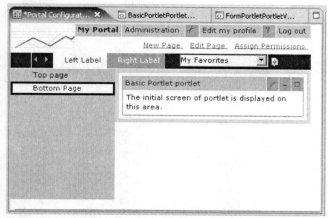

Figure 18-31   Basic portlet on the bottom page of the left label

6. Now click the **Right Label**.
7. Insert the Form Portlet onto this page (see Figure 18-32).

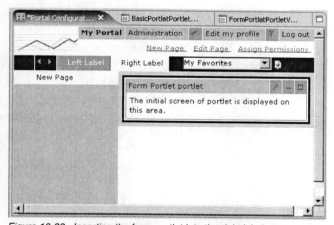

Figure 18-32   Inserting the form portlet into the right label new page

8. Click **File** → **Save All** to save all the changes made to your portal site.

18.3.6 Run the project in the test environment

Now you can run and test the project in the WebSphere Portal Test Environment. This section assumes that you have not previously defined a WebSphere Portal Test Environment server and will configure a server for you as part of the procedure.

1. Open the Web perspective.
2. Expand **Dynamic Web Projects**.
3. Right-click **MyPortal**, and select **Run** → **Run on Server**, as seen in Figure 18-33.

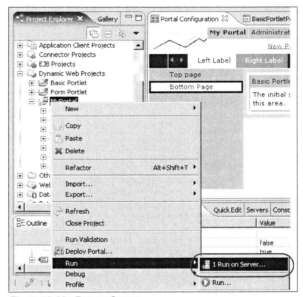

Figure 18-33 Run on Server

4. When the Define a New Server dialog appears, select **Manually define a server**, and select the desired WebSphere Portal Test Environment (V5.0 or V5.1). For example, we selected **WebSphere Portal v5.0 Test Environment** and clicked **Next**.
5. When the WebSphere Server Configuration Settings dialog appears, we accepted the default port (9081) and clicked **Next**.

6. When the Add and Remove Projects dialog appears, select each of the following projects and click **Add**:
   - Form PortletEAR
   - Basic PortletEAR
   - MyPortalEAR

7. When done adding the projects to the Configured projects column, you should have four projects (MyPortalEAR, Form PortletEAR, Basic PortletEAR, MyPortalPortletsEAR) associated with your MyPortal project so that they can run on the server. Click **Finish**.

8. Click **OK** if you receive the Repair Server Configuration dialog window (see Figure 18-34). This indicates that your portlets will be added to the server so that they run in your portal project.

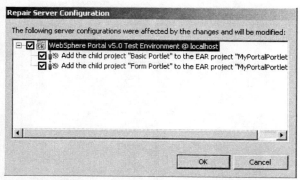

Figure 18-34   Repair Server Configuration dialog

9. The server will now start, and your portal site will load in the Web browser, as seen in Figure 18-35 on page 1039.

   Test the portal site.

   a. Navigate the portal site using the labels and page links.

   b. Enter edit mode on the Basic Portlet by clicking **Edit Page**.

   c. Submit a value using the form.

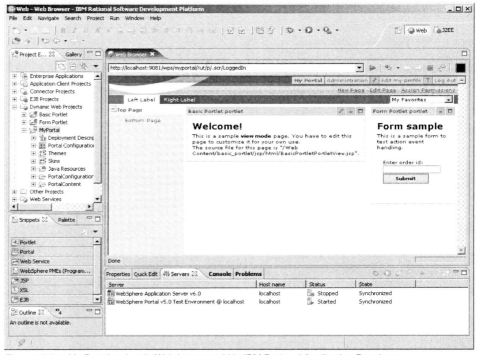

Figure 18-35 My Portal project in Web browser within IBM Rational Application Developer

Chapter 18. Develop portal applications **1039**

Part 3

Test and debug applications

19

Servers and server configuration

Rational Application Developer provides support for testing, debugging, profiling, and deploying Enterprise applications to local and remote test environments.

To run an Enterprise application or Web application in Application Developer, the application must be published (deployed) to the server. This is achieved by installing the EAR project for the application into an application server. The server can then be started and the application can be tested in a Web browser, or by using the Universal Test Client (UTC) for EJBs and Web Services.

This chapter describes the features and concepts of server configuration, as well as demonstrates how to configure a server to test applications.

The chapter is organized into the following sections:

- Introduction to server configuration
- Configure a WebSphere V6 Test Environment
- Add a project to a server
- Remove a project from a server
- Publish application changes
- Configure application and server resources

19.1 Introduction to server configuration

IBM Rational Application Developer V6.0 includes integrated test environments for IBM WebSphere Application Server V5.0/V5.1/V6.0 and IBM WebSphere Portal V5.0.2/V5.1, as well as support for many third-party servers obtained separately. In Version 6 the server configuration is the same for IBM WebSphere Application Server V6.0 (base), Express, and Network Deployment Editions. One of the many great features of V6 is the ability to simultaneously run multiple server configurations and test environments on the same development node where Rational Application Developer is installed.

In previous releases, there was a separate server configuration for WebSphere Application Server and only the base and Express servers were supported. In IBM Rational Application Developer V6.0, the new architecture supports deploying and testing on IBM WebSphere Application Server V6.0 (base), Express, and Network Deployment Editions. Also, test environment configuration for the WebSphere Application Server V6.0 Test Environment is done from the WebSphere Administrative Console.

All communication with all WebSphere V6 servers occurs through JMX calls over SOAP (start, stop, install applications, set status) using port 8880 by default.

When using Rational Application Developer it is very common for a developer to have multiple test environments or server configurations, which are made up of workspaces, projects, and preferences, and supporting test environments (local or remote).

Some of the key test environment configuration items include:

- Multiple Workspaces with different projects, preferences, and other configuration settings defined
- Multiple Rational Application Developer Test Environment servers configured
- When using WebSphere Application Server V6.0 test environments, multiple profiles, each potentially representing a different server configuration

For example, a developer may want to have a separate server configuration for WebSphere Application Server V6.0 with a unique set of projects and preferences in a workspace and server configuration pointing to a newly created and customized WebSphere Application Server V6.0 profile. On the same system, the developer can create a separate portal server configuration with unique portal workspace projects and preferences, as well as a WebSphere Portal V5.1 Test Environment. This chapter describes how to create, configure, and run both a WebSphere Application Server V6.0 and WebSphere Portal V6.1 Test Environments on the same development system.

19.1.1 Supported test server environments

IBM Rational Web Developer V6.0 and IBM Rational Application Developer V6.0 support a wide range of test server environments for running, testing, and debugging application code.

In IBM Rational Application Developer V6.0, the integration with the IBM WebSphere Application Server V6.0 for deployment, testing, and administration is the same for IBM WebSphere Application Server V6.0 (Test Environment, separate install, and the Network Deployment edition). In previous versions of WebSphere Studio, the configuration of the test environment was different than a separately installed WebSphere Application Server.

We have categorized the test server environments as follows:

- Integrated test servers

    Integrated test servers refers to the test servers included with the Rational Developer edition (see Table 19-1).

- Test servers available separately

    Test servers available separately refers to the test servers that are supported by the Rational Developer edition, but available separately from the Rational Developer products (see Table 19-2 on page 1046).

Table 19-1 Integrated test servers

Install option	Integrated test server	Web Developer	Application Developer
IBM WebSphere Application Server V6.0			
	IBM WebSphere Application Server V6.0	X	X
IBM WebSphere Application Server V5.x			
	IBM WebSphere Application Server V5.1	X	X
	IBM WebSphere Application Server Express V5.1	X	X
	IBM WebSphere Application Server V5.0.2	X	X
	IBM WebSphere Application Server Express V5.0.2	X	X
IBM WebSphere Portal			
	IBM WebSphere Portal V5.0.2.2 **Note**: Available on Windows (not Linux)	na	X
	IBM WebSphere Portal V5.1	na	X

Table 19-2 Additional supported test servers available separately

Integrated Test Server	Web Developer	Application Developer
Tomcat V5.0	X	X
WebLogic V6.1	X	X
WebLogic V7.1	X	X
WebLogic V8.1	X	X

19.1.2 Local vs. remote test environments

When configuring a test environment, the server can be either a local integrated server or a remote server. Once the server itself is installed and configured, the server definition within Rational Application Developer is very similar for local and remote servers.

In either case, local or remote, you will need to specify the SOAP connector port from the Rational Application Developer WebSphere V6.0 server configuration and the WebSphere Application Server V6.0 Profile.

19.1.3 Commands to manage test servers

Once the server is setup, there are a few key commands used to manage the test servers.

- Debug: Only available for local test servers
- Start: Only available for local test servers
- Profile: Only available for local test servers
- Restart: Available on all active WebSphere v6.0 Servers
- Restart: Can restart in different modes (normal, debug, and profile)
- Stop

19.2 Configure a WebSphere V6 Test Environment

This section describes how to create and configure a WebSphere Application Server V6 Test Environment within IBM Rational Application Developer V6.0. In this example, we create a new WebSphere V6 profile, a new Rational Application Developer server configuration, and a workspace.

19.2.1 Understanding WebSphere Application Server V6.0 profiles

New with IBM WebSphere Application Server V6.0 is the concept of profiles. The WebSphere Application Server installation process simply lays down a set of core product files required for the runtime processes. After installation you will need to create one or more profiles that define the runtime to have a functional system. The core product files are shared among the runtime components defined by these profiles.

> **Note:** In V5, the `wsinstance` command was used to create multiple runtime configurations using the same installation. With V6, profiles allow you to do this.

With WebSphere Application Server and WebSphere Application Server Express Editions you can only have standalone application servers, as shown in Figure 19-1. Each application server is defined within a single cell and node. The administration console is hosted within the application server and can only connect to that application server. No central management of multiple application servers are possible. An application server profile defines this environment.

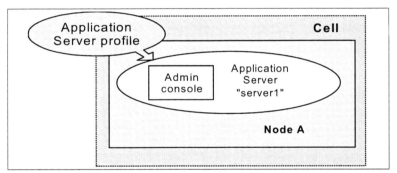

Figure 19-1 System management topology - Standalone server (Base and Express)

You can also create standalone application servers with the Network Deployment package, though you would most likely do so with the intent of federating that server into a cell for central management at some point.

With the Network Deployment package, you have the option of defining multiple application servers with central management capabilities. For more information on profiles for the IBM WebSphere Application Server V6.0 Network Deployment Edition, refer to the *WebSphere Application Server V6 Systems Management and Configuration*, SG24-6451.

Types of profiles

There are three types of profiles for defining the runtime:

- Application server profile

    > **Note:** The application server profile is used by Rational Application Developer WebSphere Application Server V6.0 Test Environment.

- Deployment manager profile
- Custom profile

Application server profile

The application server profile defines a single standalone application server. Using this profile will give you an application server that can run standalone (unmanaged) with the following characteristics:

- The profile will consist of one cell, one node, and one server. The cell and node are not relevant in terms of administration, but you will see them when you administer the server through the administrative console (scopes).
- The name of the application server is "server1".
- The application samples are automatically installed on the server.
- The server has a dedicated administrative console.

The primary use for this type of profile would be:

- To build a server in a Base or Express installation (including a test environment within Rational Application Developer).
- To build a standalone server in a Network Deployment installation that is not managed by the deployment manager (for example, to build a test machine).
- Or to build a server in a distributed server environment to be federated and managed by the deployment manager. If you are new to WebSphere Application Server and want a quick way of getting an application server complete with samples, this is a good option. When you federate this node, the default cell will become obsolete and the node will be added to the deployment manager cell. The server name will remain as server1 and the administrative console will be removed from the application server.

Deployment manager profile

The deployment manager profile defines a deployment manager in a Network Deployment installation. Although you could conceivably have the Network Deployment package and run only standalone servers, this would bypass the primary advantages of Network Deployment, which are workload management, failover, and central administration.

In a Network Deployment environment, you should create one deployment manager profile. This will give you:

- A cell for the administrative domain
- A node for the deployment manager
- A deployment manager with an administrative console.
- No application servers

Once you have the deployment manager, you can:

- Federate nodes built either from existing application server profiles or custom profiles.
- Create new application servers and clusters on the nodes from the administrative console.

Custom profile

A custom profile is an empty node, intended for federation to a deployment manager. This type of profile is used when you are building a distributed server environment. The way you would use this is:

- Create a deployment manager profile.
- Create one custom profile on each node on which you will run application servers.
- Federate each custom profile, either during the custom profile creation process or later using the **addNode** command, to the deployment manager.
- Create new application servers and clusters on the nodes from the administrative console.

Directory structure and default profiles

Within Rational Application Developer the integrated test environments are located in the <rad_home>/runtimes directory, where <rad_home> is the installation path, such as:

```
C:/Program Files/IBM/Rational/SDP/6.0
```

The IBM WebSphere Application Server V6.0 Test Environment is located in the following directory:

```
<rad_home>/runtimes/base_v6
```

We will refer to the root of each profile directory as <profile_home>:

```
<rad_home>/runtimes/base_v6/profiles/<profile_name>
```

The default profile is determined by the following:

- The profile was defined as the default profile when you created it. The last profile specified as the default will take precedence. You can also use the **wasprofile** command to specify the default profile.
- Or, if you have not specified the default profile, it will be the first profile you create.

When a profile is created, the profile is created from a template and copied to its unique <profile_home>. In addition, an entry is made to the profileRegistry.xml found at:

> <rad_home>\runtimes\base_v6\properties\profileRegistry.xml

Example 19-1 lists the contents of a sample profileRegistry.xml. In this example, two profiles exist (default, AppSrv01). Notice the profile named *default* is marked as isDefault="true".

Example 19-1 Sample profileRegistry.xml

```
<?xml version="1.0" encoding="UTF-8"?>
<profiles>
    <profile isDefault="true" name="default" path="C:\Program Files\IBM\Rational\SDP\6.0\runtimes\base_v6\profiles\default" template="C:\Program Files\IBM\Rational\SDP\6.0\runtimes\base_v6\profileTemplates\default"/>
    <profile isDefault="false" name="AppSrv01" path="C:\Program Files\IBM\Rational\SDP\6.0\runtimes\base_v6\profiles\AppSrv01" template="C:\Program Files\IBM\Rational\SDP\6.0\runtimes\base_v6\profileTemplates\default"/>
</profiles>
```

19.2.2 WebSphere Application Server V6 installation

The IBM WebSphere Application Server V6.0 Integrated Test Environment is an installation option from the main Rational Application Developer Installer.

For details on how to install the WebSphere Application Server V6.0 Test Environment, refer to "IBM Rational Application Developer V6 installation" on page 1372 (see Figure A-2 on page 1375 for install component selection).

Prior to the IBM WebSphere Application Server V6.0 Test Environment installation, the runtimes directory will look as follows:

> <rad_home>\runtimes\base_v6_stub

After the IBM WebSphere Application Server V6.0 Test Environment is installed the directory will look as follows (no more stub):

> <rad_home>\runtimes\base_v6

19.2.3 WebSphere Application Server V6 profile creation

In 19.2.1, "Understanding WebSphere Application Server V6.0 profiles" on page 1047, we reviewed the concepts for WebSphere V6.0 profiles. Profiles can be created using the **wasprofile** command line tool or the WebSphere Profile Creator wizard (pctWindows.exe), which is an interface to the wasprofile tool. For the purposes of development, we chose to use the WebSphere Profile wizard in the following example.

Create new profile using the WebSphere Profile wizard

To create a new WebSphere Application Server V6.0 profile using the WebSphere Profile Creator wizard (application server profile), do the following:

1. Start the WebSphere Profile Creation wizard.

   a. Navigate to the following directory:

   ```
   <rad_home>\runtimes\base_v6\bin\ProfileCreator
   ```

   b. Run **pctWindows.exe** to launch the WebSphere Profile Creation wizard.

   > **Note:** Alternatively, if you have installed IBM Rational Application Developer Fix level V6.0.0.1, then you can do the following:
   >
   > 1. Select **Window → Preferences**.
   > 2. Expand **Server → WebSphere**.
   > 3. Click **Create Profile**.

4. When the Welcome dialog appears, click **Next**.
5. When the Profile name dialog appears, we entered the following (as seen in Figure 19-2 on page 1052), and then clicked **Next**:
   - Profile name: AppSrv01
   - Uncheck **Make this profile the default**.

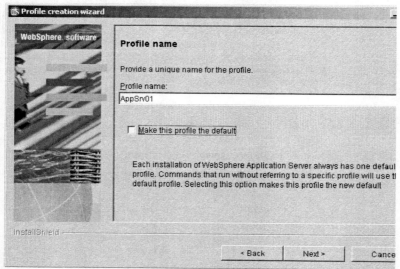

Figure 19-2   WebSphere Profile Creator wizard - Profile name

6. When the Profile directory dialog appeared, we accepted the following default directory and then clicked **Next**:

   <rad_home>\runtimes\base_v6\profiles\AppSrv01

   Where <rad_home> is the Rational Application Developer installation path.

7. When the Node and host names dialog appeared, we accepted the following defaults and then clicked **Next**:

   – Node name: rad6win1Node02

     In this case, rad6win1 is the host name of our computer, and Node01 was already used to create the default server, so the wizard used the next available node (Node02).

   – Host name: rad6win1.itso.ral.ibm.com

     This is the fully qualified host name of our computer.

8. When the Port value assignment dialog appeared, we accepted the generated port values. In this case, notice in Figure 19-3 on page 1053 that each of the port values is increased by one from the original default since a default profile existed before creating the new profile (AppSrv01).

   Take note of the port values and click **Next**.

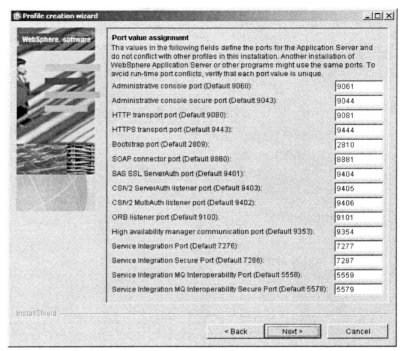

Figure 19-3 WebSphere Profile Creator - Port value assignments

> **Note:** If you want to have multiple WebSphere Profiles but only intend to run them one at a time, you may consider using the default port values for each of them. Of course, this would preclude running them simultaneously without port conflicts.

9. When the Windows service definition dialog appears, we unchecked Run the Application Server process as a Windows service, as seen in Figure 19-4 on page 1054, and then clicked **Next**.

> **Note:** We will be starting and stopping the server from Rational Application Developer. Remember, the Rational Application Developer server configuration is a pointer to the server defined in the WebSphere Profile.

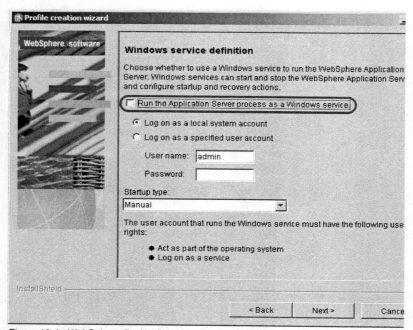

Figure 19-4 WebSphere Profile Creator - Windows service definition

10. When the Profile summary dialog appears, review the profile settings and then click **Next** to begin creating the new profile.

    The WebSphere Profile creation process takes approximately 10 minutes to complete.

11. When the Profile creation complete dialog appears, you should see a message at the top of the dialog: *The Profile creation wizard created the profile successfully.*

    By default, **Launch the First steps console** is checked. Click **Finish**.

Verify the new WebSphere Profile

After creating the WebSphere Profile, we recommend that you verify it was created properly and familiarize yourself with how to use it.

1. View the directory structure and find the new profile.

    <rad_home>/runtimes/base_v6/profiles/<profile_name>

Where *<profile_name>* is the name of the WebSphere Profile.

This is where you will find, among other things, the config directory containing the application server configuration files, the bin directory (for entering commands), and the logs directory where information is recorded.

> **Note:** For simplicity, we will refer the entire path for the profile as *<profile_home>*.

2. Start the server.

    If you ran the installation verification, the server should already be started. You can check using the following commands:

    ```
    cd <profile_home>\bin
    serverStatus -all
    ```

    If the server status is not started, then start it from the First Steps menu or with the following commands:

    ```
    cd <profile_home>\bin
    startServer server1
    ```

3. Verify the server startup and installation.

    You can do this directly from the First Steps menu. This process will start the application server and verify the proper operation of the Web and EJB containers. Messages are displayed on the First Steps window and logged in the following places:

    ```
    <profile_home>/logs/server1/startServer.log
    <profile_home>/logs/server1/SystemOut.log
    ```

4. Open the WebSphere Administrative Console either by selecting the option in the First Steps window, or by accessing its URL from a Web browser:

    ```
    http://<appserver_host>:<admin_console_port>/ibm/console
    ```

    For example:

    ```
    http://localhost:9061/ibm/console/
    ```

    The administrative console port was selected during the profile creation wizard (see Figure 19-3 on page 1053).

    Click the **Log in** button. Since security is not active at this time, you do not have to enter a user name. If you choose to enter a name, it can be any name. If you enter a name it will be used to track changes you made to the configuration.

5. Display the configuration from the console. You should be able to see the following items from the administrative console:

   a. Application servers: Select **Servers** → **Application servers**. You should see server1, as seen in Figure 19-5 on page 1056. To see the configuration of this server, click the name in the list.

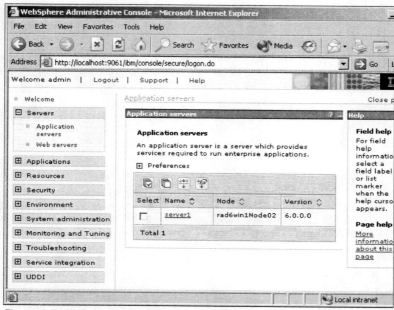

Figure 19-5   Application server defined by the application server profile

   b. Enterprise applications: Select **Applications** → **Enterprise Applications**. You should see a list of applications installed on server1.

   > **Note:** Although you cannot display the cell and node from the administrative console, they do exist. You will see this later as you begin to configure resources and choose a scope, and also in the <profile_home>/config directory structure.

   c. Click **Logout** and close the browser.

6. Stop the application server. You can do this from the First Steps menu, or better yet, use the `stopServer` command:

   ```
   cd <profile_home>\bin
   stopServer server1
   ```

   Tip: Delete a WebSphere Profile.

   To delete a WebSphere Profile, do the following:

   1. Stop the server that the profile is associated with.
   2. Delete the WebSphere Profile.
      - Delete using the `wasprofile` command:

        ```
        wasprofile -delete -profileName AppSrv01
        ```

        Where AppSrv01 is the WebSphere Profile to delete.

        Or do the following
      - Manually delete the profile.
        i. Remove the profile entry from the profileRegistry.xml.

           ```
           <rad_home>\runtimes\base_v6\properties\profileRegistry.xml
           ```
        ii. Delete the <profile_name> directory:

           ```
           <rad_home>\runtimes\base_v6\profiles\<profile_name>
           ```
        iii. Delete the <profile_name>.bat from the following directory:

           ```
           <rad_home>\runtimes\base_v6\properties\fsdb\<profile_name>.bat
           ```

19.2.4 Define a new server in Rational Application Developer

Once you have defined the WebSphere Profile or chosen to use the default profile, you can create a server in Rational Application Developer. The server points to the server defined within the WebSphere Profile you configured.

With the new server configuration architecture, there are a few considerations to be aware of:

- The profile *default* is created when the WebSphere Application Server V6.0 Integrated Test Environment feature is selected during Rational Application Developer installation. A Rational Application Developer WebSphere Application Server V6.0 Test Environment is configured to use the default profile.
- The Rational Application Developer server configuration is essentially a pointer to the WebSphere Profile.

- You must manually stop the WebSphere Application Server Test Environment within Rational Application Developer before closing the Rational Application Developer, otherwise the server (server1 of the WebSphere Profile) will continue to run as a standalone WebSphere Application Server.

> **Tip:** If you have installed IBM Rational Application Developer Fix level V6.0.0.1, then you can do the following to stop the server when the Workbench is closed:
> 1. From the Server view, double-click the server to open the Server Overview page settings.
> 2. At the bottom of the page, there is a check box to **Terminate server on Workbench shutdown**.
> 3. Save the settings.

To create a server in Rational Application Developer, do the following:

1. Open the J2EE perspective.
2. Select the **Servers** view.
3. Right-click in the Servers view, and select **New** → **Server**.
4. When the Define a New Server dialog appears, we did the following (as seen in Figure 19-6 on page 1059), and then clicked **Next**:
   - Host name: `localhost` (default)
   - Select the server type: Select **WebSphere v6.0 Server**.

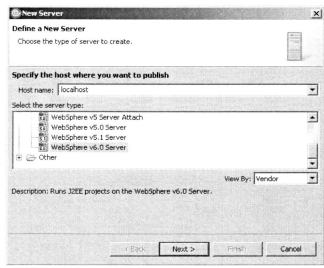

Figure 19-6   Define a New Server

5. When the WebSphere Server Settings dialog appears, we did the following (as seen in Figure 19-7 on page 1060), and then clicked **Next**:

   – WebSphere Profile name: Select **AppSrv01**.

   In our example, AppSrv01 is the WebSphere Profile we created. The *default* WebSphere Profile is the default value.

   – Server admin port number (SOAP connector port): 8881

   > **Note:** The port will need to match the SOAP port defined when creating the WebSphere Profile.

   – Server name: server1
   – Check **Run server with resources within the workspace**.
   – Server type: Select Base or Express server.
   – We left the remaining fields as the default settings.

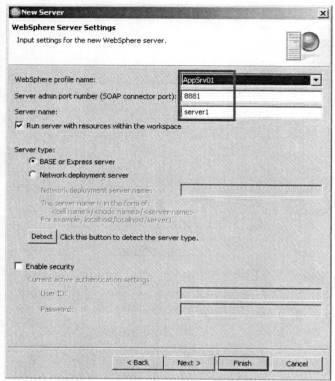

Figure 19-7 Define a New Server - WebSphere Server Settings

6. When the Add and Remove Projects dialog appears, we did not select a project at this time, and clicked **Finish**.

> **Note:** We address the topic of adding projects to a server in 19.3, "Add a project to a server" on page 1064.

The server will be created and should be displayed in the Servers view. In our example, the server WebSphere v6.0 @ localhost was created.

19.2.5 Verify the server

After you have completed defining the server within Rational Application Developer, we recommend that you perform some basic verification steps to ensure the server is configured properly.

1. Open the J2EE perspective.
2. Select the **Servers** view.
3. Double-click the server you created (for example, WebSphere v6.0 @ localhost) in the Servers view.
4. Review properties settings for the server.

   When the WebSphere v6.0 @ localhost server properties dialog opens, verify that the proper WebSphere Profile name is selected (for example, AppSrv01). Review the other settings. When done, save the file if changes were made and then close it.

5. Select the server (for example, WebSphere v6.0 @ localhost) in the Servers view, right-click, and select **Start**.

   In this example, the WebSphere v6.0 @ localhost defined in Rational Application Developer is configured to use server1 of the AppSrv01 WebSphere Profile.

6. Review the server startup output in the console. Also check the startServer.log and SystemOut.log for errors. The server logs can be found in the following directory:

   <profile_home>/logs/server1/startServer.log
   <profile_home>/logs/server1/SystemOut.log

7. Open the WebSphere Administrative Console either by selecting the option in the First Steps window, or by accessing its URL from a Web browser:

   http://<appserver_host>:<admin_console_port>/ibm/console

   For example:

   http://localhost:9061/ibm/console/

   The WebSphere Administrative Console port was selected during the WebSphere Profile Creation wizard (see Figure 19-3 on page 1053).

8. Click the **Log in** button. Since security is not active at this time, you do not have to enter a user name. If you choose to enter a name, it can be any name. If you enter a name it will be used to track changes you made to the configuration.

9. After accessing several pages of the WebSphere Administrative Console to verify it is working properly, click **Logout** and close the browser.

10. Verify the server stops properly by doing the following:
    a. From the J2EE perspective Server view, select the server (for example, WebSphere v6.0 @ localhost), right-click, and select **Stop**.

       The server status should change to Stopped.
    b. Verify that the server1 application server of the AppSrv01 WebSphere Profile has really stopped by entering the following command to check the server status:

       cd <profile_home>/bin
       serverStatus -all

       The server status output should show that the server has been stopped. If not, stop the server by entering the following command:

       stopServer server1

19.2.6 Customize a server in Rational Application Developer

Once the server has been created in Rational Application Developer, it is very easy to customize the settings.

1. Open the J2EE perspective.
2. Double-click the server you wish to customize in the Servers view.

There are a couple of key settings to point out for the server configuration, as seen in Figure 19-8 on page 1063.

- Server
  - WebSphere Profile name: Select the desired WebSphere Profile from the drop-down list.
  - Server admin port number (SOAP connector port): The SOAP connector port was defined for the WebSphere Profile at the time the profile was created. If you have more than one profile, the default behavior of the WebSphere Profile wizard is to increment this port number by 1. For example, the SOAP connector port for the *default* profile is 8880, and the AppSrv01 profile is 8881.
- Publishing

  Modify the publishing settings.
  - Select one of the following:
    - **Run server with resources within the workspace**
    - **Run server with resources on a Server**

– Enable automatic publishing: The default is for this to be enabled. This can be very time consuming, so you may consider turning this off and publishing as needed. Alternatively, change the interval of publishing.

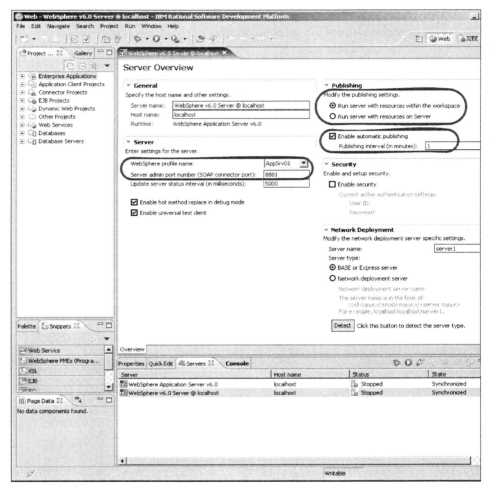

Figure 19-8   Customize server settings

3. After making changes save and close the file.

19.3 Add a project to a server

Once the server is configured, it can be further configured with server resources and be used to run applications by adding projects to it.

19.3.1 Considerations for adding a project to a server

When applications are added to a local test server or a separate installation, the actual binary files can be located in different places. The server definition in Rational Application Developer provides the selection of "Run server with resources within the workspace" or "Run server with resources on Server," as seen in Figure 19-9. This configuration page can be accessed by double-clicking the server in the Servers view.

The publishing setting applies to all applications added from a workspace. When a project or application is removed via the Add/Remove Projects from the server context menu or from the WebSphere Administrative Console, the project still remains within the workspace.

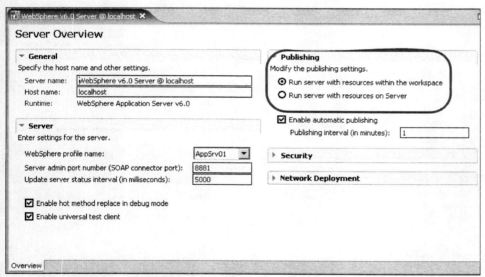

Figure 19-9 Application binary file location

19.3.2 Add a project to a server

This section describes how to add a Web application project to a server. We will use the simple JSP and Servlet Web application sample provided with Rational Application Developer.

Import the JSP and Servlet sample

To import the JSP and Servlet sample as a basis to demonstrate debug capabilities within Rational Application Developer, do the following:

1. From the Workbench select **Help** → **Samples Gallery**.
2. When the Samples Gallery window appears, select **Technology Samples** → **Web** → **JSP and Servlet**.
3. Scroll down the page and click **Import the Sample**.
4. When the Create a Sample Web Project window appears, accept the defaults and then click **Finish**.

Add the Web project to the server

To add a Web project to the server, do the following:

1. From the J2EE Perspective, select the **Servers** view.
2. Right-click the desired server to add the project, and select **Add and remove projects**.

    For example, we right-clicked the WebSphere v6.0 Server @ localhost we defined in "Define a new server in Rational Application Developer" on page 1057.

3. When the Add and Remove Projects dialog appears, we selected the **JSPandServletExampleEAR** and then clicked **Add**.
4. When the project appears in the Configured projects column, as seen in Figure 19-10 on page 1066, click **Finish**.

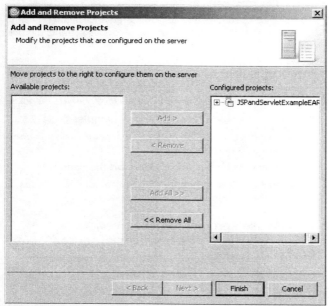

Figure 19-10   Add and Remove Projects

19.4 Remove a project from a server

As discussed previously, the Rational Application Developer server configuration is essentially a pointer to a server defined in the WebSphere Profile it is configured with. In this section we describe two scenarios for removing published projects from the server.

19.4.1 Remove a project via Rational Application Developer

In most cases, you can remove the project from the test server within Rational Application Developer as follows:

1. Open the Servers view.
2. Right-click the server where the application is published, and select **Add and remove projects** from the context menu.

3. When the Add and Remove Projects dialog appears, select the project in the Configured projects list, click the **< Remove** button, and then click **Finish**.

This operation will uninstall the application from the server defined for the WebSphere Profile your Rational Application Developer test server is configured with.

19.4.2 Remove a project via WebSphere Administrative Console

We found it necessary in some cases to uninstall the application from the WebSphere Administrative Console. For example, if you have published a project in Rational Application Developer to your test server, it will have been deployed to the server defined in the WebSphere Profile. If you then delete your Rational Application Developer server configuration or switch workspaces without first removing the project from the server, you will have a broken association between the Rational Application Developer server and the server defined in the WebSphere Profile.

> **Note:** We have listed a couple of possible resolutions to this issue:
>
> ► Create a new WebSphere Profile for each new Rational Application Developer workspace (server configuration). This approach will require more diskspace for each WebSphere Profile and server configuration, and if run simultaneously will require additional memory.
>
> For details refer to 19.2, "Configure a WebSphere V6 Test Environment" on page 1046.
>
> ► Manually uninstall the application from the WebSphere Administrative Console.
>
> The following procedure explains how to uninstall a deployed application using the WebSphere Administrative Console.

To address issues like the scenarios described, uninstall the enterprise application from the WebSphere Administrative Console as follows:

1. Start the test server in Rational Application Developer by selecting the server, right-clicking, and selecting **Start**.

2. Start the WebSphere Administrative Console either by right-clicking the server and selecting **Run administrative console**, or by accessing its URL from a Web browser:

   `http://<appserver_host>:<admin_console_port>/ibm/console`

   For example:

   `http://localhost:9060/ibm/console/`

3. Click the **Log in** button.

   WebSphere security is not enabled, thus a user ID and password are not required.

4. Click **Applications** → **Enterprise Applications**.
5. Check the desired application to uninstall.
6. Click the **Uninstall** button.
7. When prompted, click **OK**.
8. Save your changes.

19.5 Publish application changes

Depending on the type of application change, new artifacts may be published automatically.

1. The source code and configuration data are created/modified and saved.
2. The Builder runs, and then starts the AppInstaller.
3. The AppInstaller then determines the type of application change (for example, delta) and then publishes the change to the server.

Table 19-10 on page 1066 lists the actions of different components in Rational Application Developer and automatic publish actions.

Table 19-3   Automatic publish of changes

Action in Rational Application Developer	Automatic publish action	Result on server
Web module added to EAR	Module update sent to server	Module added to EAR on server and module started
Web module removed from EAR	Module update sent to server	Module removed, EAR remains started
EJB module added to EAR	Full application update sent to server	EJB module removed and EAR restarted
Enhanced EAR information added/changed in EAR	Full application update sent to server	EAR replaced and restarted
JSP added/changed/removed to Web module	Single file update sent to server	JSP added to Web module
JSP removed from Web module	Single file update sent to server	JSP removed and Web module remains started

Action in Rational Application Developer	Automatic publish action	Result on server
Servlet added/changed/removed to Web module or web.xml (IBM Extensions and Bindings) changed	Module update sent to server	Web module added to EAR and Web module restarted
EJB added/changed/removed or ejb-jar.xml (IBM Extensions and Bindings) changed	Full application update sent to server	EAR replaced and restarted

Considerations with automatic publish:

- If applications are set to run from the workspace, changes will be picked up and take affect without publishing.
- Test server restarts are minimized with Automatic Publish enabled:
    - Enabled defined resources (data sources at server level and above, JMS resources)
    - Debugging applications
    - Profiling servers
    - Enabling security
    - Changing JVM values on application server
- Automatic publish may slow system and development/test if making a large number of changes.
- Automatic publish requires server to be started, which requires more system resources.

19.6 Configure application and server resources

This section is organized into the following options for configuring application and server resources.

- Configure application resources.
- Configure server resources.
- Configure messaging resources.
- Configure security.

19.6.1 Configure application resources

In IBM WebSphere Application Server V6, application-related properties and data sources can be defined within an enhanced EAR file to simplify application deployment (see Figure 19-3 on page 1053). The properties are used by the application after being deployed. When the extended EAR is deployed, the data source is registered with WebSphere Application Server V6.0 once the target application server is restarted. To provide greater flexibility, variables can be defined for substitution with server values when the application is deployed.

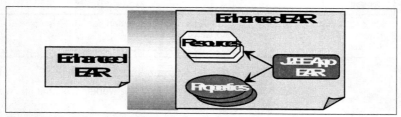

Figure 19-11   Enhanced EAR

Enhanced EAR tooling

The enhanced EAR tooling is provided from the Deployment tab of the Application Deployment Descriptor Editor, as seen in Figure 19-12 on page 1071. Deployment information is saved under the application ../META-INF/ibmconfig directory.

The following resource types can be added to the enhanced EAR:

- Virtual Hosts
- JAAS Authorization entries
- Shared Library
- Application class loader settings
- JDBC resources

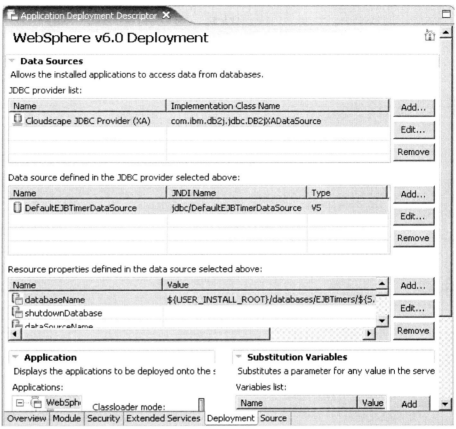

Figure 19-12 Application Deployment Descriptor Editor

Create a data source for EJB access

The data sources that support the entity beans must be specified before the application can be started. There are several ways to do it, but the easiest is to use the Enhanced EAR Editor.

> **Note:** The Enhanced EAR Editor is used to edit several WebSphere Application Server V6 specific configurations, like data sources, classloader policies, substitution variables, shared libraries, virtual hosts, and authentication settings. It lets you configure these settings with little effort and publish them every time you publish the application.
>
> The upside of the tool is that it makes the testing process simpler and easily repeatable, because the configurations it makes are saved to files that are usually shared at the team's repository. Thus, even though it will not let you configure every possible runtime setting, it is a good tool for development purposes because it eases the process of configuring the most common ones.
>
> The downside is that the configurations the tool makes will be attached to the EAR, and will not be visible from WebSphere Application Server's administrative console. The console is only able to edit settings that belong to the cluster, node, and server contexts. When you change a configuration using the Enhanced EAR Editor, this change is made at the application context. The deployer can still make changes to the EAR file using the Application Server Toolkit (AST), but it is a separate tool. Furthermore, in most cases these settings are dependent on the node the application server is installed in anyway, so it makes little sense to configure them at the application context for deployment purposes.

The following sample demonstrates how to create a data source for EJB access for the EJB project created in Chapter 15, "Develop Web applications using EJBs" on page 827.

1. On the Project Explorer view, double-click the BankEJBEAR enterprise application's deployment descriptor.
2. Select the **Deployment** page as shown in Figure 19-13 on page 1073.

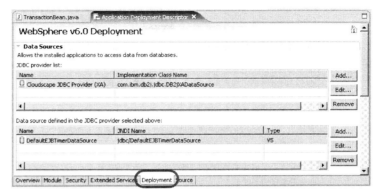

Figure 19-13   Enhanced EAR Editor

3. Scroll down the page until you find the Authentication section. It allows you to define a login configuration used by JAAS.

4. Click **Add** to include a new configuration (Figure 19-14).

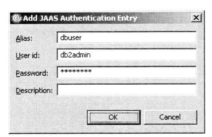

Figure 19-14   JAAS Authentication Entry

5. Enter dbuser as the entry's alias, and the appropriate user ID and password for your configuration. Click **OK** to complete the configuration.

6. Back at the Enhanced EAR editor, scroll back up to the Data Sources section. By default, the Cloudscape JDBC provider and Timer service datasource are defined. Since we are using DB2 in this example, we will need to add a DB2 JDBC provider by clicking the **Add** button right next to the provider list.

   The dialog depicted in Figure 19-15 on page 1074 is displayed.

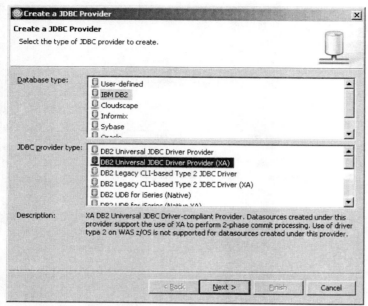

Figure 19-15   Creating a JDBC provider (page 1)

7. Select **IBM DB2** as the database type. Then select **DB2 Universal JDBC Driver Provider (XA)** as the provider type.

   > **Note:** Note that for our development purposes, the DB2 Universal JDBC Driver Provider (non XA) would work fine, because we will not need XA (two-phase commit) capabilities.

8. Click **Next** to proceed to the second page (see Figure 19-16 on page 1075).

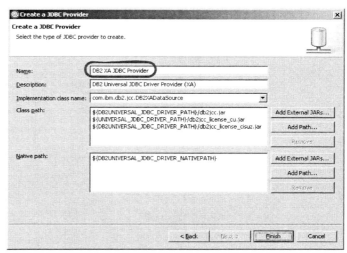

Figure 19-16   Creating a JDBC provider (page 2)

9. In this page, you only need to name the provider. We chose to call it DB2 XA JDBC Provider. The rest of the settings are good, so click **Finish**.

10. Go back to the Enhanced EAR Editor. With the new DB2 provider selected, click the **Add** button next to the defined data sources list (see Figure 19-17 on page 1076).

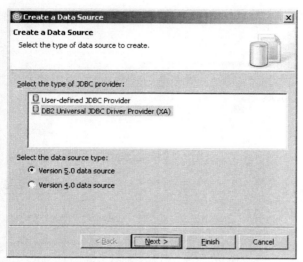

Figure 19-17   Create a Data Source (page 1)

11. Select **DB2 Universal JDBC Driver Provider (XA)** from the JDBC provider type list, and select the **Version 5.0 data source** radio button. Click **Next** to continue to the next page (see Figure 19-18 on page 1077).

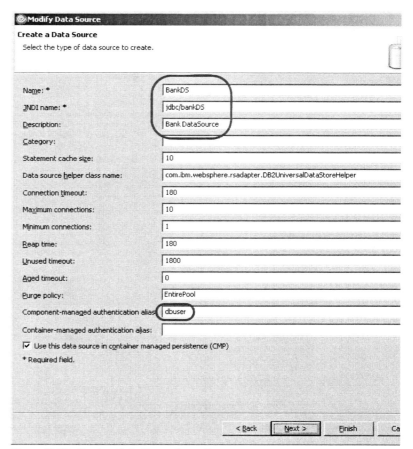

Figure 19-18 Create a Data Source (page 2)

12. Name the data source BankDS, give it the jdbc/bankDS JNDI name, fill out a description if you want, and select the **dbuser alias** from the "Component-managed authentication alias" drop-down box. Click **Next** to proceed to next wizard's last page, shown in Figure 19-19 on page 1078.

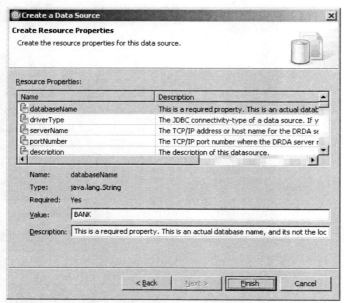

Figure 19-19   Create a Data Source (page 3)

13. Finally, just set the databaseName variable value to BANK, and click **Finish** to conclude the wizard. Save the deployment descriptor.

19.6.2 Configure server resources

Within IBM Rational Application Developer V6.0, the WebSphere Administrative Console is the primary interface for configuring WebSphere Application Server V6.0 test servers (local and remote). The Server editor replaces the Server Configuration editor from Version 5.x. The Server editor only contains details that point to the Rational Application Developer test server.

There are a couple of methods for accessing the WebSphere Administrative Server; however, in any case the WebSphere Application Server V6.0 test server must be started.

Once the WebSphere Application Server V6.0 test server is started, you can right-click the server and select **Run administrative server**. Alternatively, once the server is started you can enter one of the following URLs in a Web browser:

```
http://localhost:9060/ibm/console
http://localhost:9060/admin
```

Where 9060 is the port defined for the WebSphere Administrative Console for the application server in the WebSphere Profile.

19.6.3 Configure messaging resources

All Messaging Resources are set up through the WebSphere Administrative Console. This includes the Service Integration Bus, Bus Member, Messaging Engine, Bus Destinations, and JMS Destinations.

> **Note:** For details on how to configure messaging refer to the WebSphere Application Server online information found in the InfoCenter. Also, in this book our sample EJB application includes messaging. For details on configuring messaging for this sample, refer to Chapter 23, "Deploy enterprise applications" on page 1189.

For 2.1 message-driven beans, they must bind to ActivationSpec JNDI name, Authentication Alias, and Destination JNDI name. The Listenerport is only for 2.0 Message-driven beans.

For EJB or Web messaging client, the message references must bind to messaging resources (similar to V5).

19.6.4 Configure security

Security is enabled from the WebSphere Administrative Console for the test environment. User ID and password fields are used to authenticate to a running server to find status, publish applications, and stop or restart servers. A user ID and password are not used for the user ID and password the server runs under.

> **Note:** For more information on configuring WebSphere security, refer to *WebSphere Application Server V6 Security*, SG24-6316.

19.7 TCP/IP Monitor

The TCP/IP Monitor is a simple server that monitors all the requests and the responses between a Web browser and an application server. By default, when the TCP/IP Monitor is started, it listens for requests on port 9081, and then it forwards these requests to the application server on port 9080. For responses from the application server, the TCP/IP Monitor forwards them back.

For an example of using the TCP/IP Monitor refer to 17.4.5, "Monitor the Web Service using the TCP/IP Monitor" on page 976.

20

JUnit and component testing

The IBM Rational Application Developer V6.0 test framework is built upon the open source Eclipse Hyades test framework, and includes JUnit, which can be used for automated component testing. Rational Application Developer also includes profiling capabilities for memory, performance, and other execution time code analysis. We explore profiling in more detail in Chapter 24, "Profile applications" on page 1237.

In this chapter we introduce application testing concepts, and provide an overview on the Hyades and JUnit, as well as the features of Rational Application Developer for testing. In addition, we include working examples to demonstrate how to create, run, and automate component tests using JUnit, as well as demonstrate how to test Web applications.

The chapter is organized into the following sections:

- Introduction to application testing
- JUnit testing
- Automated component testing
- Web application testing

20.1 Introduction to application testing

Although the focus of this chapter is on component testing, we have included an introduction to testing concepts such as test phases and environments to put into context where component testing fits within the development cycle. Next we provide an overview on the Hyades and JUnit testing frameworks. The remainder of the chapter provides a working example of using the features of Hyades and JUnit within Rational Application Developer.

20.1.1 Test concepts

Within a typical development project, there are various types of testing performed within different phases of the development cycle. Project needs based on size, complexity, risks, and costs determine the levels of testing to be used. The focus of this chapter is on component testing.

Test phases

We have outlined the key test phases and categories as follows:

- Unit test: Unit tests are informal tests that are generally executed by the developers of the application code. They are often quite low-level in nature, and test the behavior of individual software components such as individual Java classes, servlets, or EJBs.

  Because unit tests are usually written and performed by the application developer, they tend to be white-box in nature—that is to say, they are written using knowledge about the implementation details and test-specific code paths. This is not to say all unit tests have to be written this way; one common practice is to write the unit tests for a component based on the component specification before developing the component itself. Both approaches are valid, and you may want to make use of both when defining your own unit testing policy.

- Component test: Component tests are used to verify particular components of the code before they are integrated into the production code base. Component tests can be performed on a developer's machine. Within the context of Rational Application Developer, a developer configures a test environment and supporting testing tools such as JUnit. Using the test environment, you can test customized code including Java beans, Enterprise JavaBeans, and JavaServer Pages without needing to deploy this code to a runtime system (WebSphere Application Server, WebSphere Portal).

- Build Verification Test (BVT): Members of the development team check their source code into the source control tool, and mark the components as part of a build level. The build team is responsible for building the application in a controlled environment based on the source code available in the source control system repository. The build team extracts the source code from the source control system, executes scripts to compile the source code (link if needed), packages the application, and tests the application build.

The test run on the application of the build produced is called a Build Verification Test (BVT). BVT is a predefined and documented test procedure to ensure that basic elements of the application are working properly before accepting the build and making it available to the test team for Function Verification Test (FVT) and/or System Verification Test (SVT).

- Function Verification Test (FVT): These tests are used to verify individual functions of an application. For example, you may verify if the taxes are being calculated properly within a banking application.

  Note: Within the Rational product family, the IBM Rational Function Tester is an ideal choice for this type of testing.

- System Verification Test (SVT): System tests are used to test a group of functions. A dedicated test environment should be used with the same system and application software as the target production environment. To get the best results from your tests, you need to find the most similar environment and involve as many components as possible, and verify that all functions are working properly in an integrated environment.

  Note: Within the Rational product family, the IBM Rational Manual Tester is an ideal choice for this type of testing.

- Performance test: Performance tests simulate the volume of traffic that you expect to have for the application(s) and ensure that it will support this stress and determine if the system performance is acceptable.

  Note: Within the Rational product family, the IBM Rational Performance Tester is an ideal choice for this type of testing.

- Customer Acceptance Test: This is a level of testing in which all aspects of an application or system are thoroughly and systematically tested to demonstrate that it meets business and non-functional requirements. The scope of a particular acceptance test is defined in the acceptance test plan.

Test environments

When sizing a project, it is important to consider the system requirements needed for your test environments. We have listed some common test environments that are used.

- Component test environment: This is often the development system and the focus of this chapter. In larger projects, we recommend that development teams have a dedicated test environment to be used as a sandbox to integrate team members' components before putting the code into the application build.
- Build verification test environment: This test environment is used to test the application produced from a controlled build. For example, a controlled build should have source control, build scripts, and packaging scripts for the application. The Build Verification Team will run a subset of tests, often known as regression tests, to verify basic functionality of the system that is representative to a wider scale of testing.
- System test environment: This test environment is used for FVT and SVT to verify the functionality of the application and integrate it with other components. There may be many test environments with teams of people focused on different aspects of the system.
- Staging environment: This staging environment is critical for all sizes of organizations. Prior to deploying the application to production, the staging environment is used to simulate the production environment. This environment can be used to perform customer acceptance tests.
- Production environment: This is the live runtime environment that customers will use to access your e-commerce Web site. In some cases, customer acceptance testing may be performed on the production environment. Ultimately, the customers will test the application. You will need a process to track customer problems and implement fixes to the application within this environment.

Calibration

By definition calibration is a set of gradations that show positions or values. When testing, it is important to establish a base line for such things as performance and functionality for regression testing. For example, when regression testing, you need to provide a set of tests that have been exercised on previous builds of the application, before you test the new build. This is also very important when setting entrance and exit criteria.

Test case execution and recording results

Sometimes the easiest way to know what broke the functionality of a component within the application is to know when the test case last worked. Recording the successes and failures of test cases for a designated application build is essential to having an accountable test organization and a quality application.

20.1.2 Benefits of unit and component testing

It may seem straightforward to many people as to why we test our code. Unfortunately, there are many people who do not understand the value of testing. Simply, we test our code and applications to find defects in the code, and to verify that changes we have made to existing code do not break that code. In this section, we highlight the key benefits of unit and component testing.

Perhaps it is more useful to look at the question from the opposite perspective, that is to say, why do developers *not* perform unit tests? In general, the simple answer is because it is too hard or because nobody forces them to. Writing an effective set of unit tests for a component is not a trivial undertaking. Given the pressure to deliver that many developers find themselves subjected to, the temptation to postpone the creation and execution of unit tests in favor of delivering code fixes or new functionality is often overwhelming.

In practice, this usually turns out to be a false economy, since developers very rarely deliver bug-free code, and the discovery of code defects and the costs associated with fixing them are simply pushed further out into the development cycle, which is inefficient. The best time to fix a code defect is immediately after the code has been written, while it is still fresh in the developer's mind.

Furthermore, a defect discovered during a formal testing cycle must be written up, prioritized, and tracked. All of these activities incur cost, and may mean that a fix is deferred indefinitely, or at least until it becomes critical.

Based on our experience, we believe that encouraging and supporting the development and regular execution of unit test cases ultimately leads to significant improvements in productivity and overall code quality. The creation of unit test cases does not have to be a burden. If done properly, developers can find the intellectual challenge quite stimulating and ultimately satisfying. The thought process involved in creating a test can also highlight shortcomings in a design, which may not otherwise have been identified when the main focus is on implementation.

We recommend that you take the time to define a unit testing strategy for your own development projects. A simple set of guidelines, and a framework that makes it easy to develop and execute tests, pays for itself surprisingly quickly.

Once you have decided to implement a unit testing strategy for your project, the first hurdles to overcome are the factors that dissuade developers from creating and running unit tests in the first place. A testing framework can help by making it easier to:

- Write tests
- Run tests
- Rerun a test after a change

Tests are easier to write, because a lot of the infrastructure code that you require to support every test is already available. A testing framework also provides a facility that makes it easier to run and re-run tests, perhaps via a GUI. The more often a developer runs tests, the quicker problems can be located and fixed, because the difference between the code that last passed a unit test, and the code that fails the test, is smaller.

Testing frameworks also provide other benefits:

- Consistency: Every developer is using the same framework, all of your unit tests work in the same way, can be managed in the same way, and report results in the same format.
- Maintenance: A framework has already been developed and is already in use in a number of projects, and you spend less time maintaining your testing code.
- Ramp-up time: If you select a popular testing framework, you may find that new developers coming into your team are already familiar with the tools and concepts involved.
- Automation: A framework may offer the ability to run tests unattended, perhaps as part of a daily or nightly build.

> **Automatic builds:** A common practice in many development environments is the use of daily builds. These automatic builds are usually initiated in the early hours of the morning by a scheduling tool.

20.1.3 Eclipse Hyades

The Eclipse Hyades Test framework provides integrated testing, tracing, and monitoring framework. Within the scope of Rational Application Developer, this includes three types of testing:

- JUnit testing
- Manual testing
- Web browser-based application testing

Although each of these areas of testing has its own unique set of tasks and concepts, two sets of topics are common to all three types of testing:

- Creation and use of data pools
- Creating a test deployment

The primary purpose of the Eclipse Hyades project is to provide a common framework for test tools, so that Eclipse-based test tools can easily communicate with one another and work together. As such, the primary users of Hyades are Eclipse test tool developers. In addition, Hyades has an important secondary audience—testers of HTTP-based applications.

20.2 JUnit testing

This section provides JUnit fundamentals as well as a working example of how to create and run a JUnit test within Rational Application Developer.

20.2.1 JUnit fundamentals

A unit test is a collection of tests designed to verify the behavior of a single unit with in a class. JUnit tests your class by scenario, and you have to create a testing scenario that uses the following elements:

- Instantiate an object.
- Invoke methods.
- Verify assertions.

> **Note:** An assertion is a statement that allows you to test the validity of any assumptions made in your code.

Example 20-1 lists a simple test case to verify the result count of a database query.

Example 20-1   Sample JUnit test method

```
//Test method
public void testGetAccount(){
      //instantiate
      Banking banking = new Banking();
      //invoke a method
      Account account = banking.getAccount("104-4001");
      //verify an assertion
      assertEquals(account.getAccountId(),"104-4001");
}
```

In JUnit, each test is implemented as a Java method that should be declared as *public void* and take no parameters. This method is then invoked from a test runner defined in a different package. If the test method name begins with `test...`, the test runner finds it automatically and runs it. This way, if you have a large number of test cases, there is no need to explicitly define all the test methods to the test runner.

TestCase class

The core class in the JUnit test framework is junit.framework.TestCase, of which all of the JUnit test cases inherit (see Example 20-2).

Example 20-2 Sample to highlight junit.framework.TestCase

```
import junit.framework.TestCase;

public class ITSOBankTest extends TestCase {

   /**
    * Constructor for ITSOBankTest.
    * @param arg0
    */
   public ITSOBankTest(String arg0) {
      super(arg0);
   }
```

As a best practice, your test case should have a constructor with a single string parameter. This is used as a test case name to display in the log and reports. All the reports will have the name of the test, which can make more sense than the entire java package and class name when seeing the report.

TestRunner class

Tests are executed using a test runner. To run this test in the text mode, use TestRunner, as seen in Example 20-3.

Example 20-3 Sample to highlight TestRunner

```
public static void main (String[] args) {
   junit.textui.TestRunner.run (ITSOBankTest);
}
```

TestSuite class

Test cases can be organized into test suites, managed by the junit.framework.TestSuite class. JUnit provides tools that allow every test in a suite to be run in turn and to report on the results.

TestSuite can extract the tests to be run automatically. To do so, you pass the class of your TestCase class to the TestSuite constructor, as seen in Example 20-4.

Example 20-4   Sample to highlight TestSuite class - TestSuite constructor
```
TestSuite suite = new TestSuite(ITSOBankTest.class);
```

This constructor creates a suite containing all methods starting with test, and that takes no arguments.

Alternatively, you can add new test cases using the addTest method of the TestSuite class, as seen in Example 20-5.

Example 20-5   Sample to highlight TestSuite class - addTest method
```
TestSuite suite = new TestSuite();
suite.addTest(new ITSOBankTest("testBankingConnection"));
suite.addTest(new ITSOBankTest("testBanking"));
```

20.2.2 Prepare for the sample

We use the Java Bank sample application created in Chapter 7, "Develop Java applications" on page 221, for the JUnit test working example.

Import the c:\6449code\java\BankJava.zip Project Interchange file into Rational Application Developer.

After importing the Java Bank sample, verify that it runs properly in the Java perspective (BankClient). For more information refer to 7.2.12, "Run the Java Bank application" on page 286.

> **Note:** The completed ITSOBankTest.java source used for the JUnit test case is included in the itso.bank.test package of the BankJava project.

20.2.3 Create the JUnit test case

Rational Application Developer contains wizards to help you build JUnit test cases and test suites. We will use this wizard to create the ITSOBankTest test class to test the AllTests JavaBean, which is a facade of a banking application that allows you to get information about your account, and withdraw and deposit funds.

Create the itso.bank.test.junit package

The completed version of the ITSOBankTest.java JUnit test case is included in the itso.bank.test package of the BankJava project. For the purposes of illustrating how to create a JUnit test case, we will create a new package named itso.bank.test.junit.

To create the itso.bank.test.junit package, which we will use for JUnit test cases, do the following:

1. Select the **BankJava** project, right-click, and select **New** → **Package**.
2. When the Java Package dialog appears, enter `itso.bank.test.junit` in the Name field and then click **Finish**.

Create a JUnit test case

To create a test case for the processTransaction method of the AllTests facade, do the following:

1. Open the Java perspective Package Explorer view.
2. Expand **BankJava** → **src** → **itso.bank.model.facade**.
3. Select **ITSOBank.java**, right-click, and select **New** → **JUnit Test Case**.
4. To use JUnit in Rational Application Developer, the JUnit packages need to be added to the build path of the Java project. This is automatically detected, as seen Figure 20-1. Click **Yes**.

> **Note:** In our example, since we imported the BankJava project with the existing JUnit test code, the JUnit packages have already been added to the Java build path for the BankJava project.

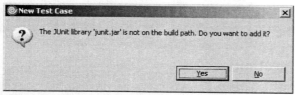

Figure 20-1   Adding JUnit library to the build class path

> **Tip:** Sometimes you may need to add the JUnit library manually to your project. In that case, right-click the project and select **Properties**. Select **Java Build Path** and switch to the **Libraries** tab. Add a JUNIT variable that points to the junit.jar file, which can be found in the following directory:
>
> <RAD_HOME>\eclipse\plugins\org.junit_3.8.1\junit.jar

5. When the JUnit Test Case dialog appears, we entered the following (as seen in Figure 20-2 on page 1092), and then clicked **Next**:
   - Source Folder: BankJava/src
   - Package: itso.bank.test.junit

     This is the package we created in "Create the itso.bank.test.junit package" on page 1090. It is a best practice to use a separate package for test cases.
   - Name: ITSOBankTest

     Test is concatenated to the original source file name *ITSOBank*.
   - Superclass: junit.framework.TestCase

     This is the default since we are creating a JUnit test case.
   - Check **public static void main(String[] args)**.
   - Check **Add TestRunner statement for:** and select **text ui**.

     This creates a main method in the test case, and adds a line of code that executes the TestRunner to run the test methods and output the results.
   - Check **setUp()**.

     This creates a stub for this method in the generated file.
   - We accepted the default values for the remaining fields.

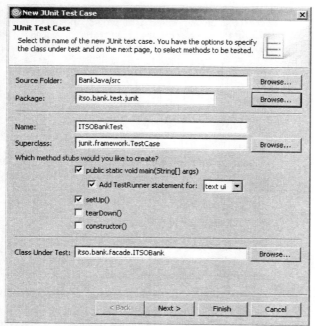

Figure 20-2   Create a JUnit test case

- *main* is the method that is executed to start the JUnit test case as a Java application. This is not required, as within Rational Application Developer, we can run Java classes as JUnit test cases.
- The "Add TestRunner statement for" check box has three options: text ui, swing ui, and awt ui. These options add a single line of code to the main method to run the test case and output the results in three different user interfaces. Text is plain text, while swing and awt are graphical outputs.
- *setUp* is a method that is executed before the tests.
- *tearDown* is a method that is executed after the tests.
- *constructor* is constructor stub for the class.
- *Class Under Test:* This is the Java class that this new test case is testing.

Note: A *stub* is a skeleton method, generated so that you can add the body of the method yourself.

6. When the Test Methods dialog appears, we checked the **processTransaction** method, as seen in Figure 20-3, and then clicked **Finish**.

> **Tip:** Try to think of the stub methods for a few scenarios to test in your test case. You can add as many methods to the generated file as you would like, and the naming conventions are up to you. This page of the wizard gets you started.

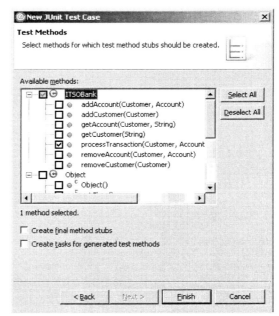

Figure 20-3 JUnit - Select test methods

The wizard will generate the ITSOBankTest.java and open the file in an editor. This file can be used to test the ITSOBank class. All that remains to do is to write the testing code.

Complete the setUp and tearDown methods

Typically, you run several tests in one test case. To make sure there are no side effects between test runs, the JUnit framework provides the setUp and tearDown methods. Every time the test case is run, setUp is called at the start and tearDown at the end of the run.

1. Expand **BankJava** → **src** → **itso.bank.test.junit**.
2. Double-click **ITSOBankTest.java** to open the file in the Java editor.
3. Add the private object code highlighted in Example 20-6 to ITSOBankTest.java.

   This private object will be instantiated before starting the test and is available for use in the test methods.

Example 20-6   Add private object to ITSOBankTest.java
```
public class ITSOBankTest extends TestCase {

    Bank bank;
    Customer customer1;
    Account account11, account12;
```

4. Add the code highlighted in Example 20-7 to the setUp method of ITSOBankTest.java.

   The code is used to create an instance of the Bank facade and instantiate customer and account.

Example 20-7   Add code to setUp method
```
protected void setUp() throws Exception {
    super.setUp();

    bank = new ITSOBank();
        try {
            customer1 = new Customer("111-11-1111","John","Ganci");
            bank.addCustomer(customer1);
            System.out.println ( "Successfully Added customer1. "+customer1);
            account11 = new Account("11",new BigDecimal(10000.00D));
            bank.addAccount(customer1,account11);
            account12 = new Account("12",new BigDecimal(11234.23));
            bank.addAccount(customer1,account12);
            System.out.println("Successfully Added 2 Accounts to Customer1... ");
            System.out.println(customer1);

        }catch(InvalidCustomerException e){
            e.printStackTrace();
        }
}
```

5. Resolve imports.

As code is added, you will need to update the imports accordingly. Sometimes this is done automatically by Rational Application Developer, sometimes you can simply press Ctrl+Shift+O and add the imports, and other times you may need to manually add the imports.

6. Save the changes to the ITSOBankTest.java file by clicking **File** → **Save**.

In our example, there is no tearDown method (not needed). This method could be used to clean up tasks such as disconnecting from a database.

Complete the test methods

When the ITSOBankTest.java was generated, the test methods were added in stub form. This section describes the steps to complete the test methods.

1. Complete the testProcessTransaction method by adding the code highlighted in Example 20-8.

   This test method adds a new customer and account, then deposits funds into that account. Then it retrieves the account balance again and verifies that the new balance is the sum of the original balance and the deposited amount.

Example 20-8   Add code to the testProcessTransaction method

```
public void testProcessTransaction() {
   try {
      BigDecimal balanceBefore = new BigDecimal( account11.getBalance().toString() );
      BigDecimal debitAmount = new BigDecimal(2399.99D);

      bank.processTransaction( customer1, account11, debitAmount,TransactionType.DEBIT);

      assertEquals(account11.getBalance(), balanceBefore.subtract(debitAmount));

   }catch(InvalidCustomerException e){
      e.printStackTrace();
      fail("InvalidCustomerException. Message: " + e.getMessage());
   }catch(InvalidAccountException e){
      e.printStackTrace();
      fail("InvalidAccountException. Message: " + e.getMessage());
   }catch(InvalidTransactionException e){
      e.printStackTrace();
      fail("InvalidTransactionException. Message: " + e.getMessage());
   }
}
```

2. Add a new test method called testInvalidProcessTransaction, as seen in Example 20-9 on page 1096.

   This method verifies that if you try withdrawing more than the account holds, you will receive the proper InvalidTransactionException exception.

Example 20-9 Add new testInvalidProcessTransaction method

```
public void testInvalidProcessTransaction(){
   try {
      BigDecimal balanceBefore = new BigDecimal(account11.getBalance().toString());
      BigDecimal debitAmount = new BigDecimal(12399.99D);

      bank.processTransaction(customer1, account11, debitAmount,TransactionType.DEBIT);

      fail("Transaction should not be processed. Negative balance");

   }catch(InvalidCustomerException e){
      e.printStackTrace();
      fail("InvalidCustomerException. Message: " + e.getMessage());
   }catch(InvalidAccountException e){
      e.printStackTrace();
      fail("InvalidAccountException. Message: " + e.getMessage());
   }catch(InvalidTransactionException e){
      assertTrue(true);
   }
}
```

3. Save the changes to the ITSOBankTest.java file by clicking **File → Save**.

   This test case is now ready to run and can already be executed from the context menu (**Run → JUnit Test**).

   Before continuing on to run the JUnit test, we need to review the assert and fail methods that we used in our test. In addition, we will also introduce the concept of a *test suite*.

   ### JUnit-supplied assert and fail methods
   The assertEquals, assertTrue, and fail methods are provided by the JUnit framework.

   JUnit provides a number of methods that can be used to assert conditions and fail a test if the condition is not met. These methods are inherited from the class junit.framework.Assert (see Table 20-1).

   Table 20-1 JUnit assert methods

Method name	Description
assertEquals	Assert that two objects or primitives are equal. Compares objects using equals, and compares primitives using ==.
assertNotNull	Assert that an object is not null.
assertNull	Assert that an object is null.

Method name	Description
assertSame	Assert that two objects refer to the same object. Compares using ==.
assertTrue	Assert that a boolean condition is true.
fail	Fails the test.

All of these methods include an optional String parameter that allows the writer of a test to provide a brief explanation of why the test failed. This message is reported along with the failure when the test is executed. Example 20-10 includes an assertEquals sample message that will fail for the working example.

Example 20-10   Sample assertEquals message

```
assertEquals(account11.getBalance().toString(), balanceBefore.add(debitAmount).toString());
```

Create a TestSuite

A TestSuite is used to run one or more test cases at once. Rational Application Developer contains a simple wizard to create a test suite as follows:

1. Expand **BankJava** → **src**
2. Right-click **itso.bank.test.junit**, and select **New** → **Other** → **Java** → **JUnit** → **JUnit Test Suite**. Click **Next**.

   Note: You may need to check **Show All Wizards** if not accessed previously.

3. When the JUnit Test Suite dialog appears, we entered the following, as seen in Figure 20-4 on page 1098, and then clicked **Finish**:
   - Source Folder: `BankJava/src`
   - Package: `itso.bank.test.junit`
   - Test suite: `AllTests`

     By default, the test suite is called AllTests. If you had multiple test classes, you could include them in one suite. We currently have a single test class only, but you can add to the suite later.
   - Check **ITSOBankTest**.
   - Check **public static void main(String[] args)**.
   - Check **Add TestRunner statement for:** and select **text ui**.

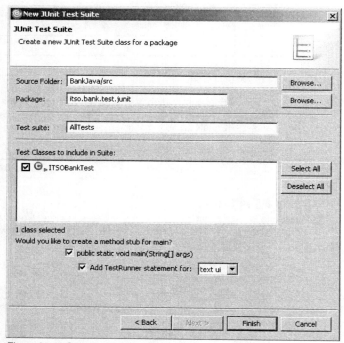

Figure 20-4 Sample JUnit Test Suite settings

The generated AllTests.java source opens, and here we can add more test classes later by using the suite.addTestSuite() method.

This code uses the text-based Test Runner tool in the JUnit framework, which runs the tests and reports the results.

4. No changes are required this time. Close the AllTests.java file.

In our example we only have a single test, and thus test suite is not required. However, as you add more and more test cases, a test suite quickly becomes a more practical way to manage your unit testing.

20.2.4 Run the JUnit test case

This section includes a couple of scenarios for running the JUnit test case. First, we examine the JUnit view and console output if the JUnit test was run after completing the test methods (before "JUnit-supplied assert and fail methods" on page 1096). Second, we add asserts to have the test create a failure (not error).

Run JUnit test case
Now that the JUnit test case has been created (no assert failure), it can be run as follows:

1. Expand **BankJava** → **src** → **itso.bank.test.junit**.
2. Right-click **ITSOBankTest.java**, and select **Run** → **JUnit Test**.

   For our working example, you should see a JUnit view like Figure 20-5 with the results of the test run (no failures, no errors).

Figure 20-5   JUnit view - No assert condition (no failures, no errors)

> **Tip:** To run just one test case, select the test case class and then **Run** → **JUnit Test**. To run all the test cases, select the test suite class (by default AllTests) and then the same action.
>
> Note the Rerun Last Test button on the JUnit view menu bar ( ).

Modify and run the JUnit test case with assert failures
In the previous example we tested only for success. A test is considered to be *successful* if the test method returns normally. A test *fails* if one of the methods from the Assert class signals a failure. An *error* indicates that an unexpected exception was raised by the test method, or the setUp or tearDown method was invoked before or after it.

The JUnit view is more interesting when an error or failure occurs. This section describes how to modify both methods in ITSOBankTest to include assert test failures.

1. Expand **BankJava** → **src** → **itso.bank.test.junit**.
2. Double-click **ITSOBankTest.java** to open the file in the Java editor.
3. Modify the testProcessTransaction method by changing the transaction type from DEBIT to CREDIT, as seen in Example 20-11, so the balance will not match, and thus get an assert failure.

Example 20-11   Modified testProcessTransaction method - CREDIT instead of DEBIT

```
bank.processTransaction(customer1,account11,debitAmount,TransactionType.CREDIT);
```

4. Modify the testInvalidProcessTransaction methods so that the transaction is attempted on an account that is unassigned to customer, as listed in Example 20-12.

Example 20-12   Modified testInvalidProcessTransaction method - Unassigned customer

```
bank.processTransaction(new Customer("374-594-3994", "a", "b"),
account12,debitAmount,TransactionType.DEBIT);
```

5. Run the modified JUnit ITSOBankTest.java test case.

   Select **ITSOBankTest.java**, right-click, and select **Run** → **JUnit Test**.

   Figure 20-6 shows the JUnit view when the test case is run as a JUnit test again. This time, failures are displayed as well as failure trace information for each failure.

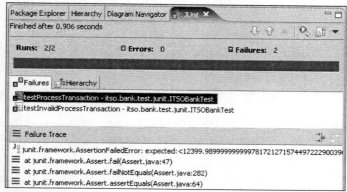

Figure 20-6   Junit view with failures

6. Select the **testProcessTransaction** method from the failures list.
7. This will update the Failure Trace window to show the stack trace of the failure. This makes it easy for you to track where the failure occurred. Double-clicking the entry in the Failure Trace list takes you to the specified line in the specified Java source file.

   Alternatively, the ITSOBankTest class can be run as a Java application by selecting **Run** → **Java Application**, which executes the main method and uses the TestRunner from the JUnit framework to run and output the test results in the console.
8. Example 20-13 displays the Console output from the test case.

   In this example, there was one success and one failure. The failure occurred when running testProcessTransaction.

Example 20-13 Console output

```
.F.Debit: Could not process Transaction. Reason: Negative/Zero Debit Amount.
Amount: $12399.99

Time: 0.02
There was 1 failure:
1) testProcessTransaction(itso.junit.bank.model.facade.java.ITSOBankTest)
     junit.framework.AssertionFailedError:
     expected:<12399.989999999997817212715744972229003906 25> but was:
        <7600.01000000000021827872842550277709960937 5>
...
FAILURES!!!
Tests run: 2,  Failures: 1,  Errors: 0
```

Each dot (.) in the first line of the output represents the start of a test. We have two tests in our test case, so there are two dots. An "F" indicates a failure, so one test failed. There is no special symbol printed for a passed test. Once all the tests have completed, the test runner shows how long they took to run and provides a summary of the results.

9. Once the error is corrected, the output should look like the Console view displayed in Example 20-14.

Example 20-14 New console output

```
..Debit: Could not process Transaction. Reason: Negative/Zero Debit Amount.
Amount: $12399.99

Time: 0.02

OK (2 tests)
```

Test the Web applications

You can also create test cases that run against one of the Web projects, BankBasicWeb or BankStrutsWeb. However, when testing anything that runs inside a servlet container, a testing framework like *Cactus* could make the testing much easier.

> **Note:** Cactus is an open source sub-project in the Apache Software Foundation's Jakarta Project. It is a simple framework for unit testing server-side Java code such as servlets, EJBs, Tag Libs, Filters, etc.
>
> The objective of Cactus is to lower the cost of writing tests for server-side code. Cactus supports so-called white box testing of server-side code. It extends and uses JUnit.

20.3 Automated component testing

The automated component testing features in Rational Application Developer allows you to create, edit, deploy, and run automated tests for Java components, EJBs, and Web Services. These features comply with the UML Testing Profile standard and they use the JUnit testing framework.

All the tests that you create with Rational Application Developer are extensions of JUnit tests. The automated component testing features extend JUnit with the following families of primitives:

- Initialization points (IP): Initialize variables or attributes of a component-under-test (CUT).
- Validation actions (VA): Verify the validity of a variable.
- Timing constraints (TC): Measure the duration of method calls.

A major difference between validation actions and the original JUnit assert methods is that with validation actions, failed assertions do not stop the execution of the entire JUnit test suite.

20.3.1 Prepare for the sample

This section outlines the tasks to complete the preparation for the automating component testing sample.

IBM Rational Agent Controller installation

The IBM Rational Agent Controller must be installed and running as a prerequisite to automated component testing.

For information on installing the IBM Rational Agent Controller included with Rational Application Developer, refer to "IBM Rational Agent Controller V6 installation" on page 1382.

Import the sample application

We use the sample Java Bank application for the automated component testing sample. If you have not already done so, import the c:\6449code\java\BankJava.zip Project Interchange file. This is the same project that was used to implement the JUnit tests in 20.2, "JUnit testing" on page 1087.

20.3.2 Create a test project

To test your components, you must first create a test project. The test project is linked to one or several development projects that contain the components you want to test. Development projects can include Java development projects, Enterprise Application projects, or Dynamic Web Projects. The components targeted for each test are known as the component-under-test (CUT).

To create a new component test project, do the following:

1. Select **File → New Project**.
2. When the New Project dialog appears, select **Component Test → Component Test Project** and then click **Next**.
3. Enter `BankComponentTest` in the Name field and then click **Next**.
4. When the Define the scope of the component test project dialog appears, check **BankJava** and then click **Finish**.
5. When the Confirm Perspective Switch dialog appears, click **Yes**.

20.3.3 Create a Java component test

To create a Java Component test, do the following:

1. From the Test perspective Test Navigator view, select the **BankComponentTest** project.
2. Select **File → New → Other**.
3. Select **Component Test → Java → Java Component Test**, and then click **Next**.
4. When the Select a test project dialog appears, select **BankComponentTest** and click **Next**.
5. If you completed the JUnit example found in 20.2, "JUnit testing" on page 1087, a Metrics Analysis pop-up dialog appears notifying you that the

ITSOBankTest class is not a valid class for further testing because it extends TestCase. This makes sense and we do not need to test this class. Click **OK**.

6. When the Select components under test dialog appears, do the following (as seen in Figure 20-7 on page 1105) and then click **Next**:
   - Check **Customer**.
   - Check **Account**.
   - Check **ITSOBank**.

Figure 20-7 on page 1105 displays the components with highlighted values or high numerical values considered high-priority test candidates.

A static analysis was performed on the Java source files associated with the BankJava project. These files were selected during the creation of the test and help to define the scope of the test. The list of files in the test project can be updated later by modifying the *Test Scope* properties of the project.

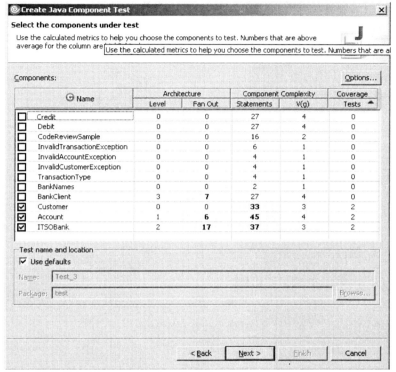

Figure 20-7   Select the components under test

7. When the Select a test pattern dialog appears, select **Scenario-based pattern** and then click **Next**.

8. When the Define a test scenario dialog appears, do the following, as seen in Figure 20-8 on page 1106:

   a. Add an instance of each class-under-test by double-clicking each constructor from the list on the left side. For our example, double-click each of the following: **ITSOBank**, **Customer**, and **Account**.

   b. On the right side of the dialog, double-click a particular method to be included in the test scenario. Double-click **addAccount**, **processTransaction**, and **addCustomer**.

   c. When you are finished building the scenario, click **Finish**.

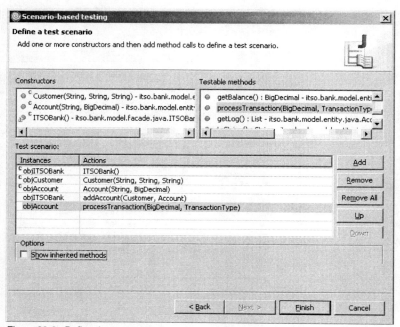

Figure 20-8   Define the test scenario

We have now created a scenario-based test, and a single test case has been created within the test suite. In the test behavior code, the test case is implemented as a single JUnit test method.

The Test Overview dialog appears, as seen in Figure 20-9 on page 1107. From this page, you can edit the name of test, add a description of the test, and open test behavior code in the Java editor.

Click **/BankComponentTest/Behavior/test/Test.java** next to Behavior, to view and start editing the test code.

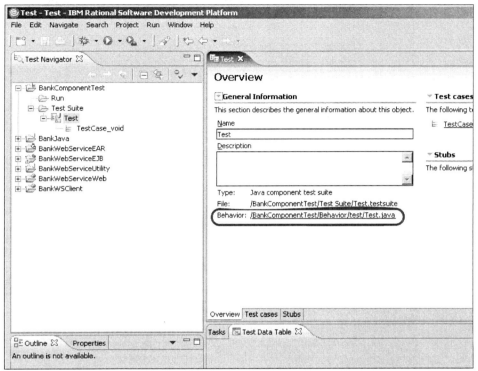

Figure 20-9   Component test for processing a transaction

20.3.4 Complete the component test code

To complete the component test, do the following:

1. The Java test file should be opened in the editor. If not opened, do the following:

   a. From the Test Perspective Test Navigator view, expand **Component Test** → **Test Suite**.

   b. Double-click **Test** to open in the editor.

2. Click **/BankComponentTest/Behavior/test/Test.java** next to Behavior, to view and start editing the test code.

3. Clean up the import statements.

   When the Test.java file is open, you will notice a minor problem with the imports. To fix the import issue, do the following:

   a. Click **import >** to expand the import statements.
   b. Click the twistie next to the import line and then delete the last unnecessary import statement, as seen in Figure 20-10.

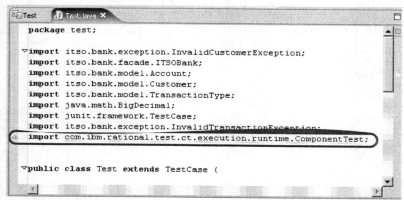

Figure 20-10 Clean up the import statements

4. Modify the code to implement the desired tests. For example:
   - Use test data tables to define test data specific to your test.
   - Use the Java editor to edit the test behavior code.
   - Create stubs for classes that the code you are testing interacts with.

   a. To view a test data table, click any test method in the editor.
   b. Maximize the Test Data Table view.

      We can now see the outline of the test. On the right-hand side there is the Test Data column, which is further divided into the In data column and Expected test result column. Note that some of the cells are plain white and the others are shaded. Our next task is to fill in the empty white cells.

   c. Fill in the test input data in the In column, as shown in Figure 20-11 on page 1109.

      You can define the data ranges for the id and balance fields by right-clicking the field and selecting **Define Set** from the context menu.

Note: Some of the entries will not be present until after modifying the code in the next step, at which time we enter the remaining *In* values.

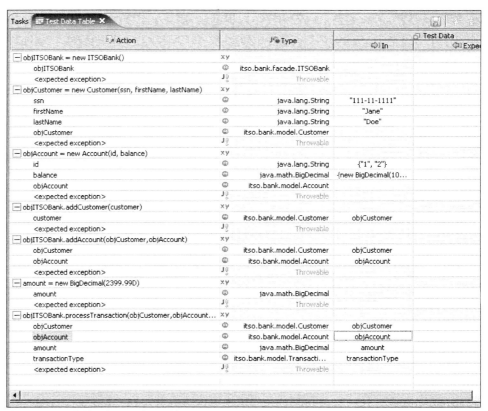

Figure 20-11 Editing the test data table

d. Save your changes by clicking the diskette icon on the toolbar, or by pressing Ctrl+S. There is a synchronization link between the table and the code, but not everything in the code gets displayed in the test table.

Note that you need to enclose the strings and define the data types. Note also that the local *amount* variable gets assigned in the Action part of the test table and that the *type* variable does not appear.

5. Example 20-15 displays the test behavior code for Test.java. The local variables should be assigned based on the actions of the previous steps.

Example 20-15   Modified test behavior code for Test.java

```
public class Test extends TestCase {

    public void test_void() throws InvalidCustomerException,
            InvalidAccountException, InvalidTransactionException {
        ITSOBank objITSOBank = null;
        Customer objCustomer = null;
        Account objAccount = null;
        objITSOBank = new ITSOBank();
        String ssn = "";
        String firstName = "";
        String lastName = "";
        objCustomer = new Customer(ssn,firstName,lastName);
        String id = "";
        BigDecimal balance = null;
        objAccount = new Account(id, balance);
        Customer customer = null;
        objITSOBank.addCustomer(customer);
        objITSOBank.addAccount(objCustomer,objAccount);
        BigDecimal amount = null;
        amount = new BigDecimal(2399.99D);
        TransactionType transactionType = null;
        transactionType = TransactionType.DEBIT;
        objITSOBank.processTransaction(objCustomer,objAccount,
            amount,transactionType);
    }
}
```

6. Now that the code has been modified, If you have not done so already, go back to the Test Data Table and enter the In values listed in Figure 20-11 on page 1109.

7. Save the modifications to the Test.java and close the file.

20.3.5 Run the component test

We can now run the test and view the results. A test runs with the behavior code and uses the additional input data you have supplied for it in a test data table.

As we noticed, you can also supply sets or ranges of values in the test data table. In that case, running a single test results in the running of many individual tests;

for example, in our case where we supplied two values for two arguments, running the test results in four individual tests.

1. From the Test Navigator, expand **BankComponentTest**.
2. Right-click **Test Suite**, and select **Run** → **Component Test**.
3. After the test is completed, expand the **BankComponentTest** → **Run** folder until you find the individual tests, as seen in Figure 20-12.

   We can see that two tests passed and two tests had some kind of failure.

Figure 20-12   Selecting test result

4. Click an individual test to display the test results in the Test Data Comparator.

   The Test Data Comparator is quite similar to the Test Data Table. There are now three columns for test data:

   – Input data (including derived input)
   – Expected output
   – Actual result

   The actual results column appears in green when the actual result matches the expected result, and in red when there are discrepancies.

   As you can see in Figure 20-13 on page 1112, we have discrepancies, as can be expected, because the first balance was too low, and because the second account was not assigned to a customer.

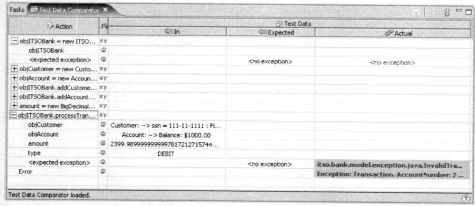

Figure 20-13   Test Data Comparator

5. Try to achieve a 100 percent successful pass by modifying the input in the Test Data Table and Java editor and running the component test again.

> **Note:** For additional information on automated component testing, we recommend that you refer to the Rational Application Developer online help and the tutorial, which can be accessed by clicking **Help** → **Tutorial Gallery** → **Do and Learn** → **Test Java components**.

20.4 Web application testing

In addition to providing a common framework for test tools and support for JUnit test generation, Hyades includes features allowing you to test Web-based applications.

The Hyades framework has an important secondary audience—testers of HTTP-based applications. You can perform the following Web-testing tasks with Hyades, without modifying the framework:

- Recording a test: The test creation wizard starts the Hyades proxy recorder, which records your interactions with a browser-based application. When you stop recording, the wizard starts a test generator, which creates a test from the recorded session.

- Editing a test: You can inspect and modify a test prior to compiling and running it.

- Generating an executable test: Follow this procedure to generate an executable test. Before a test can be run, the test's Java source code must be generated and compiled. This process is called code generation.
- Running a test.
- Analyzing test results: At the conclusion of a test run you see an execution history, including a test verdict, and you can request two graphical reports showing a page response time and a page hit analysis.

20.4.1 Preparing for the sample

As a prerequisite to the Web application testing sample, you will need to have the WebSphere Application Server V6.0 Test Environment or runtime server installed and running. We will run a simple test using the WebSphere Administration Console.

1. Open the J2EE perspective.
2. Click the **Servers** view.
3. Select **WebSphere Application Server v6.0**, right-click, and select **Start**.

20.4.2 Create a Java project

To create a Java project, do the following:

1. Open the Java perspective.
2. Create a new Java project to hold the test case behavior and other test elements.
    a. Select **File** → **New** → **Project**.
    b. Select **Java Project** and then click **Next**.
3. Enter `ITSO HTTP Test` as the project name and click **Finish**.
4. Create a source folder under the project.
    a. Right-click **ITSO HTTP Test** and select **New** → **Source folder**.
    b. Enter `src` as the folder name and click **Finish**.

20.4.3 Create (record) a test

We use the WebSphere Administration Console to demonstrate how to record a HTTP recording for a Web application (could be any application).

We now create a simple HTTP test case in Rational Application Developer, as follows:

1. Open the Test perspective Test Navigator view.
2. Right-click **ITSO HTTP Test** and select **New** → **Test Artifact**.
3. When the New Test Artifact dialog appears, select **Test** → **Recording** → **HTTP Proxy Recorder**, and then click **Next**.
4. Select the **ITSO HTTP Test** container, enter adminconsole in the Recording file name field, and then click **Finish**.

   A progress dialog box opens while your browser starts. Your browser settings are updated and a local proxy is enabled. If you are using a browser other than Microsoft Internet Explorer, see the online help for detailed instructions on how to configure the proxy. Recording has now started.

5. Start the WebSphere Administrative Console by entering the following URL in a Web browser:

   http://localhost:9060/admin

   Or:

   http://localhost:9060/ibm/console

6. Log in to the console (security is not enabled, so any user ID will work) and access some pages. A small set is sufficient.
7. When done, close the Web browser to stop recording.

   Alternatively, stop the recording by clicking the **Stop** button on the right side of the Recorder Control viewer, as seen in Figure 20-14.

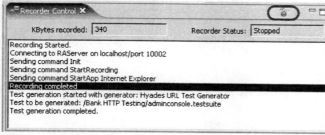

Figure 20-14   Recorder Control view

Notice the message Recording completed in the Recorder Control view seen in Figure 20-14 after closing the browser.

20.4.4 Edit the test

The Hyades URL test suite now appears under the HTTP Test project. We can inspect and modify it before compiling and running it. The test is not Java code yet, but we can check the requests and behavior and modify them.

1. Click the **Behavior** tab of the Hyades URL Test Suite.
2. Change the behavior of the test. For example, you may want to adjust the number of iterations or think times for some of the requests, as seen in Figure 20-15.
3. Save and close the file.

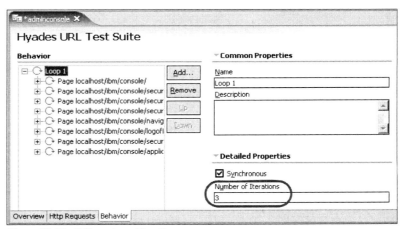

Figure 20-15   Edit number of iterations

20.4.5 Generate an executable test

Before a test can be run, the test's Java source code must be generated and compiled. This process is called *code generation*.

The compiled code is stored in the *src* folder in the same Java project as the test. Once the test's Java source code is generated, the Eclipse IDE automatically compiles the source code into an executable test.

1. In the Test Navigator, right-click **adminconsole** and select **Generate**.
2. When the JUnit Test Definition Code Generation dialog appears, we entered the following and then clicked **Finish**:
   – Java Project: ITSO HTTP Test

- Source Folder: `src`

The code is now generated and compiled.

3. To examine the code, switch to the Java perspective and you will find Adminconsole.java JUnit source in the src/test package.

20.4.6 Create a deployment definition

Before a test can be run, it must be deployed. That requires creating a *deployment* definition for the test.

A test deployment definition typically consists of one or more pairs of test *artifacts* and *locations*. Test artifacts are test suites and data pools. A location identifies the computer where you run the test suite. Hyades reads the pairing and deploys the test artifacts on the computer specified.

You can also create a test deployment that specifies only a location and does not specify test artifacts. Such a deployment is convenient when you want to run a specific test suite on a specific computer. Since we have only one test suite in our test, we need to define one deployment definition containing one location.

1. Open the Test perspective Test Navigator view.
2. Right-click **ITSO HTTP Test**, and select **New** → **Test Artifact**.
3. When the New Test Artifact dialog appears, select **Test** → **Test Elements** → **Deployment** and click **Next**.
4. When the New Deployment dialog appears, select **ITSO HTTP Test** as the folder, and enter `deployment` in the File name field, and then click **Next**.
5. When the New Deployment dialog appears, click **Next**. We have only one test suite and it will be automatically included in the deployment.
6. When the New Deployment - define the locations dialog appears, click **Add**.
   a. In the Add Location Association dialog, select **Create a new resource** and click **Next**.
   b. In the New Location dialog, select **ITSO HTTP Test** as the folder and enter `location` as the filename.
   c. Click **Finish**.
7. In the New Deployment - define the locations dialog, make sure the location entry appears in the list of locations, and then click **Finish**.

You should now have the structure in Test Navigator seen in Figure 20-16 on page 1117.

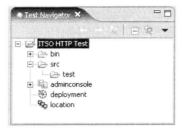

Figure 20-16   Testing artifacts in Test Navigator

20.4.7 Run the test

The test code has now been generated and deployment has been defined. To run the test, do the following:

1. Open the Test perspective Test Navigator.
2. Right-click **adminconsole**, and select **Run → Run**.
3. When the Create, manage, and run configurations dialog appears, select **Hyades URL Test** and then click **New**.
4. A new test configuration, initially named New_Configuration is created. Change the name to ITSO URL Test.
5. In Select Test to run, navigate to the **ITSO HTTP Test** project and click **adminconsole**.

   The deployment definition should now appear under the deployments selection, as seen in Figure 20-17 on page 1118.

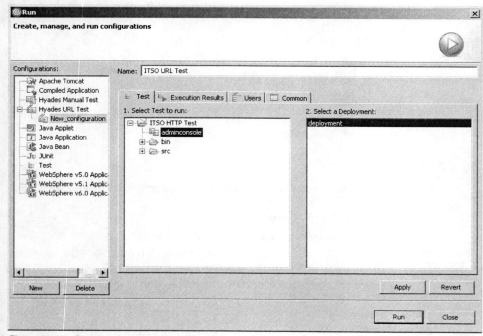

Figure 20-17   Creating the run configuration

6. Select the **Users** tab.

   You may set the number of users to emulate in the run. If you are running everything locally, do not use too high a number.

7. When done click **Apply**.

8. Select the test case to run, such as **adminconsole**, and then click **Run**.

20.4.8 Analyze the test results

When the test run is finished, the execution result ▦ appears in the Test Navigator. If you execute the test multiple times, a running sequence number is appended to the result, as seen in Figure 20-18 on page 1119.

Figure 20-18   Test execution results

1. In order to view the Page Response Time and the Page Hit Rate reports, you need to install Adobe's Scalable Vector Graphics (SVG) browser plug-in. You can get this free viewer from the Adobe Web site at:

   http://www.adobe.com/svg/viewer/install/main.html

2. Double-click the execution, and the execution summary is displayed.

   The execution summary gives the test's verdict, the time recording started, and the time recording stopped. The verdict may be one of the following:

   – fail: One or more requests returned a code of 400 or greater, or the server could not be reached during playback.

   – pass: No request returned a code of 400 or greater.

   – inconclusive: The test did not run to completion.

   – error: The test itself contains an error.

   For tests that fail, the Events tab shows you the overall verdict and allows you to drill down to the requests in each page that returned a fail code.

   Two analysis reports are available.

   – Page Response Time report: Bar graph showing the seconds required to process each page in the test and the average response time for all pages.

   – Page Hit Rate report: Bar graph showing the hits per second to each page and the total hit rate for all pages.

3. To generate the reports from the execution result, right-click the **adminconsole** test suite (the last adminconsole entry with the icon) and select **Report** from the context menu.

4. When the New report dialog appears, select **HTTP Page Response Time** and then click **Next**.
5. When the New Report - Report dialog appears, select **ITSO HTTP Test** and enter `adminconsole page response time` as the file name, and click **Finish**.
6. If you have multiple test results, the HTTP Report Generator - select result for report dialog appears next. Select a result you want to base the report on and click **Finish**.

A report like the one in Figure 20-19 should appear.

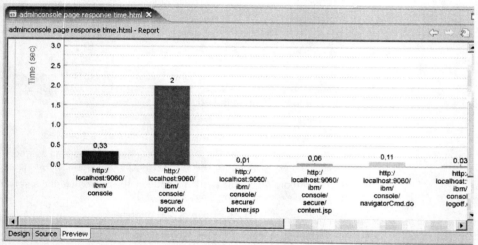

Figure 20-19   HTTP Page Response Time

The exact numbers displayed at the top of the bars do not appear unless you click one of the bars.

If you need to access the report later, you can find it under the Package Explorer view: `adminconsole page response time.html`.

21

Debug local and remote applications

The debug tooling included with IBM Rational Application Developer V6.0 can be used to debug a wide range of applications (languages and environments) either in a local integrated test environment or on remote servers such as WebSphere Application Server or WebSphere Portal.

In this chapter, we highlight the new and enhanced debug tooling features included with Rational Application Developer, as well as provide examples for using the debug tooling. In the first example, we demonstrate how to use the debugger within the Workbench and integrated WebSphere Application Server V6.0 Test Environment with Web application. Second, we describe how to debug a Web application on a remote WebSphere Application Server.

This chapter describes the following topics:

- Introduction to the debug tooling
- Prepare for the sample
- Debug a Web application on a local server
- Debug a Web application on a remote server

21.1 Introduction to the debug tooling

This section provides an overview of the following new and enhanced debug tooling features included in IBM Rational Application Developer V6.0. The debug tooling can be used on local or remote test environments.

- Summary of new Version 6 features
- Supported languages and environments
- General functionality
- Drop-to-frame
- View Management
- XSLT debugger

> **Note:** Most of the features outlined in this section include screen shots to display the menu options and dialogs. If you want to see these features on a live Rational Application Developer system, we suggest that you jump ahead to 21.3, "Debug a Web application on a local server" on page 1132. By completing the setup for this section, you will have a Web application imported to test these new and enhanced features.

21.1.1 Summary of new Version 6 features

The main areas of enhancements in Version 6 are as follows:

- Debug many different languages and environments, including mixed languages.
- User interface enhancements to make debugging the application easier.
- XSLT debugger now utilizes Eclipse Debug framework. This provides a common look and feel for the debuggers in Rational Application Developer.
- Debug option available from context menu.

    Figure 21-1 on page 1123 displays the Debug configuration options.

- Debug from any perspective.

    When you run an application using Debug on Server, you will be prompted as to whether you want to switch to the Debug perspective. You can choose to debug in the current perspective (Web, Java, etc.) as well as the Debug perspective.

- New debug predefined configuration options.

    For a list of new predefined configurations see Figure 21-1 on page 1123. You may choose to use an existing configuration or define your own settings for your application.

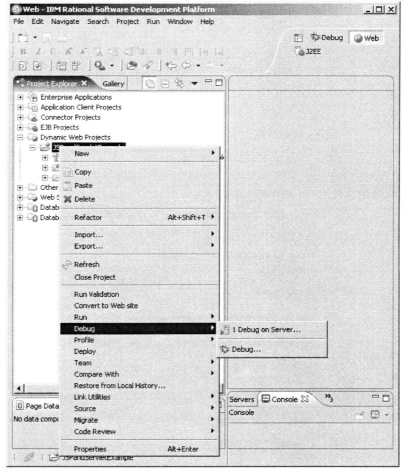

Figure 21-1   Debug - Debug on Server

21.1.2 Supported languages and environments

IBM Rational Application Developer V6.0 includes support for debugging many different languages and environments, including mixed languages:

- Java
- Compiled Languages
- Active Script (client-side JavaScript or VisualBasic script)
- SQL Stored Procedures
- EGL
- XSL Transformations (XSLT)
- SQLJ
- Mixed language (new to V6)
- WebSphere Application Server (servlets, JSPs, EJBs, Web Services)
- WebSphere Portal (portlets)

21.1.3 General functionality

In this section, we explore some features that provide general functionality throughout the debugging tools.

Breakpoint enable/disable

Breakpoints can be enabled and disabled. To enable a breakpoint in the code, double-click in the grey area of the left frame for the line of code you for which to enable the breakpoint.

Alternatively, the breakpoints can be enabled and disabled from the Breakpoints view (as seen in Figure 21-2) once they have been created. If the breakpoint is unchecked in the Breakpoints view, it will be skipped during execution.

To disable or enable all breakpoints, click the Breakpoint icon in the tool bar highlighted in the Debug perspective, as seen in Figure 21-2. If disabled, the next execution will skip the breakpoint.

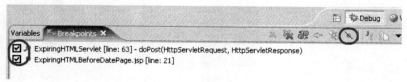

Figure 21-2 Breakpoint view - Enable/disable breakpoints

Step-by-step disable default

By default, step-by-step debugging is disabled in the Workbench preferences. To enable step-by-step debug, do the following:

1. Select **Window** → **Preferences**.
2. Expand **Run/Debug** → **Java and Mixed Language Debug**.
3. Check **Enable step-by-step debug mode by default** (as seen in Figure 21-3), and then click **OK**.

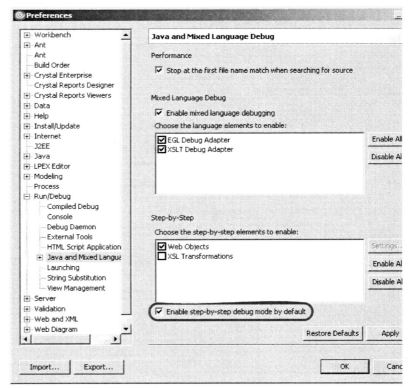

Figure 21-3 Enable step-by-step debug

Once the step-by-step debug feature is enabled, it can be toggled on and off by clicking the Step-By-Step Mode icon ( ) in the Debug view.

Enable/disable Step Filter/Step Debug in Debug view

Within the Debug view, there is a new Step Filter/Step Debug icon ( ). This feature allows step functions such as step into, step over, etc. to be used. By default this feature is disabled in the Workbench preferences.

To enable the Step Filter/Step Debug feature in the Debug view, do the following:

1. Select **Window** → **Preferences**.
2. Expand **Run/Debug** → **Java and Mixed Language Debug** → **Step Filters**.
3. Click **Add Filter**.
4. Enter the new filter and click **OK**.

Once the Step Filter/Step Debug feature is enabled, it can be toggled on and off by clicking the Step Filter icon ( ) in the Debug view.

21.1.4 Drop-to-frame

The Drop-to-frame feature allows you to back up execution of the application. This feature is available when debugging Java applications and Web applications running on WebSphere Application Server. This feature is useful when you need to test a range of values. With this feature multiple input values can be entered without having to rerun the application.

When running an application in the Debug perspective, you will see the stack frame in the Debug view, as seen in Figure 21-4. Drop-to-frame allows you to back up your application's execution to previous points in the call stack by selecting the desired frame and then clicking the Drop-To-Frame icon ( ).

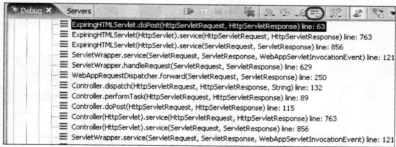

Figure 21-4   Debug view - Drop-to-frame feature

21.1.5 View Management

The View Management feature allows debug-related views to be opened in non-debug perspectives. This helps reduce user interface clutter by only opening the views necessary for debugging for the launched process. After the process has terminated the opened debug-related views are closed.

The View Management feature can be configured through either the Debug view or the Workbench preferences. The Debug perspective participates in View Management by default. Additional perspectives can be configured to participate. For example:

- Debugging the Java process opens Debug, Breakpoints, Variables, and Expressions views.
- Debugging the compiled language process opens Debug, Breakpoints, Variables, Registers, Memory Rendering, Monitors, and Modules views.

To configure the View Management from the Workbench preferences, do the following:

1. Select **Window** → **Preferences**.
2. Expand **Run/Debug** → **View Management**.
3. From the View Management tab, check the desired perspective(s) to be enabled, as seen in Figure 21-5 on page1124. This feature is used to determine which perspective(s) and supporting views will be displayed when the Debug view is opened and closed. Click **OK** when done.

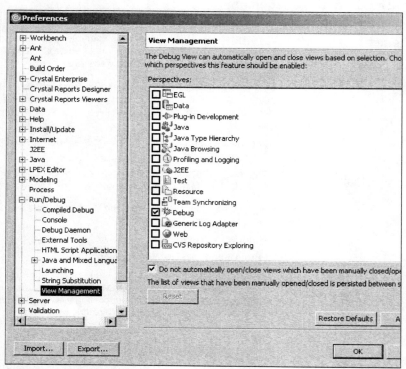

Figure 21-5   View Management

21.1.6 XSLT debugger

XSL Transformations (XSLT) is a language for transforming XML documents into other XML documents. XML Path Language (XPath) is used in matching parts of the source XML document with one or more predefined templates in the transformation script. For example, XSLT can be used to transform an XML document into an HTML document.

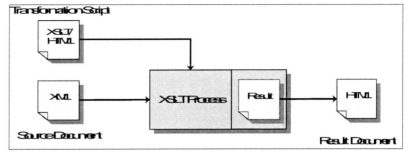

Figure 21-6   Example XSLT transform XML to HTML

In IBM Rational Application Developer V6, the XSLT debugger is implemented using an Eclipse Debug framework. Some of the new capabilities include a similar look and feel to other debuggers, the ability to set breakpoints in code, single step through code, and a XSLT Context view.

Transformations can be debugged even when the source is in DOM or SAX format. The XSLT debugger supports XSL Transformations (XSLT) Version 1.0:

http://www.w3.org/TR/xslt

We have listed some of the other key features of the new XSLT debugger:

- Launch configurations
    - Standalone XSL transformations
        - Apply XSL directly to a single XML file (able to step into Java extensions called from the transformation).
        - Allows user to verify transformations outside of a complex environment.
    - Mixed language transformations
        - Use when debugging Java to XSLT or XSLT involving Java extensions.
        - Allows user to debug transformations in real-world scenarios.
- New preferences
    - Node-by-node stepping

        Enabling allows the user to step between nodes that appear on the same line (disabled by default).
    - Built-in template rules filter
        - Enabling causes the debugger to step over built-in template rules (enabled by default).

- Built-in rules are still displayed on call stack.
– Step-by-step debugging for XSLT

    Enabling allows step-by-step functionality to additionally work with XSLT debugging (disabled by default).

► Debug activities

   – Iterate through XSLT using standard debugging operations.
   – Add/remove breakpoints (set in both the XSL source and the XML input).
   – Set watches on XPath expressions.
   – View XSLT processor execution using XSLT Context view.
   – View XSLT output using XSL Transformation Output view.

► Setting breakpoints

   – XSL files can be set anywhere between opening and closing template tags.
   – XML files must be set on the line containing the closing ">" of either the opening tag or the closing tag of an element.
   – Breakpoints set in files generated by the transformation will not be persisted between debug sessions.

► XSLT view

   – Visualizes XSLT processor's execution
   – Enables users to debug XPath expressions

► XSL Transformation Output view

   – View output from transformation in either a text or Web browser viewer.
   – Supports Xalan redirect extension.

► Troubleshooting

   – Verify launch configuration problems by checking the configuration's properties (Edit Launch Configuration properties through **Run** → **Debug**).
   – Tracing for XSLT debugging can be enabled by modifying the options file in <rad_home>\rwd\eclipse\plugins\com.ibm.debug.xsl_6.0.0.
   – Increase debugger timeout values if timeout errors occur by configuring through **Window** → **Preferences** → **Java** → **Debug**.
   – Verify that problems encountered when debugging Java in Mixed Language debugger also occur in Java debugger (mixed Language debugger is based on Java debugger).
   – Verify Java process used to launch transformation has correct arguments (view JVM launch properties by right-clicking the process in the Debug view and selecting **Properties**).

- XML capabilities need to be enabled in order to use XSLT debugging functionality.
- Configure through **Window** → **Preferences** → **Workbench** → **Capabilities**.

> **Note:** For an example of using the XSLT debugger, refer to 21.1.6, "XSLT debugger" on page 1128.

21.2 Prepare for the sample

This section describes how to set up the environment in preparation for the debug sample. We will use the ITSO RedBank Web application sampled developed in Chapter 11, "Develop Web applications using JSPs and servlets" on page 499, to demonstrate the debug facilities.

Import the sample application

To import the ITSO RedBank JSP and Servlet Web application Project Interchange file (BankBasicWeb.zip), do the following:

1. Open the Web perspective Project Explorer view.
2. Right-click **Dynamic Web Projects**, and select **Import** → **Import**.
3. When the Import dialog appears, select **Project Interchange** and then click **Next**.
4. In the Import Projects screen, browse to the c:\6449code\web folder and select **BankBasicWeb.zip**. Click **Open**.
5. Check the **BankBasicWeb** and **BankBasicWebEAR** projects, and click **Finish**.

Verify the sample application

To verify the sample application was imported properly, we recommend that you publish and run the sample Web application on the WebSphere Application Server V6.0 test server as follows:

1. Open the Web perspective.
2. Expand **Dynamic Web Projects** → **BankBasicWeb** → **WebContent**.
3. Right-click **index.html**, and select **Run** → **Run on Server**.
4. When the Server Selection dialog appears, select **Choose and existing server**, select **WebSphere Application Server v6.0**, and click **Finish**.

   This operation will start the server, and publish the application to the server.

5. When the Login page appears, enter 111-11-1111 in the Customer SSN field, and then click the **Login** button.

21.3 Debug a Web application on a local server

This section includes a Web application scenario in which the application will run, and shows hot to debug the local WebSphere Application Server V6.0 Test Environment. We use the expiring page sample included as part of the JSP, a Servlet Web application imported in 21.2, "Prepare for the sample" on page 1131.

The local debug example includes the following tasks to demonstrate the debug tooling and features of Rational Application Developer:

- Set breakpoints in a servlet.
- Set breakpoints in a JSP.
- Start the application for debugging.
- Debug view with stack frames.
- Debug functions.
- Breakpoints view.
- Watch variables.
- Inspect variables.
- Evaluate an expression.
- Debug a JSP.

21.3.1 Set breakpoints in a servlet

Breakpoints are indicators to the debugger that it should stop execution at specific places in the code, and let you step through it. Breakpoints can be set to trigger always or when a certain condition has been met.

In the ITSO RedBank sample application, before allowing the withdrawal of funds from an account, the amount requested to be withdrawn is evaluated with the amount that exists in the account. If there are adequate funds, the withdrawal will complete. If there are not enough funds in the account an InsufficientFundsException should be thrown. In this example, we set a breakpoint on the condition that tests the amount to withdraw does not exceed the amount that exists in the account.

To add a breakpoint in the code, do the following:

1. Select and expand the **Dynamic Web Projects** → **BankBasicWeb** → **Java Resources** → **JavaSource** → **itso.bank.facade**.
2. Double-click **MemoryBank.java** to open the file in the Java editor.

3. Place the cursor in the gray bar (along the left edge of the editor area) on the following line of code:

    ```
    if (account.getBalance() > amount)
    ```

    Tip: Use the Outline view to find the withdraw method to quickly find the source code listed.

4. Double-click to set a breakpoint marker, as seen in Figure 21-7 on page 1133.

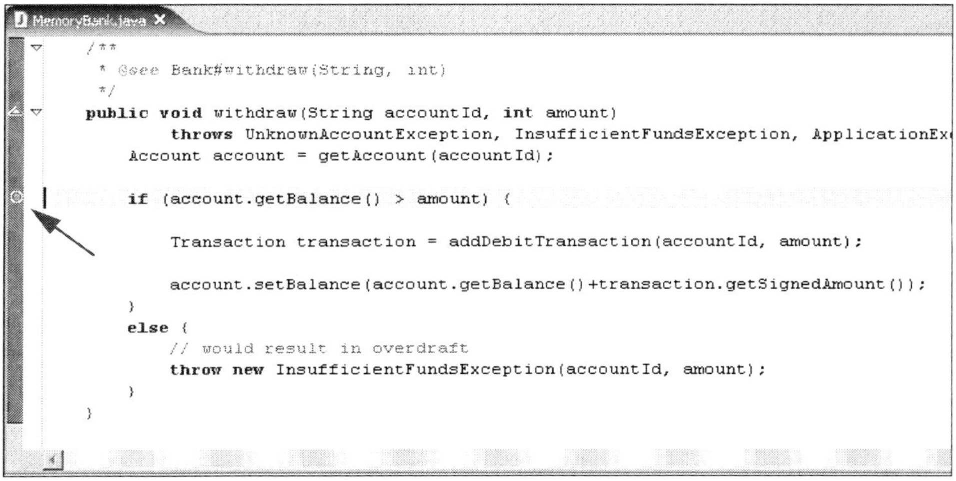

Figure 21-7   Add a breakpoint

Note: Enabled breakpoints are indicated with a blue circle. If the enabled breakpoint is successfully installed in a class in the VM at runtime, it is indicated with a check mark overlay.

5. Right-click the breakpoint in the breakpoint view, and select **Breakpoint Properties** from the context menu.

    The Breakpoint Properties window should appear with more detailed options about the breakpoint, as seen in Figure 21-8 on page 1134.

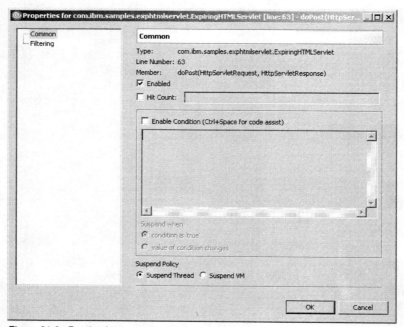

Figure 21-8 Breakpoint properties

- The Hit Count property, when set, causes the breakpoint to be triggered only when the lines have been executed as many times as the hit count specified. Once triggered, the breakpoint is disabled.
- The other property of interest here is *Enable Condition*. If set, then the breakpoint is reached only when the condition specified in the entry field evaluates to *true*. This condition is a Java expression. When this is enabled the breakpoint will now be marked with a question mark on the breakpoint, which indicates that it is a conditional breakpoint.

> **Note:** For example, check **Enable Condition**, select **condition is true**, and enter amount==1000 in the Enable Condition text box, and then click **OK**. Remember, in this application 1000 is really $10.00. When the application is run and 1000 is entered to withdraw, this conditional breakpoint will be hit in the debugger.

6. Click **OK** to close the breakpoint properties.

21.3.2 Set breakpoints in a JSP

You can also set breakpoints in the JSP source code. However, you can only set breakpoints inside Java scriptlets or other JSP tags, such as JSTL tags.

In the following example, we set a breakpoint in the listAccounts.jsp at the point where the JSP displays a list of accounts for the customer.

1. Expand **Dynamic Web Projects** → **BankBasicWeb** → **WebContent**.
2. Double-click **listAccounts.jsp** to open the file in the editor.
3. Click the **Source** tab.
4. Set a breakpoint as shown in Figure 21-9 on page 1135 by double-clicking in the grey area next to the desired line of code.

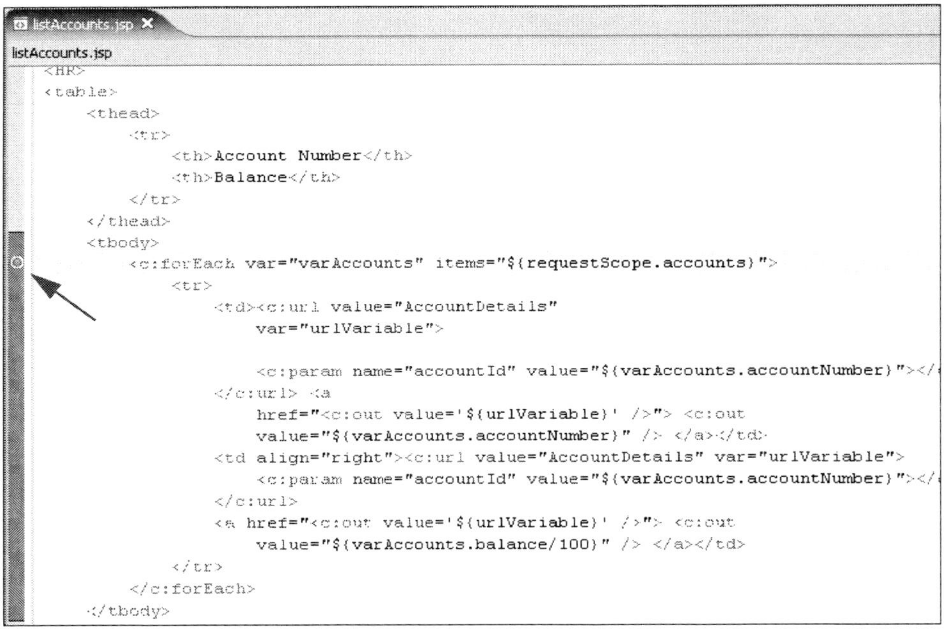

```
listAccounts.jsp
    <HR>
    <table>
        <thead>
            <tr>
                <th>Account Number</th>
                <th>Balance</th>
            </tr>
        </thead>
        <tbody>
            <c:forEach var="varAccounts" items="${requestScope.accounts}">
                <tr>
                    <td><c:url value="AccountDetails"
                        var="urlVariable">
                        <c:param name="accountId" value="${varAccounts.accountNumber}"></
                    </c:url> <a
                        href="<c:out value='${urlVariable}' />"> <c:out
                        value="${varAccounts.accountNumber}" /> </a></td>
                    <td align="right"><c:url value="AccountDetails" var="urlVariable">
                        <c:param name="accountId" value="${varAccounts.accountNumber}"></
                    </c:url>
                    <a href="<c:out value='${urlVariable}' />"> <c:out
                        value="${varAccounts.balance/100}" /> </a></td>
                </tr>
            </c:forEach>
        </tbody>
```

Figure 21-9 Set a breakpoint in a JSP

21.3.3 Start the application for debugging

Once you have set the breakpoint(s), the Web application can be started for debugging.

> **Note:** The server used for testing (for example, WebSphere Application Server V6.0 (default test server)), must be either stopped or started in debug mode. Otherwise, an error message will be displayed.

1. Stop the WebSphere Application Server V6.0 test server.
2. From the Web perspective, expand **Dynamic Web Projects**.
3. Right-click **BankBasicWeb**, and select **Debug** → **Debug on Server**.

> **Note:** If the server was started it will prompt you to restart.

4. When the Define a New Server dialog appears, select **Choose and existing Server**, select **WebSphere Application Server V6.0**, and then click **Finish**.

> **Tip:** To debug a Java application, select **Run** → **Debug As** → **Java Application** to start the debugger. The startup is the primary difference between debugging a Web application and Java application.

21.3.4 Run the application in the debugger

After starting the application in debug mode, as described in 21.3.3, "Start the application for debugging" on page 1136, you should now see `index.html` displayed in the Web Browser view, as shown in Figure 21-10 on page 1137.

Figure 21-10 ITSO RedBank index.html page

1. Click **RedBank** in the horizontal navigation bar, as seen in Figure 21-10.
2. When prompted for the customer ID (SSN), enter 111-11-1111 (as seen in Figure 21-11 on page 1138), and then click **Submit**.

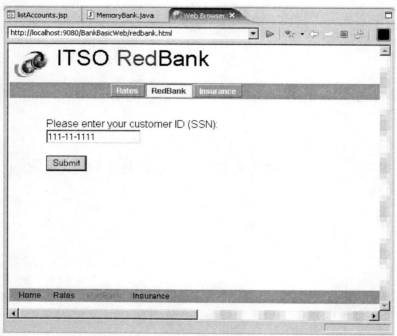

Figure 21-11   Enter customer ID (SSN)

3. When the Confirm Perspective Switch window appears, click **Yes** to switch to the Debug perspective.

   The sample will now be run in the Debug perspective.

4. Execution should stop at the breakpoint set in the listAccounts.jsp, since clicking Submit in the application will display the accounts. The thread is suspended in debug, but other threads might still be running (see Figure 21-12 on page 1139).

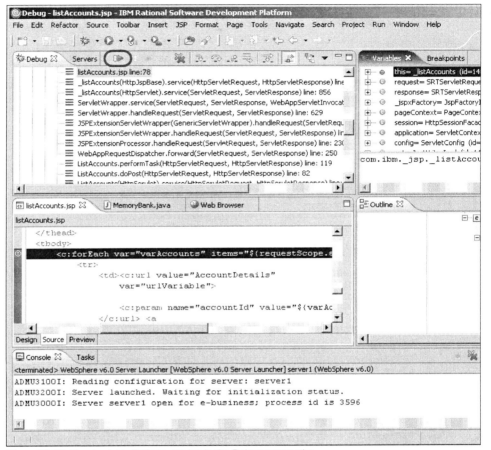

Figure 21-12   Breakpoint in listAccounts.jsp in the Debug perspective

5. Once a breakpoint is hit, you can proceed in a number of ways. For our example, we click the Resume icon highlighted in Figure 21-12.

6. Click the **Web Browser** session and resize the page as needed. Click the **001-999000888** account.

Chapter 21. Debug local and remote applications   **1139**

7. When the Account: 001-999000888 page appears, select **Withdraw**, enter 1000 (value of conditional breakpoint in MemoryBank.java), and then click **Submit**.

   The breakpoint in MemoryBank.java should be hit and displayed in the Debug perspective, similar to Figure 21-13.

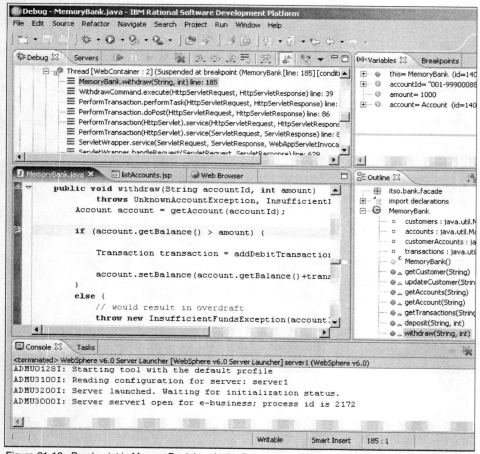

Figure 21-13   Breakpoint in MemoryBank.java in the Debug perspective

Next we discuss the different views of the Debug perspective.

21.3.5 Debug view with stack frames

When a breakpoint is reached, the debugger displays a list of stack frames before the breakpoint occurred. Each frame corresponds to a called method. The entire list is in reverse chronological order. Figure 21-14 shows the stack frame listing for the breakpoint in the MemoryBank.java withdraw method.

Figure 21-14 Stack frame listing in Debug view

When a thread suspends, the top stack frame is automatically selected. If you select another stack frame, all visible variables in that frame are shown in the Variables view.

21.3.6 Debug functions

From the Debug view, which should now be displayed in the top left pane, you can use the functions available from its icon bar to control the execution of the application. The following icons are available:

- Resume: Runs the application to the next breakpoint.
- Suspend: Suspends a running thread.
- Terminate: Terminates a process.
- Disconnect: Disconnects from the target when debugging remotely.
- Remove All Terminated Launches: Removes terminated executions.
- Step Into: Steps into the highlighted statement.
- Step Over: Steps over the highlighted statement.
- Step Return: Steps out of the current method.
- Drop to Frame: Drops to the Debug Frame view and highlights code.
- Step Filter: Enable/disable the filtering for the *step* functions.

▶ **Step-By-Step Mode:** Once the step-by-step debug feature is enabled in the Run/Debug preferences, this icon can be used to toggle the feature.

▶ **Show Qualified Names:** Toggle option to show the full package name.

In the upper right pane you can see the various debugging views that are available.

21.3.7 Breakpoints view

The Breakpoints view displays all the breakpoints set in the Workbench (see Figure 21-15).

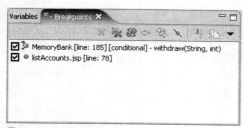

Figure 21-15 Debugging views

You can use the Breakpoints view to display and manipulate the breakpoints that are currently set. You can open the properties, remove the breakpoint, or open its source file.

21.3.8 Watch variables

The Variables view displays the current values of the variables in the selected stack frame. Follow these steps to see how you can track the state of a variable.

Click the Step Over icon to execute the current statement.

Click Step Over again and the year variable is added. The plus sign (+) next to a variable indicates that it is an object.

In our example, we set a conditional break point on amount==1000. Notice the year input variable value 1000 in Figure 21-16 on page 1143.

Figure 21-16   Displaying variables

If you want to test the code with some other value for any of these instance variables, you can change one of them by selecting **Change Variable Value** from its context menu. An entry field opens where you can change the value; for example, you can change the value of the year to 2002 and then click Resume.

21.3.9 Inspect variables

To view more details about a variable, select the variable (for example, **amount=1000**), right-click, and select **Inspect** from the context menu. The result opens in the Expressions view, as seen in Figure 21-17.

Both the Variables and the Expressions views can be split into two panes by selecting **Show Detail Pane** from the context menu.

Figure 21-17   Inspecting a variable in Expressions view

21.3.10 Evaluate an expression

To evaluate an expression in the context of the currently suspended thread, use the Display view.

Chapter 21. Debug local and remote applications   **1143**

1. While in the debugger at the breakpoint, press F6 twice to step through code until you reach the following line:

   ```
   account.setBalance(account.getBalance()+transaction.getSignedAmount());
   ```

2. From the Workbench select **Windows** → **Show view** → **Display**.
3. Enter the expression `transaction.getTimestamp()`, then highlight the expression, right-click, and select **Display** from the context menu.

   Note: When entering the expression, we used the code assist (Ctrl+spacebar) to simplify entry and enter the proper method.

   Each expression is executed, and the result is displayed (Figure 21-18).

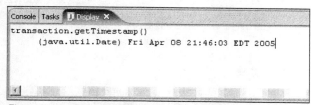

Figure 21-18   Expression and evaluated result in display view

4. The results of the Java expression can also be inspected by selecting **Inspect** from the context menu, as seen in Figure 21-19.

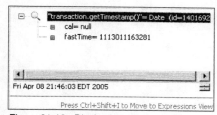

Figure 21-19   Display Inspect expression

   Note: To move the results to the Expression view, press Ctrl+Shift+I.

5. You can also highlight any expression in the source code, right-click, and select **Display** or **Inspect** from the context menu. The result is shown either in the Display or the Expressions view.

This is a useful way to evaluate Java expressions during debugging, without having to make changes in your code and recompile.

6. Select **Remove** from the context menu to remove expressions or variables from the Expressions views. In the Display view just select the text and delete it.

21.3.11 Debug a JSP

Step through the code or click the Resume icon ( ) to progress to the breakpoint in the JSP (see Figure 21-12 on page 1139).

> **Note:** If you have two JSPs in different Web applications, the wrong JSP source may be displayed. Open the correct JSP to see its source code.

Watch the JSP variables in the Variables view. The same functions as for servlets are available for JSP debugging. A JSP is compiled into a servlet. The difference is that the debugger shows the JSP source code and not the generated Java code.

When you step through JSP code, the debugger only stops at Java code; HTML statements are skipped.

Resume execution to see the next Web page, then close the Debug perspective and stop the server.

21.4 Debug a Web application on a remote server

It is possible to connect to and debug a Java Web application that has been launched in debug mode on a remote application server, and the application server has been configured to accept remote connections. Debugging a remote program is similar to debugging a local application, except that the program has already been launched and could be running on a remote host.

This example scenario will include a node where IBM Rational Application Developer V6.0 is installed (Developer node), and a separate node where IBM WebSphere Application Server V6.0 is installed (Application Server node).

21.4.1 Export the BankBasicWeb project to a WAR file

This section describes how to export the BankBasicWeb project to a WAR file so that it can be deployed on a remote WebSphere Application Server.

1. Open the Web perspective in Rational Application Developer.

2. Expand **Dynamic Web Projects**.
3. Select **BankBasicWeb**, right-click, and select **Export** → **WAR file**.
4. When the WAR Export window appears, enter the following and then click **Finish**:
   – Web project: BankBasicWeb
   – Destination: c:\temp\BankBasicWeb.war
5. Verify that the c:\temp\BankBasicWeb.war exists.

21.4.2 Deploy the BankBasicWeb.war

This section describes how to deploy the BankBasicWeb.war to a remote system where IBM WebSphere Application Server V6.0 has been installed.

1. Copy the BankBasicWeb.war from the node where Rational Application Developer is installed to the node where WebSphere Application Server is installed (for example, c:\temp).
2. Ensure that the WebSphere Application Server - server1 application server is started.
3. Start the WebSphere Application Server Administrative Console by entering the following in a Web browser and logging on:

   http://<hostname>:9060/ibm/console

4. Select **Applications** → **Install New Application**.
5. Enter the path to the war file and the context root, and then click **Next**. For example, we entered:
   – Specify path: c:\temp\BankBasicWeb.war
   – Context root: BankBasicWeb
6. We accepted the default options and clicked **Next**.
7. When you see an Application Security Warning, click **Continue**.
8. When the Step 1: Select installation options page appears, accept the default and click **Next**.
9. When the Step 2: Map modules to servers page appears, check the **BankBasicWeb** module, and then click **Next**.
10. When the Step 3: Map virtual hosts for Web modules page appears, check the **BankBasicWeb** Web module, select **default_host** from the Virtual host drop-down list, and then click **Next**.
11. When the Step 4: Summary page appears, accept the defaults and then click **Finish**.

You should see the following message if successfully deployed:

```
Application BankBasicWeb _war installed successfully.
```

12. Click **Save to Master**. Click **Save**.
13. Check **BankBasicWeb_war**, and click **Start**.
14. Click **Logout**.
15. Verify the application is working properly by entering the following URL:

```
http://<hostname>:9080/BankBasicWeb/
```

21.4.3 Install the IBM Rational Agent Controller

The IBM Rational Agent Controller provides several plug-ins for debugging, logging, profiling, and testing.

If the remote system is running WebSphere Application Server V6.0 and you only intend to use remote debug, the IBM Rational Agent Controller is not required, since the required functionality is built-in to WebSphere Application Server V6.0.

If the remote system is running WebSphere Application Server V5.1 or V5.0 and you intend to use remote debug, the IBM Rational Agent Controller is required. You will be prompted to provided the installation path for WebSphere Application Server V5.1 or V5.0 during the IBM Rational Agent Controller installation.

If you intend to use the profiling and testing features of Rational Application Developer, the IBM Rational Agent Controller is required for WebSphere Application Server V6.0, V5.1 and 5.0.

For the redbook scenario, although we are planning on debugging on a WebSphere Application Server V6.0 server, we also want to perform profiling and testing, so we installed all plug-ins for the IBM Rational Agent Controller.

For details on installing the IBM Agent Controller refer to "IBM Rational Agent Controller V6 installation" on page 1382.

21.4.4 Configure debug on remote WebSphere Application Server

The following steps explain how to configure WebSphere Application Server V6.0 to start in debug mode:

1. Start the application server.

```
<was_home>\bin\startServer.bat server1
```

2. Start the WebSphere Administrative Console by entering the following in a Web browser and then logging in:

   `http://<hostname>:9060/ibm/console`

3. In the left-hand frame, select **Servers** → **Application Servers**.
4. In the Application Servers page, click **server1**.
5. On the Configuration tab, select **Debugging Service** in the Additional Properties section to open the Debugging Service configuration page.
6. In the General Properties section of the Configuration tab, check **Enable service at startup**. This enables the debugging service when the server starts.

   > **Note:** The value of the JVM debug port (default 7777) is needed when connecting to the application server with the debugger.

7. Click **OK** to make the changes to your local configuration.
8. Click **Save** to apply the configuration changes.
9. Click **Logout**.
10. You must restart the application server before the changes that you have made take effect.

21.4.5 Attach to the remote server in Rational Application Developer

To attach to the remote WebSphere Application Server V6.0 from within Rational Application Developer V6.0, do the following:

1. From the Workbench, open the J2EE perspective.
2. In the Servers view, right-click **WebSphere Application Server v6.0** and select **Stop**.
3. Create a new remote WebSphere Application Server V6 server.

   a. In the Servers view, right-click **New** → **Server**.
   b. When the Define a New Server window appears, we entered the following, as seen in Figure 21-20, and then clicked **Next**:

      - Host name: `was6win1.itso.ral.ibm.com`
      - Server type: Select **WebSphere V6.0 Server**.

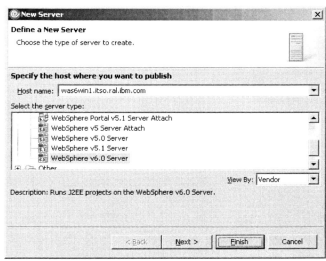

Figure 21-20   Define new remote server

c. When the WebSphere Server Settings page appears, we entered the following, as seen in Figure 21-21 on page 1150:

- Server admin port number (SOAP connector port): 8880

> **Note:** The SOAP connector port is defined in the WebSphere Profile.

- Server name: server1
- Server type: Select **Base or Express server**.

> **Note:** We recommend that you test the connection to the server by clicking the **Detect** button (see Figure 21-21 on page 1150).

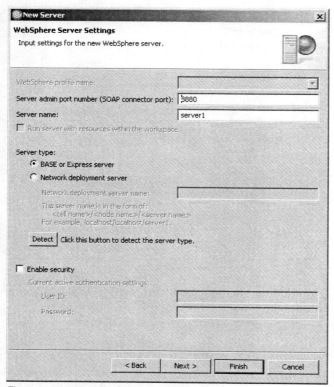

Figure 21-21   WebSphere Server Settings

   d. Click **Finish**.

      When complete, the configuration should look like Figure 21-22 on page 1151. Notice the status is `Debugging`.

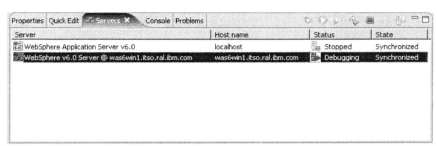

Figure 21-22   Remote server configuration

21.4.6 Debug the application on the remote server

Now that the environment is configured, we demonstrate how to debug an application running on the remote server within Rational Application Developer.

Debug sample application on remote server

The behavior of debugging for remote servers is slightly different than locally. For example, when debugging locally you can select a project and Debug on Server. This will cause the application to be invoked in the built-in Web browser and start the server. Also, the user will automatically be prompted if they want to switch to the Debug perspective.

When debugging on a remote server, some of these steps are a bit more manual in the way that they are initiated.

1. Open the Debug perspective.
2. Add the Web browser to the Debug perspective.
    a. From the tool bar of the Debug perspective, right-click **Customize Perspective**.
    b. Click the **Commands** tab.
    c. Scroll down and check **Web Browser**.
    d. Click **OK**.
3. Click the Web browser icon ( ) found on the tool bar.
4. Enter the URL for the remote Web application in the Web browser. For example, we entered the following:

   `http://was6win1.itso.ral.ibm.com:9080/BankBasicWeb`
5. Run the sample.

Once the application is started, the steps to run the application are similar to those in 21.3.4, "Run the application in the debugger" on page 1136.

> **Note:** When the page of the breakpoint is loaded, you will see an option to locate the source. Select **Folder**, then select the project **WebContent** directory (for example, in this case for a JSP).

6. Provided that a breakpoint is set, the code will be displayed at the breakpoint. You can also step through the code.
7. Define source location.
    a. You will see the message `Source not found`. Click the **Edit Source Lookup Path** button.
    b. When the Edit Source Lookup Path dialog appears, click **Add**.
    c. When the Add Source dialog appears, select **Workspace** and click **OK**.
    d. Click **OK**.

> **Attention:** From within Rational Application Developer, you can stop the remote server by right-clicking the remote server in the Servers view, and selecting **Stop**. However, you cannot start the remote server from within Rational Application Developer. You must start the remote server from the remote WebSphere Application Server node.

Part 4

Deploy and profile applications

22

Build applications with Ant

Traditionally, application builds are performed by using UNIX/Linux shell scripts or Windows batch files in combination with tools such as *make*. While these approaches are still valid, new challenges exist for when developing Java applications, especially in a heterogeneous environment. Traditional tools are limited in that they are closely coupled to a particular operating system. With Ant you can overcome these limitations and perform the build process in a standardized fashion regardless of the platform.

This chapter provides an introduction to the concepts and features of Ant within IBM Rational Application Developer V6.0. The focus of the chapter is to demonstrate how to use the Ant tooling included in Rational Application Developer to build projects (applications).

This chapter is organized into the following sections:

- Introduction to Ant
- New features
- Build a simple Java application
- Build a J2EE application
- Run Ant outside of Application Developer

22.1 Introduction to Ant

Ant is a Java-based, platform-independent, open source build tool. It was formerly a sub-project in the Apache Jakarta project, but in November 2002 it was migrated to an Apache top-level project. Ant's function is similar to the *make* tool. Since it is Java-based and does not make use of any operating system-specific functions, it is platform independent, thus allowing you to build your projects using the same build script on any Java-enabled platform.

The Ant build operations are controlled by the contents of the XML-based script file. This file not only defines what operations to perform, but also defines the order in which they should be performed, and any dependencies between them.

Ant comes with a large number of built-in tasks sufficient to perform many common build operations. However, if the tasks included are not sufficient, you also have the ability to extend Ant's functionality by using Java to develop your own specialized tasks. These tasks can then be plugged into Ant.

Not only can Ant be used to *build* your applications, but it can also be used for many other operations such as retrieving source files from a version control system, storing the result back in the version control system, transferring the build output to other machines, deploying the applications, generating Javadoc, and sending messages when a build is finished.

22.1.1 Ant build files

Ant uses XML *build files* to define what operations must be performed to build a project. We have listed the main components of a build file:

- project: A build file contains build information for a single project. It may contain one or more *targets*.
- target: A target describes the *tasks* that must be performed to satisfy a goal. For example, compiling source code into class files may be one target, and packaging the class files into a JAR file may be another target.

    Targets may depend upon other targets. For example, the class files must be up-to-date before you can create the JAR file. Ant can resolve these dependencies.

- task: A task is a single step that must be performed to satisfy a target. Tasks are implemented as Java classes that are invoked by Ant, passing parameters defined as attributes in the XML. Ant provides a set of standard tasks (core tasks), a set of optional tasks, and an API, which allows you to write your own tasks.

- property: A property has a name and a value pair. Properties are essentially variables that can be passed to tasks through task attributes. Property values can be set inside a build file, or obtained externally from a properties file or from the command line. A property is referenced by enclosing the property name inside ${}, for example ${basedir}.
- path: A path is a set of directories or files. Paths can be defined once and referred to multiple times, easing the development and maintenance of build files. For example, a Java compilation task may use a path reference to determine the classpath to use.

22.1.2 Ant tasks

A comprehensive set of built-in tasks is supplied with the Ant distribution. The tasks that we use in our example are as follows:

- delete: Deletes files and directories
- echo: Outputs messages
- jar: Creates Java archive files
- javac: Compiles Java source
- mkdir: Creates directories
- tstamp: Sets properties containing date and time information

To find out more about Ant, visit the Ant Web site at:

```
http://ant.apache.org/
```

This chapter provides a basic outline of the features and capabilities of Ant. For complete information you should consult the Ant documentation included in the Ant distribution or available on the Internet at:

```
http://ant.apache.org/manual/index.html
```

Note: IBM Rational Application Developer V6.0 includes Ant V1.4.1.

22.2 New features

IBM Rational Application Developer V6.0 includes the following new features to aid in the development and use of Ant scripts:

- The ability to run the build process in a background task like other tasks within IBM Rational Application Developer V6.0.
- The Ant editor now also offers code assist with the ability to insert snippets.
- The Ant editor now has a format function that will allow you to format your Ant files base on your preferences.

- A problems view is now available in the Ant editor to highlight syntax errors in your Ant files.

In this section we highlight the following Ant-related features in Rational Application Developer:

- Code Assist
- Code snippets
- Format an Ant script
- Define format of an Ant script
- Problem view

> **Note:** The new features outlined in this section can be explored hands on by importing the BankAnt.zip Project Interchange file, as described in 22.3.1, "Prepare for the sample" on page 1168.

22.2.1 Code Assist

To access the new features such as Code Assist in the Ant editor, do the following:

1. Open the Java perspective.
2. Expand the **BankAnt** project.
3. Double-click **build.xml** to open the file in an editor.
4. Place the cursor in the file and enter <prop, and then press Ctrl+Spacebar.
5. The Code Assist dialog will be presented, as shown in Figure 22-1 on page 1159. You can then use the up and down arrow keys to select the tag that you want.

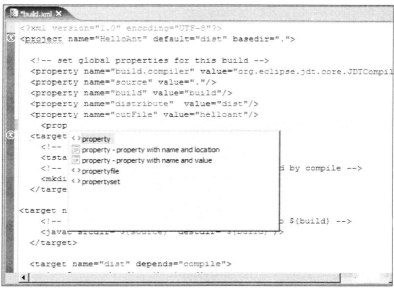

Figure 22-1   Code Assist in Ant editor

22.2.2 Code snippets

IBM Rational Application Developer V6 provides the ability to create code snippets that contain commonly used code to be inserted into files rather than typing the code in every time.

To create code snippets, do the following:

1. Open the Snippets view by selecting **Window** → **Show View** → **Other**, and the Show View dialog will be displayed.
2. Expand the **Basic** folder, select the **Snippets** view (as shown in Figure 22-2 on page 1160), and then click **OK**.

Figure 22-2   Show View dialog

3. Right-click the Snippets view and select **Customize**, as seen in Figure 22-3.

Figure 22-3   Customizing snippets

4. When the Customize Palette dialog appears, select **New → New Category**.

5. When the New Customize Palette dialog appears (as seen in Figure 22-4 on page 1161), do the following:
   - Name: Ant
   - Description: Ant Snippets
   - Select **Custom**.

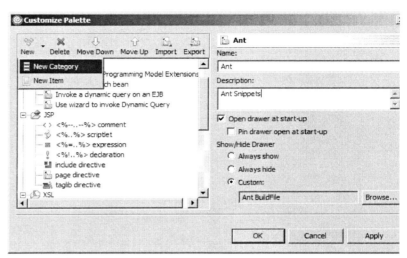

Figure 22-4 New Customize Palette dialog

6. Click **Browse** next to Custom, check **Ant Buildfiles** (as seen in Figure 22-5 on page 1162), and click **OK** to return to the Customize Palette dialog.

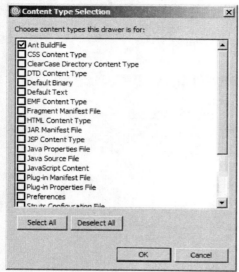

Figure 22-5   Content Type Selection view

7. From the Customize Palette dialog, select **New** → **New Item**.
8. When the Unamed Template dialog appears, enter the following:
   - Name: Comment Tag
   - Click **New** in the variables section.
   - Variable Name: comment
   - Template Pattern: <!-- ${comment} -->
9. Click **OK** on the Customize Palette dialog.

Use the code snippet

Now that you have created a code snippet you can use it in any Ant build file. To use a code snippet, do the following:

1. Double-click the **build.xml** file to open it in the editor.
2. Place the cursor under the <project tag, double-click the **Comment Tag** in the Snippets view, and the Insert Template dialog will be displayed (as shown in Figure 22-6 on page 1163).

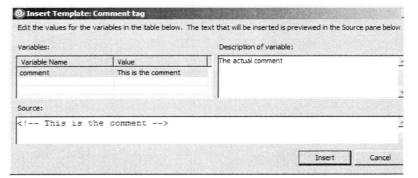

Figure 22-6   Insert Template dialog

3. In the variables table, enter Surf's up! in the comment variable.
4. Click the **Insert** button.

22.2.3 Format an Ant script

Rational Application Developer now offers you the ability to format Ant scripts in the Ant editor. To format the Ant script, do the following:

1. Double-click **build.xml** to open it in the Ant editor.
2. Right-click the editor and select **Format** from the context menu, as shown in Figure 22-7 on page 1164.

    Alternatively, you can press Ctrl+Shift+F.

Figure 22-7   Formatting the Ant file

22.2.4 Define format of an Ant script

To define the format of an Ant script, do the following:

1. Select **Window → Preferences**.
2. When the Preferences dialog appears, select **Ant**.
3. When the Ant preferences dialog appears, as seen in Figure 22-8 on page 1165, you can specify the console colors.

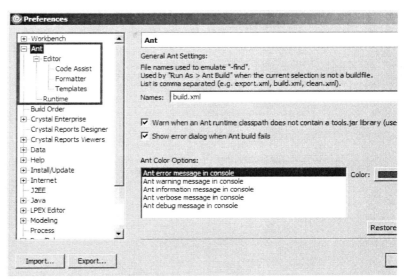

Figure 22-8 Ant preferences

4. Expand the **Ant** folder and select **Editor**.

   a. On the Appearance tab you can change the layout preferences of your Ant file.

   b. On the Syntax tab you can change the syntax highlighting preferences with a preview of the results, and on the Problem tab you can define how certain problems should be handled.

5. Expand **Editor**.

   a. In the Code Assist window you can define the code assist preferences.

   b. In the Formatter window you can define the preferences for the formatting tool for the Ant files.

   c. In the Templates window you can create, edit, and delete templates for Ant files.

6. Select **Runtime**.

   In this window you can define your preferences such as classpath, tasks, types, and properties.

22.2.5 Problem view

Rational Application Developer now offers you the problems view for the Ant file. The editor will present an error in the view by placing a *red X* on the left of the line with the problem as well as a line marker in the file on the right of the window, as shown in Figure 22-9. The problem view will list the problems as seen in Figure 22-10.

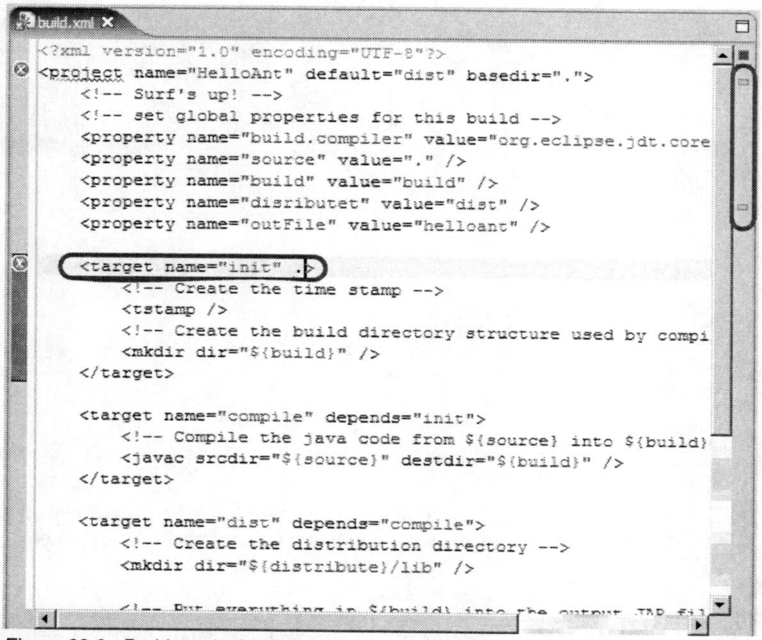

Figure 22-9   Problems in the Ant editor

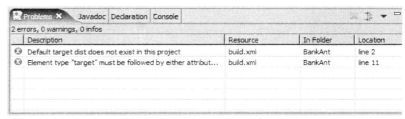

Figure 22-10   Problems view displaying Ant problems

22.3 Build a simple Java application

We created a simple build file that compiles the Java source for our HelloAnt application and generates a JAR file with the result. The build file is called build.xml, which is the default name assumed by Ant if no build file name is supplied.

The example simple build file has the following targets:

- init: Performs build initialization tasks. All other targets depend upon this target.
- compile: Compiles Java source into class files.
- dist: Creates the deliverable JAR for the module, and depends upon the compile target.
- clean: Removes all generated files. Used to force a full build.

Each Ant build file may have a default target. This target is executed if Ant is invoked on a build file and no target is supplied as a parameter. In our example, the default target is dist. The dependencies between the targets are illustrated in Figure 22-11.

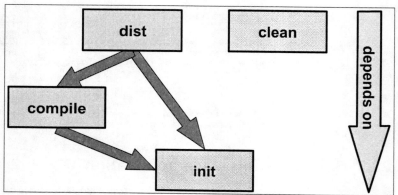

Figure 22-11   Ant example dependencies

22.3.1 Prepare for the sample

To demonstrate the basic concepts of Ant, we wrote a very simple Java application named HelloAnt, which prints a message to stdout.

We created a new Java project for this that we called BankAnt. In this project we created a Java package called itso.ant.hello and a class called HelloAnt. Since these steps are basic Rational Application Developer tasks and the application does nothing but a simple System.out.println("G'day from Australia."), we do not show them here. In addition, the source code for the chapter is included in the BankAnt project.

To import the BankAnt.zip Project Interchange file, do the following:

1. Start Rational Application Developer.
2. From the Workbench, select **File** → **Import**.
3. From the Import dialog, select **Project Interchange** and then click **Next**.
4. When prompted for the Project Interchange path and file name, and target workspace location, we entered the following:
   - From zip file: `c:\6449code\ant\BankAnt.zip`
   - Project location root: `c:\workspace`

     Enter the location of the desired workspace (for example, our workspace is found in c:\workspace).
5. After entering the zip file, check **BankAnt** and then click **Finish**.

22.3.2 Create a build file

The BankAnt project already includes the build.xml file we will create in this section.

To create the simple build file, do the following:

1. Select the **BankAnt** project in the Package Explorer view.
2. Right-click and select **New** → **File** from its context menu.
3. When the New File dialog appears, enter build.xml as the filename, as seen in Figure 22-12 on page 1169, and click **Finish**.

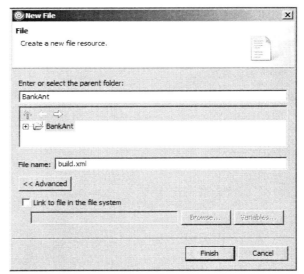

Figure 22-12   Create a build.xml file

> **Note:** IBM Rational Application Developer V6 now has the ability to link to external files on the file system. The Advance button on the New File dialog allows you to specify the location on the file system that the new file is linked to.

4. Cut and paste the text in Example 22-1 into the file.

Example 22-1   Example build.xml

```xml
<?xml version="1.0" encoding="UTF-8"?>
<project name="HelloAnt" default="dist" basedir=".">

    <!-- set global properties for this build -->
    <property name="build.compiler" value="org.eclipse.jdt.core.JDTCompilerAdapter"/>
    <property name="source" value="."/>
    <property name="build" value="c:\temp\build"/>
    <property name="distribute"  value="c:\temp\BankAnt"/>
    <property name="outFile" value="helloant"/>

    <target name="init">
      <!-- Create the time stamp -->
      <tstamp/>
      <!-- Create the build directory structure used by compile -->
      <mkdir dir="${build}"/>
    </target>

<target name="compile" depends="init">
    <!-- Compile the java code from ${source} into ${build} -->
    <javac srcdir="${source}" destdir="${build}"/>
</target>

    <target name="dist" depends="compile">
      <!-- Create the distribution directory -->
      <mkdir dir="${distribute}/lib"/>

      <!-- Put everything in ${build} into the output JAR file -->
      <!-- Add a timestamp to the output filename as well -->
      <jar jarfile="${distribute}/lib/${outFile}-${DSTAMP}.jar" basedir="${build}">
         <manifest>
             <attribute name="Main-Class" value="itso.ant.hello.HelloAnt"/>
         </manifest>
      </jar>
    </target>

    <target name="clean">
      <!-- Delete the ${build} and ${distribute} directory trees -->
      <delete dir="${build}"/>
      <delete dir="${distribute}"/>
    </target>

</project>
```

We will now walk you through the various sections of this file, and provide an explanation for each of them.

22.3.3 Project definition

The <project tag in the build.xml file defines the project name and the default target. The project name is an arbitrary name; it is not related to any project name in your Application Developer workspace.

The project tag also sets the working directory for the Ant script. All references to directories throughout the script file are based on this directory. A dot (.) means to use the current directory, which, in Application Developer, is the directory where the build.xml file resides.

22.3.4 Global properties

Properties that will be referenced throughout the whole script file can be placed at the beginning of the Ant script. Here we define the property build.compiler that tells the `javac` command what compiler to use. We will tell it to use the Eclipse compiler.

We also define the names for the source directory, the build directory, and the distribute directory. The source directory is where the Java source files reside. The build directory is where the class files end up, and the distribute directory is where the resulting JAR file is placed:

- We define the source property as ".", which means it is the same directory as the base directory specified in the project definition above.
- The build and distribute directories will be created as c:\temp\build and c:\temp\BankAnt directories.

Properties can be set as shown below, but Ant can also read properties from standard Java properties files or use parameters passed as arguments on the command line:

```
<!-- set global properties for this build -->
<property name="build.compiler"
value="org.eclipse.jdt.core.JDTCompilerAdapter"/>
<property name="source" value="."/>
<property name="build" value="c:\temp\build"/>
<property name="distribute"  value="c:\temp\BankAnt"/>
<property name="outFile" value="helloant"/>
```

22.3.5 Build targets

The build file contains four build targets:

- init
- compile
- dist

- clean

Initialization target (init)

The first target we describe is the init target. All other targets (except clean) in the build file depend upon this target. In the init target we execute the tstamp task to set up properties that include timestamp information. These properties are then available throughout the whole build. We also create a build directory defined by the build property.

```
<target name="init">
    <!-- Create the time stamp -->
    <tstamp/>
    <!-- Create the build directory structure used by compile -->
    <mkdir dir="${build}"/>
</target>
```

Compilation target (compile)

The compile target compiles the Java source files in the source directory and places the resulting class files in the build directory.

```
<target name="compile" depends="init">
    <!-- Compile the java code from ${source} into ${build} -->
    <javac srcdir="${source}" destdir="${build}"/>
</target>
```

With these parameters, if the compiled code in the build directory is up-to-date (each class file has a timestamp later than the corresponding Java file in the source directory), the source will not be recompiled.

Distribution target (dist)

The distribution target creates a JAR file that contains the compiled class files from the build directory and places it in the lib directory under the dist directory. Because the distribution target depends on the compile target, the compile target must have executed successfully before the distribution target is run.

```
<target name="dist" depends="compile">
    <!-- Create the distribution directory -->
    <mkdir dir="${distribute}/lib"/>

    <!-- Put everything in ${build} into the output JAR file -->
    <!-- We add a time stamp to the filename as well -->
    <jar jarfile="${distribute}/lib/${outFile}-${DSTAMP}.jar"
basedir="${build}">
        <manifest>
            <attribute name="Main-Class" value="itso.ant.hello.HelloAnt"/>
        </manifest>
    </jar>
```

```
</target>
```

Cleanup target (clean)

The last of our standard targets is the cleanup target. This target removes the build and distribute directories, which means that a full recompile is always performed if this target has been executed.

```
<target name="clean">
    <!-- Delete the ${build} and ${distribute} directory trees -->
    <delete dir="${build}"/>
    <delete dir="${distribute}"/>
</target>
```

Note that our build.xml file does not call for this target to be executed. It has to be specified when running Ant.

22.3.6 Run Ant

Ant is a built-in function to Rational Application Developer. You can launch it from the context menu of any XML file, although it will run successfully only on valid Ant XML build script files. When launching an Ant script, you are given the option to select which targets to run and whether you want to view the output in a special Log Console window.

To run our build script:

1. Open the Java perspective.
2. Expand the **BankAnt** project.
3. Right-click **build.xml** in either the Package Explorer or Outline view.
4. Select **Run** → **3.Run Ant...**, as seen in Figure 22-13.

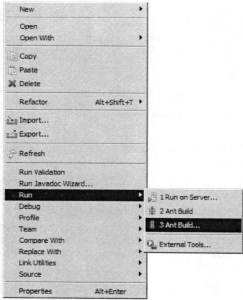

Figure 22-13   Launching Ant

5. When the Modify Attributes and Launch dialog appears, as seen in Figure 22-13 on page 1174, select the desired attributes. For example, select the **JRE** tab, select **Run in the same JRE as the workspace**, and then click **Run**.

   The default target specified in the build file is already selected as one target to run. You can check, in sequence, which ones are to be executed, and the execution sequence is shown in the Target execution order field.

   > **Note:** Since dist depends on compile, even if you only select dist, the compile target is executed as well.

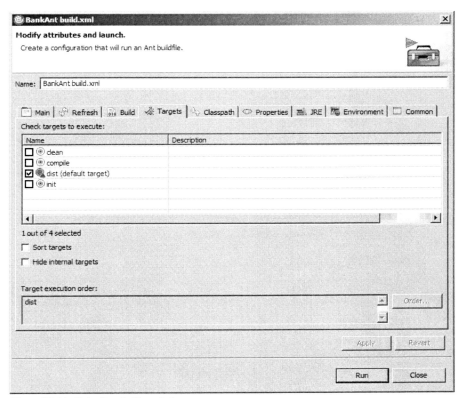

Figure 22-14 Selecting Ant targets to run

The Run Ant wizard gives you several tabs to configure or run the Ant process. The tabs allow you to do the following:

- Main: This tab allows you to select the build file, base directory, and arguments to pass to the Ant process.
- Refresh: This tab allows you to set some refresh options when the Ant process has finished running.
- Build: This tab allows you to set some build options before the Ant process is run.
- Target: This tab allows you to select the targets and the sequences the targets are to run.

- Classpath: This tab allows you to customize the classpath for the Ant process.
- Properties: This tab allows you to add, edit, or remove properties to be used by the Ant process.
- JRE: This tab allows you to select the Java Runtime Environment to use to run the Ant process.
- Environment: This tab allows you to define environmental variables to be used by the Ant process. This tab is only relevant when running in an external JRE.
- Common: This tab allows you to define the launch configuration for the Ant process.

When Ant is running, you will see output in the Log Console (Figure 22-15).

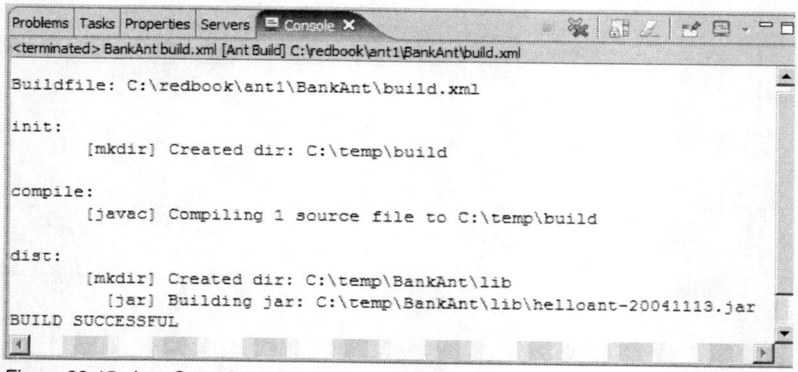
Problems
Tasks
Properties
Servers
Console
<terminated> BankAnt build.xml [Ant Build] C:\redbook\ant1\BankAnt\build.xml
Buildfile: C:\redbook\ant1\BankAnt\build.xml
init:
[mkdir] Created dir: C:\temp\build
compile:
[javac] Compiling 1 source file to C:\temp\build
dist:
[mkdir] Created dir: C:\temp\BankAnt\lib
[jar] Building jar: C:\temp\BankAnt\lib\helloant-20041113.jar
BUILD SUCCESSFUL

Figure 22-15 Log Console

22.3.7 Ant Log Console

The Log Console view opens automatically when running Ant, but if you want to open it manually, select **Window → Show view → Log Console**.

The Log Console shows that Ant has created the c:\temp\build directory, compiled the source files, created the c:\temp\BankAnt\lib directory, and generated a JAR file.

22.3.8 Rerun Ant

If you launch Ant again with the same target selected, Ant will not do anything at all since the c:\temp\build and c:\temp\BankAnt\lib directories were already created, and the class files in the build directory were already up-to-date.

22.3.9 Forced build

To generate a complete build, select the clean target as the first target and the dist target as the second target to run. You have to de-select dist, select clean, and then select dist again to get the execution order right (see Figure 22-16).

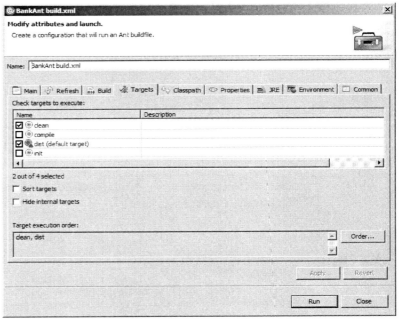

Figure 22-16   Launching Ant to generate complete build

22.3.10 Classpath problem

The classpath specified in the Java build path for the project is, unfortunately, not available to the Ant process. If you are building a project that references another project, the classpath for the javac compiler must be set up in the following way:

```
<javac srcdir="${source}" destdir="${build}" includes="**/*.java">
   <classpath>
      <pathelement location="../MyOtherProject"/>
      <pathelement location="../MyThirdProject"/>
   </classpath>
</javac>
```

22.3.11 Run the sample application to verify the Ant build

Now that you have completed the Ant build, we recommend that you verify the build by running the sample application as follows:

1. Open a Windows command window.
2. Navigate to the output directory of the Ant build (for example, c:\temp\BankAnt\lib).
3. Set the Java path by entering the following command:

   ```
   set PATH=%PATH%;c:\Program Files\IBM\Rational\SDP\6.0\runtimes\base_v6\java\bin
   ```

4. Enter the following to run the program:

   ```
   java -jar helloant-20050216.jar
   ```

   Where the timestamp in the jar filename will be dependent on when it is built.

   You should see the following output:

   ```
   G'day from Australia!
   ```

22.4 Build a J2EE application

As we have just demonstrated in the previous section, building a simple Java application using Ant is quite easy. In this section we demonstrate how to build a J2EE application from existing J2EE-related projects.

This section is organized as follows:

- J2EE application deployment packaging.
- Prepare for the sample.
- Create the build script.
- Run the Ant J2EE application build.

22.4.1 J2EE application deployment packaging

EAR, WAR, and EJB JAR files contain a number of deployment descriptors that control how the artifacts of the application are to be deployed onto an application server. These deployment descriptors are mostly XML files and are standardized within the J2EE specification.

While working in Application Developer, some of the information in the deployment descriptor is stored in XML files. The deployment descriptor files also contain information in a format convenient for interactive testing and debugging. This is one of the reasons it is so quick and easy to test J2EE applications in the integrated WebSphere Application Server V6.0 Test Environment included with Rational Application Developer.

The actual EAR being tested, and its supporting WAR, EJB, and client application JARs, are not actually created as a standalone file. Instead, a special EAR is used that simply points to the build contents of the various J2EE projects. Since these individual projects can be anywhere on the development machine, absolute path references are used.

When an enterprise application project is exported, a true standalone EAR is created, including all the module WARs, EJB JARs, and Java utility JARs it contains. Therefore, during the export operation, all absolute paths are changed into self-contained relative references within that EAR, and the internally optimized deployment descriptor information is merged and changed into a standard format. To create a J2EE-compliant WAR or EAR, we therefore have to use Application Developer's export function.

22.4.2 Prepare for the sample

For the purposes of demonstrating how to build a J2EE application using Ant, we will use the J2EE applications developed in Chapter 15, "Develop Web applications using EJBs" on page 827.

To import the BankEJB.zip Project Interchange file containing the sample code into Rational Application Developer, do the following:

1. Open the J2EE perspective Project Explorer view.
2. Select **File** → **Import**.
3. Select **Project Interchange** from the list of import sources and then click **Next**.
4. When the Import Projects dialog appears, click the **Browse** button next to zip file, navigate to and select the **BankEJB.zip** from the c:\6449code\ejb folder, and click **Open**.

> **Note:** For information on downloading and unpacking the redbook sample code, refer to Appendix B, "Additional material" on page 1395.

5. Click **Select All** to select all projects and then click **Finish**.

After importing the BankEJB.zip Project Interchange file you should see the following projects:

- BankEJBEAR
- BankEJB
- BankEJBClient
- BankBasicWeb

22.4.3 Create the build script

To build the BankEJBEAR enterprise application, we created an Ant build script (build.xml) that utilizes the J2EE Ant tasks provided by Rational Application Developer.

> **Note:** The completed version the build.xml can be found in the c:\6449code\ant\j2ee directory.

To add the Ant build script to the project, do the following:

1. Open the J2EE perspective Project Explorer view.
2. Expand **Enterprise Applications** → **BankEJBEAR**, and select **META-INF**.
3. Select **File** → **New** → **Other**.
4. When the New File dialog appears, select **Simple** → **File**, and click **Next**.
5. Enter `build.xml` in the File name field, and click **Finish**.
6. Enter the code in Example 22-2 into the build.xml file.

> **Tip:** For simplicity, we suggest that you simply import the completed build.xml or cut and paste the contents from the c:\6449code\ant\j2ee\build.xml file.

7. Modify the value for the work.dir property to match your desired working directory (for example, c:/BankEAR_workdir), as highlighted in Example 22-2.

Example 22-2   J2EE Ant build.xml script

```
<?xml version="1.0" encoding="UTF-8"?>
<project name="ITSO RAD Pro Guide Ant" default="Total" basedir=".">
```

```xml
<!-- Set global properties -->
<property name="work.dir" value="c:/BankEAR_workdir" />
<property name="dist" value="${work.dir}/dist" />
<property name="project.ear" value="BankEJBEAR" />
<property name="project.ejb" value="BankEJB" />
<property name="project.war" value="BankBasicWeb" />
<property name="type" value="incremental" />
<property name="debug" value="true" />
<property name="source" value="true" />
<property name="meta" value="false" />
<property name="noValidate" value="false" />

<target name="init">
    <!-- Create the time stamp -->
    <tstamp />
    <!-- Create the dist directory where the output files are placed -->
    <mkdir dir="${dist}" />
</target>

<target name="info">
    <!-- Displays the properties for this run -->
    <echo message="debug=${debug}" />
    <echo message="type=${type}" />
    <echo message="source=${source}" />
    <echo message="meta=${meta}" />
    <echo message="noValidate=${noValidate}" />
    <echo message="Output directory=${dist}" />
    <echo message="project.ear=${project.ear}" />
    <echo message="project.ejb=${project.ejb}" />
    <echo message="project.war=${project.war}" />
</target>

<target name="deployEjb">
    <!-- Generates deployed code for the EJBs -->
    <ejbDeploy EJBProject="${project.ejb}" NoValidate="${noValidate}" />
</target>

<target name="buildEjb" depends="deployEjb">
    <!-- Builds the EJB project -->
    <projectBuild ProjectName="${project.ejb}" BuildType="${type}" DebugCompilation="${debug}" />
    <projectBuild ProjectName="${project.ejb}" BuildType="${type}" DebugCompilation="${debug}" />
</target>

<target name="buildWar">
    <!-- Builds the WAR project -->
```

```xml
        <projectBuild ProjectName="${project.war}" BuildType="${type}"
DebugCompilation="${debug}" />
    </target>

    <target name="buildEar">
        <!-- Builds the EAR project -->
        <projectBuild ProjectName="${project.ear}" BuildType="${type}"
DebugCompilation="${debug}" />
    </target>

    <target name="exportEjb" depends="init">
        <!-- Exports the EJB JAR -->
        <ejbExport ejbprojectname="${project.ejb}" ejbexportfile="${dist}/${project.ejb}.jar"
exportsource="${source}" overwrite="true" />
    </target>

    <target name="exportWar" depends="init">
        <!-- Exports the WAR file -->
        <warExport warprojectname="${project.war}" warexportfile="${dist}/${project.war}.war"
exportsource="${source}" overwrite="true" />
    </target>

    <target name="exportEar" depends="init">
        <!-- Exports the EAR file -->
        <echo message="Exported EAR files to ${dist}/${project.ear}.ear" />
        <earExport earprojectname="${project.ear}" earexportfile="${dist}/${project.ear}.ear"
exportsource="${source}" IncludeProjectMetaFiles="${meta}" overwrite="true" />
    </target>

    <target name="buildAll" depends="buildEjb,buildWar,buildEar">
        <!-- Builds all projects -->
        <echo message="Built all projects" />
    </target>

    <target name="exportAll" depends="exportEjb,exportWar,exportEar">
        <!-- Exports all files -->
        <echo message="Exported all files" />
    </target>

    <target name="Total" depends="buildAll,exportAll">
        <!-- Buidl all projects and exports all files -->
        <echo message="Total finished" />
    </target>

    <target name="clean">
        <!-- Delete the output files -->
        <delete file="${dist}/${project.ejb}.jar" failonerror="false" />
        <delete file="${dist}/${project.war}.war" failonerror="false" />
        <delete file="${dist}/${project.ear}.ear" failonerror="false" />
```

```
        </target>
</project>
```

The build.xml script includes the following Ant targets, which correspond to common J2EE application build.

- deployEjb: This generates the deploy code for all EJBs in the project.
- buildEjb: This builds the EJB project (compiles resources within project).
- buildWar: This builds the Web project (compiles resources within project).
- buildEar: This builds the Enterprise Application project (compiles resources within project).
- exportEjb: This exports the EJB project to a jar file.
- exportWar: This exports the Web project to a WAR file.
- exportEar: This exports the Enterprise Application project to an EAR file.
- buildAll: This invokes the buildEjb, buildWar, and buildEar targets.
- exportAll: This invokes the exportEjb, exportWar, and exportEar targets to create the BankEJBEAR.ear used for deployment.

In the global properties for this script we define a number of useful variables, such as the project names and the target directory. We also define a number of properties that we pass on to the Application Developer Ant tasks. These properties allow us to control whether the build process should perform a full or incremental build, whether debug statements should be included in the generated class files, and whether Application Developer's metadata information should be included when exporting the project.

When launching this Ant script, we can also override these properties by specifying other values in the arguments field, allowing us to perform different kinds of builds with the same script.

22.4.4 Run the Ant J2EE application build

When launching the build.xml script, you can select which targets to run and the execution order.

To run the Ant build.xml to build the J2EE application, do the following:

1. Open the J2EE perspective Project Explorer view.
2. Expand **Enterprise Applications** → **BankEJBEAR** → **META-INF**.
3. Right-click **build.xml**, and select **Run** → **3 Ant Build**.

> **Note:** From the content menu for the Ant build script, the following two build options exist:
>
> ► 2 Ant Build: This will invoke the default target for the Ant build. In our example, this is the Total target, which in turn invokes buildAll and exportAll targets.
>
> ► 3 Ant Build: This will launch a dialog where you can select the targets and order, and provide parameters, as seen in Figure 22-17 on page 1185.

The Modify attributes and launch dialog will appear, as seen in Figure 22-17 on page 1185.

4. Click the **Main** tab.
   - To build the J2EE EAR file with debug, source files, and meta data, enter the following in the Arguments text area:

     `-DDebug=true -Dsource=true -Dmeta=true`

   Or:

   - To build the J2EE EAR for production deployment (without debug support, source code, and meta data), enter the following in the Arguments text area:

     `-Dtype=full`

5. Click the **Targets** tab, and check **Sort Targets**. Ensure that **Total** is checked (default).
6. Click the **JRE** tab. Select **Run in the same JRE as the workspace**.
7. Click **Apply** and then click **Run**.
8. Change to the following directory to ensure that the BankEJBEAR.ear file was created:

   `c:\BankEAR_workdir\dist`

The Console view will display the operations performed and their results.

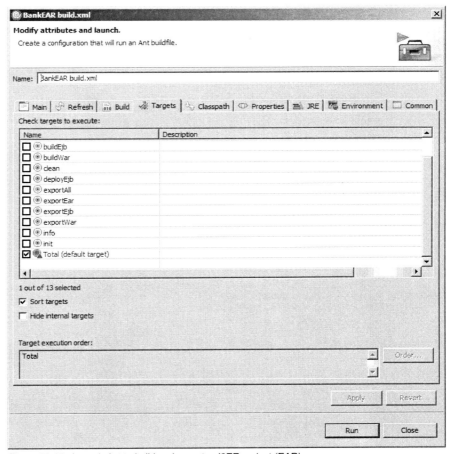

Figure 22-17 Launch Ant to build and export a J2EE project (EAR)

22.5 Run Ant outside of Application Developer

To automate the build process even further, you may want to run Ant outside of Application Developer by running Ant in *headless mode*.

22.5.1 Prepare for the headless build

Rational Application Developer includes a runAnt.bat file that can be used to invoke Ant in headless mode and passes the parameters that you specify. This will need to be customized for your environment.

The runAnt.bat file included with Rational Application Developer is located in the following directory:

```
<rad_home>\rwd\eclipse\plugins\com.ibm.etools.j2ee.ant_6.0.0
```

To create a headless Ant build script for J2EE project, do the following:

1. Copy the runAnt.bat file to a new file called itsoRunAnt.bat.
2. Modify the following values in the itsoRunAnt.bat, as seen in Example 22-3:

   ```
   set STUDIO_DIR=C:\Program Files\IBM\Rational\SDP\6.0
   set WORKSPACE=C:\workspace
   ```

Example 22-3 Snippet of the itsoRunAnt.bat (modified runAnt.bat)

```
@echo off
setlocal
REM RUNANT_DIR=This directory (which may, or may not, be your current working directory)
set RUNANT_DIR=%~dp0

:studio
REM The root directory of your Studio installation
set STUDIO_DIR=C:\Program Files\IBM\Rational\SDP\6.0
if not exist "%STUDIO_DIR%"\eclipse\jre   set STUDIO_DIR=%RUNANT_DIR%..\..\..
if not exist "%STUDIO_DIR%"\eclipse\jre   echo ERROR: incorrect STUDIO_DIR=%STUDIO_DIR%
if not exist "%STUDIO_DIR%"\eclipse\jre   goto done

:java
if not $%JAVA_DIR%$==$$ goto workspace
set JAVA_DIR=%STUDIO_DIR%\eclipse\jre\bin

:workspace
if not $%WORKSPACE%$==$$ goto check
REM #####################################################
REM ##### you must edit the "WORKSPACE" setting below #####
REM #####################################################
REM *********** The location of your workspace ************
set WORKSPACE=C:\workspace
```

22.5.2 Run the headless Ant build script

> **Attention:** Prior to running Ant in headless mode, Rational Application Developer must be closed. If you do not close Rational Application Developer, you will get build errors when attempting to run Ant build in headless mode.

To run the itsoRunAnt.bat command file, do the following:

1. Ensure you have closed Rational Application Developer.
2. Open a Windows command prompt.
3. Navigate to the location of the itsoRunAnt.bat file.
4. Run the command file by entering the following:

   ```
   itsoRunAnt -buildfile c:\workspace\BankEJBEAR\META-INF\build.xml clean
   Total -DDebug=true -Dsource=true -Dmeta=true
   ```

   The -buildfile parameter should specify the fully qualified path of the build.xml script file. We can pass the targets to run as parameters to itsoRunAnt and we can also pass Java environment variables by using the -D switch.

   In this example we chose to run the clean and exportWar1 targets, and we chose to include the debug, Java source, and metadata files in the resulting EAR file.

   > **Note:** We have included a file named output.txt, which contains the output from the headless Ant script for review purposes. The file can be found in the c:\6449code\ant\j2ee directory.

5. There are several build output files, which can be found in the c:\BankEARTest\dist directory:
   - BankBasicWeb.war, which is the BankBasicWeb project
   - BankEJB.war, which is the BankEJB project
   - BankEJBEAR.ear, which is the BankEJBEAR project with all the dependant projects included

23

Deploy enterprise applications

The term *deployment* can have many different meanings depending on the context. In this chapter we start out by defining the concepts of application deployment. The remainder of the chapter provides a working example for packaging and deploying the ITSO Bank enterprise application to a standalone IBM WebSphere Application Server V6.0 (Base Edition).

The application deployment concepts and procedures described in this chapter apply to IBM WebSphere Application Server V6.0 Base, Express, and Network Deployment editions, as well as the Rational Application Developer integrated WebSphere Application Server V6.0 Test Environment.

This chapter is organized into the following sections:

- Introduction to application deployment
- Prepare for the sample
- Package the application for deployment
- Deploy the enterprise application
- Verify the application

23.1 Introduction to application deployment

Deployment is a critical part of the J2EE application development cycle. Having a solid understanding of the deployment components, architecture, and process is essential for the successful deployment of the application.

In this section we review the following concepts of the J2EE and WebSphere deployment architecture:

- Common deployment considerations
- J2EE application components and deployment modules
- Java and WebSphere class loader
- Deployment descriptors
- WebSphere deployment architecture

> **Note:** Further information on the IBM WebSphere Application Server deployment can be found in the following sources:
> - *WebSphere V6 Planning and Design*, SG24-6446
> - *WebSphere Application Server V6 Systems Management and Configuration*, SG24-6451
> - *WebSphere Application Server V6 Scalability and Performance*, SG24-6392
> - IBM WebSphere Application Server V6.0 InfoCenter found at:
>   http://publib.boulder.ibm.com/infocenter/ws60help/index.jsp?topic=/com.ibm.websphere.base.doc/info/welcome_base.html

23.1.1 Common deployment considerations

Some of the most common factors that impact the deployment of a J2EE application are as follows:

- Deployment architecture: How can you create, assemble, and deploy an application properly if you do not understand the deployment architecture.

  > **Note:** This chapter focuses on this aspect of deployment.

- Infrastructure: What the hardware and software constraints are for the application.
- Security: What security will be imposed on the application and what is the current security architecture.
- Application requirements: Do they imply a distributed architecture?

- Performance: How many users are using the system (frequency, duration, and concurrency).

23.1.2 J2EE application components and deployment modules

Within the J2EE application development life cycle, the application components are created, assembled, and then deployed. In this section, we explore the application component types, deployment modules, and packaging formats to gain a better understanding of what is being packaged (assembled) for deployment.

Application component types

In J2EE V1.4, there are four application component types supported by the runtime environment:

- Application Clients: Run in the Application Client Container.
- Applets: Run in the Applet Container.
- Web applications (servlets, JSPs, HTML pages): Run in the Web Container.
- EJBs: Run in the EJB Container.

Deployment modules

The J2EE deployment components are packaged for deployment as modules:

- Web application module
- EJB module
- Resource adapter module
- Application client module

Packaging formats (WAR and EAR)

There are two key packaging formats used to package J2EE modules for deployment, namely Web Application Archive (WAR) and Enterprise Application Archive (EAR). The packaging technology for both is similar to that of a jar file. WAR files can include servlets, JSPs, HTML, images, etc. Enterprise Application Archive (EAR) can be used to package EJB modules, resource adapter modules, and Web application modules.

23.1.3 Java and WebSphere class loader

Class loaders are responsible for loading classes, which may be used by an application. Understanding how Java and WebSphere class loaders work is an important element of WebSphere Application Server configuration needed for the application to work properly after deployment. Failure to set up the class loaders properly will often result in class loading exceptions such as ClassNotFoundException when trying to start the application.

Java class loader

Java class loaders enable the Java virtual machine (JVM) to load classes. Given the name of a class, the class loader should locate the definition of this class. Each Java class must be loaded by a class loader.

The the JVM is started; three class loaders are used:

- Bootstrap class load: The bootstrap class loader is responsible for loading the core Java libraries (that is, core.jar, server.jar, etc.) in the <JAVA_HOME>/lib directory. This class loader, which is part of the core JVM, is written in native code.

    > **Note:** Beginning with JDK 1.4, the core Java libraries in the IBM JDK are no longer packaged in rt.jar as was previously the case (and is the case for the Sun JDKs), but instead split into multiple JAR files.

- Extensions class loader: The extensions class loader is responsible for loading the code in the extensions directories (<JAVA_HOME>/lib/ext or any other directory specified by the java.ext.dirs system property). This class loader is implemented by the sun.misc.Launcher$ExtClassLoader class.

- System class loader: The system class loader is responsible for loading the code that is found on java.class.path, which ultimately maps to the system CLASSPATH variable. This class loader is implemented by the sun.misc.Launcher$AppClassLoader class.

Delegation is a key concept to understand when dealing with class loaders. It states that a custom class loader (a class loader other than the bootstrap, extension, or system class loaders) delegates class loading to its parent before trying to load the class itself. The parent class loader can either be another custom class loader or the bootstrap class loader. Another way to look at this is that a class loaded by a specific class loader can only reference classes that this class loader or its parents can load, but not its children.

The Extensions class loader is the parent for the System class loader. The Bootstrap class loader is the parent for the Extensions class loader. The class loaders hierarchy is shown in Figure 23-1 on page 1193.

If the System class loader needs to load a class, it first delegates to the Extensions class loader, which in turn delegates to the Bootstrap class loader. If the parent class loader cannot load the class, the child class loader tries to find the class in its own repository. In this manner, a class loader is only responsible for loading classes that its ancestors cannot load.

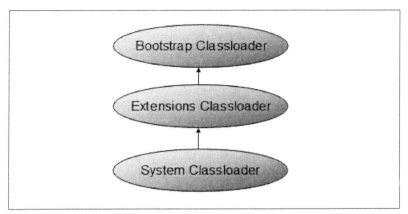

Figure 23-1 Java class loaders hierarchy

WebSphere class loader

It is important to keep in mind when reading the following material on WebSphere class loaders, that each Java Virtual Machine (JVM) has its own setup of class loaders. This means that in a WebSphere environment hosting multiple application servers (JVMs), such as a Network Deployment configuration, the class loaders for the JVMs are completely separated even if they are running on the same physical machine.

WebSphere provides several custom delegated class loaders, as shown in Figure 23-2 on page 1194.

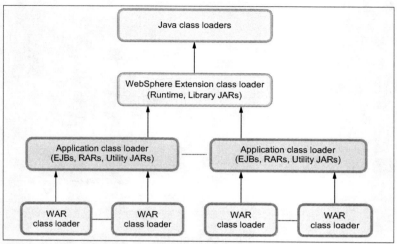

Figure 23-2 WebSphere class loaders hierarchy

In Figure 23-2, the top box represents the Java (Bootstrap, Extension, and System) class loaders. WebSphere does not load much here, just enough to get itself bootstrapped and initialize the WebSphere extension class loader.

WebSphere extensions class loader

The WebSphere extensions class loader is where WebSphere itself is loaded. It uses the following directories to load the required WebSphere classes:

- <JAVA_HOME>\lib
- <WAS_HOME>\classes (Runtime Class Patches directory, or RCP)
- <WAS_HOME>\lib (Runtime class path directory, or RP)
- <WAS_HOME>\lib\ext (Runtime Extensions directory, or RE)
- <WAS_HOME>\installedChannels

The WebSphere runtime is loaded by the WebSphere extensions class loader based on the ws.ext.dirs system property, which is initially derived from the WS_EXT_DIRS environment variable set in the setupCmdLine script file. The default value of ws.ext.dirs is the following:

```
SET
WAS_EXT_DIRS=%JAVA_HOME%\lib;%WAS_HOME%\classes;%WAS_HOME%\lib;%WAS_HOME%\i
nstalledChannels;%WAS_HOME%\lib\ext;%WAS_HOME%\web\help;%ITP_LOC%\plugins\c
om.ibm.etools.ejbdeploy\runtime
```

The RCP directory is intended to be used for fixes and other APARs that are applied to the application server runtime. These patches override any copies of the same files lower in the RP and RE directories. The RP directory contains the core application server runtime files. The bootstrap class loader first finds classes in the RCP directory, then in the RP directory. The RE directory is used for extensions to the core application server runtime.

Each directory listed in the ws.ext.dirs environment variable is added to the WebSphere extensions class loaders class path. In addition, every JAR file and/or ZIP file in the directory is added to the class path.

You can extend the list of directories/files loaded by the WebSphere extensions class loaders by setting a ws.ext.dirs custom property to the Java virtual machine settings of an application server.

Application and Web module class loaders

J2EE applications consist of five primary elements: Web modules, EJB modules, application client modules, resource adapters (RAR files), and Utility JARs. Utility JARs contain code used by both EJBs and/or servlets. Utility frameworks (like log4j) are a good example of a utility JAR.

EJB modules, utility JARs, resource adapters files, and shared libraries associated with an application are always grouped together into the same class loader. This class loader is called the application class loader. Depending on the application class loader policy, this application class loader can be shared by multiple applications (EAR) or be unique for each application (the default).

By default, Web modules receive their own class loader (a WAR class loader) to load the contents of the WEB-INF/classes and WEB-INF/lib directories. The default behavior can be modified by changing the application's WAR class loader policy (the default being Module). If the WAR class loader policy is set to Application, the Web module contents are loaded by the *application class loader* (in addition to the EJBs, RARs, utility JARs, and shared libraries). The application class loader is the parent of the WAR class loader.

The application and the Web module class loaders are reloadable class loaders. They monitor changes in the application code to automatically reload modified classes. This behavior can be altered at deployment time.

Handling JNI code

Due to a JVM limitation, code that needs to access native code via a Java Native Interface (JNI) must not be placed on a reloadable class path, but on a static class path. This includes shared libraries for which you can define a native class path, or the application server class path. So if you have a class loading native code via JNI, this class must not be placed on the WAR or application class loaders, but rather on the WebSphere extensions class loader.

It may make sense to break out just the lines of code that actually load the native library into a class of its own and place this class on a static class loader. This way you can have all the other code on a reloadable class loader.

23.1.4 Deployment descriptors

Information describing a J2EE application and how to deploy it into a J2EE container is stored in XML files called deployment descriptors. An EAR file normally contains multiple deployment descriptors, depending on the modules it contains. Figure 23-3 shows a schematic overview of a J2EE EAR file. In this figure the various deployment descriptors are designated with DD after their name.

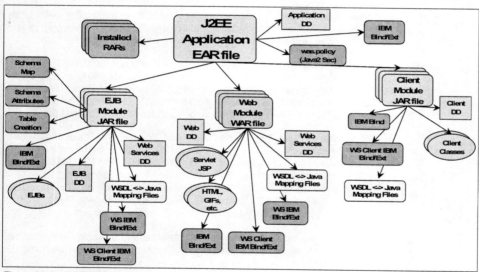

Figure 23-3   J2EE EAR file structure

The deployment descriptor of the EAR file itself is stored in the META-INF directory in the root of the EAR and is called application.xml. It contains information about the modules making up the application.

The deployment descriptors for each module are stored in the META-INF directory of the module and are called web.xml (for Web modules), ejb-jar.xml (for EJB modules), ra.xml (for resource adapter modules), and application-client.xml (for Application client modules). These files describe the contents of a module and allow the J2EE container to configure things like servlet mappings, JNDI names, etc.

Classpath information specifying which other modules and utility JARs are needed for a particular module to run, is stored in the manifest.mf file, also in the META-INF directory of the modules.

In addition to the standard J2EE deployment descriptors, EAR files produced by Rational Application Developer or the Application Server Toolkit can also include additional WebSphere-specific information used when deploying applications to WebSphere environments. This supplemental information is stored in an XMI file, also in the META-INF directory of the respective modules. Examples of information in the IBM-specific files are IBM extensions like servlet reloading and EJB access intents.

New in WebSphere Application Server V6 is also the information contained in the enhanced EAR files. This information, which includes settings for the resources required by the application, is stored in an ibmconfig subdirectory of the application's (EAR file's) META-INF directory. In the ibmconfig directory are the well-known directories for a WebSphere cell configuration.

Rational Application Developer and the Application Server Toolkit have easy-to-use editors for working with all deployment descriptors. The information that goes into the different files is shown on one page in the GUI, eliminating the need to be concerned about what information is put into what file. However, if you are interested, you can click the Source tab of the deployment descriptor editor to see the text version of what is actually stored in that descriptor.

For example, if you open the EJB deployment descriptor, you will see settings that are stored across multiple deployment descriptors for the EJB module, including:

- The EJB deployment descriptor, ejb-jar.xml
- The extensions deployment descriptor, ibm-ejb-jar-ext.xmi
- The bindings file, ibm-ejb-jar-bnd.xmi files
- The access intent settings, ibm-ejb-access-bean.xmi

The deployment descriptors can be modified from within Rational Application Developer, by double-clicking the file to open the Deployment Descriptor Editor, as seen in Figure 23-4.

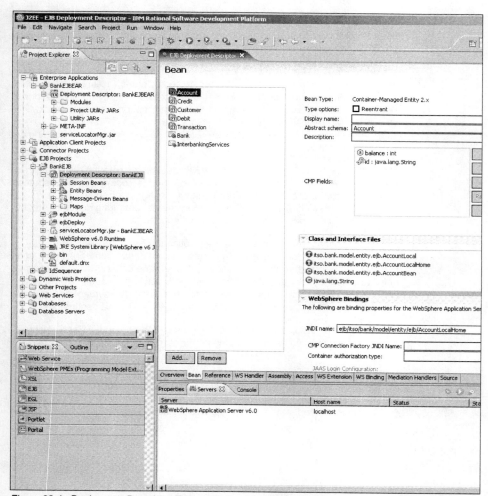

Figure 23-4   Deployment Descriptor Editor in Rational Application Developer

While the editor will show you information stored in all the relevant deployment descriptor files on the appropriate tabs, the Source tab will only show you the source of the deployment descriptor itself (for example, ejb-jar.xml or web.xml) and not the IBM extensions and bindings stored in the WebSphere-specific deployment descriptor files. If you want to view the results of updates to those files in the source, you will need to open each file individually. By hovering over the EJB Deployment Descriptor Caption tab you can see the different files that make up the EJB deployment descriptor you are editing. The descriptor files are kept in the META-INF directory of the module you are editing.

When you have made changes to a deployment descriptor, save it by pressing Ctrl+S and then close it.

Note: "Customize the deployment descriptors" on page 1220 provides an example of customizing the ITSO Bank EJB deployment descriptors for the desired database server type (Cloudscape or DB2 Universal Database).

23.1.5 WebSphere deployment architecture

This section provides an overview of the IBM WebSphere Application Server V6.0 deployment architecture.

IBM Rational Application Developer V6.0 includes an integrated WebSphere Application Server V6.0 Test Environment. Administration of the server and applications is performed by using the WebSphere Administrative Console for such configuration tasks as:

- J2C authentication aliases
- Datasources
- Service buses
- JMS queues and connection factories

Due to the loose coupling between Rational Application Developer and WebSphere Application Server, applications can deploy in the following ways:

- Deploy from a Rational Application Developer project to the integrated WebSphere Application Server V6.0 Test Environment.
- Deploy from a Rational Application Developer project to a separate WebSphere Application Server runtime environment.
- Deploy via EAR to an integrated WebSphere Application Server V6.0 Test Environment.
- Deploy via EAR to a separate WebSphere Application Server runtime environment.

Administration of the application server is performed through the use of an Internet Web browser.

In addition, the WebSphere Application Server V6 can obtain an EAR from external tools without the deployment code generated and be loaded into the Rational Application Developer or Application Server Toolkit (AST). Rational Application Developer or AST will generate the deployment code for the WebSphere Application Server and a new EAR will be saved to deploy out to the application server.

A diagram of the deployment architecture and the various mechanisms to deploy out an application are provided in Figure 23-5.

Details on how to configure the servers in IBM Rational Application Developer V6 are documented in Chapter 19, "Servers and server configuration" on page 1043.

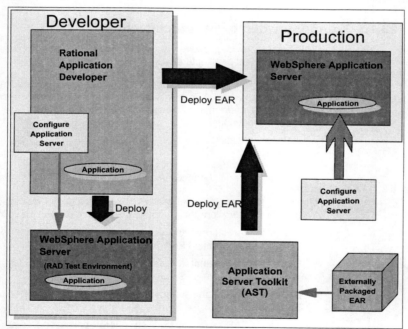

Figure 23-5   Deployment architecture

Profiles in WebSphere Application Server

WebSphere Application Server V6.0 has been split into two separate components:

- A set of shared read-only product files
- A set of configuration files known as WebSphere Profiles

The first component is the runtime part of WebSphere Application Server V6.0, while the second component is a new concept called WebSphere Profiles.

A WebSphere Profile is the set of configurable files including WebSphere Application Server configuration, applications, and properties files that constitute a new application server. Having multiple profiles equates to having multiple WebSphere Application Server instances for use with a number of applications.

> **Note:** This function is similar to the `wsinstance` command that was available in WebSphere Application Server V5.x, creating multiple runtime configurations using the same installation.

In IBM Rational Application Developer V6 this allows a developer to configure multiple application servers for various applications that they may be working with. Separate WebSphere Profiles can then be set up as test environments in Rational Web/Application Developer (see Chapter 19, "Servers and server configuration" on page 1043).

WebSphere enhanced EAR

The WebSphere enhanced EAR is a feature of IBM WebSphere Application Server V6.0 that provides an extension of the J2EE EAR with additional configuration information for resources typically required by J2EE applications. This information is not mandatory to be supplied at packaging time, but it can simplify the deployment of applications to WebSphere Application Server for selected scenarios.

The Enhanced EAR Editor can be used to edit several WebSphere Application Server V6 specific configurations, such as data sources, class loader policies, substitution variables, shared libraries, virtual hosts, and authentication settings. The configuration settings can be made simply within the editor and published with the EAR at the time of deployment.

The upside of the tool is that it makes the testing process simpler and repeatable, since the configurations can be saved to files and then shared within a team's repository. Even though it will not let you configure every possible runtime setting, it is a good tool for development purposes because it eases the process of configuring the most common ones.

The downside is that the configurations the tool makes will be attached to the EAR, and will not be visible from the WebSphere Administrative Console. The WebSphere Administrative Console is only able to edit settings that belong to the cluster, node, and server contexts.

When you change a configuration using the Enhanced EAR Editor, these changes are made within the application context. The deployer can still make changes to the EAR file using the Application Server Toolkit (AST), but it still requires a separate tool. Furthermore, in most cases these settings are dependent on the node the application server is installed in anyway, so it may not make sense to configure them at the application context for production deployment purposes.

Table 23-1 lists the supported resources that the enhanced EAR provides and the scope in which they are created.

Table 23-1   Enhanced EAR resources supported and their scope

Resource Type	Scope
JDBC Providers	Application
DataSources	Application
Substitution variables	Application
Class loader policies	Application
Shared libraries	Server
JAAS authentication aliases	Cell
Virtual hosts	Cell

The following example demonstrates how to use the Extended EAR Editor to create a data source, as an alternative to using the WebSphere Administrative Console.

1. Start Rational Application Developer.
2. Open the J2EE perspective Project Explorer view.
3. Expand **Enterprise Applications** → **BankEJBEAR**.
4. Double-click the **Deployment Descriptor: BankEJBEAR** to open in the editor.
5. Configure JAAS Authentication for DB2 Universal Database.

   Note: This step is not required for Cloudscape (no authentication required).

a. Click the **Deployment** tab, as seen in Figure 23-6 on page 1203.
b. Scroll down the page until you see the Authentication property. This allows you to define a login configuration used by JAAS Authentication.
c. Select the **dbuser** entry (default) and click **Edit**.

   Alternatively, click **Add** to create a new entry.

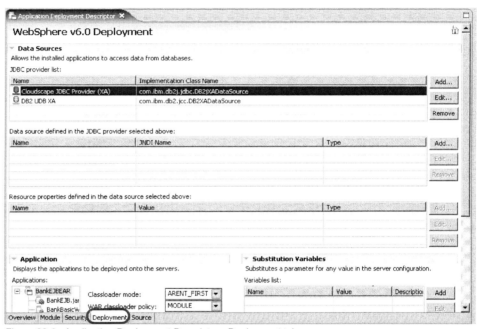

Figure 23-6   Application Deployment Descriptor - Deployment tab

d. When the Add JAAS Authentication Entry dialog appears, enter the user ID and password for the DB2 Universal Database, as seen in Figure 23-7 on page 1204.

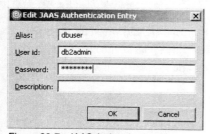

Figure 23-7   JAAS Authentication Entry

6. Add a JDBC provider.

   a. From the Enhanced EAR Editor, scroll back to the JDBC Provider section at the top of the page.

   b. Click **Add** next to the JDBC Provider list.

   c. When the Create a JDBC Provider dialog appears, select **IBM DB2** as the Database type, select **DB2 Universal JDBC Driver Provider (XA)** from the JDBC provider type (as seen in Figure 23-8 on page 1205), and then click **Next**.

   > **Note:** Note that for our development purposes, the DB2 Universal JDBC Driver Provider (non XA) would work just as well, because we will not use the XA (two-phase commit) capabilities.

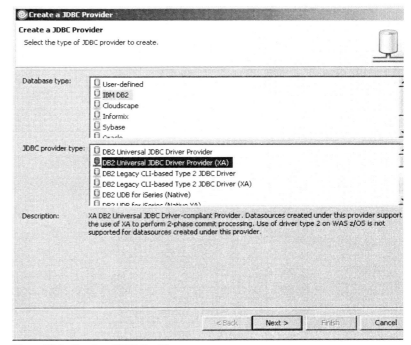

Figure 23-8   Create a JDBC Provider

d. Enter `DB2 XA JDBC Provider` in the Name field, accept the defaults for remaining fields (as seen in Figure 23-9 on page 1206), and click **Finish**.

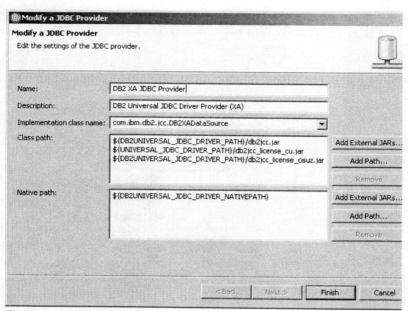

Figure 23-9   Create a JDBC Provider - Name

7. Add a data source.

    a. Select the **DB2 XA JDBC Provider** you created in the previous step under the JDBC provider list.

    b. Click **Add** next to the Data source section.

    c. When the Create a Data Source (page 1) dialog appears, select **DB2 Universal JDBC Driver Provider (XA)** (as seen in Figure 23-10 on page 1207), and then click **Next**.

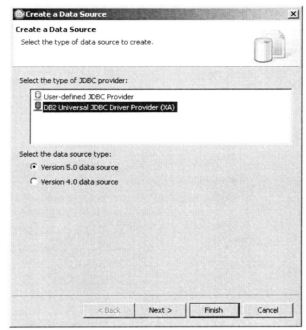

Figure 23-10   Create a Data Source (page 1)

   d. When the Create Data Source (page 2) dialog appears, we entered the following (as seen in Figure 23-11 on page 1208) and then clicked **Next**:
      - Name: BankDS
      - JNDI name: jdbc/bankDS
      - Description: Bank DataSource
      - Component-managed authenticated alias: Select **dbuser**.

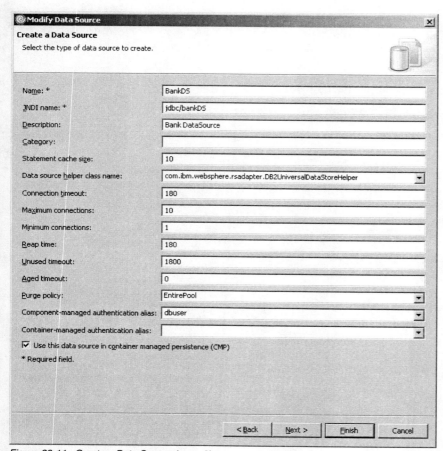

Figure 23-11   Create a Data Source (page 2)

     e. When the Create Resource Properties dialog appears, select the **databaseName** variable from the Resource Properties list, enter BANK in the variable value field (as seen in Figure 23-12 on page 1209), and then click **Finish**.

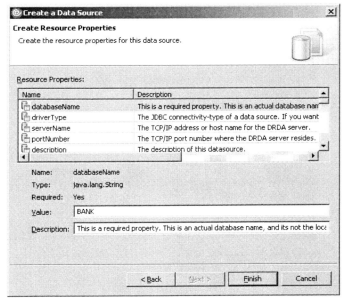

Figure 23-12   Create a Data Source (page 3)

8. Save the Deployment Descriptor.

The settings configured using the Enhanced EAR Editor will be packaged as part of the standard EAR export process and published at the time of installing the enterprise application in WebSphere Application Server.

> **Note:** For more detailed information and an example of using the WebSphere enhanced EAR refer to:
>
> ► *Packaging applications* chapter in the *WebSphere Application Server V6 Systems Management and Configuration*, SG24-6451
>
> ► IBM WebSphere Application Server V6.0 InfoCenter found at:
>
>   http://publib.boulder.ibm.com/infocenter/ws60help/index.jsp?topic=/com.ibm.websphere.base.doc/info/welcome_base.html

Chapter 23. Deploy enterprise applications   **1209**

WebSphere Rapid Deployment

WebSphere Rapid Deployment is a collection of tools and technologies introduced in IBM WebSphere Application Server V6.0 that makes application development and deployment easier than ever before.

WebSphere Rapid Deployment consists of the following elements:

- Annotation-based programming (Xdoclet)
- Rapid deployment tools
- Fine-grained application updates

Annotation-based programming (Xdoclet)

Annotation-based programming speeds up application development by reducing the number of artifacts that you need to develop and manage on your own. By adding metadata tags to the Java code, the WebSphere Rapid Deployment tools can automatically create and manage the artifacts to build a J2EE-compliant module and application.

Rapid deployment tools

Using the rapid deployment tools part of WebSphere Rapid Deployment you can:

- Create a new J2EE application quickly without the overhead of using an integrated development environment (IDE).
- Package J2EE artifacts quickly into an EAR file.
- Deploy and test J2EE modules and full applications quickly on a server.

For example, you can place full J2EE applications (EAR files), application modules (WAR files, EJB JAR files), or application artifacts (Java source files, Java class files, images, JSPs, etc.) into a configurable location on your file system, referred to as the *monitored,* or *project,* directory. The rapid deployment tools then automatically detect added or changed parts of these J2EE artifacts and perform the steps necessary to produce a running application on an application server.

There are two ways to configure the monitored directory, each performing separate and distinct tasks (as depicted in Figure 23-13 on page 1212):

- Free-form project
- Automatic application installation project

With the free-form approach you can place in a single project directory the individual parts of your application, such as Java source files that represent servlets or enterprise beans, static resources, XML files, and other supported application artifacts. The rapid deployment tools then use your artifacts to automatically place them in the appropriate J2EE project structure, generate any additional required artifacts to construct a J2EE-compliant application, and deploy that application on a target server.

The automatic application installation project, on the other hand, allows you to quickly and easily install, update, and uninstall J2EE applications on a server. If you place EAR files in the project directory they are automatically deployed to the server. If you delete EAR files from the project directory, the application is uninstalled from the server. If you place a new copy of the same EAR file in the project directory, the application is reinstalled. If you place WAR or EJB JAR files in the automatic application installation project, the rapid deployment tool generates the necessary EAR wrapper and then publishes that EAR file on the server. For RAR files, a wrapper is not created. The standalone RAR files are published to the server.

The advantage of using a free-form project is that you do not need to know how to package your application artifacts into a J2EE application. The free-form project takes care of the packaging part for you. The free-form project is suitable when you just want to test something quickly, perhaps write a servlet that performs a task.

An automatic application installation project, on the other hand, simplifies management of applications and relieves you of the burden of going through the installation panels in the WebSphere administrative console or developing wsadmin scripts to automate your application deployment.

The rapid deployment tools can be configured to deploy applications either onto a local or remote WebSphere Application Server.

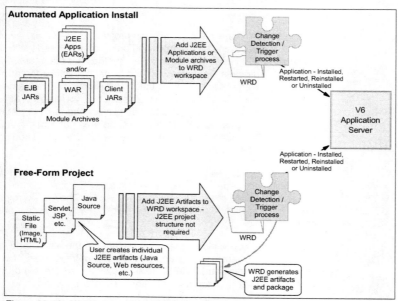

Figure 23-13   WebSphere Rapid Deployment modes

> **Note:** For more detailed information on WebSphere Rapid Deployment refer to the following:
>
> - *WebSphere V6 Planning and Design*, SG24-6446
> - *WebSphere Application Server V6 Systems Management and Configuration*, SG24-6451
> - IBM WebSphere Application Server V6.0 InfoCenter found at:
>
>   http://publib.boulder.ibm.com/infocenter/ws60help/index.jsp?topic=/com.ibm.websphere.base.doc/info/welcome_base.html

23.2 Prepare for the sample

This section describes the steps required to prepare the environment for the deployment sample. We will use the ITSO Bank enterprise application developed in Chapter 15, "Develop Web applications using EJBs" on page 827, to demonstrate the deployment process.

This section includes the following tasks:

- Review the deployment scenarios.
- Install prerequisite software
- Import the sample application Project Interchange file.
- Set up the sample database.

23.2.1 Review the deployment scenarios

Now that the Rational Application Developer integration with WebSphere Application Server V6.0 is managed the same as a standalone WebSphere Application Server, the procedure to deploy the ITSO Bank sample application is nearly identical to that of a standalone WebSphere Application Server.

There are several possible configurations in which the sample can be installed. The deployment process in this chapter accounts for the following two scenarios:

- Deploy ITSO Bank to a separate production IBM WebSphere Application Server V6.0. This scenario uses two nodes (Developer node, Application Server node).

  or

- Deploy ITSO Bank to a Rational Application Developer - integrated WebSphere Application Server V6.0 Test Environment.

23.2.2 Install prerequisite software

The application deployment sample requires that you have the software defined in this section installed. Within the example, you can choose between DB2 Universal Database and Cloudscape as your database server.

The sample for the working example environment consists of two nodes:

- Developer node (see Table 23-2 on page 1214 for product mapping)

  This node will be used by the developer to import the sample code and package the application in preparation for deployment.

- Application Server node (see Table 23-3 on page 1214 for product mapping)

  This node will be used as the target server where the enterprise application will be deployed.

Note: For detailed information on installing the required software for the sample, refer to Appendix A, "IBM product installation and configuration tips" on page 1371.

Table 23-2 Developer node product mapping

Software	Version
Microsoft Windows	XP + Service Pack 1a + Critical fixes and security patches.
IBM Rational Application Developer * IBM WebSphere Application Server V6.0 Test Environment **Note**: Cloudscape is installed by default.	6.0 + Interim Fix 0004
IBM DB2 Universal Database, Express Edition	8.2

Table 23-3 Application Server node product mapping

Software	Version
Microsoft Windows	2000 + Service Pack 4 + Critical fixes and security patches.
IBM WebSphere Application Server	6.0
IBM DB2 Universal Database, Express Edition	8.2

> **Note: DB2 Universal Database or Cloudscape**
>
> The procedures in this chapter provide information on using either DB2 Universal Database or Cloudscape. Cloudscape is installed by default as part of the Rational Application Developer installation (part of WebSphere Application Server V6.0 Test Environment).

23.2.3 Import the sample application Project Interchange file

This section describes how to import the BankEJB.zip Project Interchange file into Rational Application Developer. The BankEJB.zip contains the following projects for the ITSO Bank enterprise application developed in Chapter 15, "Develop Web applications using EJBs" on page 827:

- BankBasicWeb
- BankEJB
- BankEJBClient
- BankEJBEAR

To import the BankEJB.zip Project Interchange file containing the sample code into Rational Application Developer, do the following:

1. Start Rational Application Developer.
2. Open the J2EE perspective Project Explorer view.

3. Select **File** → **Import**.
4. Select **Project Interchange** from the list of import sources and then click **Next**.
5. When the Import Projects dialog appears, click the **Browse** button next to zip file, navigate to and select the **BankEJB.zip** from the c:\6449code\ejb folder, and click **Open**.
6. Click **Select All** to select all projects and then click **Finish**.

23.2.4 Set up the sample database

The ITSO Bank application requires the BANK database. The default procedure uses Cloudscape; however, we provide instructions for DB2 Universal Database as an alternative.

> **Important:** In our scenario, we set up the BANK database on both Developer Node and on the Application Server node, since this will be the target for deploying the application.

Depending on which database server platform you choose, the appropriate table and sample data files can be found as follows:

- Cloudscape:

    ```
    c:\6449code\deploy\database\cloudscape\Bank\Table.ddl
    c:\6449code\deploy\database\cloudscape\Bank\Loaddata.sql
    ```

    or

- DB2 Universal Database:

    ```
    c:\6449code\deploy\database\db2\Bank\Table.ddl
    c:\6449code\deploy\database\db2\Bank\Loaddata.sql
    ```

> **Attention:** The database setup procedure should be performed on the target node such as the Application Server node for our scenario, and the Developer node where Rational Application Developer is installed.

To create the BANK database, create the connections, create tables for the databases, and populate the BANK database with sample data, do the following:

1. Create the BANK database on the Application Server node and Developer node.

    – Cloudscape

    For details refer to "Create Cloudscape database via Cloudscape CView" on page 344.

or

- DB2 Universal Database

    For details refer to "Create DB2 UDB database via a DB2 command window" on page 346.

2. Create the BANK database tables on the Application Server node and Developer node.

    - Create Cloudscape tables on the Application Server node.

        For details refer to "Create Cloudscape database tables via Cloudscape CView" on page 351.

    or

    - Create DB2 Universal Database tables on the Application Server node.

        For details refer to "Create DB2 UDB database tables via a DB2 command window" on page 351.

    or

    - Create Cloudscape tables from Rational Application Developer.

        For details refer to "Create database tables via Rational Application Developer" on page 350.

3. Populate the BANK database tables with sample data on the Application Server node and Developer node.

    - Populate Cloudscape BANK database tables with sample data on the Application Server node.

        For details refer to "Populate the tables via Cloudscape CView" on page 353.

    or

    - Populate DB2 Universal Database BANK database tables with sample data on the Application Server node.

        For details refer to "Populate the tables via a DB2 UDB command window" on page 354.

    or

    - Populate Cloudscape BANK database tables from Rational Application Developer.

        For details refer to "Populate the tables within Rational Application Developer" on page 352.

4. Create the connection to the BANK database on the Developer node from within Rational Application Developer.

    For details refer to "Create a database connection" on page 347.

> **Note:** This step does not apply for setup on the Application Server node.
>
> This step only applies if you are setting up the database server within Rational Application Developer. In our example, we are preparing the database on the Application Server node, and thus this step is not needed.

5. Add the JDBC driver as a variable to the Java build path on the Developer node from within Rational Application Developer.

   To add a Cloudscape JDBC driver as a classpath variable, do the following.

   > **Note:** For DB2 Universal Database, a DB2_DRIVER_PATH variable already exists. We suggest that you double check that the path to the driver is correct for your DB2 Universal Database installation.

   a. Select **Window → Preferences**.
   b. Select **Java → Build Path → Classpath variable**.
   c. Click **New**.
   d. When the New Variable Entry dialog appears, enter CLOUDSCAPE_DRIVER_JAR in the Name field. Click **File** and navigate to the directory of the driver. Select the **db2j.jar** and then click **Open**.

      For example, see Figure 23-14 path:

      C:/Program Files/IBM/Rational/SDP/6.0/runtimes/base_v6/cloudscape/lib/db2j.jar

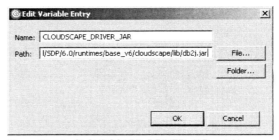

Figure 23-14   CLOUDSCAPE_DRIVER_JAR variable

   e. Click **OK** to add the variable.
   f. Click **OK** to exit the preferences window.

g. Recompile the code. By default, the Workbench preferences are configured to *Build automatically*.

23.3 Package the application for deployment

This section describes the steps in preparation for packaging, as well as how to export the enterprise application from Rational Application Developer to an EAR file, which will be used to deploy on the WebSphere Application Server.

This section includes the following:

- Packaging recommendations.
- Generate the EJB to RDB mapping.
- Customize the deployment descriptors.
- Remove the Enhanced EAR datasource.
- Generate the deploy code.
- Export the EAR.

23.3.1 Packaging recommendations

We have included some basic guidelines to consider when packaging an enterprise application:

- The EJB JAR modules and Web WAR modules comprising an application should be packaged together in the same EAR module.
- When a Web module accesses an EJB module, you should not package the EJB interfaces and stubs in the WAR modules. Thanks to the class loading architecture, EJB stubs and interfaces are visible by default to WAR modules.
- Utility classes used by a single Web module should be placed within its WEB-INF/lib folder.
- Utility classes used by multiple modules within an application should be placed at the root of the EAR file.
- Utility classes used by multiple applications can be placed on a directory referenced via a shared library definition.

23.3.2 Generate the EJB to RDB mapping

This section describes how to generate the EJB to RDB mapping for either Cloudscape or DB2 Universal Database. If you are using Cloudscape as your database server, this section is not required, but included for reference purposes. If using DB2 Universal Database, you will need to complete the DB2 section to generate the EJB to RDB mapping.

The following procedure describes how to generate the EJB to RDB mapping for the BankEJB EJBs.

1. If you are using Cloudscape, ensure the Cloudscape JDBC driver variable has been defined.

    For details refer to "Set up the sample database" on page 1215.

    For DB2 Universal Database the corresponding variable is already defined.

2. From the Data perspective, right-click the connection that you created in 23.2.4, "Set up the sample database" on page 1215, and select **Copy to Project**.

3. When the Copy to Project dialog appears, click **Browse**, expand and select **BankEJB** → **ejbModule** → **META-INF**, and click **OK**.

4. Check **Use default schema folder for EJB projects**. The folder path is then automatically entered for the appropriate database type.

5. Click **Finish**.

6. When the Confirm folder create message box appears, click **Yes**.

7. Switch to the J2EE perspective Packaging Explorer view.

8. Expand **EJB Projects**, right-click the **BankEJB** project, and select **EJB to RDB Mapping** → **Generate Map**.

9. Select **Use an existing backend folder**, select the backend folder that you created in the previous step (for example, CLOUDSCAPE_V51_1 for Cloudscape, or DB2EXPRESS_V82_1 for DB2 Universal Database), and click **Next**.

> **Note: Location of generated mapping**
>
> The mapping is generated in the following folders:
>
> ► BankEJB\Deployment Descriptor: BankEJB\Maps\Cloudscape V5.1\BANK: CLOUDSCAPE_V51_1
>
> ► BankEJB\ejbModule\META-INF\backends\CLOUDSCAPE_V51_1
>
> The Map.mapxmi file is found in this folder and will be opened as a result of generating the mapping.
>
> The mapping will increment the name of the map by one each time another map is created. In our example, the map is named CLOUDSCAPE_V51_1 since it is the first for Cloudscape. If we added another map for Cloudscape it would be named CLOUDSCAPE_V51_2.
>
> To delete a mapping, select the mapping (for example, BANK: CLOUDSCAPE_V51_1) from the **BankEJB** → **Deployment Descriptor: BankEJB** → **Maps** → **Cloudscape V5.1** folder, right-click, and select **Delete**.

10. Select **Meet-In-The-Middle** and click **Next**.
11. Select **Match by Name** and click **Next**.
12. Click **Finish**.
13. The Mapping editor will open. Follow the instructions in "Completing the EJB-to-RDB mapping" on page 897 to complete the mapping.

23.3.3 Customize the deployment descriptors

Depending on your development process you may customize your deployment descriptors prior to exporting the enterprise application to an EAR file. For example, you may wish to customize the context paths for the target WebSphere Application Server the EAR will be deployed to or change the target database from Cloudscape to DB2 Universal Database.

Alternatively, the deployment descriptors of the exported EAR could be customized using the Application Server Toolkit provided with IBM WebSphere Application Server V6.0.

> **Note:** For more information refer to "Deployment descriptors" on page 1196.

Customize the EJB deployment descriptors for Cloudscape

If you are using Cloudscape, the deployment descriptors for the sample application are already configured to use Cloudscape, thus the section is optional.

To customize the EJB deployment descriptors for use with Cloudscape, do the following:

1. Open the J2EE perspective Packaging Explorer view.
2. Expand **Enterprise Applications**.
3. Customize the BankEJB deployment descriptor.
    a. Expand the **BankEJB** project.
    b. Double-click **Deployment Descriptor: BankEJB** to open in the Deployment Descriptor Editor.
    c. Scroll down near the bottom to the section marked Backend ID.
    d. Select **CLOUDSCAPE_V51_1**.
    e. Save the Deployment Descriptor: BankEJB file.

Customize the EJB deployment descriptors for DB2 UDB

To customize the EJB deployment descriptors for use with DB2 Universal Database, do the following:

1. Open the J2EE perspective Packaging Explorer view.
2. Expand **Enterprise Applications**.
3. Customize the BankEJB deployment descriptor.
    a. Expand **EJB Projects** → **BankEJB**.
    b. Double-click **Deployment Descriptor: BankEJB** to open in the Deployment Descriptor Editor.
    c. Scroll down near the bottom to the section marked Backend ID.
    d. Select **DB2UDBNT_V82_1**.
    e. Save the Deployment Descriptor: BankEJB file.

23.3.4 Remove the Enhanced EAR datasource

The BankEJBEAR application deployment descriptor, contained in the BankEJB.zip Project Interchange that was imported in 23.2.3, "Import the sample application Project Interchange file" on page 1214, contains enhanced EAR settings to configure the datasource. These settings are needed when running the application within Rational Application Developer.

When deploying the application to a remote WebSphere Application Server system, we chose to configure the datasource using the WebSphere Application Server Administrative Console for demonstration purposes. Since the enhanced EAR datasource configuration overrides the Administrative Console configuration, the enhanced EAR datasource settings must be removed.

To remove the enhanced EAR datasource settings, do the following:

1. Expand **Enterprise Applications** → **BankEJBEAR**.
2. Double-click **Application Deployment Descriptor: BankEJBEAR**.
3. Select the **Deployment** tab.
4. Select the JDBC provider, and click **Remove**.
5. Save the deployment descriptor.

23.3.5 Generate the deploy code

Prior to exporting the EAR, we recommend that you generate the deploy code as follows:

1. Open the J2EE Perspective Project Explorer view.
2. Expand **Enterprise Applications**.
3. Right-click **BankEJBEAR** → **Deploy**.

> **Note:** After generating deployed code for the BankEJB project, you may see a number of warnings about unused imports in the Problems view. These can be safely ignored. If you wish, you can remove these warnings from the Problems view by following the process described in 15.3.4, "Configure the EJB projects" on page 849.

23.3.6 Export the EAR

This section describes how to filter the contents (include, exclude) of an EAR file, and provides a procedure to export an EAR.

Filtering the content of the EAR

When creating assets, such as diagrams, under the JavaSource folder, we found that the assets are automatically copied to the WEB-INF\classes folder. Since the WAR export utility will include all resources located in the WebContent tree, any assets located in the JavaSource tree will be included in the WAR file, regardless of the setting of the Export source files check box. For example, this is likely not a desired behavior for diagrams such as a sequence diagram.

The following procedure describes a procedure to filter the contents of an EAR for export:

1. Right-click the **BankBasicWeb** project, and select **Properties** (where BankBasicWeb is the project you wish to configure).
2. Select **Java Build Path**.
3. Select the **Source** tab.
4. Expand the **BankBasicWeb/JavaSource**, select **Excluded**, and click **Edit**.
5. When the Inclusion and Exclusion Patterns window appears, you will be presented with several options that can be used to filter contents.
   - Exclude by pattern (**Add** button)
   - Exclude individual files (**Add Multiple** button)

   For example, we used the Exclude by pattern option to filter out diagrams as follows:

   a. Click **Add**.
   b. When the Add Exclusion Patterns dialog appears, enter `**/*.dnx`, and click **OK**.
   c. Repeat the previous steps for the following patterns:
      - `**/*.iex`
      - `**/*.ifx`
      - `**/*.tpx`

   Note: Where ** is any sub folder of the JavaSource folder and the JavaSource folder itself. The /* means all files.

6. Click **OK** to close the Inclusion and Exclusion Patterns window.

Export an EAR

To export the enterprise application from Rational Application Developer to an EAR file, do the following:

1. Open the J2EE perspective Project Explorer view.
2. Expand **Enterprise Applications**.
3. Right-click **BankEJBEAR** → **Export** → **EAR file**.
4. When the EAR Export dialog window appears as shown in Figure 23-15, we entered the destination path (for example, c:\ibm\BankEJBEAR.ear) and then click **Finish**.

> **Note:** Make sure that the three options in the dialog (see Figure 23-15 on page 1224) are unchecked. Because the EAR file will be used in a production system, we do not want to include the source files or the Application Developer metadata.

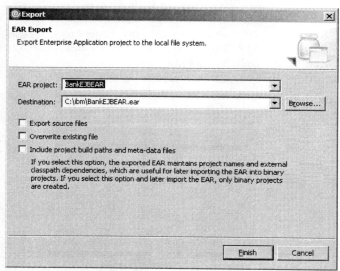

Figure 23-15   Exporting an EAR file

5. Verify that the BankEJBEAR.ear file exists in the c:\ibm folder specified during the export.

23.4 Deploy the enterprise application

Now that the application has been packaged to an EAR file, the enterprise application can be deployed to WebSphere Application Server. This section describes the steps required to configure the target WebSphere Application Server and deploy the BankEJBEAR.ear file.

> **Note:** You can deploy the BankEJBEAR.ear exported in the previous section. Alternatively, the BankEJBEAR.ear found in the c:\6449code\deploy directory of the ITSO sample code can be used.

23.4.1 Configure the data source in WebSphere Application Server

The data source for WebSphere Application Server can be created in several ways including:

- Enhanced EAR

    For details on using the enhanced EAR to configure the JDBC provider, data source, authentication, and database name refer to "WebSphere enhanced EAR" on page 1201.

- wsadmin command line interface

    For details refer to the WebSphere Application Server V6.0 InfoCenter.

- WebSphere Application Server Administrative Console

    Note: Our example uses this method.

The high-level configuration steps are as follows to configure the data source within WebSphere Application Server for the ITSO Bank application sample:

- Start the server1 application server.
- Configure the environment variables.
- Configure J2C authentication data.
- Configure the JDBC Provider.
- Create the datasource.

Start the server1 application server

Ensure that the server1 application server is started on the Application Server node. If it is, not start it as follows:

- Click **Start** → **Programs** → **IBM WebSphere** → **Application Server V6** → **Profiles** → **default** → **Start server** to start the application server named server1.

    or

- Enter the following in a command window:

    ```
    cd \Program Files\IBM\WebSphere\AppServer\profiles\default\bin
    startServer.bat server1
    ```

    or

- Start the Windows service named IBM WebSphere Application Server v6 - was6win1Node01 (where was6win1 is the host name of the system).

> **Note:** To verify that the server1 application server has started properly, you can look for the message `Server server1 open for e-business` in the SystemOut.log found in the following directory:
>
> `C:\Program Files\IBM\WebSphere\AppServer\profiles\default\logs\server1`

Configure the environment variables

Prior to configuring the data source, ensure that the environment variables are defined for the desired database server type. This step does not apply to Cloudscape since we are using the embedded Cloudscape, which already has the variables defined. For example, if you choose to use DB2 Universal Database, you must update the path of the driver for DB2 Universal Database.

1. Launch the WebSphere Administrative Console:

    — Click **Start** → **Programs** → **IBM WebSphere** → **Application Server V6** → **Profiles** → **default** → **Administrative Console**.

    or

    — Enter the following URL in a Web browser:

    `http://<hostname>:9060/ibm/console`

2. Enter a login ID (for example, admin) and then click **Log in**. The user ID can be anything at this point, since WebSphere security is not enabled.

3. Select and expand **Environment** → **WebSphere Variables**.

4. Scroll down the page and click the desired variable and update the path accordingly for your installation.

    — CLOUDSCAPE_JDBC_DRIVER_PATH

    By default this variable is already configured since Cloudscape is installed with WebSphere Application Server.

    or

    — DB2UNIVERSAL_JDBC_DRIVER_PATH

    For example, if you have decided to use DB2 Universal Database, click **DB2UNIVERSAL_JDBC_DRIVER_PATH** to enter the path value to the DB2 Java (db2java.zip). For example, we entered C:\Program Files\IBM\SQLLIB\java. Click **OK**.

5. Click **Save**, and then when prompted click **Save** to Save to Master Configuration.

Configure J2C authentication data

This section describes how to configure the J2C authentication data (database login and password) for WebSphere Application Server from the WebSphere Administrative Console. This step is required for DB2 UDB and optional for Cloudscape.

If using DB2 UDB, configure the J2C authentication data (database login and password) for WebSphere Application Server from the Administrative Console:

1. Ensure the server1 application server is started.
2. Start the WebSphere Administrative Console.

   http://<hostname>:9060/ibm/console

3. Select **Security** → **Global Security**.
4. Under the Authentication properties, expand **JAAS Configuration** → **J2C Authentication data**.
5. Click **New**.
6. Enter the following on the J2C Authentication data page if you are using DB2 UDB and then click **OK**:
   - Alias: dbuser
   - User ID: db2admin
   - Password: <password>
7. Click **Save** and then when prompted click **Save** to Save to Master Configuration.

Configure the JDBC Provider

This section describes how to configure the JDBC Provider for the selected database type. The following procedure demonstrates how to configure the JDBC Provider for Cloudscape, with notes on how to do the equivalent for DB2 Universal Database.

To configure the JDBC Provider from the WebSphere Administrative Console, do the following:

1. Select **Resources** → **JDBC Providers**.
2. Click **New**.
3. From the New JDBC Providers page, do the following and then click **Next**:
   a. Select the Database Type: Select **Cloudscape**.

   Note: For DB2 UDB, select **DB2**.

b. Select the JDBC Provider: Select **Cloudscape JDBC Provider**.

   > **Note:** For DB2 UDB, select **DB2 Universal JDBC Driver Provider**.

c. Select the Implementation type: Select **XA data source**.

   > **Note:** For DB2 UDB, select **XA data source**.

4. We accepted the default for the JDBC Provider name. Click **OK**.

   The JDBC Provider default names are as follows:
   - Cloudscape: Cloudscape JDBC Provider (XA)
   - DB2: DB2 Universal JDBC Driver Provider (XA)

5. Click **Save** and then when prompted click **Save** to Save to Master Configuration.

Create the datasource

To create the datasource from the WebSphere Administrative Console, do the following:

1. Select **Resources** → **JDBC Providers**.
2. Click the JDBC Provider created in "Configure the JDBC Provider" on page 1227. For example:
   - For Cloudscape click **Cloudscape JDBC Provider (XA)**.

   or

   - For DB2 click **DB2 Universal JDBC Driver Provider (XA)**.
3. Under Additional Properties (right-hand side of page), click **Data sources**.
4. Create the BankDS datasource for the BANK database.

   a. Click **New** from the Data sources page.

   b. Enter the following and then click **OK**:
      - Name: `BankDS`
      - JNDI name: `jdbc/BankDS`
      - Database name (Cloudscape): `c:\databases\BANK`

      > **Note:** For DB2 enter `BANK` for the database name.

   c. For DB2 you must also set the authentication. Select **dbuser** (user defined in "Configure J2C authentication data" on page 1227) from the Component-managed authentication alias drop-down list.

5. Click **Save**, and then when prompted click **Save** to Save to Master Configuration.
6. Verify the connection by checking **BankDS** and then click **Test connection**.

23.4.2 Deploy the EAR

To deploy the BankEJBEAR.ear exported in 23.3.6, "Export the EAR" on page 1222, to the WebSphere Application Server, do the following:

1. Copy the BankEJBEAR.ear from the Developer node where you exported the EAR from Rational Application Developer to a temporary directory on the Application Server node.
2. Ensure the server1 application server is started.
3. Start the WebSphere Administrative Console by opening the following location in a Web browser:

   `http://<hostname>:9060/ibm/console`
4. Select **Applications** → **Enterprise Applications**.
5. Click **Install**.
6. Enter the following and then click **Next**:
   - Select **Local file system**.
   - Specify path: `c:\temp\BankEJBEAR.ear`
7. We accepted the defaults on the generate bindings page. Click **Next**.
8. When the Install New Application wizard appears, you will need to perform the following sequence of steps to deploy the EAR.

   a. Select installation options. Accept defaults and click **Next**.

   b. Select modules to servers. Accept defaults and click **Next**.

   c. Select current backend ID. Select the currentBankendID for the specific database type then click **Next**:
   - For Cloudscape, select **CLOUDSCAPE_V51_1**.
   - For DB2 UDB, select **DB2UDBNT_V82_1**.

   d. Provide JNDI names for beans. Accept defaults and click **Next**.

   e. Provide default data source mapping for modules containing 2.x entity beans. Accept defaults and click **Next**.

   f. Map data sources for all 2.x CMP beans. Accept defaults and click **Next**.

   g. Map EJB references to beans. Accept defaults and click **Next**.

   h. Map virtual hosts for Web modules. Accept defaults and click **Next**.

i. Ensure all unprotected 2.x methods have the correct level of protection. Accept defaults and click **Next**.

j. Summary. Click **Finish**.

You should see the a number of messages, concluded by the following message:

```
Application BankEJBEAR installed successfully.
```

9. Click **Save to Master Configuration** and click **Save**.
10. Select **Applications** → **Enterprise Applications**.
11. Check **BankEJBEAR** and then click **Start**.

The status should change to started.

23.5 Verify the application

This section provides some basic procedures to verify the ITSO Bank was deployed properly and is working. Table 23-4 on page 1230 lists the sample data for the ITSO Bank loaded via the loaddata.sql in "Set up the sample database" on page 1215.

Table 23-4 ITSO Bank sample data (loaddata.sql)

Customer name	Customer SSN	Account number	Account balance
John Ganci	111-11-1111	001-999000777 (wife) 001-999000888 (kids) 001-999000999 (dad)	$1,234,567.89 $6,543.21 $98.76
George Kroner	222-22-2222	002-999000777 (wife) 002-999000888 (kids) 002-999000999 (dad)	$65,484.23 $87.96 $654.65
Daniel Farrell	333-33-3333	003-999000777 (hush $) 003-999000888 (slush) 003-999000999 (mush)	$9,876.52 $568.79 $21.56
Juha Nevalainen	444-44-4444	004-999000777 (fish) 004-999000888 (cats) 004-999000999 (builder)	$9,876.52 $1,456,456.46 $23,156.46
Ed Gondek	555-55-5555	005-999000777 (food) 005-999000888 (food) 005-999000999 (food)	$65.89 $72,213.41 $897.55
Fabio Ferraz	666-66-6666	006-999000777 (beef) 006-999000888 (more beef) 006-999000999 (barbecue)	$500.00 $100.00 $100,000.00

Customer name	Customer SSN	Account number	Account balance
Kiriya Keat	777-77-7777	007-999000777 (Vegas) 007-999000888 (beverage) 007-999000999 (ice)	$2,500,000.00 $1,000,000.00 $1.23
Nicolai Nielsen	999-99-9999	009-999000999 (Danny's)	$658,600.42

To verify that the ITSO Bank sample is deployed and working properly, do the following:

1. Ensure that the server1 application server is started.
2. Enter the following URL to access the ITSO Bank application:

   http://<hostname>:9080/BankBasicWeb/index.html

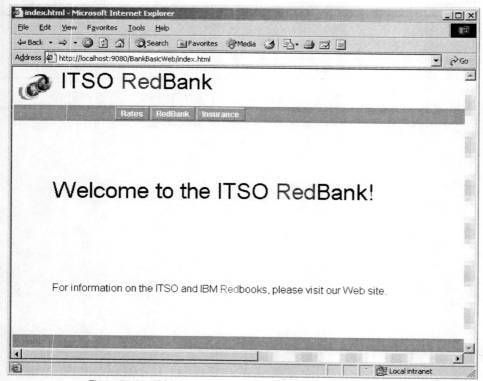

Figure 23-16 ITSO Bank home page

3. You should see something like Figure 23-16. Click **RedBank**.
4. You should see something like Figure 23-16. Enter customer ID 111-11-1111 and then click **Submit**.

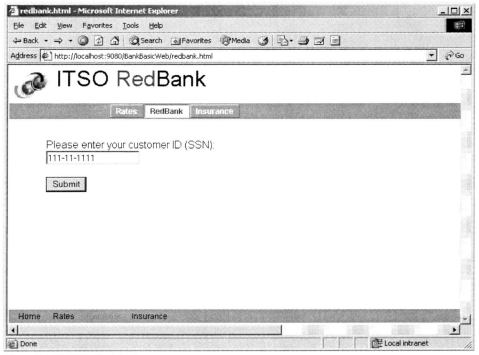

Figure 23-17   ITSO Bank login page

5. When the Accounts page appears as seen in Figure 23-18 on page 1234, click **001-999000888**.

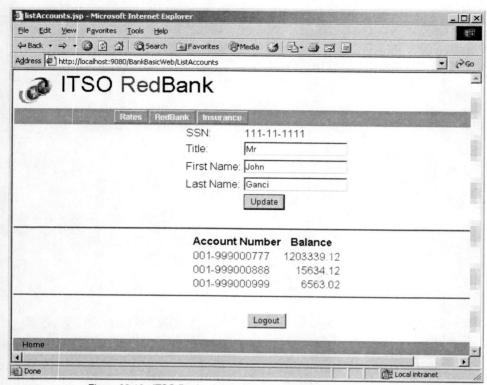

Figure 23-18 ITSO Bank - Accounts page

6. When the Account Maintenance page appears (as seen in Figure 23-19 on page 1235), do the following and then click **Submit**:

   – Select **Transfer**.
   – Amount: 54000

   > **Note:** This transfers 54000 cents, or 540 dollars.

   – Destination account: 004-999000888

> **Note:** This transfers funds to the account associated with user SSN 444-44-44444.

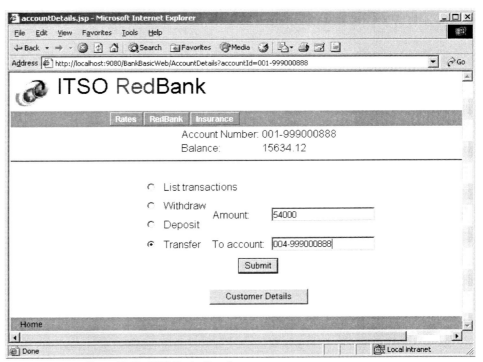

Figure 23-19   ITSO Bank - Transfer

After the transfer you should see a page like Figure 23-20 on page 1236. Notice the account balance has been updated (subtracted transfer amount).

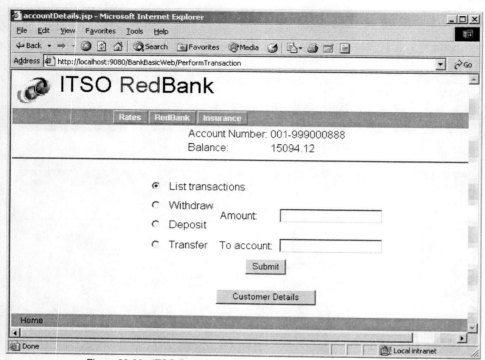

Figure 23-20 ITSO Bank - After transfer

7. Start another Web browser session, and enter the following URL to access the ITSO Bank application to simulate the other customer and account:

   `http://<hostname>:9080/BankBasicWeb/index.html`

8. Enter customer ID **444-44-4444** and then click **Submit**.

9. Click **004-999000888**.

10. Select **List transactions** and click **Submit**.

    You should see that the account has had $540.00 transferred to it. The original account balance was $1,456,456.46 and is now $1,456,996.46.

24

Profile applications

Profiling is a technique used by developers to detect and isolate application problems such as memory leaks, performance bottlenecks, excessive object creation, and exceeding system resource limits during the development phase.

This chapter introduces the features, architecture, and process for profiling applications using the profiling tooling included with IBM Rational Application Developer V6.0. We have included a working example for code coverage analysis for the Web application developed in Chapter 11, "Develop Web applications using JSPs and servlets" on page 499.

The chapter is organized into the following sections:

- Introduction to profiling
- Prepare for the profiling sample
- Profile the sample application

24.1 Introduction to profiling

Traditionally, performance analysis is performed once an application is getting close to deployment or after it has already been deployed. The profiling tools included with Rational Application Developer allow the developer to move the performance analysis to a much earlier phase in the development cycle, thus providing more time for changes to the application that may effect the architecture of the application before they become critical production environment issues.

The types of problems that IBM Rational Application Developer V6.0 profiling tooling can assist in detecting include:

- Memory leaks
- Performance bottlenecks
- Excessive object creation
- System resource limits

The profiling tools can be used to gather information on applications that are running:

- Inside an application server, such as WebSphere Application Server
- As a standalone Java application
- On the same system as Rational Application Developer
- On a remote WebSphere Application Server with the IBM Rational Agent Controller installed
- In multiple JVMs

24.1.1 Profiling features

Within Rational Application Developer, there are several profiling types. Each profiling type includes predefined profiling sets used to detect and analyze common problems such as memory leaks, performance bottlenecks, and excessive object creation.

This section describes the capabilities of the following profiling types:

- Memory analysis
- Thread analysis
- Execution time analysis
- Code coverage analysis
- Probekit analysis

Memory analysis

Memory analysis is used to detect memory management problems. In IBM Rational Application Developer V6 there is new support to provide automatic detection of memory leaks. Memory analysis can help developers identify memory leaks as well as excessive object allocation that may cause performance problems.

The memory analysis capability in IBM Rational Application Developer V6.0 has been enhanced with the addition of new views described in Table 24-1, and new capabilities found in Table 24-2.

Table 24-1   New memory analysis views

View name	Description
Leak Candidates view	A tabular view to assist the developer in identifying the most likely objects responsible for leaking memory.
Object Reference Graph view	A graphical view that shows the referential relationship of objects in a graph highlighting the allocation path of leak candidates.

Table 24-2   New memory analysis capabilities

Capability	Description
Memory Leak Analysis - Manual	Allows at the discretion of the developer to capture memory heap dumps after application warm-up; that is, when classes are loaded and initialized.
Memory Leak Analysis - Automatic	Provides timed memory heap dumps at specified intervals during the running of the Java application.

Thread analysis

Thread analysis is used to help identify thread contention and deadlock problems in a Java application. Thread contention issues can cause performance problems, while deadlocks are a correctness issue that can cause a critical runtime issue. The thread analysis capabilities provide analysis data for detecting both of these types of problems.

The thread analysis has been enhanced with the additional view displayed in Table 24-3.

Table 24-3 New thread analysis views

View name	Description
Thread View	A graphical view of all threads available, their states, and which thread is holding locks. It assists in identifying thread contentions.

Execution time analysis

Execution time analysis is used to detect performance problems by highlighting the most time intensive areas in the code. This type of analysis helps developers identify and remove unused or inefficient coding algorithms.

The execution time analysis has been enhanced with the additional views described in Table 24-4.

Table 24-4 New execution time analysis views

View name	Description
Performance Call Graph View	A graphical view focusing on data that indicates potential performance problems including statistical information.
Method Details View	A view that provides complete performance data for the currently displayed method, including information about its callers and descendants.

Code coverage analysis

Code coverage is a new capability in IBM Rational Application Developer V6.0. It is used to detect areas of code that have not been executed in a particular scenario that is tested. This capability is a useful analysis tool to integrate with component test scenarios and can be used to assist in identifying test cases that may be missing from a particular test suite or code that is redundant.

> **Note:** The profiling working example found in the following sections of this chapter demonstrate the end-to-end process of profiling a Web application for a code coverage:
> - 24.2, "Prepare for the profiling sample" on page 1246
> - 24.3, "Profile the sample application" on page 1249

New views associated with this capability are shown in Table 24-5.

Table 24-5 New views associated with code coverage

View name	Description
Coverage Navigator	A graphical view that shows coverage levels of packages, classes, and methods and their coverage statistics.
Annotated Source	Includes displays that: ► Have a copy of the code marked indicated tested, untested, and partially tested lines. ► Shows at the class and method level a pie chart with the line coverage statistic.
Coverage Statistics	A tabular view showing the coverage statistics.

Probekit analysis

Probekit analysis provides a new capability that has been introduced into IBM Rational Application Developer V6.0. It is a scriptable byte-code instrumentation (BCI) framework, to assist in profiling runtime problems by inserting Java code fragments into an application. The framework is used to collected detailed runtime information in a customized way.

A probekit file can be contain one or more probes with each containing one or more probe fragments. These probes can be specified when to be executed or on which program they will be used. The probe fragments are a set of Java methods that are merged with standard boilerplate code with a new Java class generated and compiled. The functions generated from the probe fragments appear as static methods of the generated probe class.

The probekit engine called the BCI engine is used to apply probe fragments by inserting the calls into the target programs. The insertion process of the call statements into the target methods is referred to as *instrumentation*. The data items requested by a probe fragment are passed as arguments (for example, method name and arguments). The benefit of this approach is that the probe can be inserted into a large number of methods with small overhead.

Probe fragments can be executed at the following points (see IBM Rational Application Developer V6's online help for a complete list):

► On method entry or exit
► At exception handler time
► Before every executable code when source code is available
► When specific methods are called, not inside the called method

Each of the probe fragments can access the following data:

- Package, class, and method name
- Method signature
- This object
- Arguments
- Return value
- The exception object that caused an exception handler exit to execute, or an exception exit from the method

There are two major types of probes available to the user to create, as described in Table 24-6.

Table 24-6 Types of probes available with Probekit

Type of probe	Description
Method Probe	Probe can be inserted anywhere within the body of a method with the class or jar files containing the target methods instrumented by the BCI engine.
Callsite Probe	Probe is inserted into the body of the method that calls the target method. The class or jar files that call the target instrumented by the BCI engine.

A tutorial on using Probekit is available in IBM Rational Application Developer V6 via the menu by performing the following steps:

1. Start IBM Rational Application Developer V6.
2. Select **Help → Tutorials Gallery**.
3. When the Tutorials Gallery window displays, expand **Do and Learn**.
4. Select **Use Probekit to customize Java profiling**.

This tutorial is estimated to take 45 minutes and will assist the developer in creating and using the Probekit in IBM Rational Application Developer V6.

24.1.2 Profiling architecture

The profiling architecture that exists in IBM Rational Application Developer V6.0 is based upon the data collection engine feature provided by the open source Eclipse Hyades project. More detailed information on the Eclipse Hyades project can be found at:

    http://www.eclipse.org/hyades

Hyades provides the IBM Rational Agent Controller daemon with a process for enabling client applications to launch host processes and interact with agents that exist within host processes. Figure 24-1 depicts the profiling architecture.

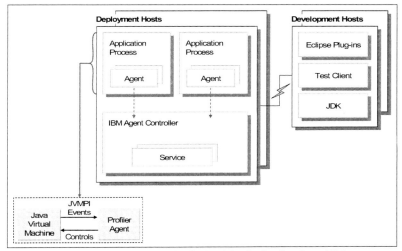

Figure 24-1   Profiling architecture of IBM Rational Application Developer V6.0

The definitions for the profiling architecture are as follows:

- Application process: The process that is executing the application consisting of the Java Virtual Machine (JVM) and the profiling agent.

- Agent: The profiling component installed with the application that provides services to the host process, and more importantly, provides a portal by which application data can be forwarded to attached clients.

- Test Client: A local or remote application that is the destination of host process data that is externalized by an agent. A single client can be attached to many agents at once, but does not always have to be attached to an agent.

- Agent Controller: A daemon process that resides on each deployment host providing the mechanism by which client applications can either launch new host processes, or attach to agents coexisting within existing host processes. The Agent Controller can only interact with host processes on the same node.

- Deployment hosts: The host that an application has been deployed to and is being monitored for the capture of profiling agent.

- Development hosts: The host that runs an Eclipse-compatible architecture such as IBM Rational Application Developer V6 to receive profiling information and data for analysis.

Each application process shown in Figure 24-1 on page 1243 represents a JVM that is executing a Java application that is being profiled. A profile agent will be attached to each application to collect the appropriate runtime data for a particular type of profiling analysis. This profiling agent is based on the Java Virtual Machine Profiler Interface (JVMPI) architecture. More details on the JVMPI specification can be found at:

    http://java.sun.com/j2se/1.4.2/docs/guide/jvmpi

The data collected by the agent is then sent to the agent controller, which then forwards this information to IBM Rational Application Developer V6 for analysis and visualization.

There are two types of profiling agents available in IBM Rational Application Developer V6:

- Java Profiling Agent: This agent is based on the JVMPI architecture and is shown in Figure 24-1 on page 1243. This agent is used for the collection of both standalone Java applications as well as applications running on an application server.
- J2EE Request Profiling Agent: This agent resides in an application server process and collects runtime data for J2EE applications by intercepting requests to the EJB or Web containers.

> **Note:** There is only one instance of the J2EE Request Profiling agent that is active in a process that hosts WebSphere Application Server.

24.1.3 Profiling and Logging perspective

After installing Rational Application Developer, you will first need to enable the Profiling and Logging capability (see "Enable the Profiling and Logging capability" on page 1247 for details).

The Profiling and Logging perspective can be accessed by selecting **Window → Open Perspective → Other → Profiling and Logging** and then clicking **OK**. If it is not listed click **Show all**.

There are many supporting views for the Profiling and Logging perspective. When selecting **Window → Show View** while in the Profiling and Logging perspective, you will see the following views:

- Console

- Log Navigator
- Log View
- Navigator
- Package Statistics
- Problems
- Profile Monitor
- Properties
- Statistical Data
- Other

> **Note:** If you select Other, you will see a listing of many more views in support of profiling.

24.1.4 Profiling sets

The profiling in IBM Rational Application Developer V6 has been structured around profiling sets and associated views. These profiling sets focus on providing the user with the ability to concentrate on particular types of analysis while profiling an application. Users who require more extensive analysis can create their own unique profiling sets to satisfy their particular needs.

The predefined profiling sets available in IBM Rational Application Developer V6 are outlined in Table 24-7.

Table 24-7 Profiling sets and available views

Profiling set	Options selected	Views available
Memory/Leak Analysis	N/A	- Package Statistics view - Class Statistics view - Object References view
	Instance Level information check box selected	- Package Statistics view - Class Statistics view - Statistics - Object References view

Profiling set	Options selected	Views available
Execution Time Analysis	Show execution Statistics (compressed data)	▸ Package Statistics view ▸ Class Statistics view ▸ Method Statistics view ▸ Coverage Statistics
	Show execution graphical details	▸ Package Statistics view ▸ Class Statistics view ▸ Method Statistics view ▸ Coverage Statistics ▸ Execution Flow view ▸ UML2 Sequence diagrams views (object, class, thread)
	Show Instance level information, Show execution graphical details	▸ Package Statistics view ▸ Class Statistics view ▸ Method Statistics view ▸ Instance Statistics ▸ Coverage Statistics ▸ Object References view ▸ Execution Flow view ▸ UML2 Sequence diagrams views (object, class, thread)
Method Code Coverage	N/A	▸ Package Statistics view ▸ Class Statistics view ▸ Method Statistics view ▸ Coverage Statistics

Important: For the Object References view you will need to ensure that *Collect Object References* is enabled to view the profiling data using the Object References view.

24.2 Prepare for the profiling sample

This redbook includes a code coverage profiling example. We will use the ITSO RedBank sample Web application developed in Chapter 11, "Develop Web applications using JSPs and servlets" on page 499, as our sample application for profiling.

Complete the following tasks in preparation for the profiling sample:
- Prerequisites hardware and software.
- Enable the Profiling and Logging capability.

- Import the sample project interchange file.
- Publish and run sample application.

24.2.1 Prerequisites hardware and software

This section outlines the hardware and software we used to run the profiling working example.

Prerequisite hardware

When developing the working example, we used the following hardware:

- IBM ThinkCentre™ M50 (8189-E1U)
  - Intel Pentium 4, 2.8 GHz CPU
  - 2 GB RAM

  > **Note:** We found memory profiling to be very resource intensive.

  - 40 GB 7200 RPM IDE HDD

Prerequisite software

The working example requires the following software be installed:

1. IBM Rational Application Developer V6.0

   For details refer to "Rational Application Developer installation" on page 1372.

2. IBM Rational Application Developer V6.0 - Interim Fix 0004

   For details refer to "Rational Application Developer Product Updater - Interim Fix 0004" on page 1380.

3. IBM Rational Agent Controller

   For details refer to "IBM Rational Agent Controller V6 installation" on page 1382.

24.2.2 Enable the Profiling and Logging capability

To enable the Profiling and Logging capability in the preferences, do the following:

1. Select **Window** → **Preferences**.
2. Expand **Workbench** → **Capabilities**.
3. Expand **Tester**, and check **Profiling and Logging** (as seen in Figure 24-2), and then click **OK**.

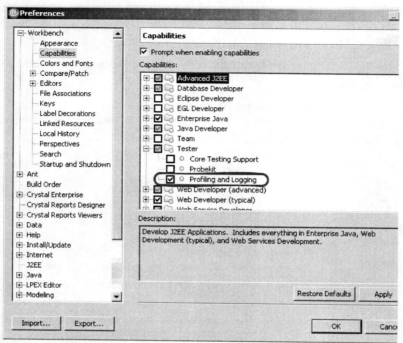

Figure 24-2 Enable Profiling and Logging capability

> **Note:** If you want to use the Probekit, you will need to enable this capability by checking the Probekit check box, as seen in Figure 24-2.

24.2.3 Import the sample project interchange file

To import the ITSO RedBank JSP and Servlet Web application Project Interchange file (BankBasicWeb.zip), do the following:

1. Open the Web perspective Project Explorer view.
2. Right-click **Dynamic Web Projects**, and select **Import** → **Import**.
3. When the Import dialog appears, select **Project Interchange** and then click **Next**.

4. In the Import Projects screen, browse to the c:\6449code\web folder and select **BankBasicWeb.zip**. Click **Open**.

5. Check the **BankBasicWeb** and **BankBasicWebEAR** projects, and click **Finish**.

24.2.4 Publish and run sample application

The sample application needs to be published to the WebSphere Application Server, prior to running the application server in profile mode.

To publish and run the sample application on the WebSphere Application Server V6.0 test server, do the following:

1. Open the Web perspective.
2. Expand **Dynamic Web Projects** → **BankBasicWeb** → **WebContent**.
3. Right-click **index.html**, and select **Run** → **Run on Server**.
4. When the Server Selection dialog appears, select **Choose and existing server**, select **WebSphere Application Server v6.0**, and click **Finish**.

   This operation will start the server and publish the application to the server.

24.3 Profile the sample application

This section demonstrates the code coverage analysis feature of profiling for the ITSO RedBank Web application.

24.3.1 Start server in profile mode

To start the WebSphere Application Server V6.0 in profile mode, do the following:

1. Ensure the IBM Rational Agent Controller Windows service is started.
2. Open the Web perspective.
3. In the Servers view, do the following to start the server in profile mode:
   - If the WebSphere Application Server V6.0 is started, right-click and select **Restart** → **Profile**.
   - If the WebSphere Application Server V6.0 is not started, right-click the server and select **Profile**.
4. After the server has started, the Profile on server dialog should appear presenting the user with a listing of agents to attach to.

Expand **PID** as seen in Figure 24-3, and select the `>` to move the PID to the Selected agents pane.

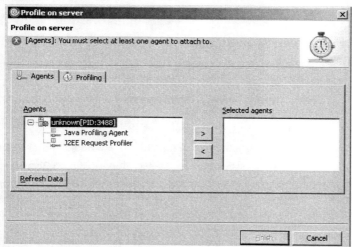

Figure 24-3   Identify Agents to attach to

5. Click the **Profiling** tab as seen in Figure 24-4 on page 1251.

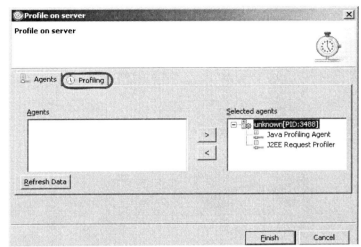

Figure 24-4   Addition of PID to the list of selected agents

6. When the Overview tab appears, check **Method Coverage Information** (as seen in Figure 24-5 on page 1252), and click **Finish**.

    When you click **Finish**, the Profiling and Logging perspective will appear.

    > **Note:** In most cases, the pre-defined profile sets will be adequate for testing; however, you may want to create a new profile set that chains together the several existing profile sets.
    >
    > To add a new profile set, click **Add** as seen in Figure 24-5 on page 1252, and enter the name of the new profile set. Click **Edit** and check the desired existing profiling sets that you wish to include in your new profiling set.

Figure 24-5   Profile on server

7. When the Profiling tips dialog appears as seen in Figure 24-6, click **OK**.

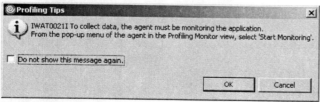

Figure 24-6   Profiling Tips

24.3.2 Collect profile information

To collect the profile information, do the following:

1. In the Profiling Monitor view of the Profiling and Logging perspective, select the two attached profiler process, as shown in Figure 24-7. Right-click and select **Start Monitoring**.

Figure 24-7   Selecting active process in the Profile Monitor view

2. Run a test of a part of the application.

   > **Note:** This step requires that you have published the project to the server as described in 24.2.4, "Publish and run sample application" on page 1249.

   a. Enter the following URL to launch the application in a Web browser:

      http://localhost:9080/BankBasicWeb/index.htm

   b. Click **RedBank**.

   c. When prompted, enter 111-11-1111 in the customer SSN field and then click **Submit**.

We have now run the part of the application that we want to obtain code coverage information for. In the next section, we will analyze this information.

24.3.3 Analysis of code coverage information

To analyze the code coverage information for our sample application, do the following:

1. In the Profiling Monitor view, right-click **Method Code Coverage**, and select **Open With → Coverage Statistics**.

2. The Coverage Statistics view will open. Enter itso.* in the Filter field and press Enter.

   The Coverage Statistics view should look similar to Figure 24-8 on page 1254.

Chapter 24. Profile applications   **1253**

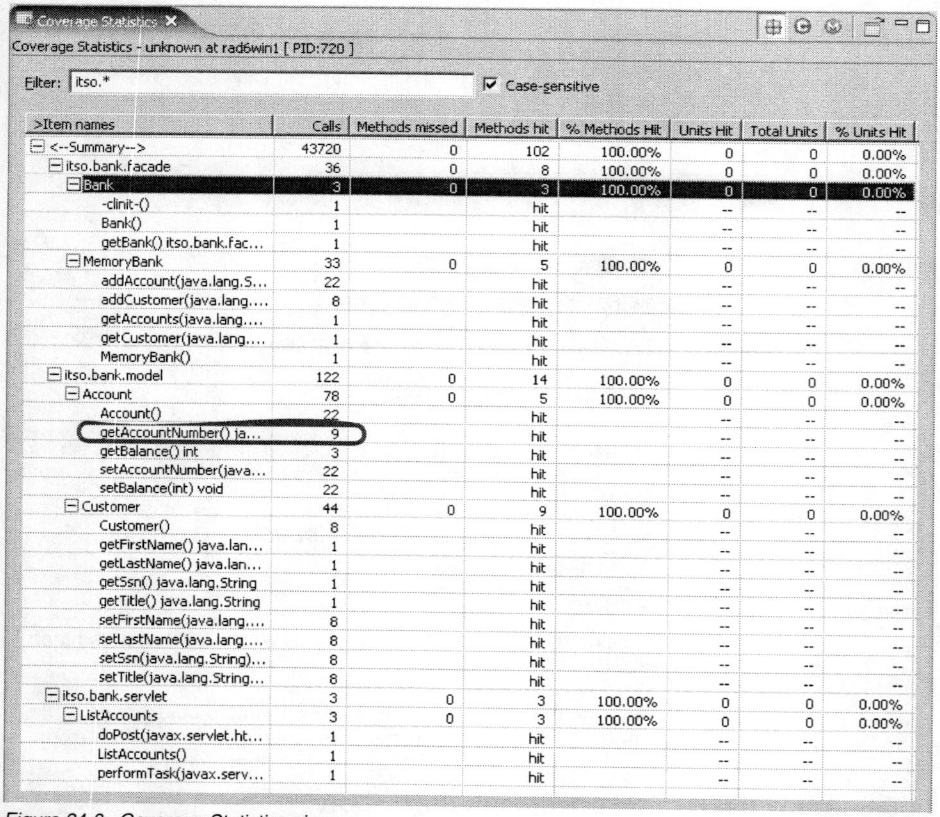

>Item names	Calls	Methods missed	Methods hit	% Methods Hit	Units Hit	Total Units	% Units Hit
<--Summary-->	43720	0	102	100.00%	0	0	0.00%
itso.bank.facade	36	0	8	100.00%	0	0	0.00%
Bank	3	0	3	100.00%	0	0	0.00%
-clinit-()	1		hit		--	--	--
Bank()	1		hit		--	--	--
getBank() itso.bank.fac...	1		hit		--	--	--
MemoryBank	33	0	5	100.00%	0	0	0.00%
addAccount(java.lang.S...	22		hit		--	--	--
addCustomer(java.lang....	8		hit		--	--	--
getAccounts(java.lang....	1		hit		--	--	--
getCustomer(java.lang....	1		hit		--	--	--
MemoryBank()	1		hit		--	--	--
itso.bank.model	122	0	14	100.00%	0	0	0.00%
Account	78	0	5	100.00%	0	0	0.00%
Account()	22		hit		--	--	--
getAccountNumber() ja...	9		hit		--	--	--
getBalance() int	3		hit		--	--	--
setAccountNumber(java...	22		hit		--	--	--
setBalance(int) void	22		hit		--	--	--
Customer	44	0	9	100.00%	0	0	0.00%
Customer()	8		hit		--	--	--
getFirstName() java.lan...	1		hit		--	--	--
getLastName() java.lan...	1		hit		--	--	--
getSsn() java.lang.String	1		hit		--	--	--
getTitle() java.lang.String	1		hit		--	--	--
setFirstName(java.lang....	8		hit		--	--	--
setLastName(java.lang....	8		hit		--	--	--
setSsn(java.lang.String)...	8		hit		--	--	--
setTitle(java.lang.String...	8		hit		--	--	--
itso.bank.servlet	3	0	3	100.00%	0	0	0.00%
ListAccounts	3	0	3	100.00%	0	0	0.00%
doPost(javax.servlet.ht...	1		hit		--	--	--
ListAccounts()	1		hit		--	--	--
performTask(javax.serv...	1		hit		--	--	--

Figure 24-8 Coverage Statistics view

The Coverage Statistics view shows which methods have been called during the tests performed on the sample application. For example, the Account.getAccountNumber method was executed nine times. This type of information is useful for function testing.

You can examine the source code for a class or method by right-clicking it in the Coverage Statistics view and selecting **Open Source**.

Part 5

Team development

25

Rational ClearCase integration

This chapter introduces the features and terminology of IBM Rational ClearCase with respect to Rational Application Developer. In addition, we provide a basic scenario with two developers working in parallel on a common Web project using Rational Application Developer and ClearCase. The focus of the example is to demonstrate the tooling and integration Rational Application Developer with ClearCase.

The chapter is organized into the following topics:

- Introduction to IBM Rational ClearCase
- Integration scenario overview
- ClearCase setup for a new project
- Development scenario

25.1 Introduction to IBM Rational ClearCase

This section provides an introduction to the IBM Rational ClearCase product as well as basic information on the IBM Rational Application Developer V6.0 integration features for ClearCase.

We have organized the section into the following topics:

- IBM Rational Application Developer ClearCase overview
- IBM Rational ClearCase terminology
- IBM Rational ClearCase LT installation
- New V6 integration features for ClearCase
- IBM Rational Application Developer integration for ClearCase

25.1.1 IBM Rational Application Developer ClearCase overview

Rational ClearCase is a software configuration management (SCM) product that helps to automate the tasks required to write, release, and maintain software code.

Rational ClearCase offers the essential functions of version control, workspace management, process configuration, and build management. By automating many of the necessary and error-prone tasks associated with software development, Rational ClearCase helps teams of all sizes build high-quality software.

ClearCase incorporates Unified Change Management (UCM), Rational's best practices process for managing change at the activity level, and control for workflow.

UCM can be applied to projects *out-of-the-box*, enabling teams to get up and running quickly. However, it can be replaced with any other process that you already have in place at your site.

ClearCase provides support for parallel development. With *automatic branching* and *merge* support, it enables multiple developers to design, code, test, and enhance software from a common, integrated code base.

Snapshot views support a *disconnected use* model for working away from the office. All changes since the last snapshot are automatically updated once you are connected again.

IBM offers two versions of the Rational ClearCase product:

- ClearCase
- ClearCase LT

ClearCase LT is a *light* version for support of small teams that do not need the full functionality of the complete ClearCase product (distributed servers, database replication, advanced build management, transparent file access). A product license for IBM Rational ClearCase LT is included with IBM Rational Application Developer V6.0.

For the *full-sized* IBM Rational ClearCase, the product also provides an add-on *MultiSite* feature.

> **Note:** Rational Application Developer includes entitlement for ClearCase LT.

More information on the IBM Rational ClearCase products can be found at:
http://www.ibm.com/software/awdtools/clearcase

25.1.2 IBM Rational ClearCase terminology

We have outlined some of the key terminology used in IBM Rational ClearCase:

- Activity: A unit of work performed by an individual. In UCM an activity tracks a change set, that is, a list of versions of files created to perform the work (for example, Developer 1 fixing problem report #123). When you work on an activity, all versions you create are associated with that activity.

- Component: A set of related directory and file elements. Typically, elements that make up a component are developed, integrated, and released together. In Application Developer, a component contains one or more projects.

- Baseline: A version of a project.

- Development stream: Each developer's own working area.

- Integration stream: A shared working area for the team, containing the versions of the components that are available to all developers.

- Deliver stream: The act of making a developer's development stream available to the integration stream, publishing a developer's work.

- Rebase: The act of retrieving a project to work on locally, or to synchronize your development stream with what is available in the integration stream.

- Check in and check out: A file that is to be edited must be checked out. This lets other developers know that the file is opened by another developer. Once a developer completes any edits on a file, it must be checked back in before making the files available to others.

- VOB (versioned object base): The permanent data repository where ClearCase stores files, directories, and metadata.

- View: A selection of resources in a VOB, a window to the VOB data.

25.1.3 IBM Rational ClearCase LT installation

IBM Rational Application Developer V6.0 includes a license for IBM Rational ClearCase LT.

Information on obtaining a copy of IBM Rational ClearCase LT can be found in TechNote-Installing_CCLT.html of the IBM Rational Application Developer V6.0 CD1. This technote describes how to obtain ClearCase LT, as well as the need to apply a patch to work properly with IBM Rational Application Developer V6.0.

For information on the IBM Rational ClearCase LT installation, refer to "IBM Rational ClearCase LT installation" on page 1385.

Figure 25-1 shows a typical development environment when using ClearCase with two developers.

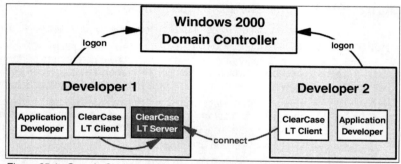

Figure 25-1   Sample ClearCase LT setup between two developers

In this chapter, we are simulating this flow by using two workspaces on the same machine.

25.1.4 IBM Rational Application Developer integration for ClearCase

IBM Rational Application Developer V6.0 includes integration support for IBM Rational ClearCase (as well as ClearCase LT), allowing easy access to ClearCase features. The ClearCase adapter is automatically activated when you start Rational Application Developer the next time after ClearCase installation.

New V6 integration features for ClearCase

Integration with Rational ClearCase via the source control management (SCM) adaptor has been enhanced in IBM Rational Application Developer V6.0 as follows:

- Dynamic views are now fully supported. Note though that ClearCase LT supports snapshot views only and the dynamic view capability is provided in ClearCase or ClearCase MultiSite®.
- Improved compare and merge, including integration with Eclipse compare/merge framework.
- Improved support for working in disconnected mode.
- Better workspace/view management.
- Better usage guidance and documentation.

ClearCase help in Rational Application Developer

Rational Application Developer provides two links to documentation for using ClearCase.

To access the help documentation in Rational Developer, select **Help** → **Help Contents** to open the new help window. Select **Developing applications in a team environment** from the Contents view.

To access the Rational ClearCase Help system, click **ClearCase Help** or click the ClearCase Help icon ( ). This icon becomes active when you connect to ClearCase.

ClearCase preferences

Ensure that the ClearCase SCM Adapter capability is enabled. Refer to 25.3.1, "Enable Team capability in preferences" on page 1264, for details.

There are a number of ClearCase preferences that you can modify by selecting **Window** → **Preferences** → **Team** → **ClearCase SCM Adapter** (see Figure 25-2 on page 1262).

We recommend that you check out files from Rational ClearCase before you edit them. However, if you edit a file that is under ClearCase control but is not checked out, Rational Developer can automatically check it out for you if you select the **Automatically checkout** option for the setting "Checked-in files are saved by an internal editor."

You can specify if you want to automatically connect to ClearCase when you start Application Developer. Select **Automatically connect to ClearCase on startup** to enable this option.

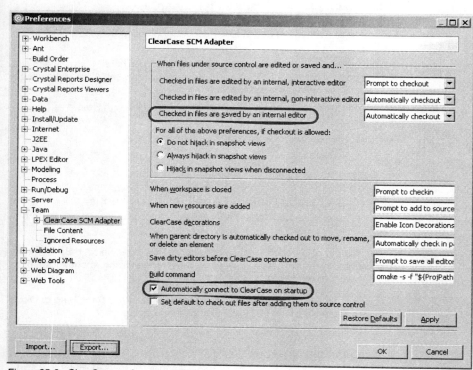

Figure 25-2 ClearCase preferences dialog

If you click **Advanced Options** and then select the **Operations** tab, there is a preference for generating backup copies when you cancel a checkout. This is enabled by default, and specifies that ClearCase generates backup copies when you perform an undo checkout operation. The backup files will have a .keep extension.

> **Note:** You must be connected to ClearCase for the Advanced Options button to be active.

The ClearCase online help in Rational Developer contains a detailed description of each option of the preferences page.

25.2 Integration scenario overview

This section describes a scenario with two developers, developer 1 and 2, working on a Web project called ITSO_ProGuide_UCM. Developer 1 is assigned the role of project integrator and is responsible for setting up the environment.

Table 25-1   Development activities

Developer 1 activities	Developer 2 activities
► Creates a new ClearCase project, ITSO_Project ► Joins the ClearCase project by creating views ► Creates a new Web project, ITSO_ProGuide_UCM ► Moves the project under ClearCase source control ► Adds a servlet, ServletA ► Delivers the work to the integration stream ► Makes a baseline	
	► Joins the ClearCase project by creating views ► Rebases his view to match the integration stream ► Imports the project into Rational Application Developer workspace
► Checks out ServletA ► Makes changes ► Checks in the servlet	► Checks out ServletA ► Makes changes ► Checks in the servlet ► Delivers the work to the integration stream
► Delivers the work to the integration stream ► Resolves conflicts by using the Merge Tool	

The setup of this scenario and its flow is shown in Figure 25-3 on page 1264. ClearCase terminology is used for the tasks.

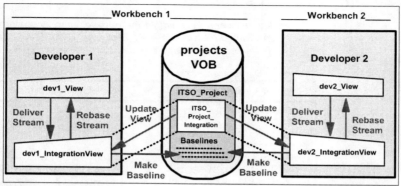

Figure 25-3 Scenario setup

Note that the integration view is like a window to the integration stream. The integration stream should be reserved for only that code that has passed the developer's inspection and is sharable to the entire team.

When finished with the changes, the developer delivers his or her development stream back to the integration stream. A project integrator (or any of the developers) can then make a new baseline freezing the latest code changes.

25.3 ClearCase setup for a new project

In this example scenario, developer 1 and developer 2 work on the same machine by switching workspaces to simulate multiple users. Alternatively, you could have developer 1 working on a machine where a ClearCase LT Server is installed, and other developers working on machines where only the ClearCase LT Client is installed. The steps are basically the same in both cases.

25.3.1 Enable Team capability in preferences

By default, the ClearCase SCM Adapter capability is disabled. To enable, do the following:

1. Select **Window → Preferences**.
2. Select **Workbench → Capabilities**.
3. Expand **Team**.
4. Check **ClearCase SCM Adapter** and **Core Team Support**.

25.3.2 Create new ClearCase project

Developer 1 creates a new project under ClearCase control as follows:

1. As developer 1, select **Start** → **Programs** → **Rational Software** → **Rational ClearCase** → **Project Explorer**.
2. Right-click **projects** and select **New** → **Project** from the context menu.
3. When the New Project Wizard appear, enter ITSO_Project in the Project name field as seen in Figure 25-4, and then click **Next**.

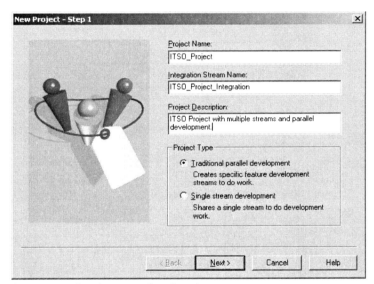

Figure 25-4   Creating new project: Step 1

4. In the Step 2 dialog ensure **No** is selected, as seen in Figure 25-5 on page 1266, and then click **Next**.

Chapter 25. Rational ClearCase integration   **1265**

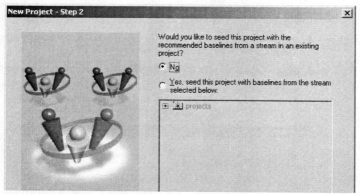

Figure 25-5   Creating new project: Step 2

5. In the Step 3 dialog (see Figure 25-6 on page 1267) click **Add**:

   a. In the Add Baseline dialog, first click **Change >>** and select **all streams**.

   b. Select the component **InitialComponent** from the drop-down list and select **InitialComponent_INITIAL** under Baselines.

   c. Click **OK**.

6. Click **Next**.

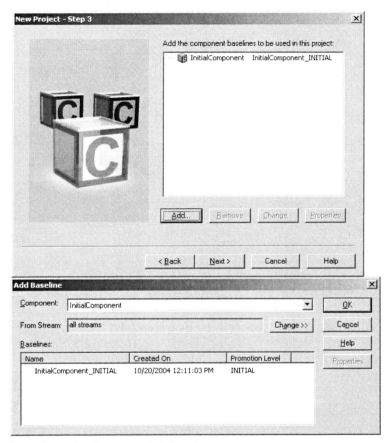

Figure 25-6   Creating new project: Step 3

7. In the Step 4 dialog (Figure 25-7 on page 1268) select **InitialComponent** under Make the following components modifiable. Leave the other values as their defaults. Click **Next**.

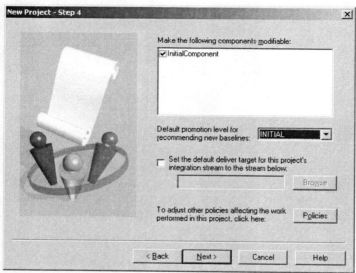

Figure 25-7   Creating new project: Step 4

8. In the Step 5 dialog, select **No** and click **Finish**.
9. Click **OK** on the confirmation dialog.

   ClearCase now creates the project and it shows up in the Project Explorer.

25.3.3 Join a ClearCase project

The next step for developer 1 is to join the project and create a new Web project in Rational Application Developer.

1. Start Rational Application Developer and enter C:\dev1_workspace as the name of the workspace for developer 1 (Figure 25-8 on page 1269).

   Do not enable the default workspace option since we will be switching workspaces several times during this exercise. Click **OK**.

   – If the Workspace Launcher dialog did not appear, change your Rational Application Developer startup setting under **Window → Preferences → Workbench → Startup** and shut down. Make sure the **Prompt for workspace on startup** option is selected.

   – If the Auto Launch Configuration Change Alert dialog appears during startup, informing of an update to your auto launch settings, click **Yes**.

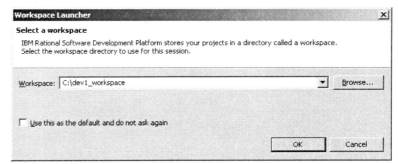

Figure 25-8   Selecting workspace for developer 1

2. Close or minimize the Welcome view.
3. Select **ClearCase** → **Connect to Rational ClearCase** (unless you specified to automatically connect to ClearCase when Rational Application Developer starts). You may also click the ClearCase Connect icon ( ).
4. Select **ClearCase** → **Create New View**.
5. In the View Creation Wizard (Figure 25-9 on page 1270), select **Yes** to indicate that we are working on a ClearCase project. Expand **projects** and select the **ITSO_Project**. Click **Next**.

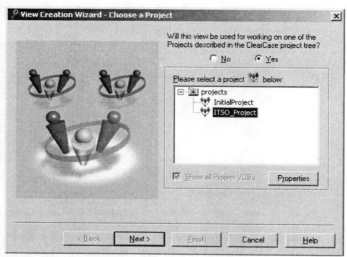

Figure 25-9   Creating a new view

6. In the Create a Development Stream dialog (Figure 25-10 on page 1271) enter `dev1_view` as the development stream name and make sure the integration stream name is ITSO_Project_Integration. Click **Next**.

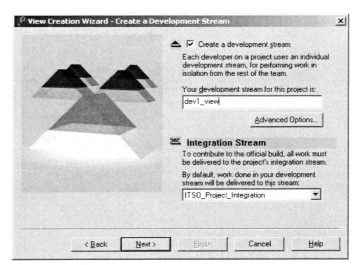

Figure 25-10 Creating a development stream

7. In the Choose Location for a Snapshot View (Development View) dialog (Figure 25-11 on page 1272) change the location to C:\ITSO\dev1_view. Click **Next** and click **Yes** on the confirmation dialog.

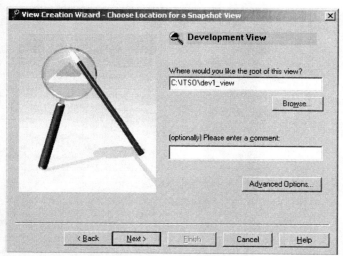

Figure 25-11   Specifying location for a development view

8. In the Choose Location for a Snapshot View (Integration View) dialog (Figure 25-12 on page 1273) change the location to C:\ITSO\Integration_view. Click **Next**.

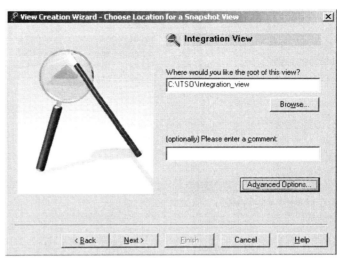

Figure 25-12 Specifying location for the integration view

9. In the Choose Components dialog, leave the **Initial_Component** selected. Click **Finish**.
10. In the Confirmation dialog (Figure 25-13) click **OK**.

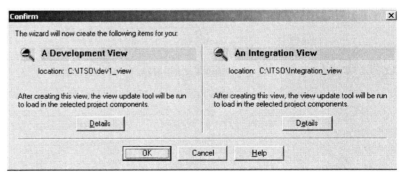

Figure 25-13 View creation confirmation dialog

11. The View Creation Status dialog is displayed after the views have been created. Click **OK**.

25.3.4 Create a Web project

Developer 1 has now created the necessary views and joined the project. The next task is to start actual development and add a new project to ClearCase control. We will create a dynamic Web project containing just one servlet for this purpose.

1. As developer 1, select **File** → **New** → **Dynamic Web Project**. In the New Dynamic Web Project dialog (Figure 25-14), enter `ITSO_ProGuide_UCM` as a project name and click **Finish**.

2. After the project is created, click **Yes** to switch to the Web perspective.

   You should now have a new project under the Dynamic Web Projects folder and the related EAR project under the Enterprise Applications folder.

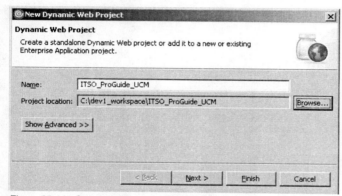

Figure 25-14   Creating dynamic Web project

25.3.5 Add a project to ClearCase source control

To add the new project under ClearCase control, do the following:

1. As developer 1, right-click the **ITSO_ProGuide_UCM** project in the Project Explorer view and select **Team** → **Share Project...** from the context menu.

2. In the Share Project dialog, select **ClearCase SCM Adapter** and click **Next**.

3. In the Move Project Into a ClearCase VOB dialog (Figure 25-15 on page 1275) click **Browse** and select the **C:\ITSO\dev1_view\sources\InitialComponent** directory. Click **OK** and then click **Finish**.

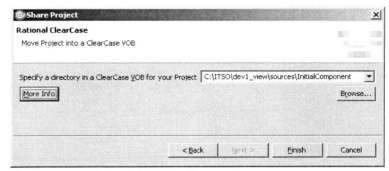

Figure 25-15   Moving project into ClearCase

4. In the Add Elements to Source Control dialog (Figure 25-16), leave all items selected and deselect **Keep checked out**. Click **OK**.

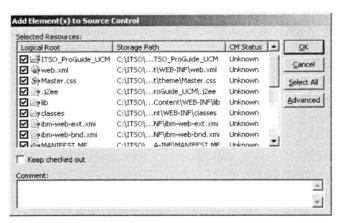

Figure 25-16   Specifying elements to add to source control

5. In the Select Activity dialog (Figure 25-16) select **New...** and enter `Developer 1 adds project to source control`. Click **OK** to return, and then click **OK** to continue. The Web project is now added to ClearCase source control.

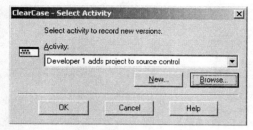

Figure 25-17   Specifying activity

In Figure 25-18 you can see that the icons belonging to the Web project now have a blue background, and the project name has a view name attached to it. This indicates that the resources are under ClearCase source control.

Figure 25-18   Resources under ClearCase source control

Project contents have been *moved* from the workspace to developer 1 view. (C:\dev1_workspace Æ C:\ITSO\dev1_view\sources\InitialComponent in our example). Open Windows Explorer and verify this result.

Note that the ITSO_ProGuide_UCMEAR project still resides under the dev1 workspace.

6. Under Enterprise Applications, select the **ITSO_ProGuide_UCMEAR** project and add this project to source control using the same method (do not create a

new activity, use the activity created when adding the Web project to source control).

Both projects are now under ClearCase source control.

25.4 Development scenario

To show how to work with ClearCase we use a simple scenario where two developers work in parallel on a common project. We will use a servlet to illustrate handling a situation when adding an element (the servlet) generates a potential update to some other element(s), like the deployment descriptor.

25.4.1 Developer 1 adds a servlet

Developer 1 defines the servlet in the Web project as follows:

1. As developer 1, right-click **ITSO_ProGuide_UCM** and select **New** → **Other** → **Web** → **Servlet** from the context menu.
2. Enter `ServletA` as the servlet name and click **Next**. Enter `itso.ucm` as the Java package name and click **Finish**.
3. Adding a servlet to the project causes an update to the deployment descriptor (web.xml) and the binding and extension information (the ibm-web-bnd.xmi and ibm-web-ext.xmi files). You are prompted to check them out (Figure 25-19). On the Check Out Elements dialog, ensure all three files are selected and click **OK**.

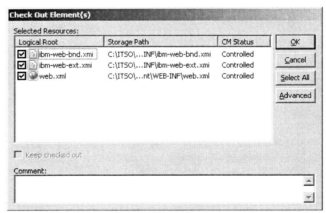

Figure 25-19 Checking out dependent elements

4. On the Select Activity dialog, select **New** and enter `Developer 1 adds servletA` as the name of the activity. Click **OK** twice. The servlet is generated.
5. On the Add Element(s) to Source Control dialog (see Figure 25-20) make sure the packages and the servlet are selected. Leave "Keep checked out" deselected and click **OK**.

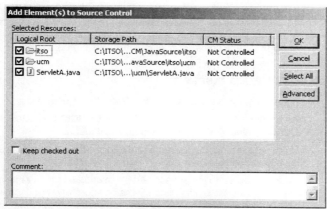

Figure 25-20   Adding new elements to source control

6. On the Select Activity dialog, select **Developer 1 adds ServletA** and click **OK**. The servlet is added to the project and to ClearCase source control.
7. Click **Yes** on the File Changed dialog.

   The three dependent files are still checked out. Expand **WebContent\WEB-INF** and note the green check marks. Before we deliver the work to the integration stream, we want to check them back in.
8. Select **web.xml** and select **Team** → **Check in** from the context menu.
9. On the Check in Elements dialog, ensure that the element is selected and click **OK**. The green check mark on the resource icon is removed, indicating that the file is no longer checked out.
10. Before we can deliver the pro**ject to the stream, the** `ibm-web-bnd.xmi` **and** `ibm-web-ext.xmi` **files must be** checked in as well. As their contents have not changed, we will simply undo their checkout. Select both of them and select **Team** → **Undo Check Out...** from the context menu.
11. Before delivering to the stream, it is also good practice to make sure that nothing else is checked out. Select **ClearCase** → **Find Checkouts...**. On the

Find Criteria dialog (see Figure 25-21) click **Browse** and select the **C:\ITSO\dev1_view\sources** directory. Keep the other defaults as shown and click **OK**.

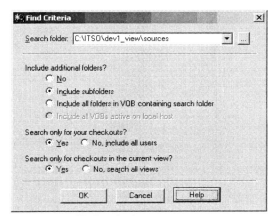

Figure 25-21   Finding checkouts

12. No checked out files should be found. Click **OK** to dismiss the dialog and then close the Find Checkouts window.

25.4.2 Developer 1 delivers work to the integration stream

Follow these steps to deliver the work into the integration stream:

1. Select **ClearCase** → **Deliver Stream**. On the Deliver from Stream dialog (Figure 25-22 on page 1280) select the development stream **dev1_view** and click **OK**.

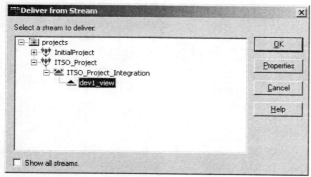

Figure 25-22   Delivering to integration stream

2. In the Deliver from Stream Preview dialog (Figure 25-23) make sure both activities are selected and that the view to deliver to is <userid>_Integration_view. Click **OK**.

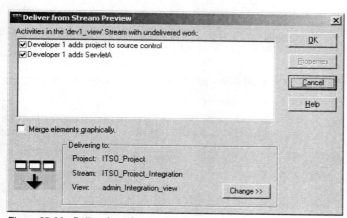

Figure 25-23   Deliver from Stream Preview dialog

3. After a while the Deliver from Stream - Merges Complete dialog (see Figure 25-24 on page 1281) is shown. Deselect **Open a ClearCase Explorer** and click **OK**.

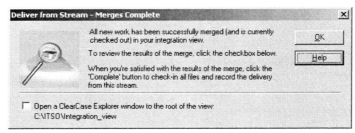

Figure 25-24   Deliver from Stream - Merges Complete dialog

4. On the Delivering to View dialog (Figure 25-25) click **Complete**.

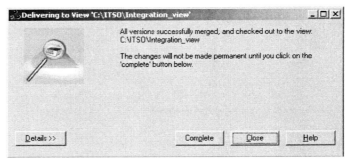

Figure 25-25   Delivering to View dialog

5. Optionally, you can click **Details** to see a list of the files delivered (see Figure 25-26 on page 1282), then click **Close**.

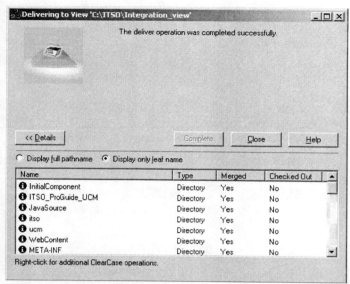

Figure 25-26 Showing files delivered

25.4.3 Developer 1 makes a baseline

To make a baseline, do the following:

1. Select **Start** → **Programs** → **Rational Software** → **Rational ClearCase** → **Project Explorer**.
2. In the left pane right-click **ITSO_Project_Integration** and select **Make Baseline** from the context menu (see Figure 25-27 on page 1283).

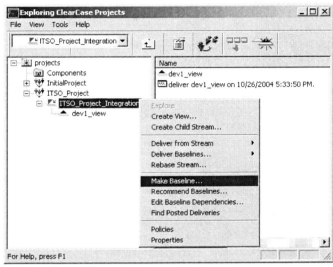

Figure 25-27   Making a baseline

3. In the Make Baseline dialog (see Figure 25-28) click **OK**.

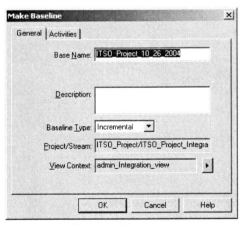

Figure 25-28   Make baseline settings

4. Click **OK** on the confirmation dialog (one new baseline was created) and then close the Make Baseline dialog.

You can now close the ClearCase Project Explorer. Developer 1 has now finished the current task. Developer 2 will now join the project and make changes to the servlet.

25.4.4 Developer 2 joins the project

Developer 2 now joins the ClearCase project and adds it to his Rational Application Developer workspace.

1. Select **File → Switch Workspace...** in Rational Application Developer for the scenario simulation purposes.
2. Enter `C:\dev2_workspace` as the workspace for developer 2. Click **OK**.
3. Close or minimize the Welcome view.
4. If you are not connected to ClearCase by the preference setting, select **ClearCase → Connect to Rational ClearCase** or click the ClearCase Connect icon ( ).
5. Select **ClearCase → Create New View**.
6. In the View Creation Wizard (Figure 25-29 on page 1285), select **Yes** to indicate that you are working on a ClearCase project. Expand **projects** and select the **ITSO_Project**. Click **Next**.

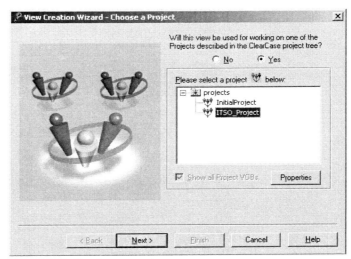

Figure 25-29   Creating a new view

7. The ClearCase View Tool dialog notifies you that there is already one stream defined for this Windows user (dev1_view). Click **OK**.

8. In the Create a Development Stream dialog (see Figure 25-30 on page 1286) enter `dev2_view` as the development stream name and verify that the integration stream name is ITSO_Project_Integration. Click **Next**.

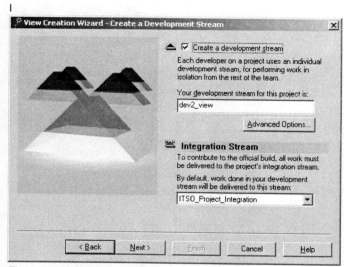

Figure 25-30   Creating a development stream - Developer 2

9. In the Review Types of Views dialog, ensure that "Create a Development view" is selected and click **Next**.

10. In the Choose Location for a Snapshot View (Development View) dialog (Figure 25-31 on page 1287) accept C:\ITSO\dev2_view as the path for the new development view and click **Next**.

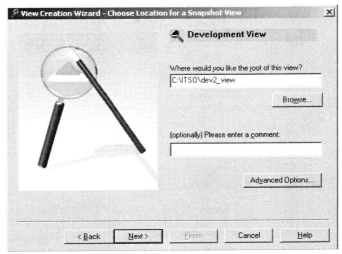

Figure 25-31   Select location for development view

11. In the Choose Components dialog, make sure **InitialComponent** is selected. Click **Finish** to create the development view for developer 2.

12. Click **OK** when the confirmation dialog is displayed and then click **OK** in the View Creation Status dialog.

25.4.5 Developer 2 imports projects into Application Developer

Developer 2 works on the same projects as developer 1 and has to import the projects:

1. As developer 2, select **ClearCase → Rebase Stream** in Rational Application Developer to update your development stream with the contents of the integration stream.

2. In the Rebase Stream dialog (see Figure 25-32 on page 1288) select **Projects → ITSO_Project → ITSO_Project_Integration → dev2_view** and click **OK**.

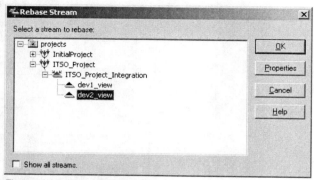

Figure 25-32   Rebase Stream dialog

3. In the Rebase Stream Preview dialog (Figure 25-33) select **InitialComponent_ITSO_Project_<date>** from the baseline drop-down list and verify that **<userid>_dev2_view** is selected as the target view. Click **OK**.

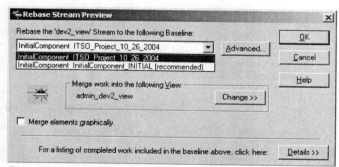

Figure 25-33   Rebase Stream Preview - Developer 2

4. Click **OK** to dismiss the Hijacked Files Warning dialog.
5. In the Rebasing in View dialog, click **Complete** to perform the rebase action. After this is done, click **Close**.

   The contents of the integration view have now been copied to the developer 2 view, but do not yet appear on this workspace.

6. In Rational Application Developer, select **File → Import → Existing Project into Workspace** and click **Next** (see Figure 25-34 on page 1289).

7. Click **Browse**, select the EAR project, and click **Finish**.

   C:\ITSO\dev2_view\sources\InitialComponent\ITSO_ProGuide_UCMEAR

R

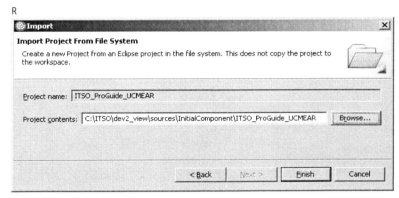

Figure 25-34   Import EAR project

8. Repeat the import process for the Web project:

   C:\ITSO\dev2_view\sources\InitialComponent\ITSO_ProGuide_UCM

   Note: By now developer 1 and developer 2 are set up with a new shared project. Both can now check out files, work with these files, check them in, and deliver their work to the stream.

25.4.6 Developer 2 modifies the servlet

As we only want to show how to work with ClearCase, we do not need to add any real code to the servlet. Adding a simple comment to the servlet will work just as well.

1. Expand **ITSO_ProGuide_UCM** → **Java Resources** → **JavaSource** → **itso.ucm** and open **ServletA.java** by double-clicking it.

2. Start entering some text inside the green comment area, indicating that developer 2 made this change. As soon as you start typing in the editor, the servlet needs to be checked out. The dialog shown in Figure 25-35 on page 1290 is displayed, asking you to check out the servlet file. Click **OK**.

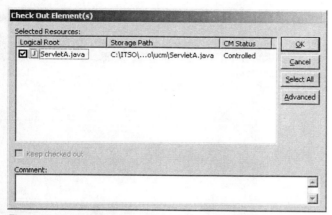

Figure 25-35 Check out elements

3. On the Select Activity dialog, create a new activity **Developer 2 updates ServletA** for this update and click **OK** to confirm. The file is now checked out, which is indicated by the green check mark on the servlet's icon .

4. After making your changes (for example, adding your name as the author), press Ctrl+S to save the servlet, and then close the editor.

5. The changed file must now be checked in. Right-click the servlet and select **Team** → **Check in** in the context menu (or use the Check in icon).

6. On the Check in Elements dialog, click **OK**. The green check marks of the resources icons are removed, indicating that the elements are no longer checked out.

   Developer 2 is now ready to deliver the changes to the stream and share the code with the other developers. Before doing this, it is a best practice to make sure that no other developer has made changes recently.

7. Select **ClearCase** → **Rebase Stream**. In the Rebase Stream dialog, select developer 2's development stream and click **OK** (Figure 25-36 on page 1291).

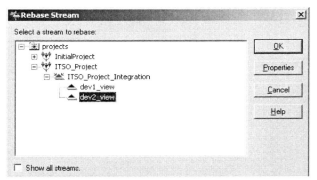

Figure 25-36   Selecting development stream to rebase - Developer 2

8. In the Rebase Stream Preview dialog (see Figure 25-37), select the latest baseline (top of the list), and make sure the <userid>_dev2_view view is selected as the target. Click **OK**.

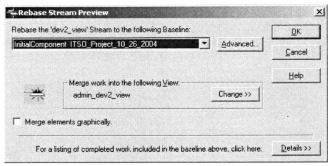

Figure 25-37   Rebase Stream Preview

9. The Rebase Stream dialog is displayed, and notifies you that the stream is currently up-to-date. Click **OK** to dismiss the information dialog and click **Cancel** to dismiss the Rebase Stream Preview dialog.

Note that what we did was to check to make sure developer 1 did not make any changes to the stream.

25.4.7 Developer 2 delivers work to the integration stream

Developer 2 is ready to integrate his work:

1. As developer 2, select **ClearCase** → **Deliver Stream**. In the Deliver from Stream dialog (Figure 25-38) select **Projects** → **ITSO_Project** → **ITSO_Project_Integration** → **dev2_view**. Click **OK**.

Figure 25-38 Deliver from Stream dialog

2. On the Deliver from Stream Preview dialog (see Figure 25-39) make sure the <userid>_Integration_view is selected as the integration view. Click **OK**.

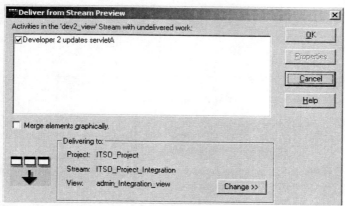

Figure 25-39 Deliver from Stream Preview

3. The integration view is now updated with the contents of the development view.
4. On the Delivering to View dialog (see Figure 25-40), click **Complete** and then **Close**.

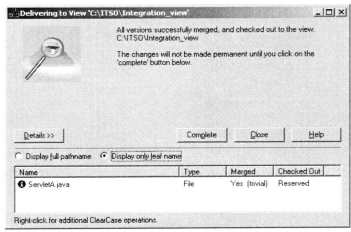

Figure 25-40 Delivering to integration view - Developer 2

25.4.8 Developer 1 modifies the servlet

ServletA has now been updated once in the integration stream since the original baseline was created. Let us see what happens when another developer makes changes to the same element and makes delivery.

1. Select **File → Switch Workspace...** in Rational Application Developer.

2. Enter C:\dev1_workspace as the workspace for developer 2. Click **OK**.

3. Expand **ITSO_ProGuide_UCM → Java Resources → JavaSource → itso.ucm** and open ServletA.java by double-clicking it.

4. Make an update to the comment as developer 1. The servlet will be checked out again.

5. On the Select Activity dialog, select **Developer 1 modifies ServletA** and click **OK**.

6. After making your changes (use some other text than previously), press Ctrl+S to save the servlet and then close the editor.

7. Check in the updated servlet.

25.4.9 Developer 1 delivers new work to the integration stream

Developer 1 is now ready to integrate his work as well:

1. As developer 1, select **ClearCase** → **Deliver Stream**. In the Deliver from Stream dialog (Figure 25-41) select **Projects** → **ITSO_Project** → **ITSO_Project_Integration** → **dev1_view**. Click **OK**.

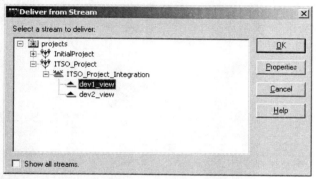

Figure 25-41   Deliver from Stream dialog - Developer 1

2. On the Deliver from Stream Preview dialog (see Figure 25-39 on page 1292) make sure the <userid>_Integration_view is selected as the integration view. Click **OK**.

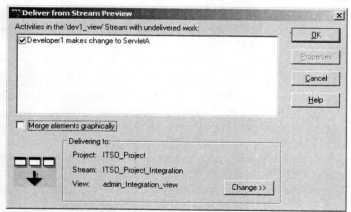

Figure 25-42   Deliver from Stream Preview

3. ClearCase notifies you that there is a conflict and the element cannot be merged automatically (Figure 25-43). Select **start the Diff Merge tool for this element** and click **OK**. Click **OK** again at the Diff Merge status dialog.

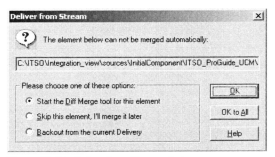

Figure 25-43 Deliver from Stream alert

4. The Diff Merge tool is now launched (see Figure 25-44). Take a few moments to become familiar with the information displayed and the options available to you.

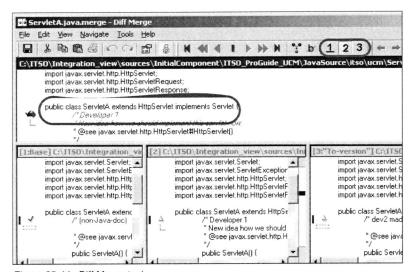

Figure 25-44 Diff Merge tool

- The top panel shows the merge result and areas of conflict. Click a line to focus on that particular conflict.
- The lower panels show the different versions that are available.
- The number icons on the toolbar (1, 2, 3) are used to indicate which version should be used in the merged result.

5. In the top panel displaying the merge result, click the line that has the arrow next to it, indicating the conflict.
6. On the toolbar, click **2** to determine that in this case the implementation by developer 1 should be used. Verify the change in the merge panel.
7. Close the Merge Tool by saving the changes (select **File** → **Save**) and close the tool.
8. On the Delivering to View dialog, click **Complete** and then **Close**.

Now all the changes to the servlet have been applied to the integration stream. You can verify this by looking at the element in the Version Tree (see Figure 25-45 on page 1297).

You can invoke the Version Tree Browser from Rational Application Developer or from Windows Explorer. Right-click the servlet file and select the **Version Tree** option from the context menu.

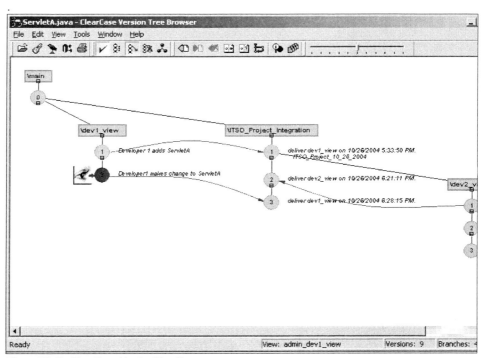

Figure 25-45   ClearCase Version Tree Browser

Note that looking at the same element as developer 2 will show the new element version in the tree, but we will not see the latest changes in that view because our view is set to look at the recommended base line. To see the delivered changes, developer 2 will need to wait for a new baseline to be created, and then rebase from that.

26

CVS integration

This chapter provides an introduction to the widely adopted open source Concurrent Version System (CVS). We will discuss the integration features of Rational Application Developer tooling for CVS by guiding the reader through an example implementation, as well as usage scenarios.

> **Note:** The example in this chapter calls for two simulated developer systems. This can be accomplished by having two instances of Rational Application Developer or two Workspaces for demonstration purposes. Refer to 3.1, "Workbench basics" on page 76, for detailed instructions.

This chapter is organized into the following topics:

- Introduction to CVS
- CVSNT Server implementation
- CVS client configuration for Application Developer
- Configure CVS in Rational Application Developer
- Development scenario
- CVS resource history
- Comparisons in CVS
- Annotations in CVS
- Branches in CVS
- Work with patches
- Disconnecting a project
- Synchronize perspective

26.1 Introduction to CVS

Concurrent Version System (CVS) is a simple open source software configuration management (SCM) system. CVS only implements version control. CVS can be used by individual developers as well as by large, distributed teams.

26.1.1 CVS features

Some of the main features of CVS are as follows:

- Multiple client-server protocols over TCP/IP that let developers access the latest code from a wide variety of clients virtually anywhere an Internet connection exists.

> **Note:** IBM Rational Application Developer V6 supports three communication protocols:
>
> - pserver (password server
> - ext
> - extssh
>
> The protocols ext and extssh require additional configuration from the Rational Application Developer preferences:
>
> - ext: **Window** → **Preferences** → **Team** → **CVS** → **Ext Connection Method**
> - extssh: **Window** → **Preferences** → **Team** → **CVS** → **SSH2 Connection Method**

- It stores all the versions of a file in a single file using forward-delta versioning, which stores only the differences among the versions.
- It insulates the different developers from each other. Every developer works in his own directory, and CVS merges the work in the repository when each developer is done. Conflicts should be resolved in the process.

> **Important:** CVS and IBM Rational Application Developer V6 have a different understanding of what a conflict is:
>
> - For CVS, a conflict arises when two changes to the same base file are close enough to be noticed by the merge command.
> - For IBM Rational Web Developer V6, a conflict exists when the local copy of a revision of a modified file is different from the revision stored in the repository.

- It uses an unreserved checkout approach to version control that helps avoid artificial conflicts common when using an exclusive checkout model.
- It keeps shared project data in repositories. Each repository has a root directory on the file system.
- CVS maintains a history of the source code revisions. Each change is stamped with the time it was made and the user name of the person who made it. It is recommended that developers also provide a description of the change. Given that information, CVS can help you find answers to questions such as: Who made the change? When was it made, and why?

26.1.2 New V6 features for team development

The key new IBM Rational Application Developer V6 features for team development are as follows:

- New team synchronize view
- Multiple synchronization of repositories
- Scheduling of synchronization
- Setting up of a commit set of defined resources located anywhere in the workspace
- Background synchronization of CVS operations of the workspace
- Checkout wizard to allow checkout by using **New** → **Project** or **File** → **Import**
- Editor interface to specify CVS date tags in standardized format
- "Blame" view to identify what and who has changed a particular file
- Additional security options to communicate with the CVS server

This list does not include all the new features, but points to the major differences compared to previous versions of WebSphere Studio products.

26.2 CVSNT Server implementation

The CVS server code for Linux and UNIX platforms is available at the project's site, as is installation and usage documentation:

```
http://www.cvshome.org
```

Since our development environment is a pure Windows environment, we choose to use CVS for NT (CVSNT) for the development environment.

The CVSNT Server implementation is organized as follows:
- CVS Server installation.
- CVS Server repository configuration.
- Create the Windows users and groups used by CVS.
- Verify the CVSNT installation.
- Create CVS users.

> **Important:** We chose to use CVSNT V2.0.58b since it has been validated against Eclipse V3.0.1. IBM Rational Application Developer V6 is built upon Eclipse V3.0.1.1 (<rad_home>\eclipse\.eclipseproduct).
>
> CVSNT was ideal for our environment because we had a pure Windows environment, and it is easy to use. We did not experience any significant problems using the CVSNT version.

26.2.1 CVS Server installation

To install CVS on the Windows platform, do the following:

1. Before installing CVSNT, we recommend reading the installation tips:

   http://www.cvsnt.org/wiki/InstallationTips

   > **Important:** The CVSNT software requires a user that has local system privileges to install and configure a service in Windows.

2. Download the CVSNT V2.0.58b Server (cvsnt-2.0.58b.exe) from the following URL to a temporary directory (for example, c:\temp) on the Build and SCM node:

   http://www.cvsnt.org

3. Execute the CVSNT installer by double-clicking the self-extracting **cvsnt-2.0.58b.exe** file from the temporary directory.

4. When the Welcome window appears, click **Next**.

5. When the License Agreement window appears, review the terms and if in agreement select **I accept the agreement** and click **Next**.

6. When the Select Destination Location window appears, we entered `c:\cvsnt` and then clicked **Next**.

7. When the Select Components window appears, we did the following and then clicked **Next**:
   - Select **Typical Installation**.
   - Under protocols, we additionally checked **Named Pipe (:ntserver) Protocol**.

8. When the Select Start Menu Folder window appears, accept default and click **Next**.

9. When the Select Additional Tasks window appears, we did the following and then clicked **Next**:
   - Check **Install cvsnt service**.
   - Check **Install cvsnt lock service**.
   - Check **Generate default certificate**.

10. When the Ready to Install window appears, review the installation options and then click **Install**.

11. When the Completing the cvsnt Setup Wizard window appears, accept the defaults and click **Finish**.

12. Restart your system.

    When the installation is complete, we recommend that you restart your system. This step will guarantee that the environment variables are set up properly and the CVSNT Windows services are started.

26.2.2 CVS Server repository configuration

After you have installed the CVS Server and restarted your system (Build and SCM node), do the following to create and configure the CVS Server repository:

1. Manually create the common root directory. For example, we created the c:\rep6449 directory using Windows Explorer or via a command window.

2. Stop the CVS services in order to create the repository, by clicking **Start** → **Programs** → **CVSNT** → **Service control panel**.

3. When the CVSNT control panel window appears, stop the following services by clicking stop:
   - Click **Stop** under CVS service.
   - Click **Stop** under CVS Lock service.

4. Click the **Repositories** tab.

5. Click **Add**.

6. When the Edit repository window appears, we entered the following (as seen in Figure 26-1 on page 1304), and then clicked **OK**:
   - Location: c:/rep6449

   > **Note:** We manually created this directory on the file system in step 1.

   - Name: /rep6449

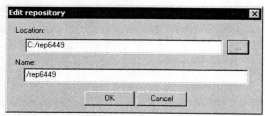

Figure 26-1 Add repository

7. When prompted with the message `c:/rep6449 exists, but is not a valid CVS repository. Do you want to initialise it?`, click **Yes**.

   When done, the Repository page should look like Figure 26-2.

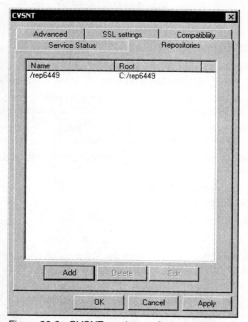

Figure 26-2 CVSNT service configuration (Repository page)

8. Click **Apply**.

9. Click the **Compatibility** tab.
10. From the Compatibility tab, check the following options (as seen in Figure 26-3), and then click **OK**:
    - Select **Generic non-cvsnt**.
    - Check **Respond as cvs 1.11.2 to version request**.
    - Check **Emulate '-n checkout' bug**.
    - Check **Hide extended log/status information**.

    These settings ensure that CVSNT is compatible with clients such as IBM Rational Application Developer V6 and other CVS clients.

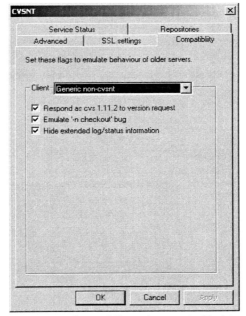

Figure 26-3 Compatibility settings required for interoperation with IBM Rational Application Developer V6 and other CVS clients

26.2.3 Create the Windows users and groups used by CVS

When setting up CVS users, we opted to use the *pserver protocol* commonly used to secure a CVS repository for the following reasons:

- The pserver protocol is desired when working from a multi operating system environment (for example, Windows and Linux clients).
- Provides a password facility that is independent of the operating system (for example, the pserver protocol does not use the password system of the native operating system).
- A single CVS administrator use can be set up and used to run the CVS commands minimizing the administration of permissions and security of all the users that will use the repository.

Add a Windows user (cvsadmin)

To add a Windows CVS administrator user do the following:

1. From the Windows desktop, right-click **My Computer**, and select **Manage**.
2. Expand **Local Users and Groups** and select **Users**.
3. From the menu bar, click **Action** → **New User**.
4. When the New user window appears, we entered the following and clicked **Create**:
   - User name: cvsadmin
   - Password: <password>
   - Uncheck **User must change password at next logon**.
5. Click **Close** on the New Users dialog, but do not exit the Computer Management tool (needed in next section).

Add Windows user (cvsadmin) to a group (Power Users)

To add the Windows user to a group that has the sufficient permissions, do the following:

1. Click **Groups** and double-click **Power Users**.
2. Click **Add**.
3. Select the **cvsadmin** and click **Add**.
4. Click **OK** to exit the Select Users or Groups window.
5. Click **OK** to exit the Power Users Properties window.
6. Exit the Computer Management console.

26.2.4 Verify the CVSNT installation

To verify the CVSNT installation, do the following:

1. Restart the system to ensure that the environment variables are loaded and the CVSNT services are started.
2. After the system has been restarted, verify that the following CVSNT Windows services have started:
   - CVSNT
   - CVSNT Lock Service

> **Tip:** The CVSNT services can also be accessed from the CVSNT Service control panel.
>
> When using the CVSNT Service control panel, we noticed that on occasion under the Service Status tab when clicking the **Stop** button for the *CVS* Lock Service and then clicking the **Start** button, that the lock service does not start running.
>
> To resolve this open the Windows Task Manager, locate the process cvslock.exe, right-click, and select **End Process Tree**. Reattempt clicking the **Start** button for the CVS Lock Service and this should set it in the running state. If further problems occur, restart the system.

26.2.5 Create CVS users

To create CVS users to access the files in the repository, do the following:

1. Open a Windows command prompt.
2. Set the cvsroot as follows:

   ```
   set cvsroot=:pserver:cvsrep1.itso.ral.ibm.com:/rep6449
   ```

   Where cvsrep1.itso.ral.ibm.com is the host name of the repository node and /rep6449 is the repository located on this host name.

   > **Note:** The host name must be specified. For example, specifying localhost will not work.

3. Log on to the CVS repository machine to manage the users, using the following command:

   ```
   cvs login cvsadmin
   ```

4. You will be prompted to enter the CVS password.

We entered the password for the cvsadmin user created in 26.2.3, "Create the Windows users and groups used by CVS" on page 1306.

5. Enter the following CVS commands to add users:

   ```
   cvs passwd -a -r cvsadmin <cvs user id>
   ```

   – Where **cvs passwd -a** indicates that you wish to add a password for a user
   – **-r cvsadmin** indicates the alias or native user name that the user will run under when connecting to the repository (set up in "Create the Windows users and groups used by CVS" on page 1306).
   – *<cvs user id>* is the user ID to be added in.

   For example, to add user cvsuser1 enter the following:

   ```
   cvs passwd -a -r cvsadmin cvsuser1
   ```

   > **Note:** The first occurrence of a user being added will create the file passwd in the directory, in our case c:\rep6449\CVSROOT. The following user will be appended into this file. It is recommended that this file not be edited directly by a text editor. It also must not be placed under CVS control.

6. A prompt will appear to enter the password, as shown in the following:

   ```
   Adding user cvsuser1@cvsrep1.itso.ral.ibm.com
   New password: ********
   Verify password: ********
   ```

7. Repeat the previous step for additional CVS users.

8. Next, provide the development users their CVS account information, host name, and connection type to the CVS server so that they can establish a connection from WebSphere Studio Application Developer in a later configuration step on the Developer node. For example:

   – Account info: Developer CVS user created (for example, `cvsuser1`)
   – Host name: <CVS_Server_host_name> (for example, `cvsrep1.itso.ral.ibm.com`)
   – Connection type: pserver
   – Password: <password>
   – Repository path: /rep6449

26.3 CVS client configuration for Application Developer

This section describes CVS client configurations to be made for use with IBM Rational Application Developer V6.0.

26.3.1 Configure CVS Team Capabilities

IBM Rational Application Developer V6, by default, does not enable the *Team Capabilities* when creating a new workspace for a user.

To enable the Team Capabilities, do the following:

1. Open IBM Rational Application Developer V6.
2. Click **Windows** → **Preferences**.
3. Select and expand the **Workbench** and click **Capabilities**.
4. Select and expand the **Team** capability and select the items showing in Figure 26-4 on page 1310.

Note: It is sufficient to set the *CVS Support* only, since the IBM Rational Application Developer V6 will automatically set *Core Team Support* as well.

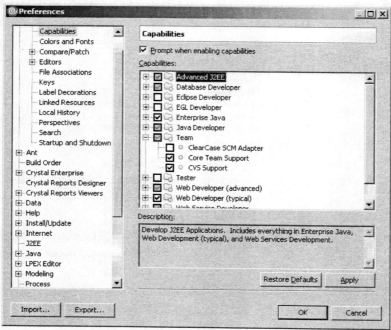

Figure 26-4   Setting the Team capability to be available

5. Click **Apply** and then click **OK**.

26.3.2 Access the CVS Repository

To access a repository that has been configured on a server for users to perform their version management, do the following:

1. Open IBM Rational Application Developer V6.
2. Click **Windows** → **Open Perspective** → **Other** → **CVS Repository Exploring**. Click **OK**.
3. In the CVS Repositories view, right-click and select **New** → **Repository Location**.
4. Add the parameters for the repository location as in Figure 26-5, check **Validate Connection Finish** and **Save Password**, and then click **Finish**.

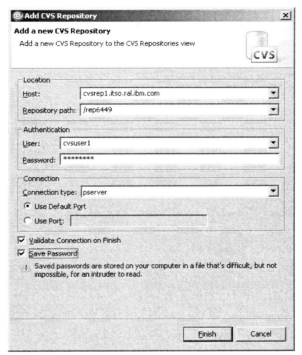

Figure 26-5 Add the CVS repository to the workspace

If everything worked correctly, you now should be able to see a repository location with HEAD, Branches, and Versions (see Figure 26-6 on page 1312).

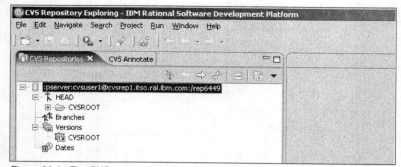

Figure 26-6 The CVS perspective of a successfully connected CVS repository

26.4 Configure CVS in Rational Application Developer

The team support for CVS had some major improvements in IBM Rational Application Developer V6.

26.4.1 Configure Rational Application Developer CVS preferences

Before you start working with CVS, you should look through the CVS preferences. Preferences that can be set for CVS include:

- Label decorations
- File content
- Ignored resources
- CVS-specific settings

Included in this section is a description of the keyword substitutions that CVS provides and how they can be used.

Label decorations

Label decorations are set to be on by default.

To view or change the label decorations, select **Windows** → **Preferences** and expand the **Label Decorations** section and select **CVS**.

CVS label decorations are set to be on if the check box is checked (see Figure 26-7 on page 1313).

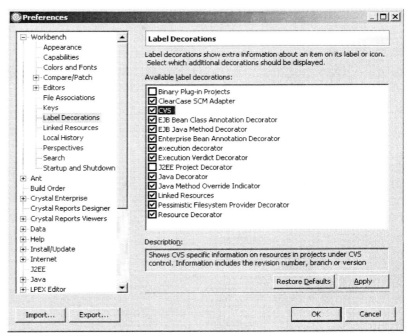

Figure 26-7   CVS decoration preferences

File content

The file content of resources can be changed to be saved into the repository as either ASCII or Binary. When working with file extensions that are not part of the file contents that are defined in IBM Rational Application Developer V6, then these files are saved into the repository as Binary by default.

To verify that a resource in the workspace is stored in the repository correctly, select **Windows** → **Preferences** and expand the **Team** → **File Content** section (see Figure 26-8 on page 1314). Verify that the file extension that you are using is present and stored in the repository as desired.

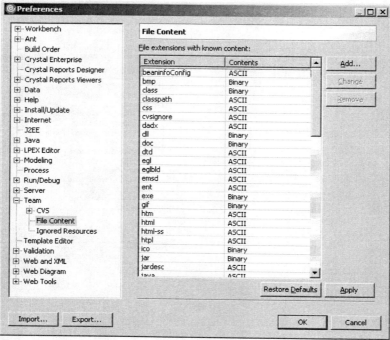

Figure 26-8   Team File Content preferences

If you find that a particular file extension is not in the list then you will need to add this extension if you do not want the resource stored with the default binary behavior. A common file that sometimes occurs when you are supplied a library is a Makefile.mak file used in making applications, which is an ASCII file.

To demonstrate adding this extension that is not present in this list, perform the following:

1. Select **Windows** → **Preferences** and expand the **Team** → **File Content** section.
2. Select the **Add** button.
3. Type the extension name mak (see Figure 26-9 on page 1315) and click **OK**.

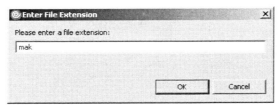

Figure 26-9   Entering a file extension

4. Find the extension in the list, click the **Content** column, and select **ASCI** from the drop-down.

   Tip: The content can also be changed by highlighting the extension and using the **Change** button.

5. Click **Apply** and then **OK** to exit the Windows preferences.

Ignored resources

Resources that are created or changed dynamically via mechanisms such as compilation or builds are not recommended to be saved in the repository. This may include class files, executables, lexer and parser code, and Enterprise Java Bean stub and implementation code.

IBM Rational Application Developer V6 has a list of these resources that is accessed by selecting **Windows** → **Preferences** and expanding the **Team** → **Ignored Resources** section.

Resources can be added to this list by specifying the pattern that will be ignored. The two wild card characters are a asterisk (*), which indicates a match of zero; or many characters and a question mark (?), which indicates a match of a character. For example, a pattern of _EJS*.java would match any file that begin with _EJS and had zero to many characters and ended in .java.

The addition of resources that need to be ignored for saving into the repository can be performed as follows using the example of a Windows dll file:

1. Select **Windows** → **Preferences** and expand the **Team** → **Ignored Resources** section.
2. Select the **Add** button.
3. Type the pattern *.dll (as shown in Figure 26-10 on page 1316) that will be ignored.

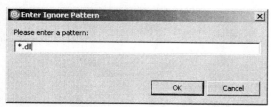

Figure 26-10   Ignored resource pattern to add

4. Click **OK** and ensure that the resource (*.dll) is checked (see Figure 26-11).

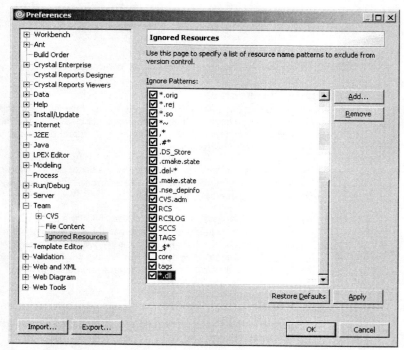

Figure 26-11   Resources that will be ignored when saving to the repository

Patterns to be removed from the ignore list can be selected and the **Remove** button clicked (see Figure 26-11 on page 1316). Alternatively, you can temporarily disable ignoring the file pattern by de-selecting it from the list, and you do not have to remove the specified file pattern from the list.

Additionally, there are two further facilities that can be used to exclude a file from version control:

- Resources marked as derived will automatically be ignored. This is implemented by builders in the Eclipse framework, such as the Java builder.

- Use of a .cvsignore file created in the same directory that it applies to. This file will contain a list of files or directories that should not be placed into the repository and is specific to CVS.

    This can be created by using the wizards to create a simple file or by selecting the resource, right-clicking, and selecting **Team → Add to .cvsignore**.

Further details on the syntax of .cvsignore can be found at:

    http://www.cvshome.org

CVS-specific settings

The CVS settings in IBM Rational Application Developer V6 are extensive and cannot be covered in full here. A list of categories for the CVS settings is provided in Table 26-1 with short descriptions. Some of the more important settings are highlighted to assist users; a description of the remaining settings can be obtained from the IBM Rational Application Developer V6 help system.

Table 26-1 Category of CVS settings available

Category	Menu location	Description
General CVS Settings	**Windows → Preferences → Team → CVS**	Settings for the default behavior in communicating with CVS
Console	**Windows → Preferences → Team → CVS → Console**	Settings for the colors to display in the CVS console and the flag to set the console display
Ext Connection Method	**Windows → Preferences → Team → CVS → Ext Connection Method**	Settings to identify the ssh external program and associated parameters

Category	Menu location	Description
Label Decorations	**Windows** → **Preferences** → **Team** → **CVS** → **Label Decorations**	Settings for displaying the state of resources in IBM Rational Application Developer V6
Password Management	**Windows** → **Preferences** → **Team** → **CVS** → **Password Management**	Manages the passwords required to connect to multiple CVS repositories
SSH2 Connection Method	**Windows** → **Preferences** → **Team** → **CVS** → **SSH2 Connection Method**	Configuration settings for SSH2 protocol to the CVS repository
Watch/Edit	**Windows** → **Preferences** → **Team** → **CVS** → **Watch/Edit**	Settings for the CVS watch and edit functionality

CVS keyword substitution

The key attributes of software development require that configuration management and versions be maintained. CVS provides a mechanism for identifying the version of the source code and other related information that is stored in the repository. This information can be accessed by developers by the defined keywords. This is known as keyword expansion.

Keyword expansion is an effective mechanism for identifying what version a resource is in the repository versus what a user has checkout locally on their workspace.

IBM Rational Application Developer V6, by default, has the keyword substitution set to *ASCII with keyword expansion (-kkv)* under the selection **Windows** → **Preferences** → **Team** → **CVS** → **Console**. This setting expands out keyword substitution based on what CVS understands, and is performed wherever they are located in the file.

Some of the available keywords (case sensitive) are listed in Table 26-2.

Table 26-2   CVS keywords

Keyword	Description
$Author$	Expands to including the name of the author of the change in the file, for example: $Author: itsodev $
$Date$	Expands to the date and time of the change in UTC, for example: $Date: 2004/10/29 18:21:32 $

Keyword	Description
$Header$	Contains the RCS file in repository, revision, date (in UTC), author, state and locker, for example: $Header: /rep6449/XMLExample/.project,v 1.1 2004/10/29 18:21:32 itsodev Exp itso $
Id	Like $Header$ except without the full path of the RCS file, for example: $Id: .project,v 1.1 2004/10/29 18:21:32 itsodev Exp itso $
$Locker$	Name of the user that has a lock on this revision. (In CVS this is not applicable.)
Log	The log message of this revision. This does not get replaced but gets appended to existing log messages. In general, this is not recommended since files can become large for no real benefit.
$Name$	Expands to the name of the sticky tag, which is a file retrieved by date or revision tags, for example: $Name: version_1_3 $
$RCSFile$	Expands to the name of the RCS file in the repository, for example: $RCSFile: .project,v $
$Revision$	Expands to the revision number of the file, for example: $Revision: 1.1 $
$Source$	Expands to the full path of the RCS file in the repository, for example: $Source: /rep6449/XMLExample/.project,v $
$State$	Expands to the state of the revision, for example: $State: Exp $. This is not commonly used.

To ensure consistency between multiple users working on a team, it is recommended that a standard header is defined for each Java code file that is created and is filled inappropriately. A simple example is shown in Example 26-1 for what could be established.

Example 26-1 Example of CVS keywords used in Java

```
/**
 * class comment goes here.
 *
 * <pre>
 * Date $Date$
 * Id $Id$
 * </pre>
 * @author $Author$
```

```
 * @version $Revision$
 *
 * ${todo} To change the template for this generated type comment go to
 * Window - Preferences - Java - Code Style - Code Templates
 */
```

To ensure consistency across all files created, each user would need to cut and paste this into their document. Fortunately, IBM Rational Application Developer V6 offers a means to ensure that consistency. To set up a standard template do the following:

1. Select **Windows** → **Preferences** → **Java** → **Code Style** → **Code Templates**.
2. Expand out the **Comments** tree.
3. Select **Types** and click **Edit**.
4. Cut and paste or type what comment header you require, as shown in Example 26-2.

Example 26-2   Comment header to paste into IBM Rational Application Developer V6

```
/**
 * class comment goes here.
 *
 * <pre>
 * Date $$Date$$
 * Id $$Id$$
 * </pre>
 * @author $$Author$$
 * @version $$Revision$$
 *
 * ${todo} To change the template for this generated type comment go to
 * Window - Preferences - Java - Code Style - Code Templates
 */
```

> **Note:** The double dollar sign ($$) (as shown in Figure 26-12 on page 1321) is required since IBM Rational Application Developer V6 treats a single dollar ($) as one of its own variables. The double dollar ($$) is used as a means of escaping the single dollar so that it can be post processed by CVS.

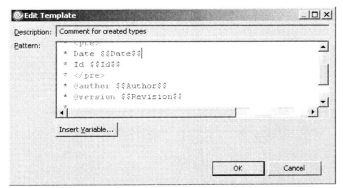

Figure 26-12 Setup of a common code template for Java files

5. Click **OK** to complete the editing.
6. Click **Apply** followed by **OK**.

After performing this operation, creating a new class, and checking in and checking out, the header will be displayed as shown in Example 26-3.

Example 26-3 Contents of Java file after check in and check out from CVS

```
/**
 * class comment goes here.
 *
 * <pre>
 * Date $Date: 2004/10/29 18:21:32 $
 * Id $Id: $Id: Example.java,v 1.1 2004/10/29 18:21:32 itsodev Exp itso $
 * </pre>
 * @author $Author: itsodev $
 * @version $Revision: 1.1 $
 *
 * ${todo} To change the template for this generated type comment go to
 * Window - Preferences - Java - Code Style - Code Templates
 */
```

26.5 Development scenario

To show you how to work with CVS in IBM Rational Application Developer V6, we will follow a simple but typical development scenario, shown in Table 26-3.

Two developers, cvsuser1 and cvsuser2, work together to create a Servlet *ServletA* and a view bean *View1*.

Table 26-3   Sample development scenario

Step	Developer 1 (cvsuser1)	Developer 2 (cvsuser2)
1	Creates a new Dynamic Web Project *ISTOCVSGuide* and adds it to the version control and the repository. Creates a servlet *ServletA* and commits it to the repository.	
2	Updates the servlet ServletA.	Imports the ISTOCVSGuide CVS module as a Workbench project. Creates a view bean View1, adds it to the version control, and synchronizes the project with the repository.
3	Synchronizes the project with the repository to commit his changes to repository and merges changes.	
4	Continues changing and updating servlet. Synchronizes the project with the repository to commit his changes to repository and merges changes.	Synchronizes the project with repository, and begins changes to servlet. Synchronizes the project after cvsuser1 has committed and needs to merge code from their workspace and the CVS repository.
5	Synchronizes and merges changes. Versions the project.	

Steps 1 through 3 are serial development—no parallel work is being done. During steps 4, 5, and 6, both developers work in parallel, resulting in inevitable conflicts. These conflicts are resolved using IBM Rational Application Developer V6 tooling.

In the sections that follow, we perform each of the steps and explain the team actions in detail.

26.5.1 Create and share the project (step 1 - cvsuser1)

IBM Rational Application Developer V6 offers a perspective specifically designed for viewing the contents of CVS servers: The CVS Repository Exploring.

Add a CVS repository

To add a CVS repository, do the following:

1. Open the CVS Repository Exploring perspective.
2. Select **New** → **Repository Location** and fill in the information (as shown in Figure 26-13) based on the repository set up in 26.2, "CVSNT Server implementation" on page 1301.

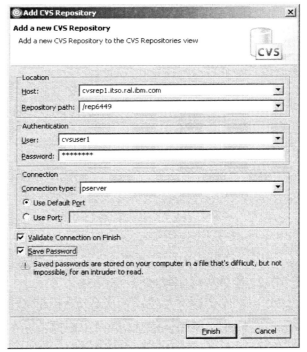

Figure 26-13 Adding a CVS repository

> **Important:** With pserver, passwords are stored on the client side in a trivial encoding and transmitted in the same encoding. The encoding is done only to prevent inadvertent password compromises, and will not prevent an attacker from obtaining the password. The other supported protocol, ssh, does not have this problem, but has to be manually set up.

3. Click **Finish**, and the CVS Repositories view now contains the new repository location (Figure 26-14).

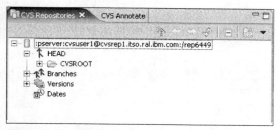

Figure 26-14 CVS Repositories view

Expanding a location in the CVS Repository view reveals branches and versions. A special branch, called HEAD, is shown detached because of its importance. It is the main integration branch, holding the project's current development state.

You can use the CVS Repositories view to check out repository resources as projects on the Workbench. You can also configure branches and versions, view resource histories, and compare resource versions and revisions.

We must first create a project and share it before making full use of the repository.

Create a project and servlet

To create a project and a servlet, do the following:

1. Switch to the Web perspective and create a new Dynamic Web Project by selecting **File → New → Dynamic Web Project**.
2. Type in the name of the project, ITSOCVSGuide, and click **Finish**.
3. In the Project Explorer, expand **Dynamic Web Projects → ITSOCVSGuide → Deployment Descriptor → Servlets**, right-click, and select **New → Servlet**.
4. Type the name of the servlet to be ServletA and click **Next**.
5. Specify the package as itso.ral.ibm.com (see Figure 26-15) and click **Finish**.

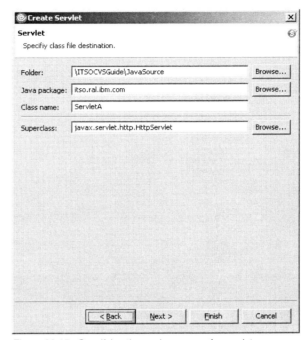

Figure 26-15   Specifying the package name for servlet

6. Expand the **Dynamic Web Projects** tree in the Project Explorer view and click on the project **ITSOCVSGuide**. Right-click and select **Team** → **Share Project**.
7. Select the option **CVS**, and click **Next**.
8. Select the radio button **Use existing repository location:** and the repository that was added previously, and click **Next**.
9. Select the radio button **Use project name as module name**, and click **Next**.
10. The window Share Project Resources (see Figure 26-16 on page 1326) will appear listing the resources to be added in. Click **Finish** to add this into the repository.

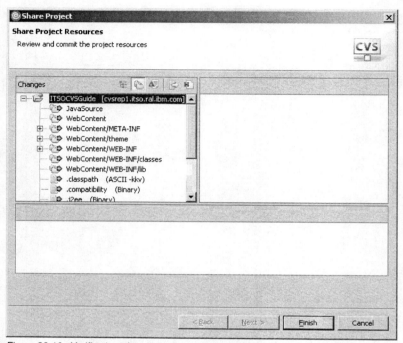

Figure 26-16 Verification of resources to commit under CVS revision control

11. A dialog will ask whether to commit uncommitted changes. Click **Yes**.

12. A dialog will ask whether to add resources to the repository. Click **Yes**.

13. A prompt for a commit comment will be presented. Type `Initial Version` and click **OK**.

> **Note:** A Run Background button is provided on the status when committing. This functionality has been introduced via the Eclipse 3.0 framework into IBM Rational Application Developer V6. This enhances productivity, allowing the user to perform other tasks while waiting for a checkin.

26.5.2 Add a shared project to the workspace (step 2 - cvsuser2)

The purpose of using CVS is to allow multiple developers to work as a team on the same project. We have created the project in one developer's workspace, shared it using CVS, and now wish to add the same project to a second developer's workspace.

1. The second developer must add the CVS repository location to the workspace using the CVS Repositories view in the CVS Repository Exploring perspective, as described in "Add a CVS repository" on page 1323.

   The difference is now that the HEAD branch in the repository, if expanded, contains the ITSOCVSGuide module, as shown in Figure 26-17.

Figure 26-17   CVS Repository with ITSOCVSGuide project

2. Select the ItsoProGuideCVS module, right-click, and click **Check Out**. The current project in the HEAD branch is added to the workspace.

Develop the viewbean

Now that both developers have exactly the same synchronized HEAD branch of the ITSOCVSGuide project on their workspaces, it is time for the second developer to create the viewbean View1.

1. Select **Window** → **Open Perspective** → **Other** → **Java** and click **OK**.
2. Expand the project tree **ITSOCVSGuide** → **JavaSource** → **itso.ral.ibm.com** and select **itso.ral.ibm.com**. Right-click and select **New** → **Class**.
3. Type the name of the class to be View1 and click **Finish** (see Figure 26-18 on page 1328).

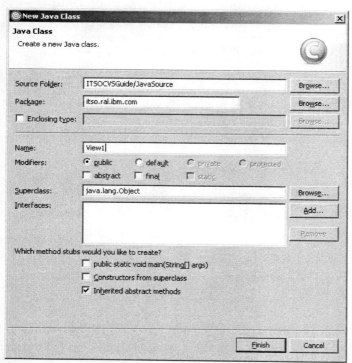

Figure 26-18   Creating the View1 viewbean

4. Create two private attributes in the class an integer named count and a string named message, as shown in Figure 26-19 on page 1329.

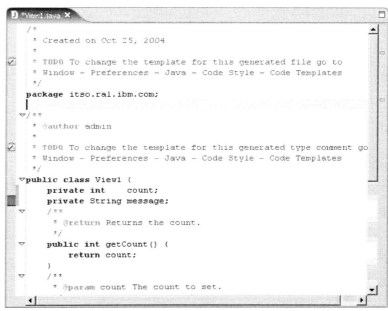

Figure 26-19 View1 code with attributes added in before a save

5. Double-click the **count** attribute to highlight it, right-click, select **Source → Generate Getters and Setters...**, and check the check box for the *message* and verify that the Access Modifier section has *public* set, as in Figure 26-20 on page 1330. Click **OK** to complete.

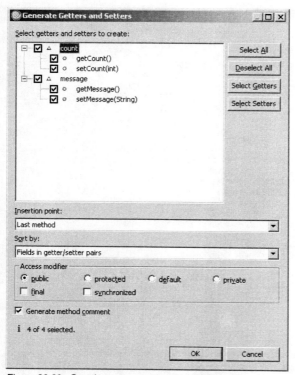

Figure 26-20 Creating setters and getters for class View1

6. Save the file by selecting **File → Save**.

> **Tip:** The greater than sign (>) in front of a resource name means that the particular resource is not synchronized with the repository. You can always use this visual cue to determine when a project requires synchronization.

Synchronizing with the repository

To update the repository with these changes, perform the following:

1. Select the **ITSOCVSGuide** project and select **Team → Synchronize with Repository...** by clicking the right button. A dialog will prompt you to change to the Synchronize view. Click **Yes**. The project is compared with the

repository, and the differences are displayed in the Synchronize view (Figure 26-21).

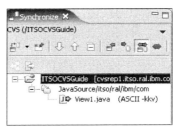

Figure 26-21   Synchronizing ITSOCVSGuide after creating the viewbean View1

This view allows you to update resources in the Workbench with newer content from the repository, commit resources from the Workbench to the repository, and resolve conflicts that may occur in the process. The arrow icons with a plus sign (+) indicate that the files do not exist in the repository.

2. Add these new resources to version control by selecting **ITSOCVSGuide** in this view by right-clicking and selecting **Commit...** .

3. When the **Add to CVS Version Control** dialog appears, click the **Details>>>** button to verify the changes and then click **Yes** (see Figure 26-22).

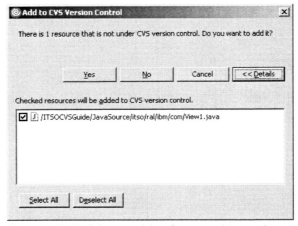

Figure 26-22   Verifying committing of resources into repository

4. The Commit dialog box will appear prompting for a comment. Enter `Added view bean for application` and click **OK**.

   > **Note:** The font in the Synchronize view turns to *italic* to indicate that there is an activity that is in progress on these files. This is useful when you are checking a large quantity of files into the CVS and have background mode on.

26.5.3 Modifying the Servlet (step 2 - cvsuser1)

While activities in the section Add a shared project to the workspace (step 2 - cvsuser2) occur, our original user, cvsuser1, is working on developing the servlet further.

1. Select the Web Perspective by clicking **Window → Open Perspective → Other → Web**.

2. In the Project Explorer expand **Dynamic Web Projects → ITSOCVSGUIDE → Java Resources → JavaSource → itso.ral.ibm.com** and double-click **ServletA.java** to open in an editor.

3. Create a static attribute called totalCount of type int and initialized to zero, as in Figure 26-23 on page 1333.

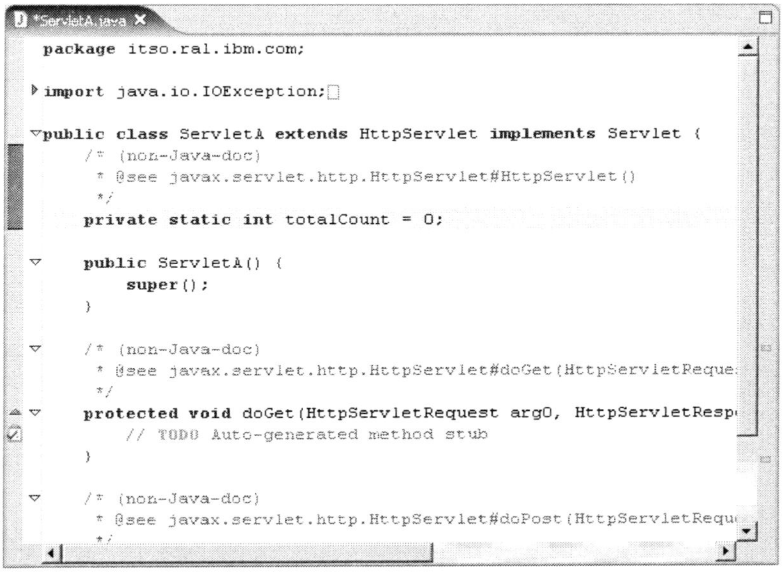

Figure 26-23   Addition of servlet attributes

> **Note:** Files that are not saved have a asterisk (*) in front of their names in the title bar of the window. This assists in identifying resources that need to be saved.

4. Save your work using **File → Save**.

26.5.4 Synchronize with repository (step 3 - cvsuser1)

The first user now synchronizes with the repository after cvsuser2 has checked their changes.

1. Open the Web perspective using **Windows → Open Perspective → Other → Web**.
2. Expand the **Dynamic Web Project** tree in the Project Explorer view and select the **ITSOCVSGuide** project. Right-click and select **Team → Synchronize with Repository...**.
3. Click **Yes** to switch to the Synchronize view.

4. Expand out the **ITSOCVSGuide** → **JavaSource** tree to view the changes. The screen in Figure 26-24 should be presented to you.

Figure 26-24   User cvsuser1 merging with CVS repository

> **Note:** The symbol [J♦] in the diagram indicates that an existing resource differs from what is in the repository. The symbol [J♦] indicates that a new resource is in the repository that does not exist on the local workspace.

5. To obtain updated resources from the CVS repository, right-click the project and select **Update**.
6. Verify that the changes do not cause problems with existing resources in the local workspace. In this case, there are none. Right-click and select **Commit...**.
7. In the Commit dialog, add the comment `Added static count variable to servlet.` and click **OK** (see Figure 26-25).

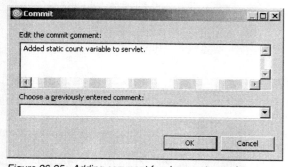

Figure 26-25   Adding comment for changes to servlet

The repository now has the latest changes to the code from both developers. The user cvsuser1 is in sync with the repository; however, cvsuser2, as yet, does not have the changes to the servlet.

26.5.5 Parallel development (step 4 - cvsuser1 and cvsuser2)

The previous steps have highlighted development and repository synchronization with two people working on two parts of a project. It highlights the need to synchronize between each phase in the development before further work is performed. This scenario highlights two developers working on the same area of the code, with one checking before the other. Each user's sequence of events is described in the sections below; however, to understand what is occurring refer to the timeline shown in Figure 26-26.

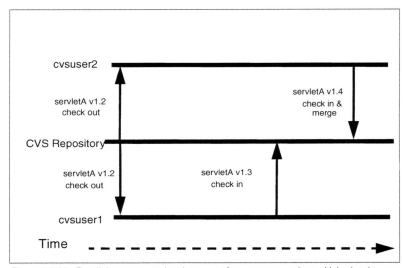

Figure 26-26 Parallel concurrent development of same resource by multiple developers

User cvsuser1 updates and commits changes

In this scenario, the user cvsuser1 modifies the dopost method to log information for an attribute. The following procedure demonstrates how to synchronize the source code and commit the changes to CVS.

1. Open the Web perspective using **Windows** → **Open Perspective** → **Other** → **Web**.

2. Open the tree under the **Dynamic Web Projects** → **ITSOCVSGuide** → **Java Resources** → **JavaSource** → **itso.ral.ibm.com** and double-click the file **ServletA.java** to open it.

3. Navigate to the doPost method by scrolling down the file and adding the code in Figure 26-27 on page 1336.

```
* @see javax.servlet.http.HttpServlet#HttpServlet()
*/
private static int totalCount = 0;

public ServletA() {
    super();
}

/* (non-Java-doc)
 * @see javax.servlet.http.HttpServlet#doGet(HttpServletRequest arg0, Ht
 */
protected void doGet(HttpServletRequest arg0, HttpServletResponse arg1)
    // TODO Auto-generated method stub
}

/* (non-Java-doc)
 * @see javax.servlet.http.HttpServlet#doPost(HttpServletRequest arg0, 
 */
protected void doPost(HttpServletRequest arg0, HttpServletResponse arg1)
    // TODO Auto-generated method stub
    totalCount = totalCount + 1;
    System.out.println("The total number of requests is:"+totalCount);
}
```

Figure 26-27 User cvsuser1 adding code to servlet in the local repository

4. Save the file by clicking **File → Save**.

5. Synchronize the project with the repository by right-clicking and selecting **Team → Synchronize Repository...**, and click **OK** to open synchronize view.

6. Fully expand out the tree in the Synchronize view. The servlet should be the only change, as shown in Figure 26-28.

Figure 26-28 Changes in servlet from the repository

7. Right-click and select **Commit...**, add the comment User1 updating the servlet, and press **OK** to commit.

1336   Rational Application Developer V6 Programming Guide

The developer cvsuser1 has now completed the task of adding code into the servlet. Changes can be picked up by other developers in the team.

User cvsuser2 updates and commits changes

The second developer updates their repository before beginning any new work to ensure that they have the latest copy of the code. This occurs before the first developer has checked in the changes to the servlet and while they are making their changes. The following steps are performed:

1. Open the Web perspective using **Windows** → **Open Perspective** → **Other** → **Web**.
2. Open the tree under **Dynamic Web Projects** → **ITSOCVSGuide** → **Java Resources** → **JavaSource itso.ral.ibm.com** and double-click the file **ServletA.java** to open it.
3. Navigate to the doPost method by scrolling down the file and adding the code in Figure 26-29. Save the code by selecting **File** → **Save**.

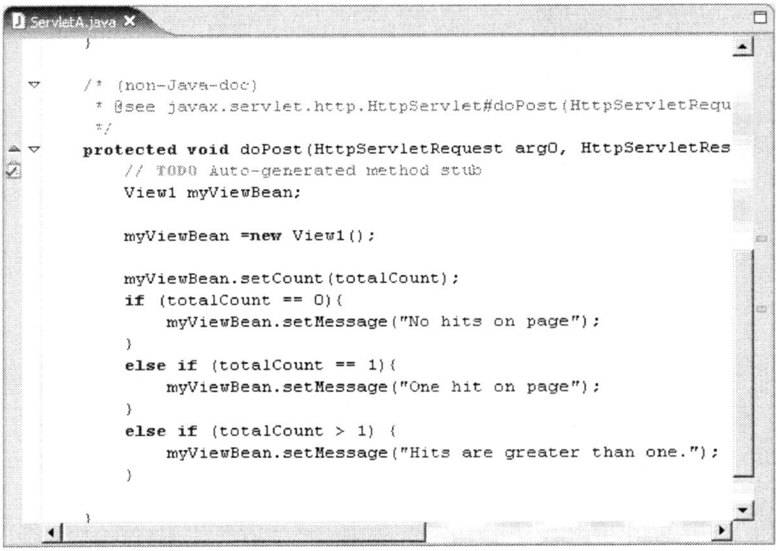

```
/* (non-Java-doc)
 * @see javax.servlet.http.HttpServlet#doPost(HttpServletRequ
 */
protected void doPost(HttpServletRequest arg0, HttpServletRes
    // TODO Auto-generated method stub
    View1 myViewBean;

    myViewBean =new View1();

    myViewBean.setCount(totalCount);
    if (totalCount == 0){
        myViewBean.setMessage("No hits on page");
    }
    else if (totalCount == 1){
        myViewBean.setMessage("One hit on page");
    }
    else if (totalCount > 1) {
        myViewBean.setMessage("Hits are greater than one.");
    }
```

Figure 26-29 User cvsuser2 adds code into the servlet

4. Synchronize with the repository by clicking the project **ITSOCVSGuide** and clicking the right button and selecting **Team** → **Synchronize with Repository**....

5. Click **Yes** to switch to the synchronize perspective and expand out the tree in the synchronize view to see change, as in Figure 26-30.

Figure 26-30   Conflict of file in CVS Repository for user cvsuser2

> **Note:** The symbol indicates that the file has conflicting changes that require merging.

6. Double-click the file **ServletA.java** to see the changes, as shown in Figure 26-31 on page 1339. On the right-hand side is the code in the repository (checked in by user cvsuser1), and on the left are the changes made by the current user cvsuser2.

Merging in this case will require consolidation between the two developers as to the best solution. In our example, we assume that the changes in the repository need to be placed before changes performed by cvsuser2 (left-hand side).

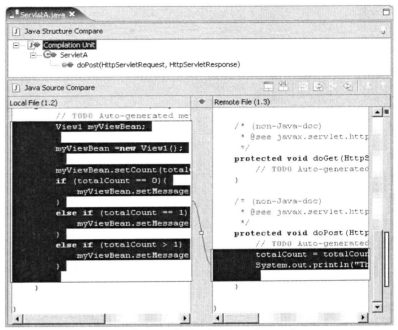

Figure 26-31   The changes between the local and remote repository

7. Click the icon (Copy current change from Right to Left). This will place the change at the end of the right-hand screen, as shown in Figure 26-32 on page 1340.

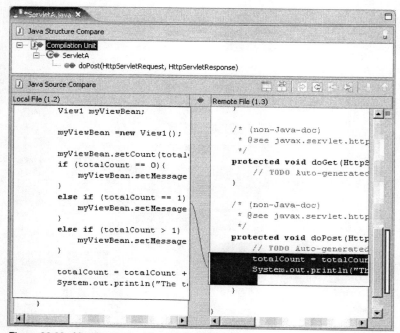

Figure 26-32 Merging changes from right to left

8. In the left pane, highlight the two lines of code added and cut and paste them to the correct location in the file, as shown in Figure 26-33 on page 1341.

Figure 26-33   Move the added code to the correct merge point

9. Verify that the code is exactly as agreed by the developers, and if so save the new merged change using **File → Save**.

10. Resynchronize the file using steps 4, 5, and 6 above in the Web perspective.

11. Verify that the changes are correct, and then in the Synchronize view right-click and select **Mark as Merged**, and then right-click and select **Commit**.

12. In the Commit dialog that appears, type the comment `Changes and merge of Servlet`, as in Figure 26-34 on page 1342.

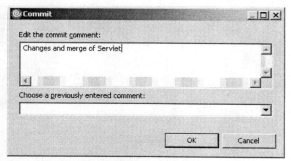

Figure 26-34   Comment for merged changes

This operation creates a version of the file, Version 1.4, which will contain the merged changes from users cvsuser1 and cvsuser2, in spite of the fact that both developers began working with Version 1.2.

26.5.6 Versioning (step 5- cvsuser1)

Now that all the changes are synchronized with the repository, we want to create a version to milestone our work.

1. Select the **ITSOCVSGuide** project in the Web perspective and Project explorer view and select **Team** → **Tag as Version...**. The Tag Resources dialog opens (seeFigure 26-35).

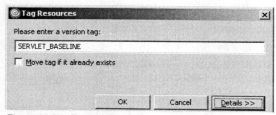

Figure 26-35   Tagging the project as a version

2. Verify that the tag has been performed by switching to the CVS Repository Exploring perspective and expand out the repository, as shown in Figure 26-36 on page 1343.

Figure 26-36   Project version

26.6 CVS resource history

The developer can view the resource history of a file of any shared project in their workspace. This is the list of all the revisions of a resource in the repository, shown in the CVS Resource History view. From this view you can compare two revisions, replace or revert the corresponding workspace file to the revision, or open an editor on a revision.

1. Open the Web perspective using **Window** → **Open Perspective** → **Other** → **Web**.

2. Expand in the Project Explorer **Dynamic Web Projects** → **ITSOCVSGuide** → **Java Resources** → **JavaSource** → **itso.ral.ibm.com** and highlight **ServletA.java**.

3. Right-click and select **Team** → **Show in Resource History** and a new view will appear, as in Figure 26-38 on page 1345.

   The CVS resource history will display the following information (Table 26-4 on page 1343).

Table 26-4   CVS resource history terminology

Resource History column	Description
Revision	The revision number of each version of the file in the repository. An asterisk (*) indicates that this is the current version in the workspace.
Tags	The tags associated with the revision. Selecting a revision line with a tag will display the tag in the lower pane of the view.
Date	The date and time when the revision was created in the repository.

Resource History column	Description
Author	The name of the used ID that created and checked in the revision into the repository.
Comments	The comment (if any) supplied for this revision at the time it was committed. Selecting a revision in the upper pane displays the comment in the lower right pane of the view.

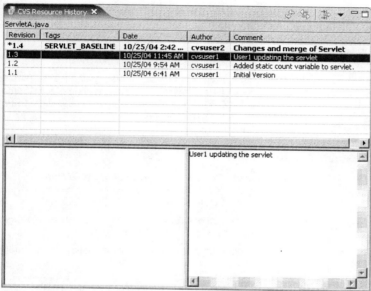

Figure 26-37   CVS Resource view for ServletA.java

26.7 Comparisons in CVS

Users on occasion require the ability to compare what changes have occurred with a version of their code against a version in the repository. There are two ways of comparing: One is to compare a file in the workspace with that in the repository; the other is to compare two files in the repository. To demonstrate these features a scenario has been provided as an example of both processes.

26.7.1 Comparing workspace file with repository

The developer has Version 1.4 of the ServletA.java resource and wants to compare the differences between their current version and 1.1 to understand changes made. They would perform the following:

1. Open the Web perspective using **Window** → **Open Perspective** → **Other** → **Web**.
2. Expand in the Project Explorer **Dynamic Web Projects** → **ITSOCVSGuide** → **Java Resources** → **JavaSource** → **itso.ral.ibm.com** and highlight **ServletA.java**.
3. Right-click and select **Compare with** → **Revision...**, and a screen similar to the CVS Resource History will display, as in Figure 26-38.

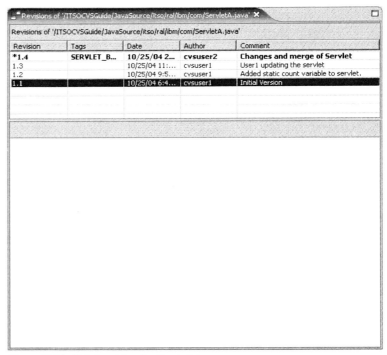

Figure 26-38   List of revisions for ServletA.java

4. Double-click the revision 1.1 version and a comparison will appear in the pane below, as in Figure 26-39.

   The changes are then displayed in a few ways. In the top right-hand corner the changes to the class are shown, which include attribute changes, and identifies the methods that have changed, while in the bottom two panes the actual code differences are highlighted. The left bottom pane has the revision in the workspace and the right bottom pane has the revision 1.2 from the repository.

   Note: The bars in the bottom pane on the right-hand side indicate the changes located in the file. By clicking them they will position the pane to highlight the changes and assist in quickly moving around large files with many changes.

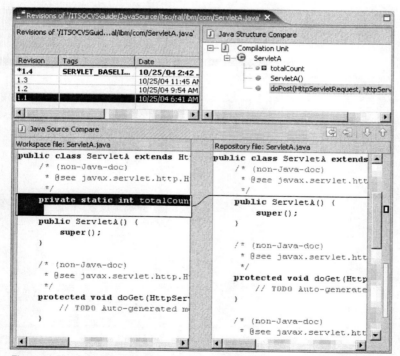

Figure 26-39 Comparison between Version 1.4 and Version 1.1 of ServletA.java

26.7.2 Comparing two revisions in repository

A developer wants to compare the differences between revision 1.1 and 1.3 in the repository of the file ServletA.java, and they have version 1.4 in their workspace and do not want to remove it. The procedure to follow is:

1. Open up the CVS Resource History using the procedure in "CVS resource history" on page 1343, which would display the view shown in Figure 26-37 on page 1344.

2. Click in the row of the first version you want to compare, say revision 1.1, and then, while pressing the Ctrl key, click in the row of the second version, which is 1.3, so that the screen looks as in Figure 26-40.

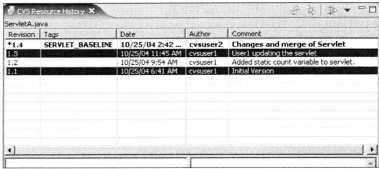

Figure 26-40   Highlight the two revisions to compare

3. Right-click, ensuring that the two revisions are highlighted, and click **Compare**, and the result will appear as in Figure 26-41 on page 1348. The higher version will always appear on the left-hand pane and the lower version in the right pane.

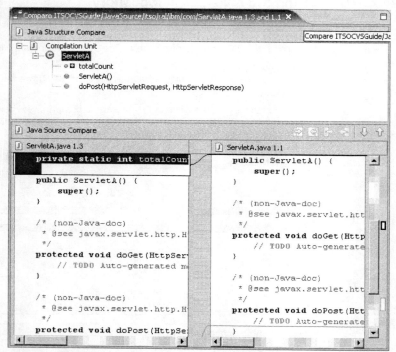

Figure 26-41 Comparisons of two revisions from the repository

26.8 Annotations in CVS

The annotation function of CVS has been included in IBM Rational Application Developer V6 to provide details of the changes that were performed on a particular revision. The annotation function displays to the request of what lines were changed in particular revisions, and the author responsible for the change (or the one to "blame"). This feature can assist developers with gaining an understanding of what has changed that may impact a functionality change in the code and identify who can assist them in their resolution of this change.

To demonstrate annotations we can go back to our example of looking at the resource ServletA.java and see what the process is and what it provides.

1. Open the Web perspective using **Window → Open Perspective → Other → Web**.
2. Expand in the Project Explorer **Dynamic Web Projects → ITSOCVSGuide → Java Resources → JavaSource → itso.ral.ibm.com** and highlight **ServletA.java**.
3. Right-click and select **Team → Show Annotation**. This will switch to the CVS Repository Exploring view and display the views as in Figure 26-42.

   The view on the left-hand side is the CVS Annotation view. The information that it displays is the user that made the change, followed by the version and the number of lines in brackets. Highlighting any of these will display the change that occurred in the top right-hand pane of the source, with the corresponding version information in the bottom right view.

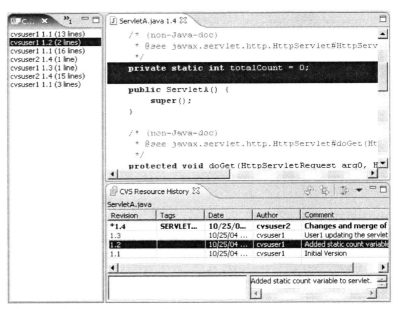

Figure 26-42 Annotation view for ServletA.java

The annotation view allows a developer to identify changes that may have occurred in a particular file and identify the root causes of issues that they may be having.

26.9 Branches in CVS

Branches are Software Configuration Management (SCM) techniques to allow current development of software based on a baseline that has been established.

In CVS there is the concept of the HEAD, which is a branch that refers to the current work that is being performed in a team environment. However, this is only useful in terms of one development team working with one release. The real-world situation is that development follows a life cycle that has development, maintenance, and enhancement based on a baseline. This is when branches can be useful and when CVS can allow you to create baselines and parallel streams of work to enhance software product development.

Typical development cycles would have a development cycle for new work, as well as a maintenance cycle in which code currently in use is enhanced and resolved of bugs. In these circumstances there would be two streams of development occurring that would be independent: The maintenance branch enhancing "operational" code and the development branch. At some point these would need to be merged together to provide a new baseline to be a production version. A representation is shown in Figure 26-43.

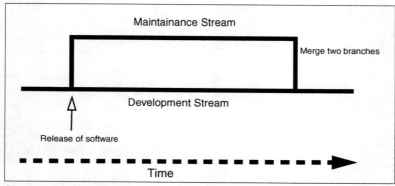

Figure 26-43   Branching of two development streams

26.9.1 Branching

Creating a branch is useful when you wish to maintain multiple versions of the software developed when they are in multiple stages of delivery.

The scenario that is identified is that a particular release has been deployed to a host machine; however, further work needs to continue to enhance the application. In addition to this, existing software needs to be enhanced and maintained so that problems identified are fixed. Branching provides the mechanism to achieve this, and a process is outlined using the simple example as follows:

1. Open the Web perspective using **Window** → **Open Perspective** → **Other** → **Web**.
2. Expand in the Project Explorer **Dynamic Web Projects** → **ITSOCVSGuide** and highlight **ITSOCVSGuide**.
3. Create a tag for what is in your repository to use as the branch root by right-clicking and selecting **Team** → **Tag as Version...**, and typing the tag name BRANCH_ROOT, and clicking **OK**.
4. Highlight the project **ITSOCVSGuide**, right-click, and select **Team** → **Branch...**.
5. Type the name of the branch in the first dialog and the branch to base it from, which is BRANCH_ROOT. Leave the check box checked to start working on this branch, as shown in Figure 26-44 and press **OK**.

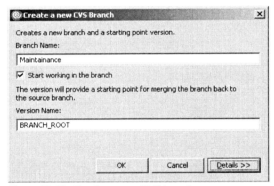

Figure 26-44   Creating a new CVS branch

Note: The version name is important; you will need it when you want to merge the branches later. It identifies the point at which the branch was created.

6. Highlight the project **ITSOCVSGuide**, right-click, select **Properties**, and click the **CVS** tag. A view, as shown in Figure 26-45 on page 1352, will be displayed with the tag name displayed as Maintainance (Branch), indicating that it has been set up correctly. Click **OK** when finished viewing.

Chapter 26. CVS integration   **1351**

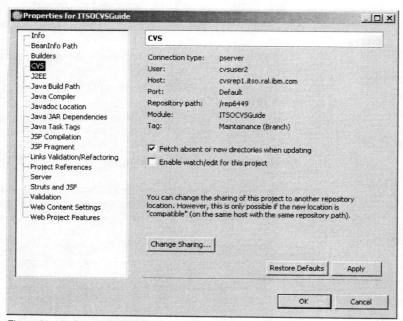

Figure 26-45   Branch information for a project in the local workspace

7. Open the CVS Repository Explorer window by clicking **Window → Open Perspective → Other → CVS Repository Explorer**.
8. Right-click the repository and click **Refresh View**.
9. Expand the tree and the branches sub tree to verify that the branch has been created in the repository, as shown in Figure 26-46.

Figure 26-46   List of branches created

Updating Branch code

Assume now that there are changes required to be made to the servlet ServletA.java and a new viewbean View2.java, which is created with no methods or attributes. This will be used to demonstrate the merge process with the changes being made in the maintainance branch and saved into the repository.

1. Open the Web perspective using **Windows** → **Open Perspective** → **Other** → **Web**.

2. Expand in the Project Explorer **Dynamic Web Projects** → **ITSOCVSGuide** → **Java Resources** → **JavaSource** → **itso.ral.ibm.com** and double-click **ServletA.java** to open it.

3. Navigate to the doPost method and at the top of the class add the statement:

   ```
   System.out.println("Added in some code to demonstrate branching");
   ```

4. Select **File** → **Save** to save the information.

5. Highlight the package **itso.ral.ibm.com** and right-click **New** → **Class**

6. Type `View2` for the name of the class and click **Finish**.

7. Highlight the project **ITSOCVSGuide** and click **Team** → **Synchronize**, and click **Yes** to switch to the Synchronize view.

8. Select the project, right-click, select **Commit...**, and click **Yes** to add the resource into CVS.

9. When the Commit dialog window appears type `Branching example`, and click **OK**.

10. Open the CVS Repository Explorer by selecting **Windows** → **Open Perspective** → **Other** → **CVS Repository Explorer**, and expand out the tree, as shown in Figure 26-47 on page 1354.

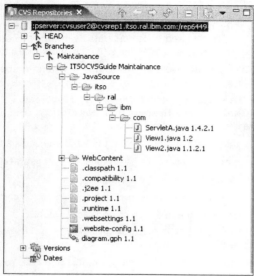

Figure 26-47 Code checked into the branch

The changes have now been committed into the branch called *Maintainance*, which will have contents that differ from the main branch. This will not be seen by developers working on the branch HEAD, which is the development stream in our scenario.

26.9.2 Merging

Merging of branches occurs when there is a point in time that requires the code from one branch to be incorporated into another branch for a major milestone. This could be a major integration step, release date, or changes are required from the branch to resolve some issues.

The scenario now is that development on the main CVS branch has completed development and is required to merge changes in the maintainance branch for release as a new version.

To merge the two branches, you have to know:

▶ The name of the branch or version that contains your changes.

- The version from which the branch was created. This is the version name that you supplied when branching.

In our case, the branch is *Maintenance*, and the version is *Branch_Root*.

Merging requires that the target or destination branch be loaded into the workspace before merging in a branch. Since in our scenario the changes will be merged to HEAD, this needs to be loaded in the workspace.

1. Open the Web perspective using **Windows** → **Open Perspective** → **Other** → **Web**.
2. Open the tree under the **Dynamic Web Projects** → **ITSOCVSGuide**, highlight the project **ITSOCVSGuide**, and right-click, selecting **Replace With...** → **Another Branch or Version...**.
3. When the dialog appears, select **HEAD** and click **OK**.
4. Highlight the project **ITSOCVSGuide** and right-click, selecting **Team** → **Merge**, which displays the dialog shown in Figure 26-48.

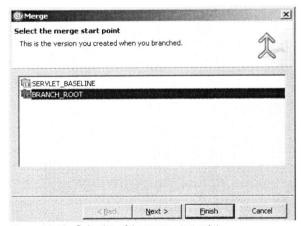

Figure 26-48 Selection of the merge start point

5. Select the branch name **BRANCH_ROOT** for the merge start point and click **Next**.
6. The merge branch dialog will be displayed requesting the branch to merge into the tag BRANCH_ROOT specified earlier. Select **Maintainance** and click **Finish**, as in Figure 26-49 on page 1356. Click **Yes** to switch to the synchronizing view.

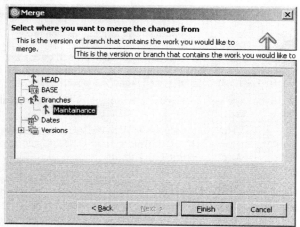

Figure 26-49   Identification of the merge target in CVS

7. Expand out the tree in the Synchronize view to display changes. Verify that there are no conflicts. If there are then the developer will need to resolve these conflicts. In our case, the merge is simple, as shown in Figure 26-50.

   Select the project **ITSOCVSGuide**, right-click, and select **Update**.

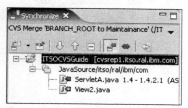

Figure 26-50   Files required to be merged

8. Open the Web perspective using **Windows → Open Perspective → Other → Web**.

9. Open the tree under the **Dynamic Web Projects → ITSOCVSGuide** and highlight the project **ITSOCVSGuide**, right-click, and select **Team → Synchronize with Repository**....

10. Click **Yes** to open the Synchronize view.

11. Expand out the Synchronize view to display the changed files ServletA.java and View2.java, as in Figure 26-51. Select the project, and right-click and select **Commit**.

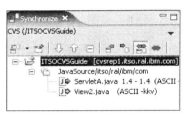

Figure 26-51   CVS updates to HEAD from the merge

12. When the commit dialog appears add the comment `Merged changes from maintainance branch` and click **OK**.

This scenario, although a simple one, highlights the technique required by users to work with branches. In a real scenario there would be conflicts found, and this would require resolution between developers. Be aware that branching and concurrent development is a complex process. IBM Rational Application Developer V6 provides the tools for merging; however, equally important are procedures on handling situations such as branching and merging of code.

26.9.3 Refreshing server-defined branches

If a branch exists on the server, you must refresh it in your workspace to be able to access it. The CVS Repositories view does not obtain a list of all branches from the server by default.

1. To define a branch manually to a repository, go to the CVS Repositories view by selecting **Window → Open Perspective → Other → CVS Repository Explorer**.

2. Select the repository and expand out the tree. Highlight the **Branches** node (see Figure 26-52 on page 1358), right-click, and select **Refresh Branches...**.

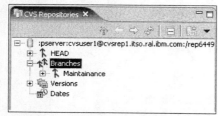

Figure 26-52   Selecting the Branches node in CVS Repository view

> **Note:** If there are no repository locations listed in the Repositories view, you have to add a location, as explained in "Add a CVS repository" on page 1323.

3. In the Refresh branches dialog specify the projects you wish to refresh (Figure 26-53 on page 1359) and click **Finish**.

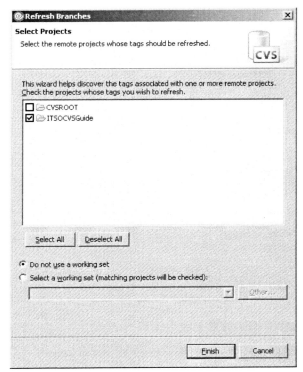

Figure 26-53   Refreshing branches

4. In the Repositories view, expand **Branches** and observe that it now contains the new SERVER_HEAD branch (see Figure 26-54 on page 1360).

   You can now check files out from this branch, if they exist.

Figure 26-54   Refreshed branch created in server displayed in CVS Repository view

26.10 Work with patches

IBM Rational Application Developer V6 provides the facility for developers to be able to share work when they do not have write access to the repository. In this circumstance the developer that does have access to the repository can create a patch and can forward it to another developer who has and can apply the patch to the project and commit changes.

See the IBM Rational Application Developer V6 online help for a description of how to work with patches.

26.11 Disconnecting a project

Developers can disconnect a project from the repository.

1. Open the Web perspective using **Windows → Open Perspective → Other → Web**.
2. Open the tree under the **Dynamic Web Projects → ITSOCVSGuide**.
3. Highlight the **ITSOCVSGuide** project, right-click, and select **Team → Disconnect**.
4. A prompt will appear asking you to confirm the deletion of the CVS control information (see Figure 26-55 on page 1361).

   Select **Do not delete the CVS meta information (e.g, CVS sub directories)**, and click **OK**.

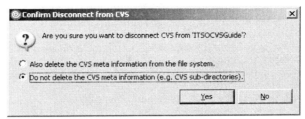

Figure 26-55   Disconnect confirmation

> **Important:** By not deleting the CVS meta information we can reconnect the project with the CVS repository more easily. Removal of the CVS meta information may impact the synchronization of the files in the workspace and the repository.

CVS adds special directories named CVS to the project and its folders. These directories can be deleted or kept on disconnect. The feature to keep these folders and files in IBM Rational Application Developer V6 hidden is provided with the Eclipse framework.

Reconnect

You can reconnect a project to the repository (**Team** → **Share Project**). Reconnect is easier if the CVS folders are still in the project. If they were deleted, you are prompted to synchronize your code with the existing repository code.

26.12 Synchronize perspective

The synchronize perspective in IBM Rational Application Developer V6 has been used in describing concepts within this chapter but has not as yet been described. The purpose of this perspective is to provide to the user of the tool with an entry point to identify changes in the team repository versus what is on the local workspace, and assist in effectively using it. Features provided with the synchronize perspective include:

- Create custom synchronization of a subset of resources in the workspace.
- Schedule checkout synchronization.
- Provide a comparison of changes in the workspace (which has been demonstrated in "Comparisons in CVS" on page 1344).

26.12.1 Custom configuration of resource synchronization

The Synchronize view provides the ability to create custom synchronization sets for the purpose of synchronizing only identified resources that a developer may be working on. This allows the developer to focus on changes that are part of their scope of work and ensure they are aware of the changes that occur without focusing on the other aspects of the application. Problems can occur with this mode of operation as well, since with normal application development changes in one part of the application can impact other parts.

> **Important:** Custom synchronization is most effective when an application is designed with defined interfaces where the partitioning of work is clear and defined. However, even in this scenario it needs to used with caution since it can introduce additional work in the development cycle for integration of the final product. Procedures need to be documented and enforced to ensure that integration is incorporated as part of the work pattern for this scenario.

The scenario to demonstrate custom synchronization requires that the ITSOCVSGuide project exists in the workspace. In addition, the developer will need to perform the following synchronization procedures:

- Full synchronization of the project ITSOCVSGuide
- Partial synchronization of the servlet ServletA.java

The procedure to perform this would be as follows:

1. Select **Window** → **Open Perspective** → **Other** → **Team Synchronizing**, which presents the window shown in Figure 26-56 on page 1363.

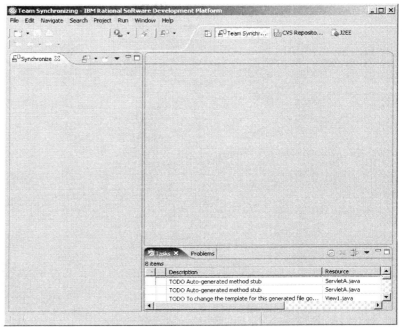

Figure 26-56 Team Synchronizing perspective

2. Click the Synchronize button ![icon] at the top the Synchronize view (left pane) and click **Synchronize...** to add a new synchronization definition.

3. In the synchronize dialog that appears as in Figure 26-57 on page 1364, select **CVS** and click **Next**.

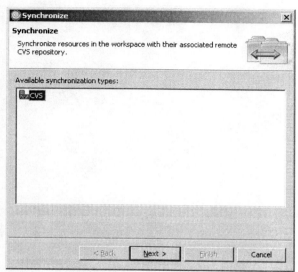

Figure 26-57   Synchronize dialog

4. Expand the project tree out to view the contents. Accept the defaults for the Synchronize CVS dialog, as shown in Figure 26-58 on page 1365, and click **Finish**.

   If there are no changes then a dialog box will appear saying `Synchronizing: No changes found`, and in the Synchronize view a message of `No changes in 'CVS (Workspace)'`.

Figure 26-58 Default synchronization of the project ITSOCVSGuide

5. To preserve this synchronization, click the Pin Current Synchronization icon.

6. Add in a new synchronization by clicking the Synchronize icon at the top of the Synchronize view.

7. In the synchronize dialog that appears, as in Figure 26-57 on page 1364, select **CVS** and click **Next**.

8. Expand the project tree fully out under JavaSource to view the contents, click **Deselect All** to deselect all the resources, and click the check box for ServletA.java.

   Verify that Selected Resources is selected, as in Figure 26-59 on page 1366, and click **Finish**. If there are no changes, then a dialog box will appear saying `Synchronizing: No changes found`, and in the Synchronize view a message of `No changes in 'CVS (Workspace)'`.

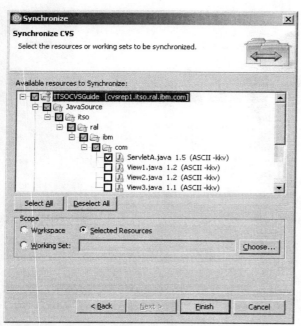

Figure 26-59 Selecting ServletA.java for synchronization

9. To preserve this synchronization, click the Pin Current Synchronization icon .

In the list of synchronizations two should appear, as shown in Figure 26-60.

Figure 26-60 List of synchronizations created

Worksets of synchronization can be defined when creating a synchronization. The workset supports three types of resources:

▶ Java

   Supports the creation of synchronization working sets consisting of pure java resources, such as java source and jar files.

- Help

    Supports the creation of synchronization working sets consisting of Help resources.

- Resource

    Supports the creation of synchronization working sets consisting of any file that can be saved into the team repository.

Working sets differ in that a name can be associated with the synchronization, allowing the developer to have a meaningful name related to the synchronization. This is not been shown in this book; however, it follows a similar procedure as described above and is left to the reader to attempt.

26.12.2 Schedule synchronization

A new feature that has been included in IBM Rational Application Developer V6 is the ability to schedule synchronization of the workspace. This feature follows on from "Custom configuration of resource synchronization" on page 1362, in which a user would like to schedule the synchronization that has been defined. Scheduling a synchronization can only be performed for synchronizations that have been pinned.

To demonstrate this feature, assume that the project ITSOCVSGuide is loaded in the workspace and a synchronization has been defined for this project and pinned. Scheduling of this project for synchronization is then performed using the following:

1. Open the synchronization view by clicking **Windows** → **Open Perspective** → **Other...** → **Team Synchronizing**.
2. In the Synchronize view click the drop-down arrow, as circled in Figure 26-61.

Figure 26-61   Synchronize view

3. A drop-down box appears. Click **Schedule...** as shown in Figure 26-62 on page 1368.

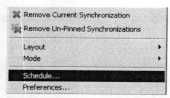

Figure 26-62   Selecting the Schedule option

4. The Configure Synchronize Schedule will be displayed. Select the radio button **Using the following schedule:** and the time period that you wish to synchronize, as shown in Figure 26-63. Click **OK**.

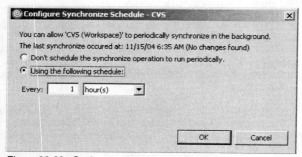

Figure 26-63   Setting synchronization schedule

By setting the synchronization schedule to an hour, the project ITSOCVSGuide will be synchronized every hour to ensure that the latest updates are available.

Appendixes

IBM product installation and configuration tips

The objective of this appendix is to highlight the key considerations and options for installation selected for IBM Rational Application Developer, IBM DB2 Universal Database, and IBM WebSphere Application Server for this redbook.

The appendix is organized into the following sections:
- IBM Rational Application Developer V6 installation
- IBM Rational Agent Controller V6 installation
- IBM Rational ClearCase LT installation
- IBM DB2 Universal Database V8.2 installation
- IBM WebSphere Application Server V6 installation
- WebSphere Application Server messaging configuration

IBM Rational Application Developer V6 installation

The purpose of this section is to highlight the key installation considerations, identify components installed while writing this redbook, and provide a general awareness to using the Rational Product Updater tool to install IBM Rational Application Developer V6 Interim Fix 0004.

This section includes the following tasks:

- Rational Application Developer installation
- WebSphere Portal V5.0 Test Environment installation
- WebSphere Portal V5.1 Test Environment installation
- Rational Application Developer Product Updater - Interim Fix 0004

> **Note:** For detailed information on the IBM Rational Application Developer V6.0 installation, refer to the following product guides found on CD 1:
>
> - *Installation Guide, IBM Rational Application Developer V6.0* (Open install.html in a Web browser.)
> - *Release note, IBM Rational Application Developer V6.0* (Open readme.html in a Web browser.)
> - *Migration Guide, IBM Rational Application Developer V6.0* (Open migrate.html in a Web browser.)
> - *Installing IBM Rational ClearCase LT - Technote* (Open TechNote-Installing_CCLT.html in a Web browser.)

Rational Application Developer installation

The IBM Rational Application Developer V6.0 product includes detailed installation documentation. This section highlights the installation issues we found while writing the redbook, as well as the components we installed.

Installation considerations

Prior to installing IBM Rational Application Developer V6.0, beware of the following installation considerations:

- UNC network shares: Do not install Rational Application Developer from a UNC network share (for example, \\server\shareA). Instead, map the network drive to a drive letter (for example, net use x: \\server\shareA) so that the Rational Application Developer installer works properly.
- Standardize installation path for team development: Standardize the Rational Application Developer installation path for your development team. We found that many files within the projects have absolute paths based on the

installation path; thus when you import projects from a team repository such as CVS or ClearCase you will get many errors.

► Installer window in foreground/background: After clicking IBM Rational Application Developer V6.0, sometimes the welcome screen does not appear in the foreground. Simply select the new window from the task list to continue.

Rational Application Developer installation

While writing this redbook, we installed IBM Rational Application Developer V6.0 as follows:

1. Start the Rational Application Developer Installer by running **launchpad.exe** from CD 1.
2. The IBM Rational Application Developer V6.0 components have separate installations from the main Launchpad Base page, as seen in Figure A-1.

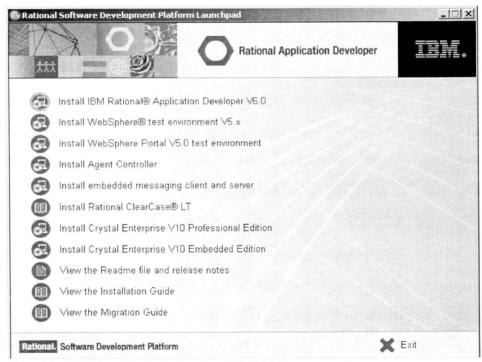

Figure A-1   IBM Rational Application Developer V6.0 installation components

Table A-1   IBM Rational Application Developer V6.0 description of install components

Component	Description

Install IBM Rational Application Developer V6.0	Core Rational Application Developer - sub components:
	▸ Integrated Development Environment (required)
	▸ IBM WebSphere Application Server V6.0 Integrated Test Environment
	▸ Additional Features:
	  – Language Pack
	  – Enterprise Generation Language (EGL)
	  – Portal tools
	  – Examples for Eclipse Plug-in Development
	
	Note: While writing the redbook, we did not install (out of scope) the Language Pack or Examples for Eclipse Plug-in Development.

IBM WebSphere Test Environment V5.x	Select from the following sub components: ▸ WebSphere Application Server V5.1 ▸ WebSphere Application Server V5.0.2 ▸ WebSphere Application Server Express V5.1 ▸ WebSphere Application Server Express V5.0.2
IBM WebSphere Portal V5.0 Test Environment	IBM WebSphere Portal V5.0 Test Environment integrated with Rational Application Developer for local testing and debug.
Install Agent Controller	IBM Rational Agent Controller is needed for debug on WebSphere Application Server V5.x (capability built-in on V6), and profiling and testing on WebSphere Application Server V6 and V5.x.
Install the embedded messaging client & server	This feature is for embedded messaging for WebSphere Application Server V5.x. In WebSphere Application Server V6 messaging is built-in.
Install Rational ClearCase LT	**Note**: Due to a defect at the time of the Rational Application Developer product release, the ClearCase LT was made available as a Web download with a supporting patch. See *Installing IBM Rational ClearCase LT - Technote* (open TechNote-Installing_CCLT.html in a Web browser found on CD 1).
Install Crystal Enterprise V10 Professional Edition	
Install Crystal Enterprise V10 Embedded Edition	

3. When Welcome window appears, click **Next**.
4. When the License Agreement window appears, review the terms and if in agreement select **I accept the terms of the license agreement**. Click **Next**.
5. When the Install Directory window appears, we accepted the default C:\Program Files\IBM\Rational\SDP\6.0 and clicked **Next**.

> **Important:** It is very important that you understand the implication of changing the default installation path. For example, if you plan on team development, we strongly recommend that all developers use the same installation path (such as default); otherwise you will run into problems.
>
> We found that many files within the projects have absolute paths based on the installation path; thus when you import projects from a team repository such as CVS or ClearCase you will get many errors.

6. When the Select Features window appears, select the appropriate features for your environment. For example, we selected the features displayed in Figure A-2 for the redbook.

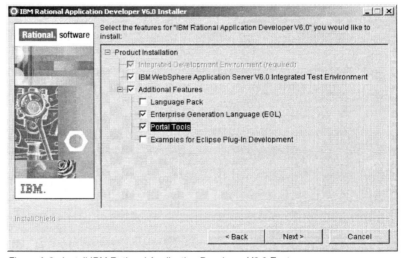

Figure A-2   Install IBM Rational Application Developer V6.0 Features

7. When the Installation Summary window appears, review your selections and click **Next** to begin copying files as seen in Figure A-3 on page 1376.

Note: The selected features take approximately 2.5 GB of disk space.

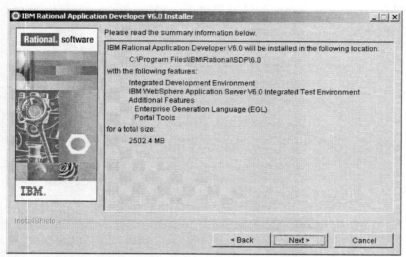

Figure A-3   IBM Rational Application Developer V6.0 install summary

The installation can take 30 minutes to 2 hours depending on the processing speed of your system and the features selected.

8. When you see the message `The Installation Wizard has successfully installed IBM Rational Application Developer V6.0`, click **Next**.

9. The installation is now complete. We unchecked the **Launch Agent Controller install** and then clicked **Finish**. We will install the IBM Rational Agent Controller separately for profiling and testing purposes.

WebSphere Portal V5.0 Test Environment installation

The development tools are installed as part of the base Rational Application Developer installation by selecting the Portal Tools feature. There are a couple of possible scenarios for the portal test environment.

► IBM WebSphere Portal V5.0 Test Environment (local)

   Install this feature from the main IBM Rational Application Developer V6.0 Installer dialog.

- IBM WebSphere Portal V5.0.2.2 (remote)

  This option requires IBM WebSphere Portal V5.0.2.2 (Express, Enable, Extend Editions); sold separately.

WebSphere Portal V5.1 Test Environment installation

The development tools are installed as part of the base Rational Application Developer installation by selecting the Portal Tools feature. There are a couple of possible scenarios for the portal test environment.

- IBM WebSphere Portal V5.1 (remote)

  This option requires IBM WebSphere Portal V5.1 (Express, Enable, Extend Editions); sold separately.

- IBM WebSphere Portal V5.1 Test Environment (local)

  The WebSphere Portal V5.1 Test Environment is included with IBM Rational Application Developer V6.0 distribution; however, it is installed via a separate installer found on the WebSphere Portal V5.1 Setup CD.

> **Tip:** Eliminate installer prompting of CDs.
>
> When installing the IBM WebSphere Portal V5.1 Test Environment from a directory or network drive (ensure drive is mapped), create the directory names as listed in Table A-2 to eliminate the need for the WebSphere Portal installer to prompt for CDs. For example, we created a directory structure on a network drive like the following:
>
> ```
> /wp51/setup
> /wp51/cd1-1
> /wp51/cd1-2
> /wp51/cd1-15
> /wp51/cd2
> /wp51/cd3
> ```

Table A-2 IBM WebSphere Portal V5.1 Test Environment CDs

IBM WebSphere Portal V5.1 Test Environment CDs included with RAD V6.0	Directory
IBM WebSphere Portal V5.1 - Portal Install (Setup)	setup
IBM WebSphere Portal V5.1 - WebSphere Business Integrator Server Foundation (1-1)	cd1-1
IBM WebSphere Portal V5.1 - WebSphere Business Integrator Server Foundation (1-2)	cd1-2
IBM WebSphere Portal V5.1 - WebSphere Business Integrator Server Foundation WebSphere Application Server V5.1 Fixpack 1 (1-15)	cd1-15

IBM WebSphere Portal V5.1 Test Environment CDs included with RAD V6.0	Directory
IBM WebSphere Portal V5.1 - Portal Server (2)	cd2
IBM WebSphere Portal V5.1 - Lotus Workplace Web Content Management™ (3)	cd3

To install the IBM WebSphere Portal V5.1 Test Environment, do the following:

1. Run **install.bat** from the WebSphere Portal Setup CD (or setup directory).
2. When prompted, select the desired language for the install wizard (for example, English) and click **OK**.
3. When the Welcome page appears, review the information and click **Next**.
4. When the Software License Agreement page appears, if in agreement, select **I accept the terms in the license agreement** and click **Next**.
5. When the Choose the setup type that best suits your needs page appears, select **Test Environment (**as seen in Figure A-4) and then click **Next**.

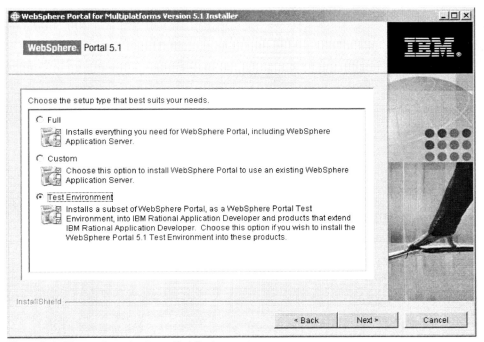

Figure A-4   Choose the setup type - Test Environment

6. When prompted, ensure instances of WebSphere Application Server and WebSphere Portal are not running. Click **Next**.

7. When prompted to enter the WebSphere Application Server installation directory used by the WebSphere Portal Test Environment, we accepted the default directory (C:\Program Files\Portal51UTE\AppServer). Click **Next**.

   Note: This requires approximately 1,650,000 KB of disk space.

8. When prompted to enter the WebSphere Portal installation directory, we accepted the default (C:\Program Files\Portal51UTE\PortalServer). Click **Next**.

   Note: This requires approximately 1,550,000 KB of disk space.

9. When prompted to enter the WebSphere Portal administrative user and password, we entered the following and then clicked **Next**:
   - WebSphere Portal administrative user: `wpsadmin`
   - WebSphere Portal administrative user password: `<password>`
10. When the WebSphere Portal install options Summary dialog appears, review the selections and click **Next**.

    The installation should now begin to copy files. The installation process takes several hours.
11. When the installation is complete click **Finish**.

> **Note:** The WebSphere Portal installation log can be found in the following directory:
> `C:\Program Files\Portal51UTE\PortalServer\log\wpinstalllog.txt`

Rational Application Developer Product Updater - Interim Fix 0004

The *Rational Product Updater* tool is used to apply fixes to IBM Rational Application Developer V6. We strongly recommend that you install the Interim Fix 004 for IBM Rational Application Developer for WebSphere Software V6.0. The Interim Fix 0004 can be installed directly over the Web using the Product Updater tool included with Rational Application Developer, or alternatively the Interim Fix 0004 can be downloaded and installed locally.

More detailed information on Interim Fix 0004 can be found at:

`http://www.ibm.com/support/docview.wss?rs=2043&context=SSRTLW&dc=D400&uid=swg24008988&loc=en_US&cs=UTF-8&lang=enclass=`

The following procedure describes how to install IBM Rational Application Developer V6.0 Interim Fix 0004 using the Product Updater tool:

1. Ensure that Rational Application Developer test servers are stopped and Application Developer is closed.
2. Start the Rational Product Updater by clicking **Start** → **Programs** → **IBM Rational** → **Rational Product Updater**.
3. Click **Find Updates** as seen in Figure A-5.

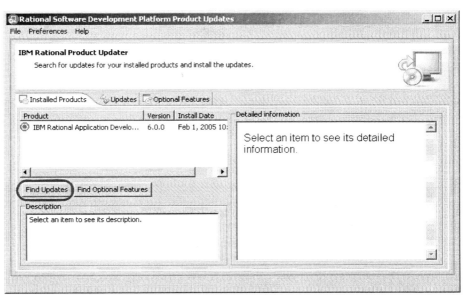

Figure A-5   Rational Product Updater

Note: The Rational Product Updater will detect that a newer version of the Product Updater is available. Download it and restart using the new version.

4. When prompted with a dialog that Interim Fix 0004 has been found, click **OK**.

Tip: If the Rational Product Updater requires an update, you are prompted to install it before you can continue. The Rational Product Updater installs the update, restarts, and retrieves a list of available updates.

5. The IBM Rational Product Updater should be populated with updated fix information. Ensure that **Interim Fix 0004** is checked. Click **Install Updates**.

Tip: Detailed information on the fix is displayed in the right-hand window by selecting the **Interim Fix**.

Appendix A. IBM product installation and configuration tips   **1381**

6. When the License Agreement dialog appears, if in agreement select **I accept the terms in the license agreements**, and then click **OK** to begin the installation.

   Depending on the speed of your computer processor, the amount of RAM, and the speed of your Internet connection, the update might take an extended period of time to download and install.

7. After the installation is complete, click the **Installed Products** tab to verify that the Interim Fixes were installed successfully.

8. Close the Rational Product Updater.

IBM Rational Agent Controller V6 installation

The IBM Rational Agent Controller is a daemon that allows client applications to launch and manage local or remote applications, and provides information about running applications to other applications. You must install Agent Controller separately before you can use the following tools:

- Profiling tools to profile your applications. Agent Controller must be installed on the same system as the application that you are profiling.
- Logging tools to import remote log files. Agent Controller must be installed and running on the remote system from which the log files are imported.
- Component testing tool to run test cases. Agent Controller must be installed on the systems on which you run the test cases.
- Run-time analysis tool for probe insertion, code coverage, and leak analysis.
- Tools for remote application testing on WebSphere Application Server version 5.0 or 5.1. (Agent Controller does not have to be installed for remote publishing of applications, or for local application publishing or testing.) Note that WebSphere Application Server Version 6.0 has this functionality built in, so Agent Controller is not required on Version 6.0 target servers.

The IBM Rational Agent Controller is available on the following platforms:

- Microsoft Windows 2000, XP, 2003
- IBM AIX®
- IBM OS/390
- IBM OS/400
- Linux on Intel
- Linux on S/390®
- SUN Solaris on Sparc
- HP/UX

Within this redbook, there are a couple of scenarios where selected components of the IBM Rational Agent Controller need to be installed.

- Chapter 20, "JUnit and component testing" on page 1081
- Chapter 21, "Debug local and remote applications" on page 1121
  - WebSphere Application Server V6.0

    If the remote system is running WebSphere Application Server V6.0 and you only intend to use remote debug, the IBM Rational Agent Controller is not required since the required functionality is built into WebSphere Application Server V6.0.

  - WebSphere Application Server V5.1 and V5.0

    If the remote system is running WebSphere Application Server V5.1 or V5.0 and you only intend to use remote debug, the IBM Rational Agent Controller is required. You will be prompted to provide the installation path for WebSphere Application Server V5.1 or V5.0 during the IBM Rational Agent Controller installation.

- Chapter 24, "Profile applications" on page 1237

To install the IIBM Rational Agent Controller for Windows, do the following:

1. Insert the IBM Rational Agent Controller CD included with IBM Rational Application Developer V6.0 in the CD-ROM drive of the system where WebSphere Application Server is installed.
2. Navigate to the win_ia32 directory and run setup.exe to start the installer.
3. When the Welcome window appears, click **Next**.
4. When prompted to make sure the Eclipse Platform is not running, click **Next**.
5. Review the terms of the license agreement, and if in agreement select **I accept the terms in the license agreement** and then click **Next**.
6. When prompted to enter the IBM Rational Agent Controller installation directory, we accepted the default C:\Program Files\IBM\AgentController and then clicked **Next**.
7. When prompted to select the components of the IBM Rational Agent Controller to install, we accepted the default (see Figure A-6) and clicked **Next**.

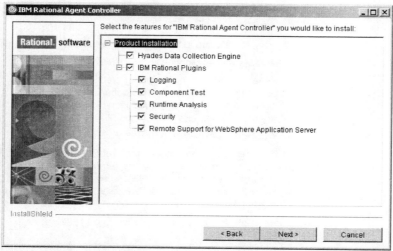

Figure A-6   IBM Rational Agent Controller component selection

8. When prompted to enter the path to the Java Runtime, we entered `c:\ibm\WebSphere\AppServer\bin\java\jre\bin\java.exe` and then clicked **Next**.

   If installing the IBM Rational Agent Controller on the node where Rational Application Developer is installed, enter the following path:

   `<rad_home>\runtimes\base_v6\java\jre\bin\java.exe`

   Where *<rad_home>* is the Rational Application Developer installation path.

9. When prompted to enter the WebSphere Application Server installation path, we left this page blank since we are installing the IBM Rational Agent Controller on a WebSphere Application Server V6.0 node. Click **Next**.

10. When the Host that can access the Hyades Data Collection Engine window appears, we accepted the default (any system) and clicked **Next**.

11. When the Specify security setting window appears, we accepted the default (Disable) and clicked **Next**.

12. When the Installation summary page appears, review the installation options and then click **Next** to begin copying files.

13. When the installation is complete, click **Finish**.

IBM Rational ClearCase LT installation

Rational Application Developer entitles you to a free license of Rational ClearCase LT. If you do not have the ClearCase LT product media, then you must first download and install the latest supported version of ClearCase LT. If you already have the ClearCase LT v2002.05 or ClearCase LT v2003.06 product media, you will also need the latest patches to support the integration with IBM Rational Application Developer V6.0.

> **Important:** Information on obtaining a copy of IBM Rational ClearCase LT can be found in TechNote-Installing_CCLT.html of the IBM Rational Application Developer V6.0 CD1.

Installing the ClearCase LT Server component also installs the ClearCase LT Client component. We recommend that you install the ClearCase LT Server component before installing ClearCase LT Client on any additional machines.

> **Tips:** When installing the ClearCase LT Server, you can be logged on either locally on your Windows machine or logged on to a Windows domain. If installing while logged on locally, you will only be able to connect to the server from your local machine. Other people in your development team will not be able to connect to your machine and use your ClearCase LT Server. The user account used when installing must be a member of the local Administrators group.
>
> To use ClearCase LT in a team environment and let other team members use your ClearCase LT Server, you must be logged on to a Windows domain with a user account having Domain Administrator privileges while installing ClearCase LT Server. The domain must also have a group for the ClearCase users and all members of your development team must be members of this group. This group should also be the Primary Group for these users. You can use the Domain Users group for this.
>
> It is highly recommended to use the Windows domain approach. Local setup can be useful for testing and demonstration purposes.

The installation instructions in this section are intended to help you install the client and server code for Rational ClearCase LT. For more detailed installation instructions refer to the *Rational ClearCase LT Installation Guide* product guide.

1. Run setup.exe from the root directory of the downloaded ClearCase LT installation image.
2. When the Rational Setup Wizard appears click **Next** to continue.

3. On the Product Selection page, select **Rational ClearCase LT** and click **Next**.
4. On the Deployment Method page, select **Desktop installation from CD image** and click **Next**.
5. On the Client/Server page, select both server and client software and click **Next**.
6. In the new welcome window that is displayed, click **Next**.
7. A warning message about potential issues with Windows change journals may be displayed next. If you have implemented change journals on the target system, check the advice on the referenced Technote and determine whether the fix is required. Click **Next** to continue.
8. Accept the licensing agreement on the next page and click **Next**.
9. On the Destination Folder page, verify the install path (we use the default of C:\Program Files\Rational). Click **Next**.
10. On the Custom Setup page, you may unselect the Web Interface, as it is not used in this exercise. Click **Next** to continue.
11. A Configure pop-up window is displayed for adjusting the Start menu and desktop shortcut settings. Click **Done**.
12. Click **Install** on the Ready to Install the program window to start the installation.
13. On the Setup Complete page, click **Finish**.
14. The ClearCase LT Getting Started Wizard is now started. The wizard guides you through the process of creating a ClearCase storage directory, a ClearCase VOB, and setting up a ClearCase project. On the first page of the wizard click **Next**.
15. On the Storage Directory page, you can select a directory to store your ClearCase VOB files. Keep the default and click **Next**.
16. On the Source VOB page, keep the default name for Source VOB and the Initial Component.
17. On the Initial Project page, keep the default project name InitialProject and select the **Parallel Stream Project option**. Click **Next**.
18. On the Summary page, click **Next**, and when the setup is done click **Close** on the final dialog.

> **Note:** After you have installed the Rational ClearCase LT product, we recommend that you review the Rational ClearCase Support page on the IBM Software Support site and make sure that the latest fixes have been applied. The Web site can be found at:
> http://www.ibm.com/software/awdtools/clearcase/support

IBM DB2 Universal Database V8.2 installation

There are several editions of IBM DB2 Universal Database; however, the core functionality is the same amongst the editions. The IBM Rational Application Developer V6.0 product packaging includes IBM DB2 Universal Database V8.2 Express Edition.

Several of the chapters found in this redbook require IBM DB2 Universal Database V8.2 to be installed. The purpose of this section is to highlight the key installation considerations for DB2 UDB specific to the redbook.

To start the DB2 UDB installation run setup.exe. We have highlighted the installation options we selected:

- Installation type: **Typical** (450 MB)
- Installation path: C:\Program Files\IBM\SQLLIB
- DB2 Administration Server user name: db2admin
- We accepted the defaults for the remaining installation settings.

> **Note:** For detailed installation instructions, refer to the IBM DB2 Universal Database V8.2 product documentation.

IBM WebSphere Application Server V6 installation

Several of the chapters found in this redbook require IBM WebSphere Application Server V6.0 to be installed. The purpose of this section is to highlight the key installation considerations for WebSphere Application Server specific to this redbook.

The IBM WebSphere Application Server V6.0 installation is started by running launchpad.bat. The IBM WebSphere Application Server V6.0 components have separate installations from the main Launchpad Base page, as seen in Figure A-7 on page 1388.

We accepted the default WebSphere Application Server installation directory, C:\Program Files\IBM\WebSphere\AppServer.

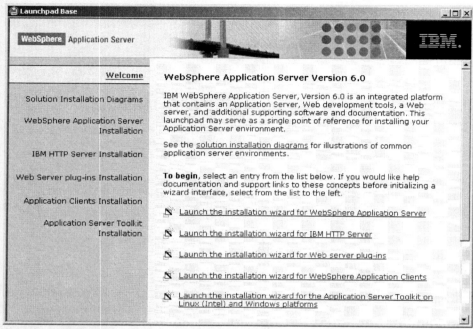

Figure A-7   IBM WebSphere Application Server V6.0 installation components

Table A-3 describes the IBM WebSphere Application Server V6.0 installation components and usage within this redbook.

Table A-3   IBM WebSphere Application Server V6.0 installation components

Installation component	Description	Use in redbook
WebSphere Application Server installation	Base WebSphere Application Server installation files.	Required * Target for deploying ITSO application sample
IBM HTTP Server installation	IBM HTTP Server installation files, which can be used with the WebSphere plug-in.	Optional

Installation component	Description	Use in redbook
WebSphere plug-ins	There are several supported WebSphere plug-ins depending on the Web server. If you install the IBM HTTP Server, you will need the IBM HTTP Server (apache) plug-in.	Optional
Application Clients installation	This included the IBM JRE V1.4.2, as well as libraries for J2EE clients.	Optional **Note**: Needed for J2EE Clients.
Application Server Toolkit installation	* Tool for assembly, deployment (EJB, Web Services) and debug J2EE applications. * No development support * WebSphere Rapid Deployment * Support for Enhanced EAR * Server Tools – support for remote server	Optional

For more detailed information on installing IBM WebSphere Application Server V6.0, refer to the following:

- IBM WebSphere Application Server V6.0 InfoCenter found at:

    http://www.ibm.com/software/webservers/appserv/infocenter.html

- *WebSphere V6 Planning and Design*, SG24-6446
- *WebSphere Application Server V6 Systems Management and Configuration*, SG24-6451

WebSphere Application Server messaging configuration

Note: This section is not required for the ITSO Bank sample application, as the ITSO Bank Enterprise Application does not use messaging, but is included for informational reasons.

The high-level configuration steps are as follows to configure messaging within WebSphere Application Server for the ITSO Bank application sample:

- Configure the service bus.
- Configure the bus members.
- Configure the destinations.
- Verify the messaging engine startup.

- Configure JMS connection queue factory.
- Configure the destination JMS queue.
- Configuration of a JMS activation specification.

Configure the service bus

To configure the service bus, do the following:

1. From the WebSphere Administrative Console, select **Service integration** → **Buses**.
2. Click **New**.
3. Enter the following and then click **OK**:
   - Name: InterbankingBus
   - Uncheck **Secure**.
4. Click **Save** and then when prompted click **Save** to Save to Master Configuration.

Configure the bus members

To configure the Bus members, do the following:

1. Select **Service integration** → **Buses**.
2. Click the **InterbankingBus** created in the previous section.
3. Under Additional Properties, click **Bus members**.
4. Click **Add**.
5. The default Bus member name is the <hostnameNode:server>. For example, our Bus name is was6jmg1Node01:server1. Accept the defaults for the remaining fields and click **Next**.
6. Click **Finish**.
7. Click **Save** and then when prompted click **Save** to Save to Master Configuration.

Configure the destinations

To configure the destinations for messaging, do the following:

1. Select **Service integration** → **Buses**.
2. Click **InterbankingBus**.
3. Under Additional Properties, click **Destinations**.
4. Click **New**.

5. When the Create new destination page appears, select **Queue** and then click **Next**.
6. Enter the Identifier. In our example we entered `interbankingQueue`. Click **Next**.
7. Select the Bus member created in "Configure the bus members" on page 1390 (for example, was6jmg1Node01:server1) and then click **Next**.
8. Click **Finish**.
9. Click **Save** and then when prompted click **Save** to Save to Master Configuration.
10. Log out of the WebSphere Administrative Console.
11. In order for the changes to take effect, you must restart the application server, in this case server1.
    a. Stop the server1 application server by clicking **Start** → **Programs** → **IBM WebSphere** → **Application Server V6** → **Profiles** → **default** → **Stop server**. Alternatively, use the `stopServer.bat server1` command.
    b. Start the server1 application server.

Verify the messaging engine startup

To verify the messaging engine startup, do the following:

1. Ensure the server1 application server has been restarted.
2. Start the WebSphere Administrative Console.
3. Select **Service integration** → **Buses**.
4. Click **InterbankingBus**.
5. Under Additional Properties, click **Bus members**.
6. Click **Node=was6jmg1Node01, Server=server1**.

   You should see the green arrow under Status to note the Messaging Engine has been started.

Configure JMS connection queue factory

To configure the JMS connection queue factory, do the following:

1. Select **Resources** → **JMS Provider** → **Default messaging**.
2. Click **JMS queue connection factory**.
3. Click **New**.

4. Enter the following and then click **OK**:

   Connection:
   - Name: `interbankingCF`
   - JNDI name: `jms/interbankingCF`

   Connection:
   - Bus name: Select **InterbankingBus**.

5. Click **Save** and then when prompted click **Save** to Save to Master Configuration.

Configure the destination JMS queue

To configure the destination JMS queue, do the following:

1. Select **Resources** → **JMS Provider** → **Default messaging**.
2. Click **JMS queue** under Destinations.
3. Click **New**.
4. Enter the following and then click **OK**:
   - Name: `InterbankingQueue`
   - JNDI name: `jms/interbankingQueue`
   - Bus name: Select **InterbankingBus**.
   - Queue name: Select **interbankingQueue**.
5. Click **Save** and then when prompted click **Save** to Save to Master Configuration.

Configuration of a JMS activation specification

The configuration for the JMS activation specification for the destination of the busification configuration is accomplished by the following simple steps:

1. Select **Resources** → **JMS Provider** → **Default messaging**.
2. Click **JMS activation specification** under Activation Specifications.
3. Click **New**.
4. Enter the following and then click **OK**:
   - Name: `interbankingAS`
   - JNDI name: `jms/interbankingAS`
   - Destination type: Select **Queue**.
   - Destination JNDI name: `jms/interbankingQueue`
   - Bus name: Select **InterbankingBus**.

5. Click **Save** and then when prompted click **Save** to Save to Master Configuration.

Additional material

The additional material is a Web download of the sample code for this redbook. This appendix describes how to download, unpack, describe the contents, and import the Project Interchange file. In some cases the chapters also require database setup; however, if needed, the instructions will be provided in the chapter in which they are needed.

This appendix is organized into the following sections:
- Locating the Web material.
- Unpack the 6449code.zip.
- Description of sample code.
- Import sample code from a Project Interchange file.

Locating the Web material

The Web material associated with this redbook is available in softcopy on the Internet from the IBM Redbooks Web server. Enter the following URL in a Web browser, and then download the 6449code.zip:

    ftp://www.redbooks.ibm.com/redbooks/SG246449

Alternatively, you can go to the IBM Redbooks Web site at:

    http://www.ibm.com/redbooks

Select the **Additional materials** and open the directory that corresponds with the redbook form number, SG246449.

The additional Web material that accompanies this redbook includes the following files:

File name   *Description*
6449code.zip   Zip file containing sample code

System requirements for downloading the Web material

The following system configuration is recommended:

Hard disk space: 20 MB minimum
Operating System: Windows or Linux
Processor: 1 GHz
Memory: 1 GB

Unpack the 6449code.zip

After you have downloaded the 6449code.zip, unpack the zip file to your local file system using WinZip, PKZip, or similar software. For example, we have unpacked the 6449code.zip to the c:\6449code directory. Throughout the samples we will reference the sample code as if you have already unpacked the zip (for example, c:\6449code).

Description of sample code

Table B-1 on page 1397 describes the contents of the 6449code.zip file after being unpacked.

Table B-1 Sample code description

Unpack directory	Description
c:\6449code	Root directory after unpack of 6449code.zip
c:\6449code\java	Chapter 7, "Develop Java applications" on page 221 ▶ Java sample code packaged in BankJava.zip Project Interchange file.
c:\6449code\database	Chapter 8, "Develop Java database applications" on page 333 ▶ Java sample code to interact with databases packaged in BankDb.zip Project Interchange file. ▶ Database scripts used to create database tables (Table.ddl) and load sample data (loadData.sql) for both Cloudscape and DB2 UDB. These scripts are shared by many redbook chapters.
c:\6449code\gui	Chapter 9, "Develop GUI applications" on page 415 ▶ Java GUI sample code packaged in BankGUI.zip Project Interchange file.
c:\6449code\xml	Chapter 10, "Develop XML applications" on page 443 ▶ XML sample code packaged in BankXMLWeb.zip Project Interchange file.
c:\6449code\web	Chapter 11, "Develop Web applications using JSPs and servlets" on page 499 ▶ Web application sample code packaged in BankWeb.zip Project Interchange file. ▶ Source code, found in the source subdirectory.
c:\6449code\struts	Chapter 12, "Develop Web applications using Struts" on page 615 ▶ Web application using Struts sample code packaged in BankStrutsWeb.zip Project Interchange file.
c:\6449code\jsf	Chapter 13, "Develop Web applications using JSF and SDO" on page 673 ▶ Web application using JSF and SDO sample code packaged in BankJSF.zip Project Interchange file.
c:\6449code\egl	Chapter 14, "Develop Web applications using EGL" on page 751 ▶ Web application using EGL sample code packaged in BankEGL.zip Project Interchange file.
c:\6449code\ejb	Chapter 15, "Develop Web applications using EJBs" on page 827 ▶ EJB application sample code packaged in BankEJB.zip Project Interchange file.

Unpack directory	Description
c:\6449code\j2eeclt	Chapter 16, "Develop J2EE application clients" on page 925 ▶ The J2EE application client sample code packaged in BankAppClient.zip Project Interchange file. The BankAppClient_with_BankEJB.zip contains the EJB projects BankAppClient is dependent (import all complete projects needed).
c:\6449code\webservices	Chapter 17, "Develop Web Services applications" on page 951 ▶ Web Services application sample code packaged in BankWebServices.zip Project Interchange file.
c:\6449code\portal	Chapter 18, "Develop portal applications" on page 985 ▶ Portal application sample code packaged in Portal.zip Project Interchange file.

Import sample code from a Project Interchange file

This section describes how to import the redbook sample code Project Interchange zip files into Rational Application Developer. This section applies for each of the chapters containing sample code that have been packaged as a Project Interchange zip file.

To import a Project Interchange file, do the following:

1. Start Rational Application Developer.
2. From the Workbench, select **File** → **Import**.
3. From the Import dialog, select **Project Interchange** (as seen in Figure B-1 on page 1399), and then click **Next**.

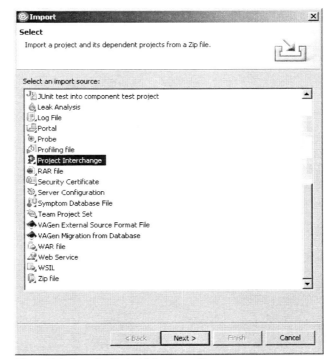

Figure B-1   Import a Project Interchange file

4. When prompted for the Project Interchange path and file name, and target workspace location, we entered the following:

    – From zip file: `c:\6449code\java\BankJava.zip`

    Enter the path and zip file name (for example, c:\6449code\java\BankJava.zip).

    – Project location root: `c:\workspace`

    Enter the location of the desired workspace (for example, our workspace is found in c:\workspace).

5. After entering the zip file, check the project and then click **Finish**.

    For example, we checked **BankJava** and clicked **Finish**, as seen in Figure B-2 on page 1400.

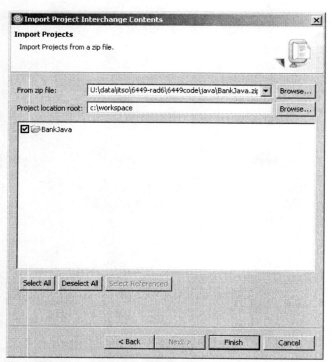

Figure B-2   Import Interchange Projects location

Related publications

The publications listed in this section are considered particularly suitable for a more detailed discussion of the topics covered in this redbook.

IBM Redbooks

For information on ordering these publications, see "How to get IBM Redbooks" on page 1404. Note that some of the documents referenced here may be available in softcopy only.

- *EJB 2.0 Development with WebSphere Studio Application Developer*, SG24-6819
- *WebSphere Studio V5.1.2 JavaServer Faces and Service Data Objects*, SG24-6361
- *IBM WebSphere Portal V5.1 Portlet Application Development*, SG24-6681
- *IBM WebSphere Portal V5 A Guide for Portlet Application Development*, SG24-6076
- *WebSphere Application Server V6: Web Services Development and Deployment*, SG24-6461
- *WebSphere V6 Planning and Design*, SG24-6446
- *WebSphere Application Server V6 Scalability and Performance*, SG24-6392
- *WebSphere Application Server V6 Security*, SG24-6316
- *WebSphere Application Server V6 Systems Management and Configuration*, SG24-6451
- *Eclipse Development using the Graphical Editing Framework and the Eclipse Modeling Framework*, SG24-6302
- *Transitioning: Informix 4GL to Enterprise Generation Language (EGL)*, SG24-6673
- *WebSphere Studio Application Developer Version 5 Programming Guide*, SG24-6957

Other publications

These publications are also relevant as further information sources:

- Crupi, Malks and Alur, *Core J2EE Patterns: Best Practices and Design Strategies*, Prentice Hall, 2003, ISBN 0131422464
- Marinescu, *EJB Design Patterns: Advanced Patterns, Processes and Idioms*, Wiley, 2002, ISBN 0471208310
- Shavor, D'Anjou, Fairbrother, Kehn, Kellerman and McCarthy, *The Java Developer's Guide to Eclipse*, Addison-Wesley, 2003, ISBN 0321159640
- Eric Gamma, et al., *Design Patterns, Elements of Reusable Object-Oriented Software*, Addison-Wesley Professional, 1995, ISBN 0-201-63361-2
- *IBM Informix 4GL to EGL Conversion Utility User's Guide*, G251-2485

Online resources

These Web sites and URLs are also relevant as further information sources:

- Sun Microsystem's Java site, with specifications, tutorials, and best practices
  http://java.sun.com/
- The Eclipse Project site, with information on the underlying platform of Rational Application Developer
  http://www.eclipse.org/
- Eclipse Hyades project
  http://www.eclipse.org/hyades
- The WorldWide Web Consortium
  http://www.w3c.org/
- Apache Jakarta Project, for information on Tomcat
  http://jakarta.apache.org/
- Apache Struts site
  http://struts.apache.org/
- The Java Community Process site, for Java specifications
  http://www.jcp.org/
- OASIS, for UDDI
  http://www.oasis-open.org/

- Web Services Interoperability Organization

  http://www.ws-i.org/

- The ServerSide.com is an enterprise Java site with articles, books, news, and discussions

  http://www.theserverside.com/

- *Writing Robust Java Code* white paper by Scott Ambler

  http://www.ambysoft.com/javaCodingStandards.pdf

- Apache Ant Project home page

  http://ant.apache.org/

- Apache Ant documentation

  http://ant.apache.org/manual/index.html

- CVS home

  http://www.cvshome.org

- CVSNT

  http://www.cvsnt.org

- CVSNT installation tips

  http://www.cvsnt.org/wiki/InstallationTips

- IBM developerWorks EGL home page

  http://www.ibm.com/developerworks/rational/products/egl/

- *Generating Java using EGL and JSF with WebSphere Studio Site Developer V5.1.2*, white paper

  http://www.ibm.com/developerworks/websphere/library/techarticles/0408_barosa/0408_barosa.html

- VisiBone HEX HTML Color Codes

  http://html-color-codes.com/

- The complete J2SE specification

  http://java.sun.com/j2se/

- Information on JDBC

  http://java.sun.com/j2se/1.4.2/docs/guide/jdbc/

- Information on the AWT

  http://java.sun.com/j2se/1.4.2/docs/guide/awt/

- Information on Swing

  http://java.sun.com/j2se/1.4.2/docs/guide/swing/

- Information on the SWT

  http://www.eclipse.org/swt/

- XML - the World Wide Web Consortium (W3C)

  http://www.w3c.org/XML/

How to get IBM Redbooks

You can search for, view, or download Redbooks, Redpapers, Hints and Tips, draft publications and Additional materials, as well as order hardcopy Redbooks or CD-ROMs, at this Web site:

http://www.ibm.com/redbooks

Help from IBM

IBM Support and downloads

http://www.ibm.com/support

IBM Global Services

http://www.ibm.com/services

Index

Symbols
.eglbld   766

Numerics
6449code.zip   1396

A
abstract facade
   implement   560
Abstract Window Toolkit   36, 416
access control
   list   833
access CVS repository   1310
accessor methods   257
accessors   254, 557
AccountDetails   514
ACID   829
ACL   833
Active Script   1124
activity   1259
add a project to a server   1064
adding emulator support   994
additional material   1395
additional supported test servers   23
aliases   357
analyze test results   1113
animated GIF   511
AnimatedGif Designer   511
annotated programming   15
Annotation-based programming   1210
Ant   1155–1156
   build
      path   1157
      project   1156
      property   1157
      target   1156
      task   1156
   build J2EE application   1178
      create build script   1180
      deployment packaging   1179
      prepare for sample   1179
      run Ant build   1183
   build simple Java application   1167
      build targets   1171
      classpath problem   1178
      clean   1173
      compile   1172
      create build file   1169
      forced build   1177
      global properties   1171
      init   1172
      project definition   1171
      rerun Ant   1177
      run Ant   1173
   documentation   1157
   headless build   1186
   introduction   1156
      build files   1156
      new features   1157
      tasks   1157
   J2EE
      applications   1178
      build script   1180
   new features
      Code Assist   1158
      Code snippets   1159
      define format of an Ant script   1164
      format an Ant script   1163
      Problem view   1166
   run   1173
   Run Ant wizard
      Build   1175
      Classpath   1176
      Common   1176
      Environment   1176
      JRE   1176
      Main   1175
      Properties   1176
      Refresh   1175
      Target   1175
   run headless build   1187
   run outside Application Developer   1185
   runAnt.bat   1186
   script   1171
   tasks   1157
      delete   1157

echo   1157
    jar   1157
    javac   1157
    mkdir   1157
    tstamp   1157
    Web site   1157
Ant build files   1156
Apache Jakarta
    Ant   1156
appearance
    preferences   100
appearance of Java elements   100
applet   501
application classloader   1195
application client module   500, 1191
application code analysis   15
application deployment   1190
application deployment descriptor
    access   630
application flow   842
application modeling with UML   15
application profiling   1237
Application Server
    Network Deployment   830
Application server profile   1048
application.xml   501
ApplicationResource.properties   652
ArrayList   269
assertEquals   1096
assertions   1087
assertTrue   1096
association   267
association relationship   267, 874
atomicity   829
attributes   254
automated component test
    run test   1110
automated component testing   1102
automatic build   85
Automatic fail-over support   830
AWT
    See Abstract Window Toolkit

B
backend folder   895
banking model   514
baseline   1259
    make   1282

Basic   753
bean   501
bean-managed persistence   836
BMP   836
bootstrap   1192
bottom up   893
BPEL
    See Business Process Execution Language
breakpoint   1124, 1132
    condition   1134
    conditional   1134
    JSP   1135
    properties   1133
    set   1132
Breakpoints view   148
    breakpoints   1142
breakpoints view   1142
Browse diagram   197
build   85, 1155
    Ant
        build file   1156
    compiler   1171
    targets   1171
build applications   1155
build verification test   1082
build.xml   1167
    J2EE application   1180
    Java application   1170
bus members   1390
Business Process Execution Language   6
BVT
    See build verification test

C
C   32, 753
C++   32
calibration   1084
Call Hierarchy view   223
capabilities   86
Cascading Style Sheets   42
change
    variable value   1143
check in and check out   1259
check out   1289
cHTML   994
Class Diagram   194, 205, 233, 243, 370
classes directory   502
classloaders   1195

classpath
   WebSphere classloaders
      RCP directory 1194
      RE directory 1194
      RP directory 1194
classpath
   add JAR 297
   Ant
      classpath 1178
ClearCase 1258
   add project 1274
   check out 1289
   connect 1269, 1284
   deliver 1279
   help 1261
   import 1287
   preferences 1261
   project 1265
   rebase 1290
   scenario 1263, 1277
   setup 1264
ClearCase LT 1259
Cloudscape CView 344
Cloudscape JDBC driver 391
CMP 836
CMP attributes 863
CMR 838
   See container-managed relationships
COBOL 753
code
   assist 121
   formatter preferences 101
Code Assist 118, 320
code coverage analysis 1240
code formatter 105
   blank lines 110
   braces 108
   comments 114
   control statements 112
   indentations 108
   line wrapping 113
   new lines 111
   white space 109
Code Review 124, 226
   add filter 126
   add rule 126
   Complete 125
   excluding matches 130
   exclusion of reources 129
   Globalization 125

J2EE Best Practices 125
J2SE Best Practices 125
Quick 124
set options 125
Code Review Details view 229
Code Review view 226
code style 102
code style and formatting 101
coexistence 26
collection type 269
COM.ibm.db2.jdbc.app.DB2Driver 392
COM.ibm.db2.jdbc.net.DB2Driver 392
command
   design pattern 515
Common Object Request Broker Architecture 34
compact Hyper Text Markup Language 994
compare a file 92
compare with 93
compatibility 27
compilation target 1172
compiler options 115
   preferences 115
component 1259
   interface 838
component interfaces 881
component test 1082
   automated 1102
component test benefits 1085
Component Test project 177
component testing 17, 1081
component-under-test 1102
composer 844
composition relationship 876
concurrency 832
Concurrent Version System 1299
condition
   breakpoint 1134
configuration
   WebSphere Application Server
      messaging 1389
conflict 1300
connect to ClearCase 1269
connection
   JDBC
      connection 334
      pooling 335
Connector project 176
consistency 829, 1086
Console view 146

constructors 262, 326, 882
container
    EJB 832
container-managed
    persistence 836
    relationships 838
container-managed persistence 892
Container-managed relationships 60
content area 533
context root 519
controller
    MVC 504, 514
converter 844
cookies 41
CORBA
    See Common Object Request Broker Architecture
Core Java APIs 33
create
    Class Diagram 551
    database 344
    database connection 347
    database schema 357
    database tables from scripts 349
    DTD file 450
    fields 554
    Java stored procedures 398
    model classes 547, 550
    packages 551
    page template 526
    simple Ant build file 1169
    SQL statements 376
    static Web resources 544
    table 357–358
    test case
        create 1093
    visual class 420
    Web Project 517
    XML schema 463
    XSL file 483
Crystal Reports integration 16
CSS
    See Cascading Style Sheets
CSS Designer 511
CSS File wizard 513
custom finders 890
Custom profile 1048
customer acceptance test 1083
CVS 1299

client configuration
    access CVS repository 1310
    enable CVS Team capability 1309
configuration 1312
development scenario 1321
features 1300
introduction 1300
new features for team development 1301
preferences 1312
Repositories view 1324
repository
    add 1323
Resource History view 1343
scenario 1321
Web site 1301
CVS Annotate view 144
CVS client configuration 1309
CVS for NT 1301
CVS preferences
    Rational Application Developer 1312
        CVS specific settings 1317
        file content 1313
        ignored resources 1315
        label decorations 1312
CVS Repositories view 143
CVS Repository Exploring perspective 143
CVS Resource History view 144
CVSNT
    create CVS users 1307
    create Windows users and groups 1306
    server implementation 1301
    server installation 1302
    server repository configuration 1303
    verfiy installation 1307

D
DADX 957
Data Definition view 145, 340
Data perspective 145, 339
data source 335, 393
    configure 628, 630
        deployment descriptor 630
    objects 335
database
    create
        Cloudscape CView 343
    create connection 347
    create database

1408 Rational Application Developer V6 Programming Guide

DB2 command window 346
create database tables
    Application Developer 350
    Cloudscape CView 351
    DB2 command window 351
defintion 355
objects 354
populate data in tables
    Application Developer 352
    Cloudscape CView 353
    DB2 command window 354
schemas 357
table 358
Database Explorer view 146, 341
databaseName property 631
DB Output view 146, 342
DB2 UDB JDBC drivers 392
DB2 Universal Database 1387
    class path environment variable 783
db2java.zip 392
DB2UNIVERSAL_JDBC_DRIVER_PATH 783
DDL file
    copy objects to workspace 362
    deploy to database 362
    generate 358, 361
    generate for database objects 365
debug 1122
    Web application on local server 1132
        breakpoints view 1142
        debug functions 1141
        debug JSP 1145
        debug view with stack frames 1141
        evaluate an expression 1144
        inspect variable 1143
        run application in debug 1136
        set breakpoint in JSP 1135
        set breakpoint in servlet 1132
        start application for debug 1136
        watch variables 1142
    Web application on remote server 1145
        attach to remote server 1148
        configure debug in WAS 1147
        debug application 1151
        deploy WAR 1146
        export project to WAR file 1145
        install Agent Controller 1147
    XSLT 493
debug features
    breakpoints 1124

drop to frame 1126
step filter 1126
view management 1127
XSLT debugger 1128
Debug perspective 146
debug tooling
    supported environments
        WebSphere Application Server 1124
        WebSphere Portal 1124
    supported languages 1124
        compiled languages 1124
        EGL 1124
        Java 1124
        JavaScript 1124
        mixed language 1124
        SQL stored procedures 1124
        SQLJ 1124
        XSLT 1124
Debug view 147, 1141
debugging
    icons 1141
    remote 1145
declaration 259
Declaration view 225
declarative programming language 752
default CMP data source 858
default workspace 82
deliver 1279
    stream 1259
delta versioning 1300
demarcation 833
deployment 1189
    common considerations 1190
    deploy the enterprise application
        configure data source in WAS 1225
        deploy the EAR 1229
    descriptors 1196
    J2EE application components
        applets 1191
        application clients 1191
        EJBs 1191
        Web applications 1191
    J2EE deployment modules
        application client module 1191
        EJB module 1191
        resource adapter module 1191
        Web application module 1191
    J2EE packaging
        EAR 1191

Index **1409**

WAR 1191
    Java and WebSphere class loader 1191
    package an application 1218
        customize deployment descriptors 1220
        export the EAR 1222
        generate deploy code 1222
        generate EJB to RDB mapping 1218
        recommendations 1218
    prepare for sample
        deployment scenario 1213
        import sample code 1214
        install prerequisite software 1213
    verify the enterprise application 1230
    WebSphere deployment architecture 1199
    WebSphere enhanced EAR 1201
    WebSphere Rapid Deployment 1210
deployment descriptor 1197
    application.xml 501
    enterprise application 501
    Web application 502
    Web module 502–503
    web.xml 502
Deployment Manager profile 1048
derived beans 870
desktop applications 32
destination JMS queue 1392
destinations 1390
development stream 1259, 1270, 1285
Diagram Navigator view 230
Display view 1143
distribution 829
document access definition extension 957
Document Type Definition 445
doGet 579
doPost 579
DriverManager 335, 390
drop to frame 1126
DTD 445
DTD editor 448
    features 452
DTD file
    create 449
    validate 456
DTO 842
durability 829
Dynamic Web Project 679
Dynamic Web project 175
dynamic Web resources 549

E

EAR 1179, 1191
EAR file 500
Eclipse and IBM Rational Software Development Platform 14
Eclipse Hyades 22, 1081, 1086
    Web application testing 1112
        analyzing test results 1113
        editing a test 1112
        generate an executable test 1113
        recording a test 1112
        run a test 1113
Eclipse Java Development Tools 21
Eclipse Modeling Framework (EMF) 22
Eclipse Platform 20
Eclipse Plug-in Development Environment 21
Eclipse Project 19
    Eclipse Platform 20
    Java Development Tools 21
    Plug-in Development Environment 21
Eclipse Software Developer Kit (SDK) 21
editing a test 1112
Editing JSP 595
editors 137
EGL 751
    debug 765
    introduction 752
    migration
        EGL migration to V6.0 764
        Informix 4GL to EGL Conversion Utility 764
        VisualAge Generator to EGL migration 764
    overview
        application architecture 756
        feature enhancements 759
        history 754
        Rational brand software 758
        target audience 754
        value proposition 755
    perspective and views 762
        EGL Debug Validation Errors 762
        EGL Generation Results 762
        EGL Parts Reference 762
        EGL SQL Errors 762
        EGL Validation Results 762
    preferences 761
    programming paradigms 752
    projects
        EGL Project 763
        EGL Web Project 763

tooling in Rational Application Developer 761
Web application components
   data 766
   Deployment Descriptor 765
   EGL Web Project 765
   EGLEAR 765
   EGLSource folder 766
   filename.eglbld 766
   JavaSource folder 766
   libraries 766
   pagehandlers 766
   WebContent folder 766
where to find more information 761
wizards
   Data Table 764
   EGL Build File 763
   EGL Data Parts 764
   EGL Data Parts and Pages 764
   EGL Package 763
   EGL Source File 763
   EGL Source Folder (EGLSource) 763
   Faces JSP File 763
   Form Group 764
   Library 763
   Program 763
EGL Data Parts and Pages wizard 784
EGL Project 763
EGL Web application 751
   add EGL components to Faces JSPs 806
   create a connection between Faces JSPs 804
   create a Faces JSP 803
   create a Web Diagram 802
   create a Web page 802
   create an EGL Web Project 773
   create Faces JSP 802
   create page template 794, 799
   create records and libraries 785
   develop the application 783
   EGL Data Parts wizard 789
   exporting an EGL project
      add runtime libraries 822
      export WAR - EAR with source 823
      reduce file size 821
   generate Java code from EGL 794
   import and run EGL sample Web application 816
   prepare
      configure data source 780
      configure EGL preferences for SQL data-base connection 779
      enable EGL development capability 771
      install EGL component 768
EGL Web Project 763
EGL wizards 763
EJB 827
   application 842
   bean class 837
   client 837
   component 834
   component interface 838
   container 832
   home interface 838
   inheritance 839
   JARs 1179
   new features 828
   overview 828
   project 844
      create 846
   QL 840
      custom finder 890
   Query Language 839
   See Enterprise Java Bean
   server 831
   specification 832
   types 836
   universal test client 915
EJB application
   develop the application
      add business logic 880
      association relationship 874
      composition relationship 876
      create custom finders 890
      create entity beans 859
      create entity relationships 872
      customize entity beans 880
      implement session facade 901
      object-relational mapping 892
   prepare for development 844
      configure data source 856
      configure EJB project 849
      create EJB project 844–845
      import Web application project 853
      setup sample database 854
   testing with UTC 915
EJB JAR 171
EJB local and remote interfaces 61
EJB module 500, 1191
EJB project 176

EJB query language 60, 839
EJB Timer Service 61
enabling transcoding for development 994
encapsulation 842
Enhanced EAR Editor 1201
Enhanced EAR tooling 1070
enterprise application 500
Enterprise Application Archive 1191
Enterprise Application project 175
Enterprise archive
    See EAR
Enterprise Generation Language 751
Enterprise Java Server 831
Enterprise JavaBean
    types
        entity 59
        message-driven 59
        session 58
Enterprise JavaBeans 57, 827
    architecture 831
    components
        client views 834
        EJB types 836
    EJB container 832
        concurrency 833
        life cycle 834
        messaging 834
        naming 833
        persistence 833
        security 833
        transaction 833
    EJB types
        entity beans 836
        message-driven beans 837
        session bean 836
    overview
        distributed 829
        persistent 829
        portable 830
        scalable 830
        secure 828
        transactional 829
entity beans 836
    create 859
    customize 880
Entity EJBs 59
entity relationships 872
E-R Modeling 195
evaluate an expression 1143

exception classes 572
execution time analysis 1240
    views 1240
export
    Java code to JAR file 299
export EAR
    export the EAR file 1223
    filtering the ontent of the EAR 1222
Expression Language 48
Expressions view 1143
extends 267
Extensible Markup Language 38, 444
Extensible Style Language 446
extensions classloader 1194–1195

F
facade 516
Faces Action 708
Faces JSP File wizard 513
fail 1096
features 12
    summary 13–14
        specification versions 14
fields 554
file
    associations 90
File Creation wizard 512
filter errors 289
filters 48
find errors in Problems view 288
folders 171
foreign key 358
form bean 619
forms 548
Fortran 753
Free Layout 544
Free Table Layout 533
function verification test 1083
FVT
    See functional verification test

G
generate EJB to RDB mapping 895
generate getter and setter 324
generating an executable test 1113
Generic Log Adapter perspective 148
getter 254, 257
graphical user interfaces 35

Abstract Window Toolkit 36
   Java components 37
   Standard Widget Toolkit 36
   Swing 36
GROUP BY 382
GUI Java application
   add event handling 434
   prepare
      Add Cloudscape JDBC driver 417
      create Java Project 417
      import model classes 419
      setup database 418
   testing 433
   verify sample application 435
   Visual Editor 423

H

HEAD branch 1327
headless
   Ant
      build 1185
headless build 1186
history 92
hit count 1134
home interface 838, 880–881
host variable 382
HTML 42, 501, 994
HTML error tag 657
HTML File wizard 512
HTTP 40
   See Hypertext Transfer Protocol
   status codes 40
HyperText Markup Language 42, 994
Hypertext Transfer Protocol 40, 43

I

IBM DB2 Universal Database V8.2
   installation 1387
IBM Eclipse SDK V3.0 21
IBM Enterprise Generation Language 753
IBM Rational Agent Controller 9, 1102, 1382
IBM Rational Agent Controller V6
   installation 1382
IBM Rational ClearCase 1258
IBM Rational Software Development Platform 4
   products 5
      Rational Application Developer 6
      Rational Function Tester 6

      Rational Performance Tester 6
      Rational Software Architect 5
      Rational Software Modeler 5
      Rational Web Developer 6
      WebSphere Business Integrator Modeler 6
IBM WebSphere Application Server V6.0 1387
IBM WebSphere Portal 56, 989
icons for debugging 1141
IDE
   See integrated development environment
IDEF1X Diagram 375
IDEF1X notation diagram 196
IE notation diagram 196
image 501
Image File wizard 513
implements relationship 267
import
   from ClearCase 1287
   generation 321–322
   Java JAR 301
imports
   resolve (Ctrl+Shift+O) 255
   resolve (Ctrl+Shift-O) 256
indexes 357
Information Engineering (IE) Diagram 374
Informix 4GL migration 764
inheritance 839
init 579
Initialization target 1172
inspect variable 1143
Installation
   CVS for NT 1302
installation
   IBM DB2 UDB V8.2 Express Edition 1387
   IBM Rational Agent Controller 1382
   IBM Rational Application Developer 1372
   Rational Application Developer
      Interim Fix 0004 1380
   Rational ClearCase LT 1385
   WebSphere Application Server V6 1387
   WebSphere Portal V5.0 Test Environment 1376
   WebSphere Portal V5.1 Test Environment 1377
Installed JREs
   preferences 119
integrated development environment 132
integrated test servers 23
integration

Index **1413**

stream   1259, 1279
interface   258, 834
Interim Fix 0004   1380
Internet
   preferences   95
Internet preferences   95
   Proxy settings   95
   Web Browser settings   96
Introduction
   application development challenges   7
   Java database programming   334
   Rational Software Development Platform   4
   version 6 terminology   7
InvalidateSession   514
ISD   958
isolation   829
itso.ant.hello   1168

J

J2EE Application Client JAR   171
J2EE Application Client project   175
J2EE Application Clients   62
J2EE Connector   18
J2EE Deployment API   19
J2EE Management API   19
J2EE modules and projects   173
J2EE perspective   149
J2EE Request Profiling Agent   1244
J2EE Visualization   219
JAAC
   See Java Authorization Service Provider Contract for Containers
JAAS
   See Java Authentication and Authorization Service
JAF
   See Java Activation Framework
JAR   501
Java
   development
      preferences   98
   Editor
      preferences   117
   Runtime Environment   119
   Scrapbook   293
   source folder   523
   test case   1110
   utility JAR   1179

Java 2 Platform Enterprise Edition   170
Java accessor methods   254
Java Activation Framework   18
Java API for XML Processing   18
Java API for XML Registries   19
Java API for XML RPC   18
Java application
   export code to JAR   299
   locate compile errors   287
      filter errors in Problems view   289
      Problems view   288
   run external   301
   run sample   269, 286
   working example   231
Java attributes   254
Java Authentication and Authorization Service   19
Java Authorization Service Provider Contract for Containers   19
Java Beans   231
Java Browsing perspective   153
Java class
   create via Diagram Navigator   250
   Java Class wizard   253
Java class loader   1192
   extensions class loader   1192
   hierarchy   1193
   system class loader   1192
Java classes   249
Java classpath variables   98
Java component test   1103
Java database application
   access database via data source   393
   access database via DriverManager   390
      load JDBC driver   390
   prepare
      setup BANK database   338
   prepare for sample   337
Java database programming   334
Java development preferences   98
   appearance of Java elements   100
   code style and formatting   101
   Java classpath variables   98
Java Editor   311
Java Editor settings   117
Java Field wizard   255
Java interface   248
Java language   32
Java Management Extensions   19
Java Message Service   18, 71

Java methods 262
Java Native Interface 36
Java package
    create via Diagram Navigator 247
    create via Java Package wizard 247
Java packages 246
Java perspective 151, 222
Java Portlet specification 56
Java Profiling Agent 1244
Java project 177, 235
Java Remote Method Invocation 34
Java Scrapbook 293
Java Search 318
Java Servlet 18, 499
Java stored procedures 394
    access via DriverManager 408
    access via JavaBean 409
    build 405
    deploy 405
    enable capability 398
    Store Procedure wizard 398
Java Transaction API 18
Java Type Hierarchy perspective 155
Java Virtual Machine 33
Javadoc 231, 303
    generate 304
        Ant script 310
        Export wizard 306
    preferences 121
JavaMail 18
Javascript Editor 511
Javascript File wizard 513
JavaServer Faces 19, 52
    application architecture 675
    benefits 674
    features 674
    overview 674
JavaServer Page 18
JavaServer Pages 46, 499
JAXP
    See Java API for XML Processing
JAXR
    See Java API for XML Registries
JAX-RPC
    See Java API for XML RPC
JDBC 34, 334
    2.0 Standard Extension API 335
    type 2 driver 392
    type 3 driver 392

JDBC provider
    configure 631
JDT
    See Java Development Tools
JMS
    See Java Message Service
JMS activation specification 1392
JMS connection queue factory 1391
JMX
    See Java Management Extensions
JNDI
    data source 335
    namespace 833
    See Java Naming and Directory Interface
JNI 1195
    See Java Native Interface
join
    project 1284
JRE 119
JSF
    See JavaServer Faces
JSF and SDO Web application
    add connection for action 712
    add navigation rules 713
    configure data source via enhanced EAR 681
    create connection between JSF pages 705
    create Dynamic Web Project 679
    create Faces Action 708
    create Faces JSP 700, 702
    create page template 684
    customize page template 695
        content area 699
        logo image and title 695
        style (fonts, size) 698
    edit JSF page
        add relational record 730
        add relational record list to page 738
        add relational record to page 733
        add reusable JavaBean 742
        add row action 741
        add SDO to JSF page 720
        add simple validation 718
        add static navigation to page 719
        add UI components 715
        add validation 727
        add variables 716
        display relational record 735
        format field for currency 740
        link button 733

link button to action 735
run sample application 746
setup database 681
JSP 46
   breakpoint 1135
   Tag libraries 47
JSP File wizard 512
JSP Page Designer 619
JSPs 595
JSR 168 993
JTA
   See Java Transaction API
JUnit 231, 1081, 1087
   assert method 1089, 1096
   automated component test 1102
   class
      TestCase 1088
      TestRunner 1088
      testRunner 1088
      TestSuite 1088
   create test case 1089
   fail method 1096
   fundamentals
      instantiate an object 1087
      invoke methods 1087
      verify assertions 1087
   methods 1096
   run test case 1098
   setUp and tearDown 1093
   view 1099
junit.framework.Assert 1096
junit.jar 1091
JVM
   See Java Virtual Machine

K
key
   class 838
   field 863
   wrapper class 864
Key themes of version 6 8
   broaden appeal 8
   extended integration 8
   maintain standards 8
   raise productivity 8
   team unifying platform 8
keyword
   expansion 1318

L
Layout Mode 544
lib directory 502, 524
licensing 23
life cycle 832, 834
links 544
Linux 1155
list 547
ListAccounts 514
listeners 49
local
   component interface 880
   history 92
local history 92
   compare with 93
   replace with 93
locate compile errors 287
location independence 835
Log Console view 1176
log files 83

M
Maintenance 1086
make 1155–1156
MANIFEST.MF 524
mapping
   strategies 893
mark occurrences 118
marker
   breakpoint
      marker 1133
MDB
   See Message Driven Bean
Meet in the middle 893
memory analysis 1239
memory analysis views 1239
merging 1354
Merging from a stream 1354
message-driven bean 837
Message-driven EJBs 59, 72
messaging 832, 834
messaging engine startup 1391
messaging resources 1079
messaging systems 70
META-INF 523
method
   accessor 257
   declaration 258

implement 325
override 325
Microsoft Windows 2000 Professional 9
Microsoft Windows 2000 Server 9
Microsoft Windows 2003 Enterprise Edition 9
Microsoft Windows 2003 Standard Edition 9
Microsoft Windows XP Professional 9
migration 26
model
    MVC 514
model classes 550
model-view-controller 51, 503
    controller 504
    dependencies between layers 505
    JSP and servlet Web application 514
    model 503
    Struts Web application 616
    view 504
multi-dimensional association 269
MVC 514
    controller 504
    pattern 505
    See model-view-controller
    Struts 617

N
namespace 833
naming 832–833
Navigator view 146, 343
no natural unique identifier 870

O
object
    caching 830
    pooling 830
Object-relational mapping
    bottom up 893
    meet-in-the-middle 893
    top down 893
object-relational mapping 892
ODBC 334
online help 132
ORDER BY 382
Outline view 148, 230, 311
override methods 325

P
Package Explorer view 223
packages
    create 551
Page Designer 509
page template 510, 526
    create dynamic JSP 530
    create static 527
    customize 531
Page Template File wizard 513
page templates versus style sheets 527
parallel development 1335
Pascal 753
pattern
    command 515
    MVC 514
PDE
    See Plug-in Development Environment
performance test 1083
PerformTransaction 515
persistence 829, 832–833
perspective layout 137
perspectives 136
    customizing 140
    CVS Repository Exploring perspective 143
    Data perspective 145
    Debug perspective 146
    Generic Log Adapter perspective 148
    J2EE perspective 149
    Java Browsing perspective 153
    Java perspective 151, 222
    Java Type Hierarchy perspective 155
    Plug-in Development perspective 157
    preferences 94
    Profiling and Logging perspective 158
    Resource perspective 159
    specify default 140
    switching 138
    Team Synchronizing perspective 160
    Test perspective 161
    Web perspective 162
pluggable JRE 296
Plug-in Development perspective 157
populate
    database tables with data 352
portabiliy 830
portal application development 14
Portal applications 55
portal applications 985

develop 992
development strategy
    choosing markup languages 994
    IBM or JSR 168 993
    JavaServer Faces 995
    Struts 995
introduction 986
run project in test environment 1037
samples and tutorials 992
tools
    coexistence and migration 1023
    deploy projects 1001
    portal administration 1022
    Portal Designer 998
    Portal Import wizard 996
    Portal Project wizard 997
    Portal Server Configuration 1016
    Portlet Project wizard 1005
    remote test server 1017
    skin and theme design 999
    WebSphere Portal test environment 1018
portal concepts and definitions
    portal page 986
    portlet 987
    portlet application 987
    portlet events 988
    portlet modes 988
    portlet states 988
Portal Designer 998
Portal Import Wizard 996
portal page 986
    add portlets 1033
    customize 1027
Portal Project
    create 1026
Portal Project wizard 997
portal samples and tutorials 992
portal test environments
    WebSphere Portal V5.0 990
    WebSphere Portal V5.1 990
portal tools 990
portlet 987
portlet application 987
portlet applications 985
portlet events
    action events 988
    message events 989
    Window events 989
portlet modes
    configure 988
    edit 988
    help 988
Portlet Project Wizard 1005
portlet states 988
    maximized 988
    minimized 988
    normal 988
    portlet modes 988
preferences 84
    capabilities 86
    ClearCase 1261
    CVS 1312
    file associations 90
    local history 93
    perspectives 94
    startup and shutdown 83
primary key 358
probekit analysis 1241
Problems view 148, 225
procedure programming languages 753
Process Advisor 191
Process Browser 192
Process Preferences 193
product configuration 1371
product features 12
product installation 1371
production environment 1084
profiles
    WebSphere Application Server 1201
profiling
    agent types
        J2EE Request Profiling Agent 1244
        Java Profiling Agent 1244
    architecture 1242
        agent 1243
        Agent Controller 1243
        application process 1243
        deployment hosts 1243
        development hosts 1244
        test client 1243
    features
        code coverage 1240
        execution time analysis 1240
        memory analysis 1239
        probekit analysis 1241
        thread analysis 1239
    prepare for profiling sample
        enable Profiling and Logging capability

1247
      prerequiste hardware and software   1247
      publish and run sample application   1249
      profile the sample application
         analysis of code coverage information   1253
         collect profile information   1253
         start server in profile mode   1249
      Profiling and Logging perspective   1244
      profiling sets   1245
Profiling and Logging capability   1244
Profiling and Logging perspective   158, 1244
profiling applications   1237
profiling sets   1245
Profiling tools   17
programming languages
   declarative   752
programming paradigms
   4GL   753
   object oriented   753
   procedural   753
programming technologies   31
   desktop applications   32
   dynamic Web applications   43
   enterprise JavaBeans   57
   J2EE Application Clients   62
   messaging systems   70
   static Web sites   39
   Web Services   66
project
   ClearCase control   1274
   create
      Java   235
   create a new   178
   directory structure   522
   disconnect from CVS   1360
   EJB   844
   join   1284
   properties   178, 180
   version   1342
Project Explorer view   149
Project Interchange file   1398
projects   171
promote   863
Proxy Settings   95

Q

Quick Assists   320
Quick Fix   320

R

ramp-up time   1086
Rapid Application Development   311
   features
      Code Assist   321
      generate getter and setter   324
      import generation   322
      Java Search   318
      navigate through the code   311
      Quick Assist   320
      Smart Insert   316
      source folding   314
      Type Hierarchy   315
      Word Skipping   317
      working sets   319
RAR   171
Rational
   ClearCase
      see ClearCase
   Web site   1259
Rational Application Developer   6
   CDs   10
   ClearCase LT integration   1257
   configure CVS   1312
   CVS preferences   1312
   database features   336
   debug
      attach to remote server   1148
   debug tooling   1121
      summary of new features   1122
   Eclipse Hyades test framework   1086
   editors   137
   EGL tooling   761
   folders   172
   installation   24, 1372
   JavaServer Faces support   677
   JUnit   1087
   licensing   23
   local vs remote test environment   1046
   log files   83
   migration and coexistence   26
   new EJB features   828
   new server   1057
   online help   132
   perspectives   136
   preferences   84
   product packaging   10
   projects   171
      Component test   177

Index   **1419**

Connector project 176
Dynamic Web project 175
EJB project 176
Enterprise Application project 175
J2EE Application Client project 175
Java project 177
Server project 177
Simple project 177
Static Web project 176
summary 173
Rational ClearCase features 1261
samples 181
server configuration 1043
startup parameters 81
Struts 619
Stuts support
    Project Explorer view 619
    Struts Component wizard 619
    Struts Configuration Editor 619
    Web Project Struts enabled 619
supported test servers 1045
test server introduction 1044
uninstall 25
views 137
Web Services tools 957
XML tools 447
Rational ClearCase
    ClearCase preferences 1261
    new features 1261
    terminology
        activity 1259
        baseline 1259
        check in 1259
        check out 1259
        component 1259
        deliver stream 1259
        development stream 1259
        integration stream 1259
        rebase 1259
        verioned object base 1259
        view 1259
Rational ClearCase LT
    development scenario 1277
    installation 1260, 1385
    integration with Rational Application Developer 1260
    scenario overview 1263
    setup for new project
        add project to ClearCase source control

1274
    create a Web project 1274
    create new ClearCase project 1265
    enable Team capability 1264
    join a ClearCase project 1268
Rational Developer 7
Rational Functional Tester 6
Rational Performance Tester 6
Rational Product Updater 25, 168, 1372, 1380
Rational Software Architect 5
Rational Software Modeler 5
Rational Unified Process 189–190
    disciplines 191
    lifecycle phases 191
    Process Advisor 191
    Process Browser 192
Rational Unified Process integration 15
Rational Web Developer 6
RCP directory 1194
RE directory 1194
rebase 1259, 1290
recording a test 1112
Red Hat Enterprise Linux Workstation V3 9
Redbooks Web site 1404
    Contact us xxvii
refactor 328
    change method signature 329
    encapsulate field 330
    extract constant 330
    extract interface 329
    extract local variable 330
    extract method 330
    inline 330
    move 329
    pull up 330
    push down 329
    redo 330
    rename 329
    undo 330
refactoring
    example 330
Relational database to XML mapping 448
relationship
    methods 879
relationships 267, 838
    create 872
remote
    client view 903
    debugging 1145

remove project from a server
    via Rational Application Developer   1066
    via WebSphere Administrative Console   1067
request sequence   618
resource adapter   1195
Resource adapter module   1191
Resource perspective   159
resoure adapter achive
    See RAR
resume   1141
RMI   832
    See Remote Method Invocation
role-based development model   131
RP directory   1194
run
    Java application outside Application Developer   301
    Java applications   290
runAnt.bat   1186
running a test   1113
RUP
    See Rational Unified Process

S

SAAJ
    See SOAP with Attachments API for Java
sample
    Java database application
        prepare
            import BankDB.zip   337
sample code   1395
    6449code.zip   1396
    description by chapter   1396
    locate   1396
    Project Interchange files   1398
scalability   830
schema   357
Scrapbook   293
SDO
    See Service Data Objects
security   832
Sequence Diagram   195, 213
server
    debugging   1136
Server project   177
server resources   1078
Servers view   148
service broker   952–953

service bus   1390
service client   953
Service Data Objects   16, 19, 52, 678
service integration   1390
service provider   952
service requester   952–953
service-oriented architecture   951–952
    service broker   953
    service provider   952
    service requester   953
servlet   577
    add to Web Project   576–577
    create   577
    implement command interface   586
servlet container   501
servlets   44, 576
session bean   836, 901
    business methods   904
    create   902
session EJBs   58
session facade   901
set breakpoint   1133
setter   254, 257
setUp   1093
Simple Object Access Protocol   954
Simple project   177
site appearance   524
site navigation   517, 524
Smart Insert   316
snippet   295
SOA   951
SOAP with Attachments API for Java   18
software
    configuration management   1258
sound   501
source folding   314
specification
    Enterprise JavaBeans (EJB)   18
    IBM Java Runtime Environment   18
    J2EE Connector   18
    J2EE Deployment API   19
    J2EE Management API   19
    Java Activation Framework   18
    Java API for XML Processing   18
    Java API for XML Registries   19
    Java API for XML RPC   18
    Java Authentication and Authorization Service   19
    Java Authorization Service Provider Contract for

    Containers 19
    Java Management Extensions 19
    Java Message Service 18
    Java Servlet 18
    Java Transaction API 18
    JavaMail 18
    JavaServer Faces 19
    JavaServer Page (JSP) 18
    Service Data Objects 19
    SOAP with Attachments API for Java 18
    Struts 19
    Web Services 18
specification versions 14, 18
SQL
    statement
        execute 383
SQL commands 334
SQL Query Builder 384
    example 384
SQL statement 376
SQL Statement wizard 376
    define conditions for WHERE clause 380
    define table joins 379
    execute SQL statement 383
    groups and order 382
    parse the statement 382
    select tables and columns 377
    use a variable 382
    view SQL statement 382
staging environment 1084
Standard Widget Toolkit 36, 416
standardization 830
start server in profile mode 1249
startup parameters 81
stateless 901
static and dynamic 500
Static Method Sequence Diagram 195, 203
static pages
    create a list 547
    create tables 544, 546
    forms 548
    links 544
    text 544
Static Web project 176
static web sites 39
step debug 1126
step filter 1126
step into 1141
step over 1141–1142

stored procedure 394
Stored Procedure wizard 398
structured types 357
Struts 19
    configuration file editor 659
    controller 616
    create components
        realize a JSP 648
        realize Struts action 645
        realize Struts form bean 641
        Struts Action 634
        Struts Form Bean 634
        Struts Web Connection 636
        Struts Web Connections 650
        Web Diagram 633
        Web Page 635
    introduction 616
    model 616
    MVC 617
    tag library 655
    view 616
Struts Action 634
Struts Component wizards 619
Struts Configuration Editor 619
Struts Form Bean 634
Struts validation framework 653
Struts Web application
    import and run sample 665
        import BankStrutsWeb.zip 665
        prepare sample database 666
        run sample application 666
    prepare for sample 620
        Dynamic Web Project Struts enabled 622
Struts Web Connection 636
Struts-bean tags 655
Struts-html tags 655
Struts-Logic tags 656
Struts-Nested tags 656
Struts-Template tags 656
Struts-Tiles Tags 656
Stuts tag library 655
style sheets 511
    customize 535
sualization 219
SubType 224
summary
    features
        annotated programming 15
        application code analysis 15

application modeling with UML 15
component testing 17
Crystal Reports integration 16
Eclipse 14
Enterprise Generation Language 17
JavaServer Faces 16
profiling tools 17
Rapid Web Development 15
Rational Unified Process 15
Service Data Objects 16
test server environments 14
Web Services 14
SuperType 224
supported
   databases
      Cloudscape 9
      DB2 Universal Database 9
      Informix Dynamic Server 10
      Microsoft SQL Server 10
      Oracle 10
      Sybase Adaptive Server Enterprise 10
   platforms
      Microsoft Windows 2000 Professional 9
      Microsoft Windows 2000 Server 9
      Microsoft Windows Server 2003 9
      Microsoft Windows XP Professional 9
      Red Hat Enterprise Linux Workstation V3 9
      SuSE Linux Enterprise Server V9 9
SuSE Linux Enterprise Server V9 9
suspend 1141
SVT
   See system verification test
Swing 36
SWT
   See Standard Widget Toolkit
system verification test 1083

T

tables 357, 546
tag libraries 47
Tasks view 146
TCP/IP Monitor 959, 1079
Team Synchronizing perspective 160
tearDown 1093
template
   page templates 535
templates 121
terminate 1141

terminology 7
test
   component test 1081
   introduction 1082
   JUnit 1081, 1087
test calibration 1084
test case
   create 1089
test environments 1084
test execution 1085
Test perspective 161
test phases
   build verification test 1082
   component test 1082
   customer acceptance test 1083
   function verification test 1083
   performance test 1083
   system verification test 1083
   unit tests 1082
test results recording 1085
test server environments 14
TestCase 1088
TestSuite 1088, 1097
text 544
theme 524
thread analysis 1239
thread analysis views 1240
Tomcat 23
top down 893
Topic Diagram 195
Topic Diagrams 199
transaction 832
   demarcation 833
transactions
   EJB 829
transfer object 842
triggers 357
Type Hierarchy view 224

U

UDDI registry 982
UML 194
   more information 220
UML Visualization 370
   browse diagram 196
   Class Diagram 196
   Sequence Diagram 196
   Static Method Sequence Diagram 196

Topic Diagram 196
UML visualization 195
Unified Change Management 1258
Unified Modeling Language
    See UML
uninstall 25
unique identifier 870
unit test 1082
    benefits 1085
    case 1085
Universal Description, Discovery and Integration 955
universal test client
    EJB 915
Universal Test Client (UTC) 915
UNIVERSAL_JDBC_DRIVER_PATH 783
UNIX 1155
URL 391
utility classes 501
Utility Java projects 302

V

value object 842
variable
    change value 1143
Variables view 147
version
    project 1342
version 6 terminology 7
versioned object base 1259
versioning 1342
video 501
view 1259
    CVS Repositories 1324
    CVS Resource History 1343
    Display 1143
    Expressions 1143
    JUnit 1099
    MVC 515
view management 1127
views 137, 357
    Breakpoints view 148, 1142
    Call Hierarchy view 223
    Code Review Details view 229
    Code Review view 226
    Console view 146
    CVS Annotate view 144
    CVS Repositories view 143
    CVS Resource History view 144
    Data Definition view 146
    Database Explorer view 146
    DB Output view 146
    Debug view 147
    Declaration view 225
    Diagram Navigator view 230
    Navigator view 146
    Outline view 230
    Outlines view 148
    Package Explorer view 223
    Problems view 148, 225
    Sensor Results view 149
    Servers view 148
    Tasks view 146
    Type Hierarch view 224
    Variables view 148
visual class 420
visual development 194
Visual Editor 415–416
    add JavaBeans to visual class 428
    binding 438
    change component properties 428
    code synchronization 427
    create visual class 420
    customize appearance 424
    launch 419
    layout 423
    open existing class 422
    overview 423
    resize JavaBean component 427
VisualAge Generator to EGL migration 764
VOB 1259

W

W3C 444
WAR 170, 1179, 1191
WAR classloader 1195
watch variables 1142
watching variables 1142
Web
    content folder 523
    project
        create 507
Web application 501
    debug on local server 1132
    debug on remote server 1145
Web Application Archive 1191

Web application module 1191
Web application test 1112
Web application testing
   sample
      analyze test results 1118
      deployment definition 1116
      edit the test 1115
      generate an executable test 1115
      record a test 1113
      run test 1117
Web applications 43, 499
   concepts and technologies 500
   introduction 500
   using EGL 751
   using EJBs 827
   using JSF and SDO 673
   using JSPs and servlets 499
      prepare for sample 513
   using Struts 615
Web archive
   See WAR
Web Browser Settings 96
Web development tooling
   AnimatedGif Designer 511
   CSS Designer 511
   file creation wizard 512
   Javascript Editor 511
   Page Designer 509
   page templates 510
   Web perspective and views 506
   Web Project 507
   Web Site Designer 508
   WebArt Designer 511
Web Diagram 197
Web module 500
Web perspective 162, 506
Web Project 507
   directory structure 517
Web Service wizard 964
Web Services 14, 18, 66, 951
   client development 958
   create from an EJB 980
   create Web Service from JavaBean 964
   EJB from WSDL 958
   enable development capability 960
   introduction
      related standards 955
      service-oriented architecture 952
      SOA implementation 953
   JavaBean from WSDL 958
   monitor using TCP/IP Monitor 976
   prepare for development 959
   publish using UDDI 982
   security 980
   test the client proxy 971, 973
   test tools 959
      TCP/IP Monitor 959
      test environment 959
      Universal Test Client 959
      Web Services Explorer 959
Web Services Description Language 954
Web Services Explorer 971
Web Services tools 957
Web Site Designer 508, 525
   launch 525
web.xml 502
WebArt Designer 511
WEB-INF 502, 524
WebLogic 23
WebSphere Administrative Console 1390
WebSphere Application Server
   (base) Edition 1189
   Base Edition 1189
   configure data source 1225
   deployment architecture 1199
   enable debug 1147
   enhanced EAR 1201
   Express Edition 1189
   installation 1050
   messaging 1389
   Network Deployment Edition 1189
   profile creation 1051
   profiles 1201
   v6.0 Profiles 1047
WebSphere Business Integrator 6
WebSphere Business Integrator Modeler 6
WebSphere class loader 1193
   application class loader 1195
   extensions to class loader 1194
   handling JNI code 1195
   hierarchy 1194
   Web module class loader 1195
WebSphere enhanced EAR 1201
WebSphere Portal 985, 989
WebSphere Portal V5.0 Test Environment 1376
WebSphere Portal V5.1 Test Environment 1377
WebSphere Profile wizard 1051
WebSphere Profiles 1047

application server profile 1048
custom profile 1049
deployment manager profile 1048
WebSphere Rapid Deployment 1210
   annotation-based programming 1210
   modes 1212
   tools 1210
WebSphere Studio 7
Wireless Markup Language 994
WML 994
Word Skipping 317
Workbench
   basics 76, 78
Working sets 319
workload optimization 830
ws.ext.dirs 1194–1195
WYSIWYG 419, 509

X
X/Open SQL 334
Xdoclet 1210
XML 38, 444
   Metadata Interchange 335
   namespaces 446
   overview 444
   processor 444
   schema 445, 458
     create new 463
     generate from DTD file 458
     generate from relational table 461
     generate from XML file 461
     graph 370
     validate 489
   transform 491
   where to find information 497
XML and relational data 448
XML editor 448
XML Path Language 446
XML schema editor 448
XML to XML mapping editor 448
XML tools
   DTD editor 448
   XML editor 448
   XML schema editor 448
   XPath Expression wizard 448
   XSL editor 448
XPath 446–447
XPath expression wizard 448

XSL 446, 483
   edit 485
XSL debugging and transformation 448
XSL editor 448
XSL Transformations 446
XSL-FO 446
XSLT 446
   debug 493
XSLT debugger 1128

Z
zSeries 759